Bringing Your Linux Server to Life

Linux is rapidly gaining recognition as a robust, high-performance operating system. It is because of this that it is also becoming know~ alternative to Windows NT for small computer clusters in need of support in the area of desktop applications lags behind that of Microsoft vv.i.dow.., Linux is remarkably well suited as a server platform. Server applications that implement file storage, an Internet mail service, World Wide Web service, routing support, IP firewall support, dial-up networking, and more are available—generally free of charge—as part of the operating system distribution. Linux is most certainly the network solution for you!

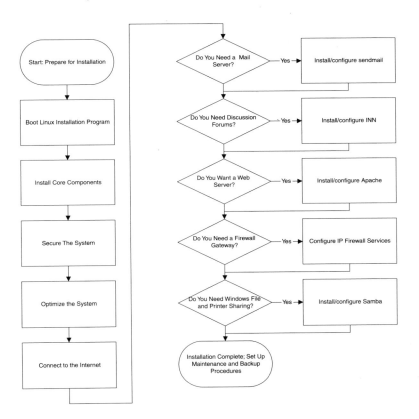

THE INSTALLATION ROADMAP.

This book is designed to help you get your Linux network up and running—and even prepare you for the possibility that your system might fail to operate, forcing you to move to a replacement system. The installation roadmap outlines the process you will take as you progress through this book. Refer to it when you need to see the big picture of where you're at in the process—or maybe even to backtrack if you find that something didn't work quite the way you thought it should. I'll be with you each step of the way in setting up your new Linux network. I hope you enjoy the experience…and good luck!

Quick Reference: Linux Commands

Common Linux Commands and Frequently Used Options

`cat /etc/services`	Dump the file `/etc/services` to the screen
`cd ~root`	Change to the root user's home directory
`df`	List mounted disk drives and their capacity
`du`	List disk usage in current directory
`dmesg`	List contents of the kernel message buffer
`find /tmp -name "*.zip" -print`	Find all files ending with `.zip` in `/tmp` and its subdirectories
`grep root /etc/passwd`	List any lines from `/etc/passwd` that contain the word root
`kill -HUP 1`	Send hangup signal to process 1
`last -10`	List the last 10 logins on the system
`ls -al`	Show detailed list of files in current directory
`mail`	Invoke the simple mail client
`man man`	Show manual page on the `man` command
`mkdir newdir`	Create a new directory named `newdir`
`mount /mnt/cdrom`	Mount a file system to the mount point `/mnt/cdrom` (must be defined and associated with a drive in `/etc/fstab`)
`netstat -t`	List active TCP connections
`ping www.mcp.com`	Ping remote host `www.mcp.com`
`ps axu`	Provide detailed list of running processes
`su`	Switch to the root user account
`tail -f /var/log/messages`	Show the last 10 lines of the system log and continue monitoring until Ctrl-C is hit
`tar czf archive.tgz .`	Pack contents of current directory into the compressed archive file `archive.tgz`
`tar xzf archive.tgz`	Unpack the contents of the compressed archive `archive.tgz`
`traceroute www.mcp.com`	Show the network path to `www.mcp.com`
`w`	Show users currently logged on and system statistics

Commands of the vi Editor

A	Append text at the end of the current line	x	Erase character under the cursor
i	Insert text at cursor position	y	Copy marked text to internal buffer (like the Windows clipboard)
d	Delete marked text		
dd	Delete current line	ZZ	Save and exit
Esc	Return to command mode after text has been typed	:	Command line mode
		/	Search for text typed
J	Join current line with next line	:q	Quit if there is no unsaved data
p	Paste internal buffer after cursor position	:q!	Quit unconditionally, discarding unsaved data
u	Undo last action		
v	Begin marking text (use cursor keys to select)	:vi	Return to visual editing mode
		:w	Write data to file
V	Begin marking text lines (use the up/down arrow keys to select)		

Linux®:
A Network Solution
for Your Office

Viktor T. Toth

SAMS

An imprint of Macmillan Computer Publishing
201 West 103rd Street, Indianapolis, IN, 46290, USA

Linux®: A Network Solution for Your Office

Copyright © 1999 by Sams

International Standard Book Number: 0-672-31628-5

Library of Congress Catalog Card Number: 98-86477

Printed in the United States of America

First Printing: *July 1999*

00   99   98   4   3   2   1

Trademarks

Warning and Disclaimer

Acquisitions and Development Editor
Laura Bulcher

Managing Editor
Brice Gosnell

Project Editor
Sara Bosin

Copy Editor
Pamela Woolf
Bart Reed

Indexer
Kevin Kent

Proofreader
Andrew Beaster

Technical Editor
Aron Hsiao

Software Development Specialist
Michael Hunter

Interior Design
Gary Adair

Cover Design
Alan Clements

Copy Writer
Eric Borgert

Layout Technicians
Stacey DeRome
Ayanna Lacey
Heather Miller

Contents at a Glance

Part I: Introduction

1	Introduction	9
2	The Linux Workhorse	23

Part I: Setting Up

3	System Installation	55
4	Internet Configuration and Basic Security	85
5	Internet Concepts	103
6	The Domain Name System	125
7	Making the Connection	145

Part III: Basic Services

8	Running a Mail Server	169
9	Mailing Lists and Newsgroups	193
10	Web Service	209

Part IV: Advanced Networking

11	Firewalls	235
12	Using External Routers	249
13	File Services for Windows: Samba	261
14	Time Services	281

Part V: Managing Your System

15	User Accounts	293
16	Logs	305
17	Backups	321
18	Scheduled Tasks, Scripts, and Programming	339
19	Configuring Workstations	361
20	Security Revisited	385

Part VI: When Something Goes Wrong

21   Diagnosing Your System   405

22   Moving to Backup Hardware   431

Part VII: Appendixes

A   Configuring the Kernel   445

B   Linux Resources on the Internet   459

C   Linux Publications   463

D   Linux Support Organizations   467

Index   471

Table of Contents

Preface   **1**

PART 1: Introduction   **7**

1   **Introduction**   **9**

Linux: The Roots   10

     A Brief History   10

     Flavors of UNIX   11

How Good Is Linux?   12

     Linux as a Server Operating System   12

     Linux on the Desktop?   13

     Linux Reliability   14

     Source Availability   14

Installation Roadmap   15

     Initial Setup   16

     Basic Services   18

     Advanced Networking   18

System Management   19

     Daily Operations   20

     Disaster Recovery   21

Summary   21

2   **The Linux Workhorse**   **23**

Anatomy of a Horse   23

     Processes   25

     Devices   30

     File Systems   32

     Access Control   34

Interacting with the System: Shells in a Nutshell   36

     Popular UNIX Shells   36

     A Comparison: bash Versus COMMAND.COM   37

The Keyboard   40

Getting Help with Man Pages   42

Editing Files   44

Using vi   44

Other Editors   47

The X Window System   48

X Implementations   49

Windows X Servers   49

Summary   50

PART 2: Setting Up   **53**

3   System Installation   **55**

Preparing for Installation   55

System Inventory   57

Hardware Preparation   58

Partitions and the Boot Process   58

Partitioning Basics   58

How the System Boots   59

Partition Schemes   60

File System Types   63

Choosing a Partitioning Scheme   65

Linux: First Boot   66

Starting from the CD-ROM   66

Creating a Floppy Disk Set   67

Starting from the MS-DOS Prompt   67

Hardware Detection   68

Software Package Installation   69

Network Configuration   69

Test System Installation   71

Setup Program Initialization   72

Hardware Configuration   73

Disk Partitioning and Swap Space Setup   75

Package Selection and Installation   76

Network Configuration   78

Supplementary Configuration Options   79

User Accounts   80

Boot Setup   80

The Linux Kernel   83

Summary   83

4   Internet Configuration and Basic Security   85

Users, Groups, and Passwords   86

Users and Groups   86

Adding New Users   89

Password Security   90

The Root Login   91

Privileges and Permissions   92

File System Permissions   92

Changing File Permissions   93

System Services   95

System Startup   95

The Internet Superserver   99

Summary   102

5   Internet Concepts   103

Internetworking   103

Local Area Networking   104

Wide Area Networking   104

Routes and Routers   105

Internetworks   107

The Internet Protocol   109

IP Numbers and Subnets   109

IP Address Assignment   111

Dynamic Address Assignment   112

Private Networks   113

Firewall Routers   114

Other Internet Protocols 114

    Beneath IP: PPP, SLIP, and PLIP 115

    Connection-oriented and Connectionless Protocols 116

    ICMP 117

    Higher Level Protocols 117

Tools 119

    Configuration Tools 119

    Diagnostic Tools 120

Other Standards 121

    Email Related Standards 121

    Hypertext Documents 122

    Assigned Numbers 122

    Batch Delivery 122

Summary 123

6   The Domain Name System **125**

Domain Names and Name Servers 125

    The /etc/hosts File 126

    Name Service 127

    Top-Level Domains 127

    The /etc/resolv.conf File 128

    DNS Tools 129

Domain Name Registration 131

    Picking a Domain Name 131

    Checking Existing Domain Names 131

    Registering with the InterNIC 132

    Registration Through Your ISP 133

    Country Domain Registrars 133

Running a Name Server 133

    The named Configuration File 134

    The Root Cache 136

    Zone Files 137

    Checking Your Configuration 139

Summary 142

7	**Making the Connection**	**145**
	Preparing for the Connection	145
	Finding the Right ISP	145
	Setting Up Your Modem	149
	Using PPP	150
	PPP Components	150
	The Dial-Up Process	151
	Auto-Dialing	151
	Routing and Forwarding	152
	Obtaining IP Numbers for Your Network	153
	Incoming Connections	154
	Incoming Data Calls	154
	PPP for Incoming Calls	157
	Running a FAX Server	158
	Connecting the Test System	159
	Dial-up Instructions	159
	Testing the Login Procedure	159
	Running pppd	160
	Running diald	162
	Using External Routers	164
	Summary	165
	Manual Pages	165
PART 3: Basic Services		**167**
8	**Running a Mail Server**	**169**
	The Mail Delivery Process	169
	Mail User Agents	171
	Mail Transport Agents	172
	Mailboxes and Protocols	173
	SMTP: The Simple Mail Transfer Protocol	173
	UNIX-Style Mailboxes	174
	Message Headers and Formats	175
	POP3: The Post Office Protocol	176

	Mail Forwarding and Aliases	177
	UUCP: UNIX to UNIX Copy for Batch Delivery	177
	Configuring sendmail	179
	Rulesets	179
	The `sendmail.cf` File	180
	Using Macro Tools	180
	Message Filtering	182
	Configuring the Test System	183
	Activating sendmail	184
	Creating `sendmail.cf`	185
	Adding Rules to Prevent Spam	187
	Configuring UUCP Delivery	188
	Summary	191
	Manual Pages	192
9	**Mailing Lists and Newsgroups**	**193**
	Mailing Lists	194
	Using the `.forward` File	194
	Using `/etc/aliases`	195
	List Manager Programs	195
	Newsgroups	197
	Basic Concepts	197
	A Guided Tour	198
	Servers and Messages	199
	Public Versus Private Newsgroups	200
	Servers, Clients, and NNTP	200
	Newsgroups and Articles	201
	News Server Configuration	201
	Test System Example	202
	Managing the Server	206
	Summary	207
	Manual Pages	207

10   Web Service   **209**

Basic Concepts   209

    Formats and Protocols   210

    Uniform Resource Locators   211

    The File Transfer Protocol   211

    The Hypertext Transfer Protocol   212

    Secure Sockets   213

Setting Up an FTP Server   214

    Server Installation   214

    Configuring the Internet Superserver   214

    Configuring Anonymous Access   215

    Server Management   216

Running Apache   217

    Starting Apache   217

    Server Configuration   219

    Setting Up Web Pages   221

Advanced Web Server Features   223

    Virtual Hosts   223

    Restricted Access   226

    Adding SSL Support   226

    Forms Processing   227

    Logs   229

Summary   230

Manual Pages   231

PART 4: Advanced Networking   **233**

11   Firewalls   **235**

What Firewalls Do   235

    Packet Filtering   236

    IP Masquerading   237

    Accounting   238

    Application Support   239

Do You Need a Firewall?   240
   Firewalls and Dial-Up Systems   240
   What a Firewall Doesn't Do   240
   Why Firewalls Make Life Harder   241
What to Protect Against   241
   Forged IP Numbers   242
   NetBIOS Connections   242
Setting Up a Linux Firewall   243
   Kernel Support   244
   The `ipfwadm` Command   244
Summary   247
Manual Pages   248

12   Using External Routers   249
Routing Revisited   249
   Routing with Linux   249
   Routing Externally   250
   Segmented Networks   252
   Multisegment Routing   254
   External Routers and Firewalls   256
Special Router Devices   256
   Using an External ISDN Router   256
   The Trouble with Cable Modems   257
Summary   259
Manual Pages   259

13   File Services for Windows: Samba   261
What Can Samba Do?   261
   Resource Sharing in Windows   261
   Samba and SMB   262
   Samba Components   262
Setting Up Samba   263
   Where Can Samba Be Obtained?   263
   The Samba Configuration File   263

Global Configuration Settings   264
   System Identification   264
   Basic Security   264
   Logging   265
   Encrypted Passwords   265
   Printing   266
   Test System Example   266
Configuring Shared Directories   267
   Sharing Users' Home Directories   267
   Other Shared Directories   267
   Test System Example   268
Configuring Shared Printers   268
   Background Printing under Linux   268
   Sharing a Printer   269
   Test System Example   269
Samba and Encryption   271
   The Problem with Windows NT   271
   SMB Passwords   272
Using Samba   273
   Accessing Shared Drives from Windows   274
   Setting Up a Network Printer in Windows   275
   Accessing Shared Resources from Linux   277
   Using smbclient   277
   The SMB File System   278
Summary   279
Manual Pages   280

14 Time Services   **281**
The Need for Synchronization   281
   Synchronizing Hosts   281
   Synchronizing to an External Service   282
UNIX, the Internet, and Timekeeping   282
   Your Computer and Its Clock   282
   The CMOS Clock   283

Simple Time Services   283

The Network Time Protocol (NTP)   283

Installing and Using NTP Software   284

Installing the NTP Server   285

NTP Servers on the Internet   285

Setting Up a Standalone Server   286

Synchronizing Other Linux Machines with `ntpdate`   287

Synchronizing Windows Hosts   288

Summary   289

Manual Pages   290

PART 5: Managing Your System   **291**

15   User Accounts   **293**

What Is a User Account?   293

User Identifiers   294

The Home Directory   294

Email Addresses   295

The Shell   295

Managing User Accounts   296

The `/etc/passwd` File   296

Creating and Removing Accounts   296

Shadow Passwords   299

Password Encryption   299

The Shadow File   300

Password Policies   300

Obtaining and Installing the Shadow Password Suite   301

User Quotas   302

Quotas and the Kernel   302

Quota Support Tools   302

Summary   303

Manual Pages   304

16   Logs   305

The System Log   305

    Log Messages   305

    Running `syslogd`   306

    Logging over the Network   306

    Configuring `syslogd`   307

    Kernel Logging   309

Boot Notification   310

Reading the Log Files   311

    The Meaning of Log Entries   311

    Logs and Text-Processing Commands   313

    Continuous Monitoring   313

Other Log Files   314

    Login Records   314

    Transfer Logs   315

    Web Server Logs   315

    UUCP Logs   315

    News System Logs   316

Log Maintenance   316

    Rotating Logs   316

    Test System Log Files   317

Summary   318

Manual Pages   319

17   Backups   321

Backup Strategies   321

    Backing Up Is Not Enough   321

    Planning for Restores   322

Backing Up Files   323

    Backing Up Data   323

    Configuration Files   324

    Customizations   324

The Tools of Backup   325
    Choosing Your Backup Hardware   325
    Using Backup Hardware   326
    Tapes and File Systems   327
    Backup Commands   327
    Restore Commands   331
Advanced Topics   332
    Backup Scheduling and Media Rotation   333
    Incremental Backups   333
    Using Encryption   334
    Backups Over the Network   335
Summary   336
Manual Pages   337

18   Scheduled Tasks, Scripts, and Programming   339
Scheduling Program Execution   339
    The cron Daemon   340
    Running Commands with at   341
Shell Scripts   342
    Simple Programs   342
    Conditional Execution   343
    Variables   344
    Special Parameters and Predefined Variables   347
    Input, Output, and Redirection   348
    Here Documents   350
    Using Output As Parameters   351
Other Often Used Languages   351
    Other Shells   351
    Perl   352
    C   352
Examples   353
    crontab Entries   353
    Cleaning Logs   355

Network Backup 356

Checking for Server Operation 356

The No-Shell Shell 357

Password Generation 358

Summary 359

Manual Pages 360

19   Configuring Workstations   361

Using a Linux Router 362

Setting Up the TCP/IP Protocol 362

Configuring the IP Address 364

Setting Up the Network Gateway 365

Setting Up Name Service 366

Using a Linux Mail Server 367

SMTP and POP3 Service 367

Setting Up Microsoft Outlook Express 367

Accessing Network News 372

The NNTP Server 372

Adding a News Account to Outlook Express .. 372

Using Samba Services 375

Accessing Remote Directories 375

Printing over the Network 377

Other Applications 380

Web Authoring Tools 380

X Applications 381

Summary 382

Manual Pages 383

20   Security Revisited   385

Access Security 385

Physical Security 385

Dial-up Security 386

Network Security 387

Local Area Networks 388

Remote Connections 389

Personnel Security   390

    The Case of the Disgruntled Employee   390

    Carelessness and Ignorance   390

Application Security   390

    Shell Accounts   391

    Web Scripts and Other Utilities   391

Malicious Programs   393

    Viruses   393

    Trojan Horses   394

    Worms   394

Protective Measures   395

    Password Policies   395

    Access Rights   396

    Secure Protocols   397

    Software Upgrades   398

    User Education   399

    Firewalls   399

    About the Root Account   399

    The Truth About Email Attachments   400

    Bogus Warnings   401

Summary   402

PART 6: When Something Goes Wrong   **403**

21   Diagnosing Your System   **405**

Pre-Boot Diagnostics   405

    Signs of Life   406

    The Blank Screen   406

    Remote Access   407

    If You Can Get In   407

Hardware Problems   408

    Power Supply   408

    Dead Motherboard   409

    Flash BIOS   410

Beep Codes and Diagnostic Codes	411
Swapping Components	412
Intermittent Failures	413
BIOS Settings	414
Software Problems	414
Boot Failures	415
Low Memory	415
Insufficient Disk Space	416
Processor Overload	418
Missing or Corrupt DLLs	420
Disk Corruption	420
Kernel Panics	422
Boot Options	422
Booting from the Backup Kernel Image	423
Booting from Floppy	423
Booting from Installation Disks	424
Case Studies	424
A Bad Hard Disk	424
The Case of the Broken Tape Drive	426
Swap File Trouble	427
The Case of the Dead CD-ROM	428
A Broken BIOS	428
Summary	429
Manual Pages	429
22 Moving to Backup Hardware	**431**
Anatomy of a Transplant	431
The Processor and the Motherboard	431
The Hard Disk	432
Other Peripherals	434
Moving Software	435
Moving the System	435
Moving the Kernel	437

Moving Applications   437

Moving User Data   438

More Case Studies   438

Screaming Gamers   438

An April Morning   439

Summary   441

Manual Pages   442

PART 7: Appendixes   **443**

A   Configuring the Kernel   **445**

Modules and Kernel Customization   445

Kernel Recompilation   446

Preparing LILO to Boot the Old Kernel   446

Running the Kernel Configuration Scripts   448

B   Linux Resources on the Internet   **459**

Web Sites   459

FTP Sites   460

Newsgroups   461

Whois Databases   462

C   Linux Publications   **463**

Useful Books   463

Magazines   465

D   Linux Support Organizations   **467**

Caldera Systems, Inc.   467

Corel Corporation   467

Dell Computer Corporation   468

InfoMagic   468

Linux System Labs   468

Linuxcare, Inc.   468

Red Hat Software   469

Specialized Systems Consultants (SSC)   469

Walnut Creek CD-ROM   469

Index   **471**

About the Author

Viktor Toth is a Hungarian-born author and self-employed software developer. His professional career started in 1979, when he wrote the first Hungarian-language book on Ernö Rubik's Magic Cube. In the years that followed, he developed a variety of microcomputer and mainframe software applications for clients in Hungary, Austria, Germany, and the United Kingdom. In 1986, he authored his second book, a technical reference for programmers of the Commodore 16 home computer.

Living in Canada since 1987, Viktor earns his living as an application developer. At present, he's having great fun with several professional radio receivers and spectrum analyzers, as he's developing a test and measurement application. In recent years, he created a variety of engineering and database applications, and also took part in a number of studies on consulting assignments.

Writing professionally in English since 1995, Viktor is the author of Visual C++ 4 Unleashed, Visual C++ 5 Unleashed, and Programming Windows 98/NT Unleashed, and is the co-author of several other Unleashed programming titles.

Viktor doesn't believe in "religious wars" or "OS advocacy": Windows, OS/2, and Linux happily coexist in his home office. The first Linux version he installed some six years ago on an old, retired 386SX system was 0.96; he has been using Linux ever since as a network operating system and development platform. He set up Linux-based comprehensive Internet solutions for several clients, and he continues to maintain some of these systems. He also used Linux to develop applications such as a real-time test system for a telephone company switching office.

Viktor lives with his wife in the capital of Canada, Ottawa, surrounded by several hundred pounds of computing equipment (his), knitting yarn (hers), an ever more unruly cat, and books. He spends his copious amounts of free time managing one of the oldest multiuser games in existence, MUD2, at the Internet site mud2.com (running Linux of course.)

Tell Us What You Think!

As the reader of this book, *you* are our most important critic and commentator. We value your opinion and want to know what we're doing right, what we could do better, what areas you'd like to see us publish in, and any other words of wisdom you're willing to pass our way.

As an associate publisher for Sams, I welcome your comments. You can fax, email, or write me directly to let me know what you did or didn't like about this book—as well as what we can do to make our books stronger.

Please note that I cannot help you with technical problems related to the topic of this book, and that due to the high volume of mail I receive, I might not be able to reply to every message.

When you write, please be sure to include this book's title and author as well as your name and phone or fax number. I will carefully review your comments and share them with the author and editors who worked on the book.

Fax: 317.581.4770

Email: opsys@mcp.com

Mail: *Associate Publisher*
Sams
201 West 103rd Street
Indianapolis, IN 46290 USA

Preface

My first encounter with the Linux operating system was in 1993, when I signed up as a volunteer forum operator (sysop) for the UNIX forum of the ill-fated National Videotex Network, or NVN. NVN is long gone now, one of the victims of the vicious fight for dominance in the online services market. Linux, on the other hand, is here to stay, as a professional-quality operating system with many features and a price that's quite literally unbeatable.

Despite the years I spent working with Linux (and enjoying it most of the time), I don't consider myself a Linux "advocate." That is to say that I do not intend to convince you that Linux is the best operating system out there or that you should immediately junk your Microsoft CD-ROMs. I do, however, intend to prove that there are certain tasks for which Linux provides a superior solution.

In other words, this book is not for the "Linux crowd"; these people already know what a magnificent operating system Linux is and use it daily. No, this book is for the rest of us who'd like to put Linux to good use today instead of waiting for a glamorous day in the future when Linux becomes a true Windows competitor. My aim is to show that it can be done—that Linux, even today, can be a great money-saver when used in areas where it has strengths. I also intend to show that Linux does not need to compete with Windows; the two can exist together, benefiting everyone.

Take, for example, a system used by a company of approximately 20 employees as a corporate mail server, network router, firewall gateway, World Wide Web server, and PPP server for dial-up connections. A powerful machine, one would think. Then again, the machine I have in mind—a very real system performing its tasks even at this very moment—is an old 80486 with only eight megabytes of memory and a few hundred megabytes of hard disk space.

Of course, the cost of hardware means little by itself. Talking of "total cost of owner-ship" is the rage these days. Perhaps a fairly solid argument in this regard comes in the form of a single line of text, printed by a simple Linux utility (the uptime program) on yet another "live" production system:

```
8:37am  up 57 days, 19:52,  3 users,  load average: 0.07, 0.06, 0.03
```

Incidentally, an uptime of 57 days is not at all unusual; these systems typically run with-out crashes or other problems for several hundred days in a row. A well-configured Linux system is a low-maintenance system indeed!

That's not to say that everything is rosy: configuring a Linux machine can be difficult. Indeed, this was the very reason why I proposed this book to Macmillan in the fall of 1998. Over the years I've spent setting up and maintaining small office Linux servers, I've acquired valuable experience. Although I'm a professional developer myself, I do not believe that this experience belongs to the exclusive domain of "geeks." On the con-trary, I firmly believe that nonprogrammers (who nevertheless know a thing or two about computers and aren't afraid of formatting a hard disk or installing a network card) can make good use of it.

Actually, I have one such nonprogrammer in mind: a personal friend who is co-owner of a small business here in Ottawa. He's not a programmer, but as manager of a business that's involved with computer consulting and software development projects, he has been using a computer at work for many years. Using the material that's presented here, he should be able to haul out an old 486-class computer from his storage room, set up Linux on it, and get his company on the Internet, complete with a Web site, a mail server, and other goodies in a matter of days.

Or, to put it in other words, this book is for real people who wish to implement real solu-tions while cutting through the hype. I'm not writing for "dummies" (much as I'd like to claim otherwise, I have no idea how to teach Linux system administration to someone who can't tell a power switch from a screwdriver). But then again, in my experience, most people who are seriously considering Linux as a network operating system feel comfortable with basic system management tasks and can even replace a broken hard drive or faulty network card in their computers.

My confidence in Linux as a solid business platform is based not on faith or ideology but on several years' worth of practical experience with this uniquely capable operating sys-tem. I hope I'll be able to pass on this experience to others. Will I succeed? You, the reader, will be the judge of the quality of my work presented here.

Included with this book is a CD-ROM containing Caldera OpenLinux 1.3. Although this is no longer the most recent version of this distribution, unless you're possessed by the daemon of "versionitis" and you just must have the latest software version installed on your systems, this CD-ROM will remain a useful tool for several years to come. For one thing, essential Linux components can easily be upgraded from the Internet. For another, I've found it better, at least on production systems, to stick with a known CD-ROM as your baseline distribution rather than trying to install the latest distribution every time one becomes available.

I should also mention that much of the material in this book is not specific to the distribution found on the attached CD-ROM. Most chapters contain information that remains equally valid regardless of which Linux distribution you use. Many chapters also contain an account of my experiences on a test machine that I used while writing this book to build a Linux test system that could act as a small office server. These chapters are organized in such a way that makes it easy to separate general information from any notes specific to this test installation.

The test installation itself is very similar to configurations I've built over the years— some of which I still actively manage. These systems provide Internet routing and fire-wall gateway services and act as Web servers and Internet mail servers, and more, serving up to 30 users in the case of one installation, and over 200 online game users in the case of another.

The planned test configuration is that of a multipurpose Internet server that performs the following functions:

- Act as an Internet router, connecting computers on a local area network (LAN) to an Internet Service Provider (ISP) using demand-dial to conserve online time
- Perform network firewall functions such as network aliasing, packet filtering, and accounting
- Act as a Domain Name Server (DNS) host for computers on the local area network
- Act as a dial-up server for incoming calls
- Provide Internet mail (POP3 and SMTP) services for the LAN, with protection against email spam and unauthorized relaying
- Perform batch mail transfer using the UUCP protocol
- Act as a WWW (HTTP) server for an intranet or the Internet
- Provide File Transfer Protocol (FTP) services
- Act as a newsgroup server using Usenet news (NNTP) technology
- Provide file and printer sharing for Windows clients using Samba

Needless to say, many real-life situations do not require that all these services be installed. This list, as well as many of the lists in this book, is a "shopping list." Feel free to pick and choose those items you need, ignoring the rest.

Although this book contains many examples, this is not a cookbook of any sort. I believe that such an approach is inherently doomed to failure when the goal is to aid readers who want to administer a Linux server. Such a server can be a complex, living thing that will serve you at home or in your office for many years; keeping the beast alive absolutely requires that you go beyond copying cookbook recipes and actually understand what's going on in your system, and why.

Many of the software packages described in this book are quite complex. Some of them are so big, entire books have been written about them! Needless to say, it's impossible to cover all their features in a small chapter. Instead, I'm focusing on their most typical modes of operation, demonstrating how you can install them and make them work in a simple configuration. To go beyond that, you'll need to refer to the documentation included with the package, the online manual pages, or other books dedicated to the specific subject. To help you with this, manual page references and Web addresses are included in this book.

Being an author of titles aimed at programmers, putting this book together was a new experience for me. It would have been impossible without the patience and valuable comments of my development editor, Laura Bulcher. Thanks, Laura, for putting up with me!

In closing, I should also express say my thanks to the thousands of volunteers whose work made this amazing operating system possible, proving to the world that free, open software can match, and often exceed, "commercial-grade" software in terms of quality and versatility.

Conventions Used in This Book

Linux: A Network Solution for Your Office is designed to help you get your new Linux network up and running. In doing so, this book uses the following conventions:

- **Bold monospace** text indicates information that you type.
- You'll see monospace text for URLs, onscreen messages, and command output.
- Any words that are being defined or emphasized will appear in *italics*.

TEST SYSTEM

I do, in fact, practice what I preach. The Test System sections are an account of my experiences on a test machine that I used in tandem with writing this book. When I talk about my own system, you'll see it treated with notations similar to those at the beginning and end of this section.

▲

NOTE

You'll find notes throughout the book. They indicate something I'd like you to remember or take a look at, or they might point you to other portions of the book.

WARNING

Warnings are your cue to pay attention. I'll take advantage of these to point out important cautions or information you should take to heart.

## Part I

Introduction

1 Introduction

2 The Linux Workhorse

## Chapter 1

Introduction

Everybody is talking about Linux these days. Gone are the days when this operating system belonged to the exclusive domain of computer geeks wanting to run a *real* computer system (that is, one running an operating system other than MS-DOS) in their basement. If reports on the all-news cable networks and newspaper articles mean anything, Linux has grown to be a major contender in the ever-changing market of computer operating systems.

But what, exactly, is Linux? How does it differ from that ubiquitous desktop operating system from Redmond? And most importantly, what does Linux mean to you if you are just someone trying to create meaningful business solutions on a moderate budget? How can this be accomplished?

It is the purpose of this book to provide answers to these questions in the most practical fashion by demonstrating how Linux can be used as a server operating system to create meaningful, reliable, robust business solutions. But don't touch that Linux CD-ROM just yet; you need to briefly review the basics first.

View the first two chapters of this book as a very superficial reference containing the basics about Linux's essential concepts. These are things you should to know *before* you attempt to install a Linux system. Or to put it in another way, unless you are familiar with the ideas presented here, it's unlikely that you'll manage to create a successful installation, and even if you do, you'd have no idea what you just did and why.

Linux: The Roots

No need to worry, this is not an attempt to fill pages with another recounting of the colorful quarter-century long history of the UNIX family of operating systems. However, to better understand what Linux can do for you, it is necessary to put it in context.

Linux is, for all practical intents and purposes, a version of the popular UNIX family of operating systems. Its main distinguishing characteristic is price; most commercial UNIX versions cost a lot of money, whereas Linux is free. The money you pay for a Linux CD covers the cost of distribution or any add-on products the distributor has included on the CD. The Linux license itself is not only distributed with no royalty, but the rights are also granted to redistribute. In other words, you can actually start copying and selling your own Linux distribution right away. However, you can only charge a fee for the cost of copying, packaging, and distributing, or for value-added materials. You cannot charge for the software license, and furthermore, you must grant the same freedom to copy and redistribute to your licensees. This is the essence of the GNU Public License, also called the *copyleft* license, under the terms of which Linux has been released.

A Brief History

According to Linux lore, Linux was born out of frustration; specifically, the frustrations of one Finnish man, Linus Torvalds, who believed that a previous free operating system project, the GNU project, was not likely to produce a working kernel anytime soon. So he sat down and wrote his own operating system. A man of simple pleasures, isn't he?

Perhaps the secret to Mr. Torvalds' success lies in the fact that, unlike the goals of the GNU project, his original objective was not to create a portable operating system that runs on all kinds of computer platforms—he merely wanted to create an operating system that runs on the most popular (and cheapest) of all platforms, that of IBM-compatible PCs. He also concentrated on the task of creating the operating system's core module, the kernel, instead of building a large number of supporting utilities first. (In fact, to date, Linux relies on many such utilities and building blocks that come from the GNU project.)

Of course that initial version of Linux was essentially a primitive experiment; it took years before Linux became ready for prime time. It also took the work of thousands of seasoned programmers who created many essential system components and ported Linux to a variety of hardware platforms in their spare time. Why would programmers do that? "Because it is there," to quote George Mallory, the mountaineer who in 1924 disappeared while trying to climb Mount Everest. It's not every day that a programmer has the opportunity to contribute to a world-class operating system. Not only are there programmers willing to do it for free, but I bet some would even consider paying for the privilege!

By the time I had my first encounter with Linux in 1993, it was a rapidly maturing operating system. Some rough edges notwithstanding, it had all the features of UNIX that I was familiar with. It also had a unique feature not shared by other UNIX implementations: it ran quite well on the machine I was using for test purposes at the time, an old 386SX computer with 4MB of memory.

Flavors of UNIX

While there are many different UNIX implementations out there, most of them belong to one of two families: BSD and System V.

UNIX System V is based on the "original" UNIX, as developed by AT&T Bell Labs. If you see the label, SVR5, it actually stands for System V Release 5, which is the latest version of this operating system. For the Intel platform, SVR5 is marketed as UnixWare, by SCO of Santa Cruz, California.

BSD stands for Berkeley Standard Distribution. Berkeley UNIX was developed as a research-oriented alternative to System V. Perhaps the best known variant of BSD UNIX is the operating system of Sun workstations, SunOS.

Both of these families brought about many new features and enhancements over the years. For instance, one System V enhancement was *shared memory*, a feature that allowed simultaneously executing applications to share data. An important Berkeley enhancement was called *Berkeley sockets*, a data communication mechanism that became a fundamental tool for network programming on the Internet.

Fortunately, Linux incorporates most important System V and BSD features. This makes it possible to easily port applications from other UNIX implementations to Linux. Indeed, this was probably one reason behind Linux's early popularity; not only was the operating system available for free and running on low-end PCs, it was also compatible with many existing programs. And, because even in the days prior to Linux it was already common practice to distribute scientific- or research-oriented software packages over the Internet in source code form, would-be users were often able to accomplish the port themselves, even if they had limited programming experience.

How Good Is Linux?

Linux is free software. Not too long ago, this statement automatically implied software of inferior quality, software that is suitable, at best, for hobbyists and enthusiasts, but not for serious work.

As Open Source software gains increasing credibility in the mass media, this perception has all but disappeared. Open Source software is used for a growing number of serious applications.

Linux as a Server Operating System

Indeed, according to recent statistics, Linux has become the most popular operating system in use by small Internet service providers (ISPs). There are signs that even Microsoft is taking notice; apart from Windows NT, Linux is the only server operating system that continues to gain market share.

What server features does Linux offer? At the core, you have the Linux kernel, equipped with the networking and security features found in most versions of UNIX. These include the following:

- IP networking, which is the networking standard on which the Internet is built
- Support for a variety of local area network interfaces (LAN cards)
- Support for dial-up networking, ISDN, and other wide area network (WAN) systems, including support for incoming data calls
- Router features such as packet forwarding, which allows Linux to act as a gateway for a network connected to the Internet
- Firewall features such as packet filtering, accounting, and masquerading, which makes it possible to turn Linux into a sophisticated corporate firewall

These features are provided by the operating system core, also known as the *kernel*. While these features alone make Linux useful, a large variety of server applications are also available. These allow Linux to provide the following:

- A high-capacity email server using sendmail
- A sophisticated WWW server with optional secure socket (SSL) support using Apache

- UNIX-style shared data services using NFS (Network File System)
- UNIX-style network printing support
- MS-DOS/Windows style file and printer sharing support using Samba
- Novell NetWare/IntraNetWare connectivity and NDS using NetWare for Linux
- Commonly used Internet services including FTP (File Transfer Protocol) and Telnet
- Additional UNIX-style services such as Remote Procedure Call (RPC) support or Network Time Protocol (NTP) support

The best news is that most of the service applications required to implement these features come free of charge and can be easily installed even on low-cost hardware—computers that would be considered totally unsuitable for running Windows NT, for instance.

Linux on the Desktop?

Linux's strengths as a network server operating system are indisputable. However, although many of its advocates would like to portray otherwise, Linux is not always an adequate replacement for a well-equipped Windows machine on the office desktop. While efforts to bring quality office automation applications, such as Corel's WordPerfect, to Linux are commendable, they have not made Linux an overnight Windows competitor.

One reason is the windowing system used with Linux. Many good things can be said about the X Window System's client/server design and modular architecture, but it lacks many features and utilities that Windows users take for granted. Copying text and graphics from one window and pasting it into another is second nature for most seasoned Windows users; yet even this simple operation is not necessarily possible under X, as most applications do not offer compatible clipboard support. More advanced features, such as object embedding like that of OLE, or high performance multimedia services aren't supported on the operating system level and must be implemented by applications or extensions to the system. There is also a lack of standardized utilities, which makes it more difficult for users to learn and effectively use X.

Another reason why Linux is not (yet) a good desktop alternative is the lack of application support. In this area, however, rapid change is taking place. Led by Corel and Netscape, an increasing number of recognized software companies are lining up behind this operating system.

Linux Reliability

When you select an operating system, an important consideration is its reliability. How stable is it? How well does it maintain its integrity when an application crashes? How well does it recover from a system crash? This is especially important when the operating system is used for a server where unattended operation is a requirement; but even with workstations, reliability is a concern. Remember the terrible reputation of 16-bit versions of Windows with their UAEs (Unidentified Application Errors) and GPFs (General Protection Faults), which almost invariably brought down the entire operating system? Working with these was a real pain. It was while using these early Windows versions that I acquired the habit of saving what I write after every paragraph or even more often.

Today users are more accustomed to operating systems that run for days or weeks without a crash or reboot. In my personal experience, Linux fares very well in this regard, better in fact than Windows NT. Linux servers that I manage practically never crash; they are brought down only because of maintenance or reconfiguration. It is not unusual to see an uptime—measured in days—that runs into three digits. The record I saw was well in excess of six months, but I've heard rumors of Linux systems that stayed up for a year or more, despite heavy use. These facts appear to confirm that Linux is indeed an industry-strength operating system well suited for demanding tasks.

Source Availability

Linux, as well as most Linux server applications, come with full source code. That means that in addition to the executable code that lets you run the operating system, you also get the human readable version—the engineering blueprints. This allows you to implement custom changes, fixes, and extensions, and create your own private version of the operating system.

This can be a blessing because, at least in theory, the availability of source code means that you do not have to rely on external parties for support. If you encounter a bug in the operating system or one of its components and you have the necessary expertise, you might be able to fix the bug yourself instead of waiting for a fix from the software's author.

Such expertise, however, is not readily available; not everyone qualifies as a Linux kernel programmer. Worse yet, some people with a little bit of programming background fancy themselves as kernel programmers, which they aren't; chances are that their fixes create more problems than they solve. I encountered the work of one such expert in the early days of Linux. The first version of the X Window System refused to run on my video card because, as it turned out, someone helpfully rearranged blocks of source code in the driver module for no apparent reason other than to make it "look better."

And this is where the availability of the source code can turn into a curse. Insufficient expertise combined with a lack of discipline often results in local Linux servers running mangled versions of the operating system that no longer exhibit the robustness and reliability of controlled Linux distributions. Fear of such a proliferation of uncontrolled operating system versions is what caused some system administrators to shy away from Linux in the past.

My advice is that you shouldn't touch the source code, unless

- You're a kernel programmer and know what you're doing
- You have a problem that requires an immediate solution
- You have tried the latest fixes and patches and they didn't solve the problem

Even if you do touch the source code, keep in mind that any such changes should be treated as temporary. Contact the authors of the relevant components immediately and let them know the problems you had and the fixes you implemented. Also keep your eyes open for a Linux patch that provides a *supported* version of your changes.

Of course sometimes you touch the source code for another reason: You need a customized version of Linux to be used in a special environment, such as an unmanned weather station in the Australian outback or as a controller for a scientific experiment aboard the Space Shuttle. Although these are all real-life examples, such exotic uses of Linux are, however, clearly beyond the scope of this book.

Installation Roadmap

The stated purpose of this book is to provide practical advice in setting up a production Linux system in a small office. Chapter 2, "The Linux Workhorse," contains some practical advice and information you need to know before you insert a Linux installation CD into a computer's CD-ROM drive. Starting with Chapter 3, "System Installation," most of this book is dedicated to guiding you through the installation of a basic Linux system, and installing and configuring many commonly used server components (see Figure 1.1).

FIGURE 1.1
A Linux installation roadmap.

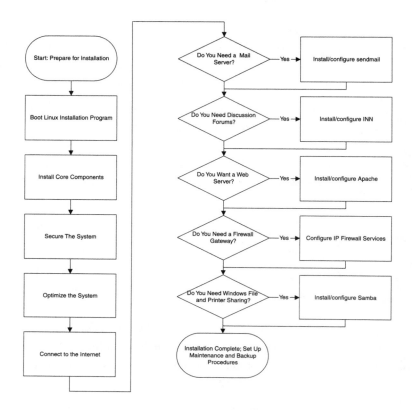

Initial Setup

The first installation step is obvious: A basic Linux system must be copied and configured on your computer's hard disk. Prior to this step, several questions need to be answered, such as whether the target system is going to be a *dual boot* computer (that is, a machine capable of loading more than one operating system), and how the destination hard disk should be partitioned and formatted.

After core system files are copied, you need to set up user accounts. In some cases, it might also be necessary to reconfigure, or *recompile* the kernel to best match your computer's hardware configuration.

When the operating system is up and running, it must be secured. This is very important! Any system that acts in a server role must be protected against intrusion. You might not have reasons to fear malicious hackers or disgruntled employees, but your system can become victim to an honest mistake against which it could have been easily protected had it been properly configured in the first place. And malicious hackers exist; even as I write this, thousands of scam artists on the Internet are running software that is specifically designed to look for unsecured mail and FTP servers that they can exploit for sending bulk email or exchanging stolen software. The most important step you can take to improve security is the removal of unwanted services; many Linux distributions, by default, install a number of service applications that you might not need, and which might exist only to provide potential security holes for hackers to exploit. It's also a good idea to be thoroughly familiar with the service applications that do remain installed, and know what they do, how they behave, how they report or log events.

Having your system properly configured (so that it can correctly manage all hardware components) and secured, it is time to connect it to the Internet. How that is accomplished depends on a number of factors: your needs, your budget, and the availability of services in your geographic area. Is your system part of a LAN? Is it going to provide routing for other computers on that network? Is it going to be used as a firewall gateway? Is your connection going to be permanent (up 24 hours a day) or on-demand? In addition to IP connectivity, what other services do you require from your would-be ISP? These are all questions that need to be asked, and answered, in order to set up a functioning connection that matches your needs.

Providing any kind of a service on the Internet requires that you have a permanent *domain name*. When you connect via an ordinary ISP account, you are usually assigned a domain name or an IP address on-the-fly, which is always different when you reconnect. That's not a problem when you are cruising the Web, but others won't be able to locate your server when its name and location are subject to change. Besides, most people wouldn't be satisfied with an address such as `ppp-23-45-67.nodethree.easternregion.myisp.net` printed on their business card instead of something simple such as `www.mud2.com`. In order to offer your own domain name, you may need to register it (and pay a fee), and you or your ISP will also have to provide the corresponding DNS (domain name service) database entries.

Prerequisites in place, it is time to connect. Most long-distance Internet connections are accomplished using PPP, the *Point-to-Point Protocol*. PPP works over modem connections, ISDN lines, and more. You can also configure your system to accept incoming PPP connections, whether it is for yourself when you travel or for employees dialing in from their homes.

When you get to this point during system installation and configuration, you will have a fully configured and connected Linux system. This system, however, is not really a server yet: for that, server applications need to be added and configured.

Basic Services

Because email is consistently listed as the most popular service for users on the Internet, it is only appropriate to deal with it first. You don't have to set up your own mail server; many ISPs offer a limited number of personal email accounts on their own server. However, setting up your own email server offers many advantages, not the least of which is the flexibility of being able to manage your own mail accounts, as opposed to having to send a request to your ISP every time an account needs to be added or deleted. The most widely used email server program is *sendmail*. An industry standard, sendmail can be extremely difficult to configure (mostly due to an arcane syntax in its configuration file) but the result—an industry-strength, secure, high-performance mail server—is worth the effort. This server also cooperates well with popular email applications, such as pine and elm under UNIX, Microsoft Outlook, Outlook Express, or Netscape Communicator under Windows.

For many years, Usenet News was one of the most widely known Internet features. The underlying newsgroup technology remains popular for setting up discussion groups on the Internet or intranets. Newsgroups can be set up with a moderate level of effort and offer public discussion forums that can be easily accessed using many popular applications, including Outlook Express and Netscape Communicator.

Of course, if your Linux server is permanently connected to the Internet, you'll probably want to set up a Web server. Who wouldn't these days? Besides, apart from the convenience of having direct control over your server, you may also be able to save considerable sums of money when compared with placing a Web site on an ISP's Web server. Setting up a simple Web service using the popular Apache server is not a terribly difficult task, although there are pitfalls as usual (and security issues that you must deal with.) Along with the Web server, you might also want to configure the FTP service. After the Web server is running, you can add options such as Microsoft's FrontPage extensions (if you want to run the FrontPage program on client computers) or a secure sockets layer (SSL) implementation if you want to offer secure transactions.

Advanced Networking

Your system is up and running. Your mail server is operating fine, and you watch with satisfaction as your Web server's log files grow, indicating that your Web site is getting more popular every day. What's next?

Popularity means exposure: the more people visit your server, the more likely one of them will try more than just downloading your company's home page. To protect against such an occurrence, you decide to configure your Linux server as a firewall gateway. Such a gateway effectively *hides* other machines on your network, while still permitting useful data traffic. Unfortunately, there is no such thing as a free lunch; increased security means that you'll have to accept a few compromises. Before you configure Linux as a firewall, you must understand what these compromises are, and what a firewall can and cannot protect you against.

Up to this point, it was assumed that you use your Linux server as your router/gateway, that is, the computer that physically connects to your ISP. That doesn't have to be so; often, you might opt for an external router device instead. Linux can be configured to utilize such a router; it can also be configured to stand between the router and the rest of your network and perform firewall gateway functions.

In the 1980s when LANs for MS-DOS based computers first became popular, their primary function was to offer access to shared storage and printing services. Although shared storage is no longer the money-saver it used to be (not when you can buy hard disks at $25 per gigabyte) it is still convenient to be able to share files by copying them to a network location. Similarly, printers might be cheap but it might not be practical to place one on everyone's desk. The alternative is to connect a printer to a network server. Linux can act as a server for Microsoft Windows' client computers using an application called Samba (named after the SMB protocol that is at the core of Windows networking.) Configuring Samba isn't difficult but there are a few tricks and pitfalls; and, as usual, security can be an issue as well.

Are you annoyed when your computer's clock is 15 minutes ahead? When every computer on your network shows a different time? The solution is to set up a time service on your Linux server, which can be configured to synchronize itself from publicly accessible time servers on the Internet. You can then configure client computers to keep their own clocks synchronized with the server. I am used to seeing a clock on my Windows NT taskbar that is accurate to the second. This is not just merely an issue of convenience, this can also help ensure that shared files are updated with the proper date/time stamp, or that networked applications run with the same date/time setting on different computers.

System Management

Setting up a Linux system is just one half of the story. The system must also be monitored and managed, possibly on a daily basis. Linux servers usually run without a complaint for months at a time, but it still helps to perform administrative tasks on a regular basis to look for signs of trouble. And, of course, the system should be backed up regularly to prevent disaster.

Daily Operations

The first item that is to be managed is the list of user accounts. Even in small organizations, people come and go; new employees are hired, others leave. People's needs will also change; an employee who until now only had an email account might now need to have write access to a portion of the company Web page for editing, or might require the ability to dial in from home using a modem.

An often overlooked system management task is monitoring system logs. Like any decent server operating system, Linux keeps several log files in which important system events, as well as errors and warnings, are recorded. These log files should be checked from time to time for suspicious content, and they also need to be trimmed, otherwise they may end up occupying undue amounts of disk space. In addition to the operating system, many server applications keep logs themselves; for instance, the Apache Web server keeps at least two log files for each virtual host.

Backups are your best—and sometimes only—protection against catastrophic data loss. Before you can start backing up your system, however, a few questions need to be answered. What media will your backups use? How are you going to be able to access backup data in case your system is physically damaged? Do you have a need to compress or encrypt your backup files? Are you going to store data from more than one machine on your backup media?

This book is not about programming, and it is not written for programmers, but a little bit of programming can go a long way when it comes to system management. A script no more complex than a simple MS-DOS batch file can help you perform unattended backups, the trimming of log files, and more. It is also useful to become familiar with Linux's capability to run scheduled tasks in the background at a predetermined time.

Another chore of the Linux system administrator is setting up client workstations to communicate with the server. Installing and configuring other operating systems is clearly beyond the scope of this book. Instead, this book addresses specific issues such as configuring Windows networking or setting up software such as mail clients, Web browsers, and Web authoring tools.

Lastly, a system administrator must also maintain the system's security. This is accomplished through an appropriately formulated security policy, and through monitoring the system and its log files. Most importantly, a thorough knowledge of your system's configuration and an understanding of potential security problems are your best guarantee against a disaster, be it a result of ill will or carelessness.

Disaster Recovery

Every computer user's worst nightmare is a system crash that irreversibly damages or destroys the computer, its configuration, or the data stored on it. Because computers are just machines that are subject to wear and tear, such disasters not only can happen, they *do* happen. Therefore, it is essential to be prepared, maintain backups, and have a plan to recover from such an eventuality.

When a system crashes or behaves in an unexpected fashion, the first step toward recovery is diagnosis—you must find out what is wrong before you can fix it. Diagnosing a system is pretty difficult if you cannot even start it up! Therefore it is important to know how you can boot up your computer from a floppy disk or CD-ROM and access data such as log files and configuration information on your hard disk. After you have access, you can diagnose hardware problems by reviewing logs and performing other tests, and you can fix many problems by adjusting configuration settings. Even if repair or replacement of hardware is necessary, being able to boot into your system might help you identify the problem, copy essential files, or even start up the system with the broken components disabled, and offer limited service until a replacement arrives.

Sometimes none of it is sufficient. In order to continue providing services, you need to move your system to a backup computer. Easier said than done, especially if the hardware specifications of your primary and backup systems are not identical. Setting up a backup system, restoring data to it from backup media, and connecting it to the network to take the place of your primary machine is the topic of Chapter 22, "Moving to Backup Hardware."

Summary

Linux is rapidly gaining recognition as a robust, high-performance UNIX-compatible operating system. While support in the area of desktop applications lags behind that of

Microsoft Windows, Linux is remarkably well suited as an Internet server platform. Server applications that implement an Internet mail service, World Wide Web service, routing support, IP firewall support, dial-up networking, and more are available, generally free of charge, as part of the operating system distribution. Linux, as well as many applications, comes with full source code; while this can provide maintenance problems of its own, it can also mean new support solutions not available with other operating systems.

Linux installation begins with a few preparatory steps, such as creating a hardware inventory or deciding how your hard disks are to be partitioned. Placing a copy of the operating system on the hard drive is the next step, following initial configuration of security settings, network setup, and installation of server applications.

After your system is up and running, you will have to establish routine maintenance procedures. Such procedures ensure that the system remains healthy, maintains up-to-date backups, and provides a means to recover when disaster strikes.

## Chapter 2

The Linux Workhorse

Because of its reliability and the near flawless service that I received from Linux over the years, I believe in calling this operating system a workhorse.

Know thy horse before you attempt to ride. Before you can move on to the practicalities of installing and running Linux, it is a good idea to become familiar with your horse's basic anatomy. This chapter provides a brief overview of some of the most fundamental UNIX concepts, demonstrated through practical examples that you'll be able to try out yourself once you have a running Linux system. Feel free to use this chapter as a reference you can return to anytime later if necessary.

This chapter is not meant as a complete reference of basic Linux commands and operations. In most cases, you should be able to obtain additional information through online help. However, if you believe you can use a printed guide or reference on the basics, I recommend *Learning the UNIX Operating System*, by Grace Todino and John Strang.

Anatomy of a Horse

Like any well-kept horse in good working condition, Linux is an animal of four legs. And although Linux is not a member of the class *Mammalia*, its hind legs, like the rear legs of most mammals, play a more fundamental role than the front pair (see Figure 2.1).

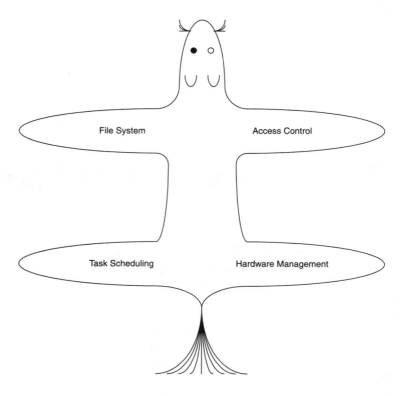

What on Earth am I talking about? The hind legs of an operating system are its core components performing the following services:

- Task scheduling
- Hardware management

Task scheduling is what you call the operating system's capability to load and execute programs. In the case of a multitasking operating system such as Linux, this gets more complicated as the operating system manages multiple applications at the same time, allowing them to share the computer's processor, memory, and other resources without conflict.

Hardware management is what the operating system does to hide the gory details and make it possible for application programmers to think in terms of higher level abstractions. For instance, this capability lets an application program print a line of text with no knowledge of the precise type of the display hardware involved, or of low-level operations such as moving bits representing characters of text to display memory.

Without this pair of hind legs, no operating system can exist. Even the most primitive operating systems have the capability to perform a minimal set of hardware-related services and to execute programs.

To continue with the horse analogy, Linux's front pair of legs is nearly as important as the hind pair:

- File system
- Access control

The file system is what turns bits, bytes, or blocks of data stored on your computer's hard disk into the familiar concepts of files and directories.

The access control mechanism assigns *rights* to objects such as hardware devices, running processes, and files. It is what makes an operating system *multiuser*. It's one thing to make a computer run several programs at once; it's another, equally complex exercise to allow multiple users to execute programs simultaneously without interfering with each other. In other words, the ability to edit a text file while at the same time working on a spreadsheet makes a great workstation. The ability to edit a text file while someone else is working on a spreadsheet on the same computer is what makes Linux a true server operating system.

Before proceeding with the practical tasks of setting up a working Linux system, it is best to first make a small detour and examine in more detail how the four legs of the Linux "horse" are implemented, and how they manifest themselves to the system's administrator. This is important background information that helps you better understand what you are doing when you finally take a deep breath and pop a Linux CD-ROM into a computer for installation.

Processes

Linux has the capability to run multiple programs (or processes) simultaneously. It is what is called a *preemptive* multitasking operating system. In recent years, this phrase was often seen even in non-technical publications and articles when characterizing Microsoft Windows 3.1 as a non-preemptive system.

The difference lies in the operating system's capability to maintain control of the computer's processor. In a preemptive operating system, after a process runs for a certain amount of time (also called the *time-slice*), the operating system forcefully regains control and allows other processes to run. In a cooperative operating system such as

Microsoft Windows 3.1, this is not so; a process must explicitly be written so as to relinquish control. Needless to say, preemptive operating systems tend to be more reliable because they can retain control of the processor even in the presence of runaway applications.

Like most other UNIX variants, Linux organizes processes into a hierarchy. With the sole exception of the "mother of all processes" each process has a parent; one parent can have multiple descendants, so processes can have siblings.

EXAMPLE
To see the running processes on a Linux system, you would typically use the ps command. For instance, if you issue **ps j** on a Linux system, you might get a list of running programs similar to the following:

```
 PPID   PID  PGID   SID TTY TPGID  STAT   UID   TIME COMMAND
16209 16210 16210 16210  p1 18530  S      501   0:00 -bash
16210 18530 18530 16210  p1 18530  R      501   0:00 ps j
```

What this list tells you is that the user who issued the ps command is currently running two processes; the bash shell (I'll talk about shells in just a moment) and the ps command itself. It's also fairly easy to decrypt the first two columns: PID stands for Process ID, and PPID stands for Parent Process ID. The parent of the ps process is process 16210, which is the bash shell. But what about the parent of bash process 16209?

That process, as well as a number (possibly dozens) of other processes are not seen in this list for one reason: The ps command only displays processes under the control of the current user by default. On a multiuser system such as Linux, processes can coexist under the control of different users as well as the operating system itself. Indeed, on most normal Linux installations, a number of processes would always be running under the operating system's control and providing services such as a mail server, Web server, and more. If you typed **ps ajx** instead of **ps j**, you would have received a much lengthier list:

```
 PPID    PID  PGID   SID  TTY  TPGID STAT   UID    TIME COMMAND
    0      1     0     0    ?     -1   S       0   1:48 init [4]
    1      2     1     1    ?     -1   SW      0   0:00 (kflushd)
    1      3     1     1    ?     -1   SW<     0   0:00 (kswapd)
    1     12    12    12    ?     -1   S       0   0:17 /sbin/update
    1     13    13    13    ?     -1   S       0   0:00 /sbin/kerneld
    1     49    46    46    ?     -1   S       0   0:00 /usr/sbin/
                                                   ➥crond -l10
    1     69    69    69    ?     -1   S       0   1:28 /usr/sbin/
                                                   ➥syslogd -r
```

▼

▼

1	71	71	71	?	-1	S		0	0:00 /usr/sbin/klogd
1	75	75	75	?	-1	S		0	0:02 /usr/sbin/inetd
75	16209	75	75	?	-1	S		0	0:03 /usr/bin/X11/ ➥color_ xterm -s
1	77	77	77	?	-1	S		0	0:13 /usr/sbin/named
1	79	79	79	?	-1	S		0	0:00 /usr/sbin/lpd
1	94	94	94	?	-1	S		0	0:01 gpm -t bm
1	96	96	96	?	-1	S	<	0	0:05 /usr/local/bin/ ➥xntpd
1	97	97	97	1	97	S		0	0:00 /sbin/agetty 38400 ➥tty1 lin
1	98	98	98	2	98	S		0	0:00 /sbin/agetty 38400 ➥tty2 lin
1	99	99	99	3	99	S		0	0:00 /sbin/agetty 38400 ➥tty3 lin
1	100	100	100	4	100	S		0	0:00 /sbin/agetty ➥38400tty4 lin
1	101	101	101	5	101	S		0	0:00 /sbin/agetty ➥38400tty5 lin
1	102	102	102	6	102	S		0	0:00 /sbin/agetty ➥38400tty6 lin
1	2458	2458	2458	?	-1	S		0	0:00 /usr/sbin/httpsd
2458	5109	2458	2458	?	-1	S		60000	0:03 /usr/sbin/httpsd
2458	5118	2458	2458	?	-1	S		60000	0:00 /usr/sbin/httpsd
2458	5124	2458	2458	?	-1	S		60000	0:00 /usr/sbin/httpsd
2458	5135	2458	2458	?	-1	S		60000	0:00 /usr/sbin/httpsd
1	9519	9519	9519	?	-1	S		0	0:10 sendmail: ➥accepting connect
16209	16210	16210	16210	p1	18530	S		501	0:00 -bash
1	18030	18030	18030	?	-1	S		0	0:00 /usr/local/sbin/ ➥mgetty -n 2
16210	18530	18530	16210	p1	18530	R		501	0:00 ps aj

At the top of the list is process 1, init, or the "mother of all processes" mentioned earlier. This is the only process that has no parent (PPID=0); all other top-level processes (that is, processes started by the operating system) are descendants of the init process.

With this more complete listing, it is now possible to trace the complete family tree (see Figure 2.2) of your ps command. The immediate parent, bash (16210) is a descendant of process 16209, a color_xterm process. (Don't worry about it for now, it's simply a program that allows text input and output in a window on a graphical display.) That program, in turn, is a descendant of process 75, the inetd daemon.

▼

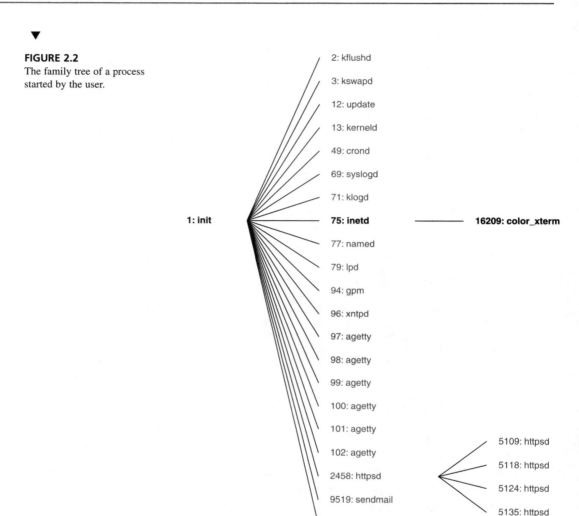

FIGURE 2.2
The family tree of a process
started by the user.

The inetd server, like several other key service processes, was initiated by the operating system at startup. Its parent, therefore, is the init process with process ID 1.

Most top-level processes are started by the operating system to perform a specific server function. One common example is the sendmail daemon: this is the process that turns your Linux machine into an Internet mail server.

Needless to say, system administrators have full control over what services should be started on their system. For instance, it is possible to disable sendmail (or never even install it in the first place) on a system which is not expected to provide Internet mail services. The administrator can also start or stop processes on-the-fly, dynamically altering the system's runtime configuration as necessary. This actually can lead to some confusion; the steps required to start sendmail by hand, for instance, are quite different from the steps needed to ensure that it is started by default when the system is booted.

Service applications that run in the background with no visible user interface are called *daemons*. One of the most important daemons is the `inetd` daemon, also often called the Internet Superserver. This is one of the key processes on an Internet-connected system because it can start most other Internet-related services on demand. It is essential that you know how this process works, how it can be configured to disable unwanted services that might become security holes, and how to set up your server to provide exactly the services you need. Needless to say, this subject is discussed often, starting in Chapter 3, "System Installation."

Processes can be stopped. After you have identified the process you want to terminate, you can use the `kill` command to stop its execution.

PART

I

CH

2

EXAMPLE   When using the `kill` command to stop a process, you need to supply the process ID on the command line. For instance, to stop the `ps` process (`PID=18530`) from the preceding listing, you would type

```
kill 18530
```

Sometimes a mere `kill` doesn't suffice. An additional parameter can be used to specify what type of *signal* to send to the target process in place of the default termination signal. For instance, you can send a hang-up signal (`HUP`), which is what a process normally receives when the user terminates his terminal session (by closing the window, disconnecting the modem, and so on) during program execution.

```
kill -HUP 18530
```

Or, you can send a `kill` signal, which is guaranteed to terminate every process:

```
kill -KILL 18530
```

As a rule of thumb, if you want to forcefully stop a process (perhaps because it stopped responding), sending a hang-up signal first is a good idea. Many programs are designed

▼   to respond to this condition and terminate in an orderly fashion, saving data, closing

▼   files, and shutting down data connections. If the hang-up signal fails to terminate the
process, try a `kill` without parameters first (which, incidentally, is the same as using the
`TERM` parameter). Use the `-KILL` parameter as a last resort; because this signal is not *trap-*
pable, any process that receives it terminates immediately, with no chance to perform
▲   cleanup.

Devices

Every operating system has the capability to provide some form of high-level access to
hardware devices. That is, the operating system hides the actual hardware operations that
are required to emit (or input) a unit of data on the device.

For instance, when a line of text is printed on a character display, a number of low-level
operations are involved. The display hardware must be instructed to switch to a character
display mode if it isn't in such a mode already. It must be instructed to initialize display
memory. A character set must be selected. The position of the current line must be calcu-
lated and translated into a memory address in display memory. Characters of text must
be translated into display code and attribute codes (including character color), and these
must be moved to the appropriate location in memory. To make things worse, the actual
way to carry out these steps is different from one display card to the next.

Programming would be a mess if every application program was required to perform an
elaborate dance every time it had to display text. (Incidentally, in the not too distant past
that was the case on many computer systems. It *was* a mess.) Fortunately, operating systems are designed, among other reasons, specifically to eliminate this type of device
dependence in application programs. Instead of performing all these customized steps for
every type of display adapter it must recognize, an application can ask the operating system to display a line of text at the current cursor position. The actual mechanics of doing
so are known only to the operating system and are performed seamlessly behind the
scenes. Not only does it make it easier to create application programs, it also guarantees
compatibility; programs will run on any hardware that the operating system supports,
even on hardware that wasn't conceived when the program was written.

There are many types of hardware devices. They usually fall into one of two categories:
character devices and block devices. As the names suggest, the distinction is that character devices operate on one character at a time, whereas block devices usually move large
(typically fixed-size) blocks of data at once.

Character devices include the text display, the printer, the keyboard, serial ports, and modems. Block devices include floppy disk drives, hard disks, and CD-ROM drives.

The method used for identifying hardware devices varies from one operating system to the next. Linux, like most other UNIX versions, uses a particularly convenient method for device identification: each device has a special file assigned in the file system. These files are usually stored in the directory named /dev. On any fully configured Linux installation, this directory contains several hundred entries, each corresponding to a different device. For instance, /dev/sda1 represents the first partition on the first (SCSI) hard disk on my Linux test system; /dev/ttyS0 represents the first serial port, better known as COM1 to users of MS-DOS or Windows.

PART

I

CH

2

OPTIONS

Table 2.1 contains a short list of some of the most commonly used devices under Linux.

TABLE 2.1 Common Linux Hardware Devices

Device Name	Description
/dev/audio	Waveform audio device
/dev/cdrom	Alias for primary CD-ROM drive
/dev/console	Active virtual console
/dev/fd0	Floppy drive 0 (drive A)
/dev/fd0h720	Synonym for floppy 0 with a 720KB diskette
/dev/fd0h1200	Synonym for floppy 0 with a 1.2MB 5.25" diskette
/dev/fd1	Floppy drive 1 (drive B)
/dev/ftape	Synonym for primary floppy tape drive
/dev/hda	Primary master IDE device
/dev/hda1	First partition on hda
/dev/hda2	Second partition on hda
/dev/hdb	Primary slave IDE device
/dev/hdc	Secondary master IDE device
/dev/hdd	Secondary slave IDE device
/dev/inportbm	Microsoft InPort bus mouse
/dev/logibm	Logitech bus mouse

▼

continues

▼ **TABLE 2.1** Common Linux Hardware Devices (Continued)

Device Name	Description
/dev/midi	MIDI device
/dev/modem	Synonym for serial port with modem attached
/dev/mouse	Synonym for preferred mouse device
/dev/null	The null device (bit bucket)
/dev/psaux	PS/2 mouse port
/dev/rmt0	Synonym for first tape drive
/dev/scd0	First SCSI CD-ROM drive
/dev/sda	First SCSI disk drive
/dev/sda1	First partition on first SCSI disk drive
/dev/sda2	Second partition on first SCSI disk drive
/dev/sdb	Second SCSI disk drive
/dev/st0	First SCSI tape drive
/dev/tty0	First virtual console
/dev/tty1	Second virtual console
/dev/ttyS0	First serial port
/dev/ttyS1	Second serial port
/dev/ttyp0	First virtual terminal
/dev/ttyp1	Second virtual terminal

▲

File Systems

It's reasonable to assume that anyone reading this book has used an MS-DOS computer before and is familiar with the concept of files organized into a hierarchy of directories. Linux's file system concept is quite similar; it too organizes files into a hierarchical collection of directories.

There are two key differences, however. First, Linux uses no drive letters. Instead, there is a *root file system,* which roughly corresponds to drive C: on your MS-DOS computer. Other file systems are *mounted* to correspond with directory entries on the root file system. The other difference is that Linux can routinely utilize many different types of file systems, whereas MS-DOS normally recognizes only its own.

EXAMPLE

To make sense of this geek speech, take a look at the output produced by the `mount` command on one of my machines:

```
/dev/sda1 on / type ext2 (rw)
/dev/sdb1 on /home type ext2 (rw)
/dev/sda3 on /usr2 type msdos (rw)
none on /proc type proc (rw)
/dev/scd0 on /cdrom type iso9660 (ro,noexec,nosuid,nodev)
```

The root file system is identified by a single forward slash (`/`); this replaces the well-known backslash (`\`) character used in MS-DOS. This listing shows that the physical device corresponding to the root file system is `/dev/sda1`. In plain (okay, plainer) English, it means that the first partition (`1`) of the first SCSI drive (`sda`) is in use as the root file system. This is known as drive C: to MS-DOS users.

The first partition of the second drive (which would be drive D: for MS-DOS), or `/dev/sdb1` is mounted to the `/home` directory. So when an MS-DOS user types **D:\MYDIR\MYFILE.TXT**, you would instead type `/home/mydir/myfile.txt`. It is traditional on UNIX systems to set up home directories for individual users under the `/home` directory tree. So for instance, my home directory would be `/home/vttoth`. (This is so regardless of whether `/home` is actually the *mount point* for a separate disk partition—as is the case here—or just an ordinary subdirectory.)

The next entry specifies that the first SCSI drive's third partition is mounted to `/usr2`. Whatever happened to the second partition on this drive? Well, there are no rules that say all partitions need to be mounted. (If you are really curious, on this system the second partition is used as swap space for virtual memory. Because it contains no file system, it does not have to be—indeed, it cannot be—mounted.)

Another important thing about this third entry is the type of the file system. For the first two entries, it was `ext2`, which is short for the *second extended file system*—the file system most commonly used by Linux. This is a very good file system with one significant drawback: It is not compatible with MS-DOS or Windows. A partition formatted with this file system type on a multiboot system cannot be seen when MS-DOS or Windows is booted unless third-party extensions are used (and even so, DOS or Windows must be booted from a different partition). Fortunately, Linux is also capable of utilizing the FAT file system of MS-DOS. The example here shows just that, an MS-DOS formatted hard disk partition mounted as `/usr2`. There are many other file system types, including the popular `umsdos`, which offer many (but not all) of the features of a *true* Linux file system while retaining MS-DOS compatibility. It is a good idea to develop an understanding of

▼   the pros and cons of the various file systems *before* you begin your Linux installation; afterward, it's rather difficult, if not outright impossible, to correct a mistake without reinstalling.

The fourth entry reveals an interesting feature of Linux: a file system is mounted, but there is no corresponding disk device! This very special file system provides file-like objects that make it easy to examine the current state of the operating system and its running processes. The proc file system is discussed in detail in later chapters.

Lastly, the final entry in the device list represents a SCSI CD-ROM drive. The file system type is ISO9660 (9660 is the number of the International Standards Organization specification for organizing CD-ROM content) and the additional options essentially specify that this is a read-only file system that can be mounted by any user. (Normally,

▲   only privileged users can mount or unmount file systems.)

Access Control

Processes, devices, files—these are all resources that application programs can request from the operating system. However, accessing these devices cannot take place without control. Otherwise users would be able to read and modify other users' confidential files, interfere with other users' running sessions or, worse yet, modify key system files, thus rendering the entire system inoperable. Such actions don't require any malicious intent; it's enough if a user loads, for example, the file /etc/passwd (a crucial system file containing usernames and account information) with the cryptic and difficult to learn vi editor and saves a corrupted copy by accident. Users will be locked out of the system just as efficiently as they would be after an attack by a master hacker.

The operating system prevents these mishaps and accidents by assigning access rights and ownership to objects in the system, namely all processes, hardware devices, and files under its control.

EXAMPLE   You can see the permission system at work by checking the settings of the file /etc/passwd, using the command ls -l /etc/passwd:

```
-rw-r—r—   1 root      root         2571 Jan  8 06:41 /etc/passwd
```

The first column in this listing shows the file's access rights; the second column displays the file's owner; the third column displays the group of users to which file ownership is

▼   assigned.

▼   Translated, this line means that the user root has read and write privileges to the file; members of the group root have read-only privilege; and other users are also assigned read-only privilege. In other words, everyone can read the file, but only the user root has the right to modify its contents. So if a user who is unfamiliar with the vi editor happens to load this file, there's no danger that it might be changed accidentally; any attempt to

▲   save the file results in an error.

Under most variants of UNIX, and certainly under Linux, the *root user* (also called the *superuser*) essentially has unrestricted privileges to perform any action on the system. In essence, the root user is the omnipotent system god—the user with the ability to do anything. (Which might explain the god-like arrogance of some seasoned UNIX system administrators!)

PART
I
CH
2

Such unrestricted power is not without its danger. Books written for UNIX system owners and administrators are full of warnings like this:

> **WARNING**   Never use the root account for regular work on your system. Use root privileges only for actions that require those privileges.

This is a very important warning, so don't be surprised if you see it repeated often in this book as well. If you log on as a regular user, any mistakes you make will be limited to files and objects to which you have write access. If you log on as root, your mistakes will have a global effect. If you log on as a regular user and run, for example, a program containing malicious code (such as a virus), the virus will only be capable of affecting files and objects you control. If you log on as root and run malicious code, it will be capable of doing anything, including wiping out system files, formatting your hard drive, and more.

The presence of the all-powerful root account on the system also represents a security limitation. No user can hide anything from the prying eyes of the root user. Or, to use security lingo, system administrator functions cannot be compartmentalized. Sometimes an organization's security policies require that an administrator be able to see only files and objects he is assigned to administer, not other files and objects. The presence of the super administrator root account on Linux and most versions of UNIX is incompatible with such a requirement.

Fortunately, establishments with such high security requirements have plenty of secure operating system products to choose from. (They usually have the money to pay for them, too.) Nevertheless, even in ordinary small business installations, security should not be taken lightly; international spies are unlikely to show up, but user errors, malicious code, viruses, Trojan horses, and simple software bugs are a matter of everyday reality. At the very least, you need to understand what the main security issues and limitations are.

Interacting with the System: Shells in a Nutshell

Shell—this is a word you'll hear often when dealing with Linux. It is a synonym for *command interpreter*, or *command processor*, a program with the main purpose of providing the user with a command line from which other programs can be launched.

Sound familiar? Even MS-DOS has a shell, the venerable COMMAND.COM. Although COMMAND.COM is grossly primitive when compared with commonly used UNIX shells, the basic functionality is the same. Simple built-in commands implement a few essential functions, while external programs can be launched by typing their name on the command line.

Just as any power user of Windows still uses the command prompt to accomplish tasks efficiently, the shell is an invaluable tool in the hands of UNIX power users and system administrators. Indeed, often the shell is the only tool; unlike in the world of Windows, the presence of a graphical environment under UNIX cannot be taken for granted.

Popular UNIX Shells

In case you're wondering, the use of *shells* was not a mistake; the plural form was intentional. Even under MS-DOS, replacements for COMMAND.COM exist, although they are not widely used. Under most UNIX systems, several shell programs are readily available to choose from; Linux is no exception. The most popular among these are the C shell, the Bourne shell, the Korn shell, and their derivatives or clones.

Why do you need so many? The main reason is that a UNIX shell is much more than the simplistic command interpreter of MS-DOS. Shells in UNIX are actually quite powerful programming tools; complex scripts can be written to perform many system administration tasks using only the shell's command language.

And it is here, in the command language, where the differences lie. The C shell provides a command syntax that closely resembles that of the C language. It is often said that the C shell is most preferred by programmers (but, even though I am a programmer myself, I have no such preference).

The Korn shell was developed by David Korn and is copyrighted by AT&T. A variety of public domain versions circulate on the Internet, for instance the Z shell on many Linux systems.

The Bourne shell, originally created by Steve Bourne of Bell Labs, is the oldest, most commonly used shell type. Under Linux, a public domain variant called the Bourne Again Shell, or bash, is very popular. Since bash is also fairly good—offering many advanced features not found in the original Bourne shell—and it is installed by many Linux distributions as the default shell program, it is going to be used throughout this book in examples and discussions related to shell commands and programming.

A Comparison: bash Versus COMMAND.COM

The command processor of MS-DOS, COMMAND.COM, might be inferior to UNIX shells, but it is also well known to many users. Even in the days of Windows 95 and its Explorer, seasoned users still use the MS-DOS Prompt.

OPTIONS   Table 2.2 contains a cross-reference of many commonly used MS-DOS commands and their equivalents in the bash shell. Built-in commands are italicized to distinguish them from commands that invoke external programs.

TABLE 2.2   MS-DOS/Linux Command Cross Reference

MS-DOS		Linux Description
cd	cd	Change directory
copy	cp	Copy file(s)
del	rm	Remove file
dir	ls	List files

▼   *continues*

▼   **TABLE 2.2**   MS-DOS/Linux Command Cross Reference (Continued)

MS-DOS	Linux	Description
echo echo		Display text
fc diff		Compare files
fdisk	fdisk	View/edit hard disk partition table
format	mkfs	Make a file system
md mkdir		Make (create) directory
more more		View file one page at a time
move mv		Move file
rd rmdir		Remove directory
ren mv		Rename file
type cat		Display file contents

▲

The names of many commands are different under MS-DOS and Linux, and often they also work differently. Just as COMMAND.COM, bash also implements many commands as built-ins, while other commands exist in the form of external programs. However, the set of built-in commands differ; for instance, type is a built-in command in MS-DOS, but its closest Linux equivalent, cat, is an external program.

The syntax of these commands also varies from one operating system to another. Many Linux commands offer a series of options not available in their MS-DOS equivalents. Perhaps surprisingly, a few Linux commands do not have the same flexibility in command-line options as do their MS-DOS counterparts.

EXAMPLE   For instance, in MS-DOS it is possible to type **dir /s** to list the contents of a directory and all its subdirectories. The Linux ls command does have a similar option, but it cannot be used in combination with wildcards. For instance, whereas you can type **dir /s *.exe** in MS-DOS, under Linux you need to use more arcane syntax:

```
find . -name "*.exe" -print
```

There are a few extremely useful Linux utilities that have no MS-DOS equivalents. Perhaps the best example is the Linux grep command, which allows you to find text in a file, or find files that contain the specified text. For instance, if you want to find all files in the current directory that contain the text *find me*, type

▼   **grep "find me" .**

▼ The command `find` allows you to locate files that match specific criteria. This command, when combined with other commands such as `grep`, can yield powerful combinations. For instance, if you want to find all files containing the text *find me* not just in the current directory but on the entire hard drive, type

```
find / -xdev -type f -exec grep -q "find me" \{\} \; -print
```

Because this command effectively scans all files and directories on your hard drive, it might take a long time to execute. It might also slow down interactive response on production systems that have, for instance, a running Web server.

This last example also provides a glimpse at the true power of UNIX. The syntax of commands might be arcane, but after you master them, you can accomplish a lot with a few simple command lines. Indeed, UNIX *shell programming* is often considered an art by itself. Shell scripts are so much more powerful than their MS-DOS batch file counterparts; they are regularly used to perform surprisingly complex tasks, such as the processing of forms returned by Web servers.

All UNIX shells offer the capability to run an application in the background. To do so, append the ampersand (&) character to the command line. Of course it does not make sense to run an application in the background unless you know you won't be interacting with it. One example would be to perform a background search with the search output redirected to a file:

```
find / -exec grep "find me" \{\} \; -print >results.txt &
```

It is important to remember that just because a program runs in the background doesn't mean that its output won't appear on your terminal. It can be quite confusing if unexpected text suddenly appears, for instance, while you're in the middle of an editing session. This is why if a program in the background is expected to generate output, it is a good idea to redirect its output to a file, as in the preceding example. Sometimes you might also need to redirect the program's *standard error* output; to do so, use `2>` instead of `>`.

One last confusing feature is hidden files. MS-DOS provides not one, but two file attributes (the `HIDDEN` and `SYSTEM` attributes) both of which cause a file not to be listed by the `dir` command. UNIX has no such attributes; however, by convention filenames that begin with a period are hidden unless referenced explicitly. For instance, if you type `ls -l` in a new user's home directory, no files are listed. However, typing `ls -al` lists several hidden files, including the `.` and `..` pseudo-directories whose meaning is the same as

▼ under MS-DOS:

▼
```
drwxr-xr-x    2 vttoth    users          1024 Feb 11 21:35 .
drwxr-xr-x    5 root      root           1024 Feb  7 17:38 ..
-rw-r—r—      1 vttoth    users           773 Feb 11 13:44 .bash_history
-rw-r—r—      1 vttoth    users            49 Nov 25 1997 .bash_logout
-rw-r—r—      1 vttoth    users           913 Nov 24 1997 .bashrc
-rw-r—r—      1 vttoth    users           650 Nov 24 1997 .cshrc
-rw-r—r—      1 vttoth    users           111 Nov  3 1997 .inputrc
-rwxr-xr-x    1 vttoth    users           186 Sep  2 00:39 .kshrc
-rw-r—r—      1 vttoth    users           392 Jan  7 1998 .login
-rw-r—r—      1 vttoth    users            51 Nov 25 1997 .logout
-rw-r—r—      1 vttoth    users           341 Oct 13 1997 .profile
-rwxr-xr-x    1 vttoth    users           182 Sep  2 00:39 .profile.ksh
```

Many of these files are startup scripts for different shells. Startup scripts are executed when the user logs on to the system; in effect they're the same as the AUTOEXEC.BAT file under MS-DOS, except that instead of initializing the system as a whole, they contain

▲   initialization commands specific to the user.

The Keyboard

You would think that anyone reading a book about installing and maintaining a Linux server already knows how to use the PC keyboard and needs no further instruction on the subject. That is largely true, but there are a few small differences—some quite annoying—that are worth mentioning.

Not only is the function of some of the keys different under Linux, there exist key combinations with no MS-DOS equivalents. For instance, under MS-DOS it is not possible to suspend a running application. MS-DOS also does not offer *virtual consoles*, a Linux feature that lets you have several simultaneous command sessions even when no windowing system is installed. There are also differences in the meaning of some special character codes; this affects not only the keyboard but the interpretation of text files as well.

EXAMPLE   One important key remains the same under Linux and MS-DOS: Ctrl+C can be used under Linux just as it can under MS-DOS to stop a running program. In fact, under Linux this key tends to work more reliably and stop all but the most stubborn applications. (Exception: applications that protect themselves against Ctrl+C by capturing the TERM signal). Ctrl+C is equivalent to sending the

▼   TERM signal to the process using the kill command discussed earlier.

▼ In MS-DOS, Ctrl+Z indicates the end of a file. If you are entering data from the keyboard, Ctrl+Z indicates the end of data entry. Under Linux, the equivalent key combination is Ctrl+D. For instance, if you want to create a file from the command line by typing its contents, you would use the following:

```
$cat >newfile.txt
This is the contents of my new file.
This is the last line, after which a Ctrl-D terminates entry.
^D
$
```

PART

I

CH

2

The dollar sign ($) is not something you type; it is the system prompt, much like C:> under MS-DOS. Just like under MS-DOS, it might be preceded by the computer's name, the current directory, or other information depending on how your system is configured.

Ctrl+Z, however, does have a meaning under Linux. It allows you to *suspend* a running application and bring up the command prompt. The suspended application can be brought back into the foreground using the fg command. It is also possible to force an application to the background using the bg command; such an application will be unsuspended, but you'll no longer be able to interact with it from the keyboard. This is equivalent to launching the application with an ampersand on the command line.

One of the most annoying features of UNIX is how it interprets the Del and Backspace keys. Because of convention, the Del key usually has the same role as Backspace under MS-DOS: it is used to delete the character to the left of the cursor and move the cursor left. The Backspace key—which as many MS-DOS users know, is the same as hitting Ctrl+H—has no special meaning.

Fortunately, when you fire up Linux on a PC-compatible computer, most installations remap the keyboard by default and cause Backspace to behave as expected. However, this might not be the case if you connect to a Linux machine via the modem or over the Internet. So remember, if Backspace doesn't work as expected, use the Del key.

Another useful set of keys consists of the keys Alt+F1 through Alt+F6. On most Linux machines, you can have multiple command sessions going over multiple virtual consoles. These keys allow you to switch between virtual consoles. Usually, six virtual consoles are available. (This number of consoles is merely a convention used on most Linux
▼ installations; the system itself supports more than six virtual consoles if so configured.)

▼   Last but not least there's another problematic difference that, although not directly related to the keyboard, can be the cause of a lot of grief. By convention, every line in an MS-DOS text file is terminated by the CR+LF character combination (a carriage return code, followed by a line feed code.) When you press the Enter key while in an editor, the editor adds this pair of character codes to the edited file. In contrast, UNIX convention dictates that a single LF be used to indicate the end of a line. When you copy files back and forth between UNIX and MS-DOS systems, this can be a real problem. Worse yet, many file transfer applications perform this conversion for you automatically, whether you ask for it or not. The result is that they often convert bytes in non-text files such as ZIP archives, images, or executable programs, in which the bytes corresponding with the carriage return or line feed character codes have no special meaning. Such a corrupted file is typically unusable. (If you ever download a 10MB ZIP archive via FTP only to find out later that you forgot to disable text mode translation before commencing the

▲   download, you'll know what I mean.)

Getting Help with Man Pages

Doing things from the command line has a drawback that should be immediately obvious: there is an intuitive user interface—no Help button to click and no Help menu to choose options from.

Still, you're not entirely Help-less when using the UNIX command line. In fact, the concept of *online help* has been known to UNIX users long before the first version of WIN-HELP.EXE was released by Microsoft.

Help for UNIX commands most commonly comes in the form of *man pages*. Man is an abbreviation for manual; it is also the name of the command that is used to display said pages.

Suppose for instance that you want to know how the bash shell can be invoked from the command line. You can type **man bash** at the operating system prompt. In response, a page similar to Figure 2.3 is displayed. Most man pages are longer than what fits the screen, but that's not a problem, because you can use the Spacebar to go forward or the B key to view previous screen pages. To exit, press Q.

FIGURE 2.3
A manual page.

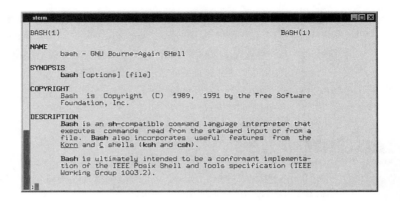

Sometimes typing **man** does not produce the desired result. Often enough, help is available, but the man page does not show what you were looking for. For instance, when you type **man mount**, you probably expect to see the manual page for the mount command; what you get instead is a page that explains usage of a C-language subroutine.

That is because manual pages are organized into sections. The man command brings up the first page that matches the keyword you specify, with lower numbered sections taking precedence. Common subroutine calls are in section 2, whereas system administration commands are in section 8. Thus, typing **man mount** displays the mount entry from section 2, a subroutine description.

Fortunately, you can specify the number of the section that you want to see. Typing **man 8 mount** brings up the desired manual page.

OPTIONS

Man pages on Linux installations are commonly organized into the following sections:

- 1. User commands
- 2. System calls
- 3. Subroutines
- 4. Devices
- 5. File Formats
- 6. Games
- 7. Miscellaneous
- 8. System Administration
- 9. Kernel Reference
- N. New

PART

I

CH

2

Recently, a new format was adopted for documentation. So-called *Texinfo* pages can be invoked using the info command. One advantage of this format is that it's navigable; you can follow references without having to leave the Texinfo system. If you invoke a command's man page, it might contain a notice stating that more up-to-date information might be available in Texinfo format.

Editing Files

One of the most dreaded features of UNIX is the text editor. For some inexplicable reason, the concept of a user-friendly text editor seems totally incompatible with UNIX. There are powerful editors alright, loaded with features never dreamt of by users of DOS's EDIT.COM or the Windows Notepad. The trouble is that most of those features are accessible only through arcane key combinations that are impossibly difficult to memorize (and very easy to forget.)

Using vi

The vi editor can be many things, but *popular* is not an adjective I'd be tempted to use. That would imply that vi is liked by its users, which is rarely the case; nevertheless, vi or its clones remain the most widely installed editors on UNIX systems. Whenever you log on to a UNIX machine, chances are that typing **vi** on the command line will bring up the full-screen editor (see Figure 2.4). Linux is no exception: two popular Linux clones, elvis and vim, are found on almost any Linux installation.

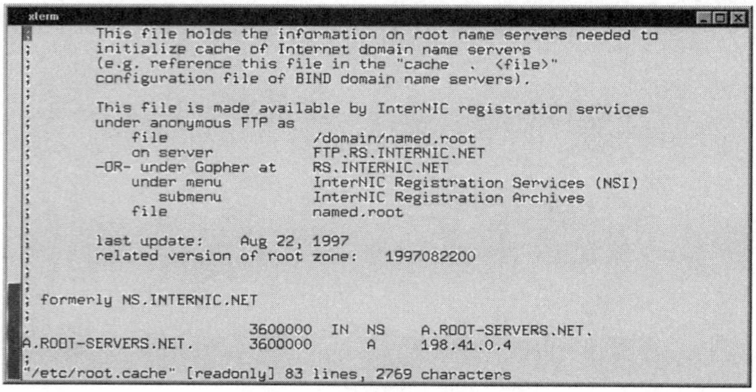

FIGURE 2.4
Using the vi editor.

So far so good, but when you're faced with a program that doesn't seem to respond to reasonable keystrokes and you don't even know how to exit it, what do you do?

One reason why vi appears so counterintuitive is that the editor has two modes of operation. When you start it, it is in Command mode; keyboard keys that you type are not inserted into the file as text, but are interpreted as command keys instead, with a special meaning assigned to each key. For instance, typing **x** causes the character under the cursor to be deleted. To actually insert text into the file you're editing, you need to type **i** (for Insert).

This odd behavior of the vi editor is due to the fact that it evolved from a *line editor* (remember EDLIN.COM from the early days of MS-DOS?) A line editor does not provide a full-screen interface where you can navigate with the cursor keys, but offers a command set instead for viewing and altering lines of text.

EXAMPLE

When vi is started, it is in a command mode not unlike the command mode of a line editor. The difference is that there is a full-screen display of the file's contents and you can move the cursor using the cursor keys. Here are a few of vi's many commands that are currently available (note that vi is case-sensitive, so upper- and lowercase letters might have a different meaning):

▲

OPTIONS

A	Append text at the end of the current line
i	Insert text at cursor position
d	Delete marked text
dd	Delete current line
J	Join current line with next line
p	Paste internal buffer after cursor position
u	Undo last action
v	Begin marking text (use cursor keys to select)
V	Begin marking text lines (use the up/down arrow keys to select)
x	Erase character under the cursor
y	Copy marked text to internal buffer (like the Windows clipboard)
ZZ	Save and exit
:	Command line mode
/	Search for text typed

PART
I
CH
2

EXAMPLE   Most vi commands can be preceded by a number. For instance, typing **10x** causes 10 characters to be erased under the cursor. Numbers can also be used in combination with cursor keys. For example, typing **10** followed by the left arrow key moves the cursor left by 10 character positions.

Using the A or i commands switches the editor to input mode. In this mode, vi works very much like a full-screen editor; any text you type will appear at the current cursor position. At this point you have limited use of the arrow keys, the Backspace key and the Del key. Some versions of vi allow you to navigate to anywhere onscreen, while others confine the cursor to the text you just entered. To exit input mode, press the Esc key. Note that as you delete characters while in input mode, they might not disappear from the screen until you actually press Esc. The editor was designed in the days of character terminals, often connected through slow telecommunication facilities; consolidating character deletions this way significantly improved interactive response over slow lines. (Even today, when you use vi over a less than fully reliable Internet connection, this feature might prove useful. Unfortunately, it can also be confusing.)

Pressing the colon (:) invokes a command line at the bottom of your screen. Here is a list of a few useful commands that can be entered here:

- q   Quit if there is no unsaved data
- q!   Quit unconditionally, discarding unsaved data
- vi   Return to visual editing mode
- w   Write data to file

These few commands, while they are by far the most commonly used, represent only a tiny subset of the capabilities of the vi editor. Most versions of vi allow the editing of multiple files, provide commands for search and replace, offer a means for building simple macros, provide special features for editing programs in different languages, and more.

A good book for learning the basics of vi is *Learning the vi Editor,* by Linda Lamb, published by O'Reilly & Associates. You also can check Amazon.com or Barnesandnoble.com for other books on vi.

Other Editors

Although vi is the most widely installed UNIX editor, it isn't the only one. Perhaps the next most popular (and this one is indeed popular because its users like it a lot more than vi users like theirs) is Emacs. Emacs (the name stands for Editing Macros) is a powerful, customizable, extensible editor with many features especially useful for programmers. It isn't necessarily easier to use, however. It might not be plagued with vi's idiosyncratic behavior, but learning convoluted key sequences starting with the Esc key isn't any easier. Still, many users prefer Emacs over vi.

Another, simple but useful editor is Pico. The name stands for Pine Composer. (Pine is the name of a popular UNIX email application developed at the University of Washington.) Pico is usually installed along with Pine and is invoked by Pine whenever you edit an email message. One major advantage of Pico is its user interface. As with other editors, it also relies on obscure keystrokes for invoking editor functions, but with Pico, those keys are actually listed on the bottom of your screen while you're editing a file! You no longer have to frantically search the manual (if you have one) or invoke the online man page from another command window or terminal to find out how to quit from the program.

Sometimes, the use of a full-screen editor is not an option. Perhaps you are connecting to the system from a terminal with no full-screen capabilities. A more likely reason is that you might want to perform file editing under script control.

EXAMPLE

Two commonly used line editors are ed and sed. ed is more oriented toward interactive editing. For instance, the following session shows how all occurrences of *dog* can be replaced with *cat* in the file `myfile.txt`:

```
$ ed myfile.txt
1172
,s/dog/cat/g
w
1172
q
$
```

sed (the name stands for Stream Editor) is most useful for changing a file's contents under script control. For example, the following command replaces all occurrences of *dog* with *cat* in the file `myfile.txt` and writes the result to `myfile2.txt`:

▲   ```
sed -e "s/dog/cat/g" myfile.txt >myfile2.txt
```

PART
I
CH
2
```

The X Window System

Everything discussed so far involves programs and commands entered at the command line of a character terminal. I can almost hear you ask: "Is this guy out of his mind? Does he really expect folks to use archaic keyboard commands at the turn of the new century?"

Yes! Graphical utilities might be available for some administrative tasks, but if you want to configure and run a robust, secure, efficient Linux server, using command-line tools is your best option. This is especially true if you occasionally need to access your system remotely, such as through a modem or Telnet connection. Furthermore, you might not even want to install a graphical user interface (GUI) in the first place. (The fact that it forces you to install a resource-hogging GUI whether you need it or not has always been considered to be one of the drawbacks of Windows NT.)

That said, even command-line tools are easier to use when you use a windowing system. While Linux allows multiple simultaneous sessions on a text screen through virtual consoles, switching back and forth between them is not as convenient as seeing several command windows onscreen at once.

UNIX is not integrated with any particular windowing system. There are no built-in preferences that make one windowing system more desirable than another. Nevertheless, for many years now, the windowing system of choice has been the X Window System, or X for short, developed originally at the Massachusetts Institute of Technology.

X is a curious combination of power and backwardness. It is an incredibly versatile system, designed from the start to operate over network connections. Surprisingly, it lacks well-established standardized support for many high-level features Windows users take for granted. Even the capability to transfer data via the clipboard can be a problem between incompatible applications, for example.

X is also idiosyncratic. As the UNIX-Haters Handbook remarks, it is probably the only system that completely reverses the concepts of *client* and *server*. Under X, your workstation is the *server*, while X programs that run on either your machine or a remote machine across the network are *clients*, connecting to your X server for graphical display.

X Implementations

There are several X implementations for Linux. Practically all Linux installations come with a free implementation of X, called XFree86. This implementation is a solid, robust version that has been with Linux since the days preceding version 1. For most basic needs, XFree86 should suffice; if there are specific features (for example, support for the OpenGL graphics library), which you must have, you might want to look into one of the many commercial implementations, such as Metro-X from MetroLink or Accelerated-X from Xi Graphics.

Windows X Servers

Thanks to the client/server architecture of X, it is possible to run X applications on one computer, yet have them display their windows on another. In fact, the workstation on which the X server runs doesn't even have to be a Linux or UNIX machine.

EXAMPLE

Take my case: for several years now, I've been using a commercial product called X-Win32 under Windows NT. This X server allows me to run Linux applications and interact with them from the Windows NT desktop of my main workstation (see Figure 2.5). This is a very convenient arrangement. If you intend to manage or control a Linux machine from a Windows workstation over the network, using a Windows-based X server such as X-Win32 is highly recommended.

FIGURE 2.5
Linux and Windows applications on a common desktop.

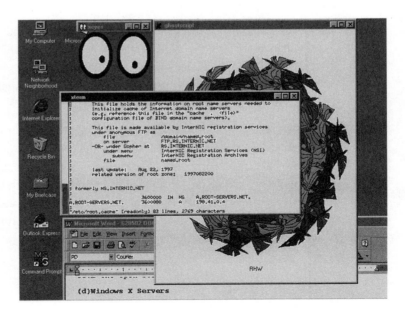

(d)Windows X Servers

▼

PART

I

CH

2

▼   When your X server resides on another machine, it is not necessary to install an X server on the Linux machine. However, you still have to install shared files and directories in
▲   order to run X applications on that computer.

Summary

Linux, like most other operating systems, has four fundamental features. It manages the computer's hardware components and provides a means to run other programs, which in turn utilize the operating system's services. File systems provide a means to organize data on storage devices. And, access control ensures that users and the programs they run do not accidentally or intentionally access or alter each other's data.

One fundamental feature is that Linux is a multitasking operating system, allowing several processes to run at once. Processes are organized into a tree hierarchy, with the `init` process acting as the mother of all processes. On a running system, active processes can be listed using the `ps` command.

Hardware devices under Linux can be *character devices* or *block devices*. Character devices move one character of data at a time; examples are the keyboard, printers, and modems. Block devices move large, usually fixed size blocks of data at a time. An example for a block device is the hard disk, which is divided into fixed size sectors of data that are read or written at once.

The file system organizes blocks of data on disk into files and directories. Linux can handle many different types of file systems, including MS-DOS file systems or the file systems on CD-ROMs. Linux's native file system is the *second extended file system*, or e2fs, an efficient, robust file system that provides most features expected under a modern UNIX-style operating system.

Linux's access control mechanism assigns ownership and permissions to objects such as files, directories, hardware devices, and running programs. All objects are owned by users who have a valid account on the system. Users are organized into groups. For every object, its owner can define the level of access others have to it. The root user, also referred to the superuser, has access to everything on the system. For this reason, it is strongly recommended that this account not be used except for administrative tasks where root privileges are required.

Another characteristic of Linux is how the user interacts with it. The primary means of interacting with a Linux system is through a command interpreter, also called a shell. Shell programs are comparable to COMMAND.COM under MS-DOS. There are several popular UNIX shell programs available, most of which have versions that operate under Linux. The most widely used Linux shall is bash.

Users can obtain online help for most system commands through the man command. For instance, typing **man cp** invokes online help for the cp command. More up-to-date documentation for some commands can be found using the info command.

Another way a user interacts with Linux is through text editors. The most widely used is vi. The editor is not easy to learn because of its obscure command set, but it is powerful and can be found on most system installations. Other editors include Emacs, Pico, and several line editors.

Don't forget, Linux is not without a GUI. XFree86, a free implementation of the X Window System, is available on nearly all Linux installations. For administrative tasks, some X utilities are available, but most are more easily performed from the command line. For Linux in a server environment, the installation of X is not required, and on lower-end systems it is not even recommended. The presence of X does, however, make administrative tasks easier even if command-line tools are used, thanks to the possibility of using multiple command windows onscreen.

Part **II**

Setting Up

3 System Installation

4 Internet Configuration and Basic Security

5 Internet Concepts

6 The Domain Name System

7 Making the Connection

System Installation

Installing and configuring an operating system is a never-ending process, which includes fiddling with performance settings, adding new features and services, updating drivers and other components, installing new hardware, and so on. These activities seem to go on continuously when you have several computer systems under your care.

Often, when you speak of installing an operating system, you understand the phrase to mean a very specific series of actions. Specifically, the result is that you are able to boot the new system from the hardware, and it is capable of performing the basic functions of an operating system—manage the hardware and provide a platform for launching applications.

This chapter covers the steps of installing a Linux system. In this chapter, you are also going to see a step-by-step description of my specific experiences installing and configuring a Linux test system.

Preparing for Installation

Installing any operating system takes some planning and forethought, especially if the target computer is a multiple boot system. Before you begin installation, you need to make a system inventory so that when the system installer asks certain questions, you won't be embarrassed or caught off-guard. You also need to decide on a partitioning scheme for your hard drive(s). It's a good idea to have a backup plan in case something goes wrong. Figure 3.1 provides an overview of the steps you need to take prior to beginning the installation.

FIGURE 3.1
Preparing for installation.

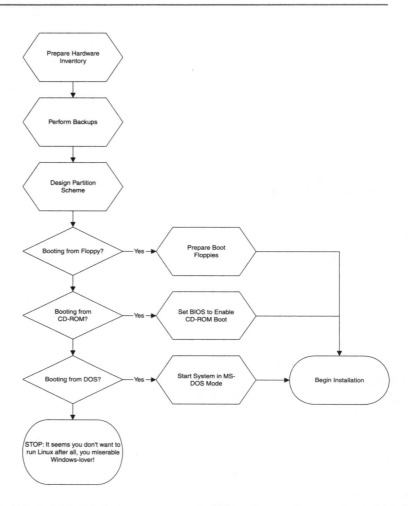

So many things can go wrong during an installation. Perhaps you intended to install the system to drive C: (letting it reformat the drive), but you didn't realize until too late that the installer swapped the C: and D: drive letters. Perhaps the operating system installer *upgraded* your disk partitions to an incompatible format. Or perhaps it overwrites key areas in a way that you cannot recover your previous installation. All these things, however rare, have been known to happen from time to time.

System Inventory

Knowing the hardware that is in your computer is generally a good idea. It's almost essential during system installation, even when using a plug-and-play operating system such as Windows 98 (just in case plug-and-play turns into plug-and-pray!).

TEST SYSTEM   I practice what I preach. I also prepared a hardware inventory for my test system, shown in Table 3.1.

TABLE 3.1   Test System Hardware Inventory

Item	Type
Mainboard	ASUS TX-97E
Processor	Pentium-166 MMX
Memory	64MB EDO RAM
Floppy 0	3.5" 1.44MB
Floppy 1	5.25" 1.2 MB
SCSI Controller	Adaptec 2940W
Drive 0	Iomega JAZ 1 GB
Drive 1	IBM DORS 2GB
CD/DVD-ROM	Creative PC-DVD (IDE0 Master)
Video	ATI All-in-Wonder (PCI, Mach64/RAGE-II, 4MB)
Network	NE-2000 compatible, IRQ=11, I/O=0x340
	Xircom PE-III (on parallel port)
Sound	SoundBlaster-16 ASP (non-PnP, IRQ=5, DMA=1,5, I/O=0x220, 0x300)
Modem	USR Sportster 33600 External
Mouse	Microsoft WheelMouse (PS/2 port)
Other	NI GPIB-TNT data acquisition card (IRQ=9, DMA=7)

PART
II

CH
3

Although I do not intend to install Linux drivers for the Xircom network adapter or the GPIB card, they are present in the system and can potentially interfere with the installation process, so it's a good idea to keep their existence in mind.

Hardware Preparation

Some hardware components store settings in non-volatile memory. These include many popular video cards, some *jumperless* network adapters, and more. Unfortunately, the utilities used to adjust these settings are almost invariably for MS-DOS only. Your computer might have other utilities, such as diagnostic programs, BIOS FLASH software, or other tools that run only under MS-DOS. For all these reasons, it is a good idea to keep a bootable DOS floppy disk around, on which all these utilities, along with a few important DOS programs such as FDISK.EXE, are stored. In fact, I have several such disks—one of which is actually capable of booting my test machine up with DOS-level networking support—so that I can copy files back and forth if necessary. (Needless to say, your MS-DOS system should be a licensed copy. This is not likely to be an issue because just about every computer nowadays comes with a bundled DOS or Windows license.)

Whatever utilities you might need to use, make sure all your hardware components are set up correctly. Sure, operating system installers generally recognize when there is a resource conflict or an invalid setting, but why take the chance? And why do extra work? Installations generally go much smoother—and need to be redone a lot less often—if the system has been properly configured from the start.

Of course the computer's hard drive needs to be configured, but that's a whole story by itself; take a look.

Partitions and the Boot Process

Because I am using a removable drive as my primary hard drive on my test system, I am lucky. I do not need to create an installation that can boot into multiple operating systems. When Linux runs, it *owns* in its entirety the 1GB JAZ cartridge that I reserved for this purpose.

For many people this is not necessarily the case, especially if you're working with a computer that is not dedicated for Linux only use. But even if it is, you might already have data on it in an MS-DOS partition that you want to keep. (Just in case, you *are* creating a backup, right?)

Partitioning Basics

Partitioning is a means to divide a hard disk into several logical units. Each logical unit can be independently formatted, even to different formatting standards. Thus you might have a hard disk with two partitions, one of which contains MS-DOS and Windows, while another houses Linux. One of the partitions is usually marked as the *active* partition, which means that when the system boots, it loads whatever operating system is installed on this partition. There are special programs, however, that may let you override this behavior and, for instance, select the partition you want to boot from manually at system startup. One such program is the OS/2 boot manager, while another is LILO, the Linux Loader.

> **NOTE**   Boot manager programs allow you to choose the partition and the operating system that is to be booted at system startup. They are not to be confused with partition managers, designed to overcome capacity limitations in older BIOSes and older versions of MS-DOS. Partition managers, which extend BIOS capability in this manner, are generally not compatible with Linux and must be removed before Linux installation, possibly necessitating a reformatting of the hard drive. Newer partition managers, however, might not present a problem.

PART

II

CH

3

How the System Boots

To better understand the significance of partitioning, take a look at the boot process—the sequence of events that occurs after you press the power button.

First, the computer's *BIOS* (Basic Input Output System) comes to life and performs a series of initializations. This includes sizing system memory, initializing adapter cards and, of course, initializing floppy disks and hard disks.

Next comes the actual attempt to *boot*, or load an operating system from disk. Most modern BIOSes let you specify the order in which disk drives are accessed. By default, the first drive accessed is drive A:—the first floppy drive on the system. The BIOS reads the first block on the floppy disk (the *boot sector*) and if it contains a certain sequence of bytes (the *boot signature*), it assumes that the data just loaded is a program and begins executing it. This program is the *boot loader*, responsible for loading further components of the operating system and initializing them.

The hard disk process is somewhat more complicated. Here too, the first block (the *master boot record*) is loaded and, if a proper signature was found, it is executed. However, this program does not normally start the loading of an operating system right away. Instead, it reads another data block from the hard disk that contains the *partition table*; that table stores information about whatever partitions are defined on the hard disk, their type, and active status.

At this point, the boot program normally loads the first block of data from the partition that is marked active. If this block contains a valid boot signature, execution is passed to it. From this point forward, the boot process is identical to what happens with a floppy drive (see Figure 3.2.). The boot program loaded from the MBR might also have a primitive user interface that lets you choose between operating systems or partitions instead of defaulting to the active partition.

This multistage boot process can be difficult to understand, but it offers a lot of flexibility. For instance, a while back I used to use a computer that was capable of booting into four different operating systems. The process, shown in Figure 3.3, went like this: The MBR contained the Linux Loader (LILO) that let me choose between Linux on the one hand or my MS-DOS formatted partition on the other. If I picked the latter, the Windows NT boot loader came up and presented me with a choice of Windows NT, Windows NT in VGA mode, or MS-DOS. Picking MS-DOS brought up the Windows 95 startup menu, with the option to boot into Windows 95 with or without Safe mode enabled, or the option to boot my previous operating system, (in this case MS-DOS 6.22 with Microsoft Windows 3.1).

Partition Schemes

So what kind of partitions should you use with Linux?

The simplest case is when you use a single partition to take up all the space on your hard drive. Linux file systems do not suffer from limitations like those under MS-DOS, which makes the use of large partitions extremely wasteful. (Incidentally, this is what led Microsoft to introduce the FAT32 format type.)

Like Windows, Linux can use hard disk space as virtual memory. This allows the operating system to run more programs than what would normally fit into the system's physical memory (RAM), but the cost is decreased performance. This performance hit can be reduced if you reserve a swap partition dedicated for use as virtual memory.

Virtual memory, due to its very nature, is accessed frequently. A hard disk's speed is, to a large extent, a function of the time it takes for the read/write head to travel from outer to inner tracks along the disk's surface. Thus it stands to reason that placing frequently accessed areas toward the middle of the hard drive can improve performance.

FIGURE 3.2
The default boot process.

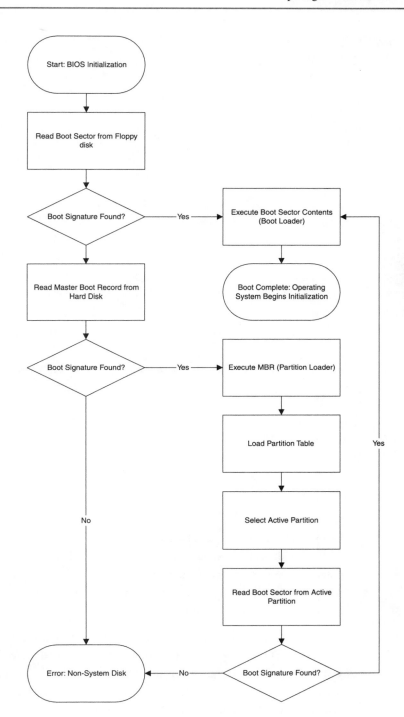

FIGURE 3.3
A multiboot configuration.

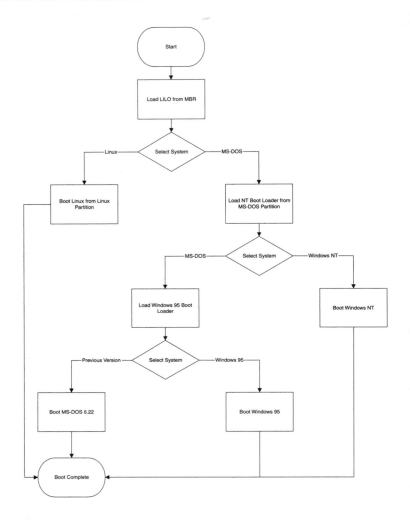

Unfortunately, with modern hard disk drives this is not always possible. These drives perform address translation both to provide a simulated disk geometry that your computer's BIOS can understand and also to remap bad sectors. Still, sandwiching the swap partition between two regular partitions may yield a slight improvement in performance; in any case, it certainly won't do harm.

So far, what has been discussed, of course, assumes that you're starting off with a blank hard drive. The situation is more complicated if the hard drive already contains data that you intend to keep. If this data is in a format other than a standard MS-DOS formatted partition, you're probably out of luck. However, with MS-DOS formatted partitions, you actually have two choices to make things work.

First, you can leave the partition intact and install Linux using the UMSDOS file system. This file system stores Linux files on an MS-DOS partition, using extra areas to store extended information, such as Linux-style long filenames and permission settings. The main advantage of UMSDOS is compatibility. However, this file system has an impact on performance, it is insecure, and on large drives, it is as inefficient as regular MS-DOS file systems are.

Second, you can use a repartitioning utility such as FIPS, which is included on the CD-ROM accompanying this book. This utility can *shrink* an existing MS-DOS partition, freeing up space. Before you use it, however, you must first use a disk defragmenter/optimizer program that consolidates unused space; otherwise, you could not shrink your partition without losing data.

> **WARNING**   Repartitioning utilities are inherently dangerous. Always back up your hard disk before trying to alter its partition table!

Of course if all else fails, you can always create a backup (which you should do anyway), repartition your hard disk, and then restore the data from backup.

File System Types

After partitions are created, they have to be formatted. The type of formatting—the file system type—you choose can have a significant impact on your system's security, reliability, and performance.

FAT File Systems

The most commonly used file system on PC-compatible computers is the FAT file system of MS-DOS. FAT stands for file allocation table, which is a key feature of this file system type.

In the days when the biggest hard disk was 10MB in size, FAT file systems were limited to 32MB. Worse yet, MS-DOS allowed only one FAT file system on a hard disk even though the partition table had room for four partitions. The other three were assumed to belong to other operating systems. To overcome this limitation, the concept of an extended partition was introduced, which could contain sub-partitions, called *logical* partitions.

With later versions of MS-DOS, Microsoft introduced the FAT16 partition type, which allowed the use of much larger partitions, all the way up to 2GB. Unfortunately, this approach had a major drawback. On a FAT partition, the disk was divided into up to 65535 allocation units (*clusters*), which represent the smallest unit of disk space that can be marked used or free. On large disk drives, the allocation unit was up to 32KB in size, which meant that storing even the smallest file, such as a 100-byte batch file, required 32KB of space. Depending on the number of files and the average file size, this often meant that 30 percent or more of the disk was lost due to this wasteful allocation scheme.

Then came FAT32, introduced with the OSR2 version of Windows 95. FAT32 uses a much larger allocation table with smaller cluster size, significantly reducing waste. In the meantime, along with Windows 95 Microsoft also introduced long filename support (VFAT) to overcome the dreaded 8.3 filename limitation of MS-DOS.

HPFS and NTFS

FAT32 with long filenames might represent a considerable improvement over the original FAT allocation scheme, but it still lacks many advanced file system features.

IBM, the developer of the OS/2 operating system, provided a solution to many FAT32's file system's shortcomings in the form of HPFS, the High Performance File System. HPFS offered better performance and reliability, but still lacked features such as the capability to assign ownership and permissions to a file. These capabilities are essential for a secure operating system, which is why the designers of Windows NT introduced yet another file system type: NTFS, the New Technology File System.

The Linux Extended File System

The file system format most commonly used for Linux these days is the Ext-2 File System (e2fs), or Second Extended File System format. The e2fs is a robust, reliable, efficient file system offering good performance, which makes it the recommended file system for Linux installations. The only drawback of e2fs is that some other operating systems do not recognize this format; thus, on a machine capable of booting multiple operating systems, e2fs might not always be the desirable choice.

UMSDOS

In the past, some would-be Linux users shied away from experimenting with this operating system when they found out that in order to try it, their hard disk had to be repartitioned. UMSDOS provides a solution to this problem: It is essentially a Linux file system that sits *on top of* an MS-DOS file system. When running MS-DOS, Linux files appear as ordinary MS-DOS files; when running Linux, the UMSDOS drivers utilize extended information to support file ownership, permissions, and other UNIX-style file system features.

It is important to note that UMSDOS retains all the drawbacks of a FAT file system, including its security shortcomings, less than stellar performance, and inefficient use of large hard disks. Therefore, UMSDOS is best when used for experimenting with Linux, but should not be used in most production environments.

Swap Partitions

Swap partitions provide an efficient mechanism for virtual memory. No file system is mounted on a swap partition; instead, swap partitions are activated using the swapon command. This command is rarely issued manually. It is invoked as part of the system initialization process.

PART

II

CH

3

Choosing a Partitioning Scheme

So given the multitude of file system types and the confusion of partitioning schemes, which scheme should you choose?

The first choice should always be E2FS, possibly in a combination with a swap partition. On hard drives that are dedicated for Linux use, this is the ideal solution.

The next best choice is UMSDOS. This file system type is ideal if you're trying to install Linux on a machine with an existing DOS or Windows operating system that you intend to continue using. UMSDOS does not require any repartitioning; it uses your existing FAT partitions.

On some systems, a combination of MS-DOS and e2fs partitions works best. Because Linux can access MS-DOS partitions, it is capable of reading and writing files there, so exchanging data between the two operating systems is possible. MS-DOS or Windows, however, cannot see the contents of a Linux e2fs partition without additional software.

TEST SYSTEM   On my test system, two SCSI hard drives are present. The first, a
JAZ drive, will contain a 1GB cartridge entirely dedicated to Linux.
The second is a 2GB internal hard drive, which is already formatted using the MS-DOS
FAT file system. The following chart shows my partitioning scheme for these two
devices.

/dev/sda1	1	900	921584	Linux (e2fs)
/dev/sda2	901	1021	123904	Linux Swap
/dev/sdb1	1	261	2096451	MS-DOS (FAT16)

Of these, the partitions on the first hard drive (sda) will need to be created during installation. The second hard drive should be left alone.

Linux: First Boot

So you think you're ready to install Linux? You have your Linux CD-ROM handy. You
have prepared an inventory of your computer's hardware. You know how you intend to
partition your hard drive, and it has sufficient empty space for use with Linux. What's
next?

You want to start the Linux installation program, that's what. Most Linux installations,
including the version of Caldera OpenLinux that accompanies this book, can be started
in three different ways.

Many newer computers support booting from standard ATAPI or SCSI CD-ROM drives.
The traditional method of installation is to use boot floppy disks. And, if your computer
already runs MS-DOS, many Linux CD-ROMs support starting the installer from the
MS-DOS prompt.

Starting from the CD-ROM

Although most newer computers support booting from a bootable CD-ROM, you might
have to change your BIOS settings to enable this feature (for instance, you might need to
change the boot sequence setting from A,C to A,CDROM,C.) Booting from the CD-
ROM is by far the simplest method of starting up any operating system installer, including Linux.

If this method works on your system, all you need to do is to insert the Linux CD into
your computer's CD-ROM drive and restart your system. After some initial BIOS messages about bootable ATAPI CD-ROMs, the Linux installation program will start.

Creating a Floppy Disk Set

Linux CD-ROMs typically contain the utilities necessary for creating boot floppy disks. You can then boot your system with these disks in drive A, which will bring up a minimal Linux installation and provide access to your CD-ROM and hard drive and a means to start the installer program.

If you are using the Caldera OpenLinux CD accompanying this book, the relevant tools can be found by accessing the CD-ROM from MS-DOS or Windows. In the directory `D:\COL\LAUNCH\FLOPPY` (where `D:` is the DOS drive letter of your CD-ROM drive), you will find the following files:

```
INSTALL.144
INSTALL.288
MODULES.144
RAWRITE3.COM
```

Of these, `RAWRITE3.COM` is an MS-DOS utility that can write a disk image file to create a non-MS-DOS floppy disk. The other three files are disk image files that contain a bootable Linux configuration. Most users will need two floppy disks, onto which `INSTALL.144` and `MODULES.144` are to be copied with `RAWRITE.COM`. Those who have a 2.88MB floppy disk drive can use `INSTALL.288` instead. If you are unsure as to what kind of floppy drive you have, assume it is a 1.44MB drive.

Usage of `RAWRITE3.COM` should be self-evident. The program asks for a source disk image file and the letter of the target floppy drive. For each disk image you intend to copy, you should have a formatted floppy disk ready; the disk does not have to be empty, but keep in mind that all previous content on it will be erased.

Other distributions also contain similar tools and disk images. Many distributions contain a variety of disk images of which you must choose one that best matches your system's hardware (for example, a disk image with SCSI and networking support).

If you prepare installation floppy disks this way, it's probably a good idea to keep them around for later use. If you need to reinstall or repair a Linux installation in the future, these disks might be useful.

Starting from the MS-DOS Prompt

Not too long ago, the only way to start Linux was from a bootable Linux disk or hard disk partition. Then came `LOADLIN.EXE`, a new utility that made life for the casual Linux user or hobbyist who wanted to give Linux a test drive much easier.

In short, LOADLIN.EXE does one thing: it starts Linux from the MS-DOS prompt.

Launching an operating system from within another isn't a trivial thing to do. LOADLIN.EXE can do what it does because MS-DOS is not a 32-bit operating system that would prevent an application program from taking over. For this reason, LOADLIN.EXE can only be used from a true MS-DOS prompt, not from a DOS window under Windows 95/98 or Windows NT. (Although I never tried, I suspect it might be possible to run LOADLIN.EXE from a Windows 3.1 DOS window. However, because as far as Windows 3.1 is concerned, LOADLIN.EXE is an application that never returns control to the operating system, this practice could result in data loss.)

When using the Caldera OpenLinux CD-ROM included with this book, LOADLIN.EXE can be launched from the directory D:\COL\LAUNCH\DOS (where *D:* is the drive letter of your CD-ROM drive.) This method also starts up the installation program found on the CD.

Hardware Detection

Running an operating system for the very first time on a computer is tricky business. Because the system is not configured yet, it has to *discover* the computer's hardware configuration with or without help from the user.

An operating system has three methods available to detect the presence of hardware components and their configuration. It can utilize the capabilities of plug-and-play hardware. It can run drivers that safely check for the presence of respective hardware and determine the configuration through *autoprobing*. And it can prompt the user to enter configuration parameters.

The primary method utilized by Linux is autoprobing. Linux configurations used for first-time boot usually contain support for most popular hardware devices. As drivers are loaded, they each check for the presence of the respective hardware component; if the component is present, the driver is initialized, otherwise it remains inactive.

Unfortunately, this method doesn't always succeed. For instance, sometimes the method used for auto-detection cannot detect all versions of the supported hardware. Recently, I added an Adaptec 2920 SCSI card to a computer running Linux. Even though I modified the kernel configuration to include support for this hardware, I found that the operating system failed to load; the SCSI controller and consequently disk drives connected through this controller were not found. In this case, the solution fortunately proved simple. All I needed to do was to add fdomain=0x6100,11 as a Linux startup option to force the driver to detect the SCSI controller at the specified address and interrupt number. (Finding the cause and solution was another matter; it took a fair amount of research on the Internet before I happened upon the right Web page that contained the explanation.)

This example demonstrates why it is a good idea to have a complete system inventory. But even when an installation proceeds flawlessly, a system inventory is still useful because it allows you to verify whether all hardware components on your system have been correctly configured.

Software Package Installation

TEST SYSTEM   Linux distributions contain a lot more than a *naked* copy of the operating system. Linux CD-ROMs are packed with server tools, development utilities, the graphical X Window System, networking tools, productivity applications, and more. Even if you have plenty of disk space, it's probably not a good idea to install packages indiscriminately; their presence can destabilize your system, and they might also represent a security hole. Therefore, at least when you're building a production system, install only the packages you need. Most distributions also contain a package management tool that lets you add or remove packages anytime later.

On the test system, I intend to install packages to support the following functions:

1. Creation of a customized Linux kernel that best matches my hardware

2. Network testing and configuration

3. Capability to run Internet services, including a mail server, WWW server, and more

▲   4. Documentation for installed packages

Because the test system will not be used as a workstation, I do not plan to install the X Window System or productivity applications.

Network Configuration

If your computer has a network card and you intend to connect it to the network during installation, you will need to specify network parameters during setup. Consider this section a crash course on the basics of IP networking; a more detailed introduction will follow in Chapter 5, "Internet Concepts."

PART
II

CH
3

All modern network configurations are implemented in the form of layers. The bottom layer is the networking hardware (the Ethernet adapter in your computer); the top layer is the application program that performs a networking function (for example, a Web browser). So, what's in between?

The first layer is the hardware driver. This driver physically manages the networking hardware.

The next layer is the low-level network protocol in use. UNIX systems typically use the Internet Protocol (IP), for this purpose. Other protocols include Novell's IPX or Microsoft's NetBIOS.

On an IP network, several data transmission protocols are available. For instance, TCP (used by most applications, including email programs and Web servers) provides a virtual connection between two machines on the network. Through this connection, data can flow in two directions.

On top of a protocol-like TCP, high-level protocols are implemented. One such protocol, HTTP (Hypertext Transfer Protocol), is used for delivering WWW content.

During operating system installation, you need to concern yourself with the first two layers: the driver for your network card and the IP configuration.

Depending on the network card you use, its configuration can be automatic or you might need to supply configuration parameters. If the card is an ISA adapter, you might also have to configure it using switches, jumpers, or a configuration utility that runs under MS-DOS.

After the network card is up and running, you need to configure the IP. The most important setting is the network adapter's IP number. This number uniquely identifies your computer on the network; if your network is directly connected to the Internet (that is, not through a firewall), the IP number must be unique worldwide.

So what IP number should you choose? If you have an existing network, chances are you already have a valid numbering scheme. If you do not yet have a network, perhaps you already have a block of IP numbers assigned for your use by your ISP. If neither of these are true, use one of the IP numbers specifically reserved for use by private networks— networks that are either not connected to the Internet or connected via a firewall.

Each IP number is actually a set of four numbers, each between 0 and 255, separated by periods. One reserved block of IP numbers is in the form of `192.168.xxx.yyy`, where *xxx* and *yyy* are arbitrary numbers. If you are preparing a server for a network that is yet to be built, use `192.168.1.1` as the server's IP number. (Remember: You can always change the IP number later if necessary.)

In addition to the IP number associated with the network card, each machine has a *local host* address: `127.0.0.1`. This address, by convention, always refers to the local machine.

IP numbers are often associated with names. For instance, when you visit the Web site of Macmillan Publishing, you use `www.mcp.com`, not `198.70.146.70` as the company's Web address. The translation from symbolic names to IP addresses is done by the DNS (domain name system). During installation, you might need to specify a DNS server. If you intend to configure the system you're working on as a DNS server, use `127.0.0.1` as the DNS server address. If you already have a DNS server on your network, use that server's address instead.

During installation, you'll also be asked to specify your machine's DNS name. If you're installing a machine on an existing network, chances are that in addition to an IP address, a name has also been assigned to it. If not, you can use an arbitrary name for now. Chapter 6, "The Domain Name System," contains information about how a registered DNS domain name can be obtained for your network and how you can assign names to individual machines within the domain.

Test System Installation

TEST SYSTEM Now I'll put this nice theory into practice. Using the Caldera OpenLinux installation that is on the accompanying CD-ROM, I began an installation on my test system.

The Caldera OpenLinux 1.3 installation program is called LISA, the OpenLinux Installation and System Administration utility. LISA guides you through a series of installation steps that help you configure your hard drive, install desired system components, set up the network, and get your system up and running.

The main steps of the setup procedure are as follows:

- Setup program initialization
- Hardware configuration
- Disk partitioning and swap space setup
- Package selection and installation

PART

II

CH

3

▼

- Network configuration
- Boot setup
- System restart

Setup Program Initialization

The Caldera OpenLinux setup program can be started from a floppy disk, CD-ROM, or from the MS-DOS prompt.

To start from a floppy disk or CD-ROM, insert the disk into your computer and reboot the system. If you're using a bootable CD-ROM, you might need to adjust your BIOS configuration to allow booting from CD-ROM.

To start from MS-DOS, type **D:\COL\LAUNCH\DOS\LOADLIN.EXE** from the MS-DOS prompt (not from an MS-DOS window under Windows).

My test machine supports booting from CD-ROM, so I started the installation program from the CD-ROM. First, I was greeted with a boot screen that offered me a chance to specify startup options. During initial installation, no startup options are necessary, so I waited a few seconds for the system to start booting, and LISA started execution. (If it had failed, I would have attempted installation after removing non-essential hardware components, such as my sound card, from the system. I would also have tried to install from floppy disks or from within MS-DOS.)

Caldera OpenLinux is an internationally distributed package, and its installation program supports several languages. It also supports non-U.S. keyboard layouts. Reasonably, the user's language preference and keyboard layouts are the first two questions the installer asks (see Figure 3.4). It would obviously be difficult to navigate through a complex installation process in a language you don't understand, with a keyboard whose keys are in the wrong position!

FIGURE 3.4
Selecting the LISA installation language.

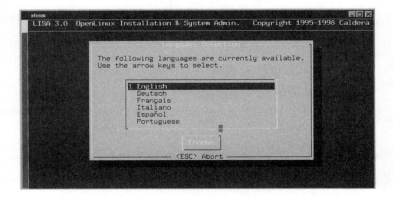

▼

▼   LISA also has the capability to run the installation using a previously created configuration, but because I was preparing a new installation, I had no saved configurations to use.

Hardware Configuration

The first action that the installer needs to perform is configuring the operating system to match the computer's hardware. In particular, it has to be capable of accessing your computer's hard disks, CD-ROM drives, and optionally, your network connection.

The installer's first dialog box (see Figure 3.5) asks whether you want to disable plug-and-play hardware. Use this option only if you suspect that the presence of some plug-and-play components causes (or might cause) the installer to fail.

FIGURE 3.5
The Change LISA Setup
dialog box.

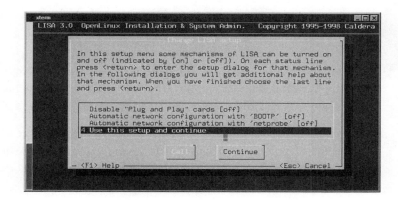

You are also given the option to automatically configure network settings. These options are typically used when configuring workstations on a network that is already up and running. Leaving the options turned off allows you to specify network settings by hand at a later stage, which is precisely what you need.

After the Change LISA Setup dialog box is dismissed, the installer proceeds by detecting all IDE devices on your system and showing you the result. On my system it displayed my CD-ROM drive (see Figure 3.6). However, it failed to list any of my hard disk drives.

The reason, of course, is that I am using SCSI hard disk drives, which are not detected automatically. Before these drives are recognized, the driver for my SCSI adapter needs to be loaded.

The opportunity to load additional drives is presented immediately, when LISA asks whether all devices have been recognized. Answering in the negative brings up another
▼   dialog box where LISA offers cautious *autoprobing* to detect additional hardware.

▼
FIGURE 3.6
IDE hardware detection.

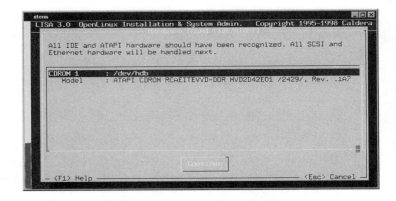

Autoprobing is a feature whereby the installer attempts to load various device drivers that check for the presence of the corresponding device. Unfortunately this method can lock up your computer. The probing action that is used to check for the presence of one device might cause another device to stop responding. Which is why autoprobing should not be used if you have a system inventory and you can specify what hardware devices are present on the system. (Note that it is safe to try autoprobing first; if the system locks up, reboot, restart the installation, and specify hardware devices manually.)

I selected no autoprobing, and then Kernel Module Manager was displayed. One of its options, Load Kernel Modules, can be used to load a new device driver. I selected the Load driver for SCSI adapter option, picked item 6 (AHA274X/284X/294X), and loaded the module (see Figure 3.7). It was not necessary to specify additional parameters, which is generally the case for PCI adapters like this one.

FIGURE 3.7
Loading a driver module.

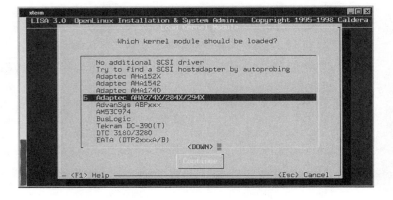

▼

▼ I also had to add support for my network card. Once again, I had to return to the Load Kernel Module command. This time I picked the Load Driver for Network Card option, and selected item 30 (NE2000/NE1000). This time it was necessary to specify additional parameters—namely the I/O port (0x340) and the interrupt number (11) before the driver could be loaded.

With these actions, initial hardware configuration was complete. The system now correctly recognized all my hard disks, CD-ROMs, and network adapters.

Disk Partitioning and Swap Space Setup

After the initial hardware configuration, LISA offers the option of changing your hard disks' partitioning. Because I dedicated an entire disk (an entire JAZ cartridge, to be precise) for use with Linux, I wanted to change its partitioning.

> **NOTE**
>
> Repartitioning a hard disk that contains data almost certainly results in complete data loss! If you need to install Linux on a disk that contains data, consider using the FIPS utility to *shrink* the existing (MS-DOS) partition and make space for a Linux partition. Alternatively, you might consider installing Linux on the existing MS-DOS partition using UMSDOS. However, I wouldn't recommend either of these methods on a machine used as a server.

When LISA displayed the list of hard disks on my system (see Figure 3.8), I selected the Iomega drive, /dev/sda, for partitioning.

FIGURE 3.8
Selecting a hard disk drive for partitioning.

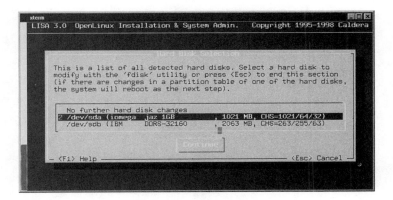

▼

▼   At this point, LISA started the Linux `fdisk` program. This program, like its MS-DOS cousin, can be used to display or modify a hard disk's partition table. It has a simple help system that lists all the program commands along with a one-line description for each. Usage is self-explanatory. First, I used the `d` command to erase all existing partitions. Then I used the `n` command to add two new partitions; and I used the `t` command to modify one of these new partitions to be a *Linux swap* type. In the end, I had a partition table that looked the following code when listed in `fdisk` using the `p` command:

```
Disk /dev/sda: 64 heads, 32 sectors, 1021 cylinders
Units = cylinders of 2048 * 512 bytes
   Device Boot    Start      End    Blocks   Id  System
/dev/sda1             1      900    921584   83  Linux native
/dev/sda2           901     1021    123904   82  Linux swap
```

It is always a good idea to use a swap partition for virtual memory if possible. As a rule of thumb, the size of the swap partition should be approximately twice the size of your system's RAM. My test computer has 64MB of RAM, and the swap partition I created is 121MB.

After partitioning is complete, LISA offers to activate the newly created swap partition.

Package Selection and Installation

At this point, the first phase of the installation has completed. All hardware components have been set up; now is the time to start setting up software.

LISA first asks you to specify the installation source, which can be a CD-ROM drive, a hard disk directory, or a network source. In my case, the installation source was a CD-ROM drive; selecting this option caused LISA to display a list of available CD-ROM devices. The drive that is already detected is highlighted (see Figure 3.9).

FIGURE 3.9
CD-ROM drive selection.

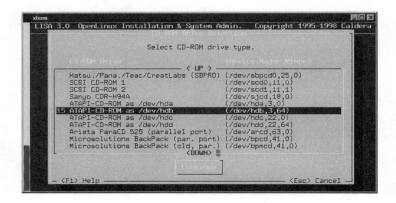

▼   Next, LISA asks you to specify the destination partition. This, *root partition* will contain
all system files. Whereas other partitions can be dynamically attached (mounted) while
the system is running, the root partition is always active. It contains the operating system
and all essential program and configuration files. On my test system, the newly created
`/dev/sda1` partition will serve as the root partition (see Figure 3.10).

FIGURE 3.10
Selecting the root partition.

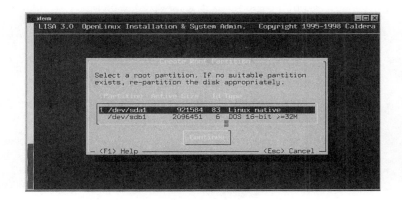

At this time LISA offers the option to *format* the partition. The term is obsolete; in reality, during this phase the file system is created on the selected partition. Nevertheless, the
effect is the same: if the partition previously contained data, that data will be erased.
LISA also offers the option to check for defective sectors, but it isn't necessary except
on really old IDE and even older MFM/RLL disk drives. All modern disk drives have the
capability to automatically detect and remap failing sectors. Checking for defective sectors on these devices is a waste of time.

After the file system has been created, LISA finally presents you with a list of software
packages to install (see Figure 3.11).

FIGURE 3.11
Package pre-selection.

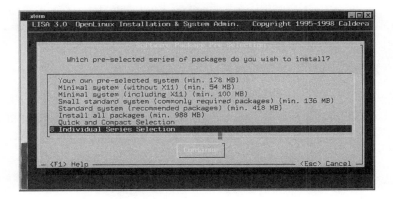

▼

▼   Because I know what I am doing, I have opted to perform an individual series installation. This allows me to pick specifically the tools and utilities I need, instead of accepting someone else's idea as to what's good for me. The packages I selected implement the services covered in this book:

- From the *basis* series, I pre-selected all software packages.
- From the *develop* series, I opted to preselect the minimum and recommended packages. Additionally, I specified the following items: aout-libs-devel, binutils-aout, byacc, gcc-aout, imap, ld.so-devel, libc-devel-static, libg++-devel, libg++-devel-static.
- From the *doku* series, I chose to pre-select the minimum and recommended packages and apache-docs, faq, howto-en-ascii, ldp-en-ascii, lilo-doc, sendmail-doc, uucp-doc, vim-help.
- From the *misc* series, I pre-selected the minimum packages, and added aout-libs and mgetty.
- From the *network* series, I chose the minimum and recommended, and bind, bind-doc, diald, inn, minicom, pine, uucp, whois.

Conspicuously absent from my selection list is the X Window System. This is intentional. As explained earlier, X is not required in order to create and efficiently manage a Linux-based server system. It is also possible to implement many server functions on old hardware that is not sufficiently powerful to run X well. Of course, if you're still only experimenting with Linux and not setting up a server intended for production use, feel free to install a standard OpenLinux configuration.

After you are finished selecting software, it's time for a coffee break; depending on the choices you made and the speed of your machine and its CD-ROM drive, it can be several minutes to a half hour or more while LISA installs and configures all packages.

When installation is complete, LISA will also run configuration scripts for any packages that require this step.

Network Configuration

After all software packages are installed, the next step is to configure the network.

LISA first asks for the machine name. For the purposes of this book, I used a fictitious domain name: linux.sys. Please note that in real life, there is no top-level domain that
▼   ends with .sys.

▼   Since I have a network card, LISA also asks for its IP parameters. The IP address for this
card, labeled eth0, is set to 192.168.1.1. LISA also asks for a network mask and broadcast address; these are set to 255.255.255.0 and 192.168.1.255, respectively. (More
information is provided on this subject in Chapter 5.)

Next LISA asks whether I have a router. Actually I do, but that's not the point; I am configuring this test system as a server that exists independently of my office LAN. After it's
fully configured, it's this server that will become a router for other machines, so the
answer is No. (If I were to use my ISDN router, for instance, I would have answered Yes
and specified the IP address of that router when asked.)

LISA also asks for my DNS server. Because I intend to configure the test machine as a
DNS server, I specified its loopback address, 127.0.0.1, as the DNS server's address.

Lastly, LISA asks if I am using NIS. NIS, the Network Information System (also known
as YP or Yellow Pages) allows you to configure a network with distributed domain and
user information. I do not intend to use NIS, so the answer is No.

Supplementary Configuration Options

Before LISA can proceed to set up user accounts, a few more items still need to be configured.

First the system time. LISA asks whether to run the computer's battery-powered CMOS
clock on local time or Greenwich Mean Time (UTC). On a dedicated Linux system, it's a
good idea to pick UTC. On a multiboot system, choose Local Time because that's what
other operating systems such as Windows expect to see. I picked Local Time for the
same reason.

Next, configure the time zone selection. Choose the time zone that matches your geographic location. I selected zone 30, Canada/Eastern.

LISA also asks for your mouse type. If you have a mouse connected to the round mouse
port of your computer's motherboard, chances are it is a PS/2 mouse. Most mice are
either serial mice or PS/2 mice; do not select another type unless you are sure it matches
your hardware.

Lastly, LISA also offers the option to configure a printer. There is no printer attached to
▼   my test system, so I skipped this part.

PART
II
CH
3

▼
User Accounts

Before your system can be used, user accounts must be configured. In addition to the root account (the superuser) at least one regular account should also be configured. As a rule of thumb, you should never use the root account for any tasks that can be accomplished using a non-privileged account.

During system installation, LISA let me specify the password for the root account.

> **WARNING**   The root password should be selected with care. Anyone who can access the system over the network can—if they possess the root password—perform any action on the system, including reading confidential data or formatting hard disks. Worse yet, using root access on a computer on your office LAN, they can also monitor all LAN traffic and potentially compromise the security of other computers.

LISA also offered the opportunity to create a regular account. By default, it offers the account name col (for Caldera OpenLinux.) I changed this to vttoth, which is my preferred username on UNIX systems. It also reflects a long-standing convention of creating account names from the user's last name and first initials.

> **NOTE**   Keep account names to a length of eight characters or less. Some programs are confused by usernames that are longer. As for passwords, although longer passwords are accepted, on most systems only the first eight characters are actually used, so you do not gain extra security by using a longer password.

When creating the new account, LISA asks which shell program to use. I picked the default, GNU bash. As with most other options, you can change this option anytime later.

Boot Setup

System installation is complete, but you still need to set up the new system's boot configuration. This involves configuring booting from the hard disk, as well as specifying
▼   which services are to be run at system startup.

▼   At this point LISA begins to configure LILO, the Linux loader. I asked LILO to set up
the boot manager on the first SCSI hard disk (see Figure 3.12).

FIGURE 3.12
Installing LILO on the hard
drive.

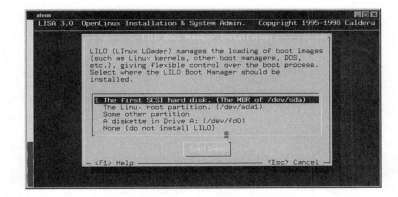

Next, LISA offers a set of choices. These correspond to operating system images that
LISA installed earlier, and optionally, other bootable partitions on the system.

In my case, LISA installed two Linux images on my hard disk, and it just so happens
that the two actually refer to the same file, so selecting one over the other makes no difference. LISA also lists the MS-DOS partition on my second hard drive as a boot option
(see Figure 3.13).

FIGURE 3.13
LILO boot image selection.

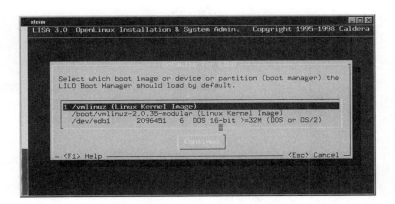

I picked /vmlinuz as the boot image and accepted the defaults LISA offered for the initial RAM disk and LILO boot parameters. This RAM disk image is required when you
▼   use the original LISA-installed Linux kernel if any device required to boot the system

▼ needs a kernel module to run, as is the case with many SCSI-based systems. During boot, the kernel finds additional modules in the RAM disk. In other words, without the RAM disk, Linux might not be capable of booting.

After all these choices have been made, LISA invokes lilo, the LILO configuration utility. If LILO is successfully installed, the system is bootable. However, the task of boot configuration is not yet complete. What remains is the selection of system services that are to be started when the system boots.

Given the choice of packages you decided to install, LISA makes an intelligent set of selections as to which services are to be enabled at startup. I had to modify very little to create a configuration to my liking.

Starting with LISA's default set of choices, I decided to turn off the Auto Mount daemon that is typically used for NFS (Network File System), because I don't intend to use it. I also turned off the Internetwork Packet eXchange (because I only use the IP not IPX on my LAN), and the remote kernel statistics server (see Figure 3.14).

FIGURE 3.14
Selection of automatically started services.

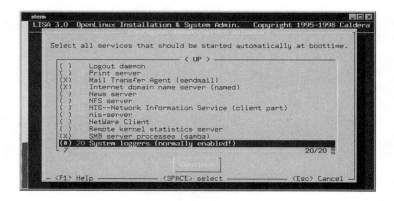

I also turned on the Mail Transfer Agent (sendmail), the Internet domain name server (named), the InterNetNews news transport system (innd), and the SMB server processes (samba). All these services are covered in the chapters that follow.

Now you are really done! At this point LISA offers the option to save the newly created configuration to floppy disk, and then proceeds with booting the system.

Notice I said booting, not rebooting; LISA loads the system with the newly created configuration, it does not actually restart the computer. This can be a problem! It is
▼ possible—in fact, this is precisely what happened to me once—for LISA to boot the

▼   system fine, but after reboot, your system will not function properly. Therefore, it's a
good idea to force a system reset after the login prompt appears (the well-known *three-
finger salute*, Ctrl+Alt+Del, causes an orderly reboot) and ensure that your configuration
loads as intended. Of course, do make sure you've removed all bootable floppy disks and
▲   CD-ROMs.

The Linux Kernel

The kernel is the core of the operating system. It usually exists on your system in the
form of the file /vmlinuz. Essentially it is a program that implements the operating system's essential features. By its very nature, the kernel is hardware dependent, and must
be configured to work on a particular computer. The desired configuration can be
achieved using kernel modules or by recompiling the kernel.

Modern versions of Linux support the concept of a *modular* kernel. A modular kernel
consists of the core kernel file and a variety of additional modules, each implementing
support for a specific device or feature. Kernel modules can be loaded and unloaded
dynamically.

This is, in fact, how Caldera OpenLinux can be installed on any system using only a pair
of floppy disks. Older Linux distributions often used dozens of different floppy disk
images containing *stock* kernels so, as the first installation step, you needed to pick the
image that best matched your system. Caldera OpenLinux uses a modular kernel instead,
which can be booted on any system as long as the proper modules are present.

A modular kernel is useful, but sometimes you might want to experiment with creating a
customized kernel that matches your system. Or you may be using a Linux distribution
that, unlike the Caldera OpenLinux distribution on the accompanying CD-ROM, does
not offer a well-designed modular kernel as an option. Appendix A, "Configuring the
Kernel," provides explanations and an example for this complex procedure.

Summary

Initial installation of a Linux system consists of placing a copy of the operating system
and essential utilities on your computer's hard drive, and configuring the system and
these utilities.

Before you begin installation, prepare for it by creating a system inventory, deciding on a partitioning scheme and collecting optional network parameters. If the target system contains data, make sure you have good backups.

To prepare an optimal partitioning scheme for your hard disk, you must understand the boot process. Using LILO, you can create a standalone Linux system or a configuration that boots multiple operating systems.

You also need to understand the differences between various file system types. With Linux, the preferred file system type on your hard disk is the Second Extended File System. However, because this file system is incompatible with other operating systems, you might opt to use UMSDOS, a file system that implements UNIX-style features on top of an MS-DOS partition.

A Linux installation can be started from a bootable CD-ROM, from within MS-DOS using the `LOADLIN.EXE` utility, or from bootable floppy disks. Such floppy disks can be created using the `rawrite` utility.

Linux installation begins with hardware detection. Additional steps include configuring your network, selecting and installing software packages, and creating a boot configuration.

Although you can run Linux using a modular kernel, creating a customized kernel that closely matches your system's hardware might in some cases improve performance or stability. Such a kernel can be created through the process of recompiling, which is explained in Appdenix A.

Internet Configuration and Basic Security

Consider this: **You are** about to move to a new house in a rough neighborhood but unfortunately you are visually impaired and unable to examine the house. You do not know how many doors and windows it has, where they are, and in what condition. Even for the doors and windows that you do know about, you aren't sure who might have a copy of the key.

Are you looking forward to the move?

Connecting a system to the Internet or even an office network is not an entirely dissimilar affair. The Internet is indeed a rough neighborhood. I do not mean to perpetuate myths about evil hackers who roam the Net ready to break into any unsecured system and wreak havoc there. True hackers (the talented kind) are few and far between, and they usually concentrate their efforts on targets more challenging and exciting than a poor little Linux box that just popped into existence.

However, thousands of shady operators scan the network incessantly, looking for just such systems that they can then use to distribute junk email, exchange stolen software, or illicit materials. They might not know much about computers, but they know enough to run scanner programs that were written by their much smarter cousins. Becoming their victim can have unpleasant consequences, the least of which is an overload of your network connection, rendering it unusable.

And even on systems connected only to a LAN, accidents happen. A user might have just discovered TELNET.EXE on his new Windows 95 computer, used it to connect to your new server, and not knowing a thing about Linux, caused all sorts of problems there.

So the task at hand is simple: ensure that you do know about all the openings of your new house (small cracks in the walls included) and that you have accounted for all the keys.

Users, Groups, and Passwords

The first line of defense against unauthorized access on any UNIX system is password security. In order to log on to the system and run programs on it, you must possess a valid user identifier and a password.

Users and Groups

Linux, like most other UNIX systems, stores information on all users in the file /etc/passwd. This file contains a colon-separated list of user identifiers and attributes.

For each user, the following information is recorded in /etc/passwd:

- Login name
- Password
- Numeric account identifier
- Numeric group identifier
- Comment (usually personal information)
- Home directory
- Startup shell

The user's login name is the identifier used for logging on to the system. For instance, my login name on many systems is vttoth.

Passwords are stored in encrypted form, either in the /etc/passwd file or, if a facility called *shadow passwords* is installed, in a separate file. If this is the case, /etc/passwd usually contains the letter X or an asterisk in place of the encrypted password.

Internally, Linux identifies users by a number. This number is recorded in /etc/passwd, and just like the user's login name, it must be unique.

The group number is the numeric identifier of the primary group to which the user belongs. Groups are listed separately in /etc/group.

The Comment field can contain any text that does not contain the colon character. By convention, this field either contains the user's full name or a comma-separated list with the user's full name, office (department), office phone, and home phone. If these fields are defined, they are used by services such as the Internet *finger* service.

The home directory is the directory that the user's login shell switches to when it is started. Typically users are only able to create files in their home directory, although they may be able to read files in many other directories.

Lastly, the login shell is the shell program that starts when the user logs on. It can be any one of the programs listed in the file /etc/shells.

TEST SYSTEM

After the initial installation was complete, this is what /etc/passwd looked like on my test system:

```
root:x:0:0:root:/root:/bin/bash
bin:x:1:1:bin:/bin:
daemon:x:2:2:daemon:/sbin:
adm:x:3:4:adm:/var/adm:
lp:x:4:7:lp:/var/spool/lpd:
sync:x:5:0:sync:/sbin:/bin/sync
shutdown:x:6:11:shutdown:/sbin:/sbin/shutdown
halt:x:7:0:halt:/sbin:/sbin/halt
mail:x:8:12:mail:/var/spool/mail:
news:x:9:13:news:/var/spool/news:
uucp:x:10:14:uucp:/var/spool/uucp:
operator:x:11:0:operator:/root:
games:x:12:100:games:/usr/games:
gopher:x:13:30:gopher:/usr/lib/gopher-data:
ftp:x:14:50:FTP User:/home/ftp:
man:x:15:15:Manuals Owner:/:
majordom:x:16:16:Majordomo:/:/bin/false
postgres:x:17:17:Postgres User:/home/postgres:/bin/bash
nobody:x:65534:65534:Nobody:/:/bin/false
vttoth:x:100:100:Viktor T. Toth:/home/vttoth:/bin/bash
```

Perhaps it's a bit surprising that as many as 20 different accounts exist on the system. Only one of these is a *true* user account, however; the rest are created by the system to perform specific functions. These accounts do not have valid passwords or login shells assigned to them, so they cannot be used to log on to the system.

▲

Groups represent an important mechanism that makes it possible to fine-tune security privileges granted to individual users. For instance, it is possible to create a file with the following permissions:

root:	read/write
members of group goodguys:	read
rest of the world:	none

Groups are listed in the file /etc/group in a colon-separated list. Each row contains a group name, a group password (rarely used), the group numeric identifier, and the group members.

It is not necessary to list a user as a group member for the group that is the user's primary group (as defined in /etc/passwd). However, if a user belongs to more than one group, his account identifier should appear for any of the additional group to which he belongs.

By way of a real-life example, I am the administrator of an online game called MUD2. Several game administration files on that system are stored with read/write permissions assigned to the game administrator account, as well as any member of the mud group. By making my ordinary user account on this system a member of the mud group, I am able to perform many administrative functions without having to switch to the superuser account.

TEST SYSTEM   On my test system, the LISA installation program created a default /etc/group file as follows:

```
root::0:
wheel::10:
bin::1:bin,daemon
daemon::2:bin,daemon
sys::3:bin,adm
adm::4:adm,daemon
tty::5:
disk::6:
lp::7:daemon,lp
mem::8:
kmem::9:
operator::11:
mail::12:mail
news::13:news
uucp::14:uucp
man::15:
majordom::16:
database::17:
```

▼
```
games::20:
gopher::30:
dip::40:
ftp::50:
users::100:
```
▲
```
nobody::65534:
```

Groups can be administered using the gpasswd command. The command can be used to set up group passwords, assign group administrators, and add and remove group members. (Note that this command is not present on all Linux installations.)

TEST SYSTEM   The following are a few useful and important commands.

- The su command (substitute user) lets you switch from one account to another. Needless to say, you need to know the password of the account you're switching to unless you're the root user. Using su with no parameters switches you to the root account.

- The passwd command lets you change your password. If you're root, you can also change the password of other users.

- The chsh command can be used to change your login shell. Only a shell from the list in /etc/shells can be selected.

- The chfn can be used to change the *finger-compatible* contents of the Comment field in /etc/passwd. This utility lets you specify your name, office, office phone, and home phone, and stores this information in /etc/passwd in a form that is understood by the UNIX finger service.

- The newgrp command can be used to change (temporarily) your default group. You can only switch to a group you are a member of, or to a group that has a password (you'll be prompted to enter the password.)

▲
- The groups command lists all the groups a user belongs to. Without parameters, it lists the groups of the current user.

PART

II

CH

4

Adding New Users

To add a new user to the system, you must perform the following steps:

- Add an entry to /etc/passwd

- If using shadow passwords, add a corresponding entry to /etc/shadow

- Create the user's home directory

- Copy initialization files to the user's home directory

These steps can be performed by hand (not recommended), or by using the `useradd` or `adduser` command-line utilities. Many Linux installations also offer more sophisticated user management utilities. If for any reason, you decide to manually edit files such as `/etc/passwd`, be extremely careful; a wrong move can compromise your system's security or even render the system unusable.

TEST SYSTEM

The Caldera OpenLinux administration utility, LISA, provides a set of simple functions for user and group administration. These can be accessed directly by invoking LISA with the `−useradm` command-line flag (see Figure 4.1).

FIGURE 4.1
LISA user administration module.

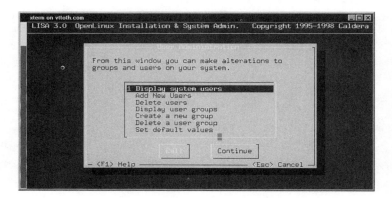

▲

Password Security

A seemingly obvious, yet frequently forgotten rule is that your password should not be easy to guess! Picking the name of your spouse or your mother or using your favorite color as the password is a very bad idea. Something more obscure, such as the average velocity of an African or European sparrow, is a much better choice. Even better are passwords picked completely at random, which contain no recognizable words and consist of a combination of upper- and lowercase letters and numbers: for example, `Y5Bxi8Ne`.

Of course such a random password is hard to remember, so you might be inclined to make a compromise. That's okay as long as the password you pick is not something others who know you can easily figure out. Some people use the first letter of each word from short sentences they can easily remember. This is a good idea, as long as the sentence in question is not something others can easily find out about.

On many UNIX installations, user passwords are stored, in encrypted form, in the file `/etc/passwd`. The encryption is one-way, meaning that there is no way to recover your password from the encrypted version. This is because the encryption used doesn't yield unique results; many different passwords can yield the same encrypted result.

Although the password encryption technique used for `/etc/passwd` is good, modern computers are even better. It no longer takes a herd of supercomputers to find a password that matches an encrypted one in the file `/etc/passwd`. This is an inherent weakness of this password mechanism; because `/etc/passwd` is readable by anyone on the system (since that's where basic user information is stored), users with access to this file can run a password cracking utility on this file to find out the passwords of others.

The solution to this problem is *shadow passwords*. This essentially entails a modification of system utilities and libraries that access the password file. When shadow passwords are installed, `/etc/passwd` no longer contains valid encrypted passwords; these are stored instead in the shadow password file, `/etc/shadow`. Unlike `/etc/passwd`, the `/etc/shadow` file is *not* readable by ordinary users. Similarly, group passwords (if used) are stored in `/etc/gshadow`.

The shadow password suite can also be used to enforce password changing policies. For instance, it can be used to set an expiration time on the user's password, forcing the user to change the password regularly.

Last but not least, make sure no account in `/etc/passwd` has a blank password. A blank password allows for a password-free login under that account name.

The Root Login

As you know, the superuser's root account provides unrestricted access to the system. For this reason, it is important that root's security not be compromised.

The root account should always have a secure password. Even if there are no other users on your system, if you connect to the Internet, others can get in. An unsecure root password (or worse yet, a blank root password) essentially leaves the door wide open to any intruder.

It is possible to restrict root logins to specific terminals. The file `/etc/securetty` lists the names of those devices on which root logins are permitted. If this file exists, any attempts to log on as root on a terminal not listed will be denied.

PART

II

CH

4

Typically, /etc/securetty contains only a list of virtual consoles, tty1 to tty8, for example. This configuration allows root logins to anyone at the machine's keyboard, but denies root access over network connections. It is still possible to gain root privileges on a non-root terminal using the su command, but first you must log on as a regular user.

Never use the root account for tasks that can be performed using a non-privileged account. This way you limit your exposure to disasters caused by malicious code or simple operator mistakes.

Privileges and Permissions

Security of a Linux system is implemented primarily through assigning ownership and permissions to system files and directories.

File System Permissions

All files and directories under Linux are *owned* by a specific user and group. Each file and directory has three sets of permissions assigned—user, group, and world.

Each set consists of three flags: read, write, and execute permission. The meaning of the read and write permission settings is obvious. The execute permission marks a file as an executable program or, in the case of a directory, the executable permission means that the user can change to that directory to make it his current directory.

For instance, typing **ls -l /bin/bash** reveals the ownership and permissions of the file that contains the bash shell program:

```
-rwxr-xr-x   1 root      root        300964 Aug 19 10:30 /bin/bash
```

The first group of ten letters and symbols specifies the file's attributes. The first letter specifies if the file is actually a directory or other special file type. The remaining nine letters represent (in groups of three) the user level, group level, and world level permissions associated with this file.

It is important that you don't assign unnecessary permissions to a file. Any extra permission represents a potential security hole. Changing the permissions of /etc/shadow (normally readable only by root) will negate the security benefits of the shadow password suite installed on your system.

Changing File Permissions

A combination of three commands is used to change the ownership and permissions of files. The chown command can be used to change a file's owner and optionally, its group owner. The chgrp command can be used to change a file's group owner only. Lastly, the chmod command can be used to change a file's permission settings.

Here is how you can change the file myfile.txt to be owned by the user root, group users, and to be readable by everyone:

```
chown root myfile.txt
chgrp root myfile.txt
chmod a+r myfile.txt
```

Usage of chown and chgrp is quite obvious, but chmod deserves more attention due to its arcane syntax. The command can accept new attributes in numeric or symbolic form. Although the symbolic form is supposed to be a mnemonic form, it is usually easier to remember the numeric form instead.

In the numeric form, permissions are represented by a group of four digits. Each digit can be a number between 0 and 7 (that is, an octal digit). The first digit represents special flags. The second represents user-level permissions; the third represents group-level permissions; and the fourth represents world-level permissions. Each digit is computed as a sum of the number 4 (if the read permission is set), 2 (if the write permission is set), and 1 (if the execute permission is set.) So the permissions rwxr-xr-x would be encoded as 0755. To change permissions for the file myfile to this set, type

chmod 0755 myfile

Of the three special flags, two are very important. These suid (set effective user identifier) and sgid (set effective group identifier) flags allow a file containing a program to execute under the user identifier of the file's owner. This is, for example, how the passwd program works; it always executes as though it was run by the root user, so it can update the contents of the file /etc/passwd, a file normal users cannot write to. Typing **ls -l /usr/bin/passwd** reveals the presence of this flag, as the letter X, which normally indicates execute permissions, is replaced by the letter S.

```
-r-sr-xr-x   1 root      bin         7351 Aug 19 04:30 /usr/bin/passwd
```

PART

II

CH

4

To set a file's user identifier at runtime using the numeric form of the `chmod` command, use the value 4 in the first digit. To set a file's group identifier, use the value 2. For example, to set `myfile` to execute under the effective user identifier and group identifier of its owner, type

```
chmod 6755 myfile
```

Be careful when using this feature. Adding `suid` permissions to the wrong command can, in effect, grant superuser privileges to anyone who uses that command!

The mnemonic form of `chmod` allows you to change individual permission settings without regard to the rest. For instance, you can grant all users on the system permission to execute `myfile` by typing

```
chmod a+x myfile
```

To revoke read and write permissions to the file by anyone other than the file's owner, type

```
chmod o-rw myfile
```

Generally, the mnemonic form consists of three parts. The first part specifies which permission levels are to be modified. The second part consists of the plus sign, minus sign, or the equal sign, and defines whether new permissions are to be added to the existing set, whether existing permissions are to be revoked, or whether the file's permissions are to be set exactly to the new specifications. The third group of letters identifies the desired permission settings.

The first and third part of the mnemonic form can contain multiple letters. For instance, to add read and write permissions to a file by all users except the file's owner, type

```
chmod ug+rw myfile
```

Multiple specifications are allowed and must be separated by a comma. For example, here is how you revoke read and write permissions to a file by anyone, and then assign read and write permissions to it by the file's owner:

```
chmod u+rw,o-rw myfile
```

The `chmod`, `chown`, and `chgrp` commands can be run recursively by supplying the `-R` argument on the command line. For instance, to change the owner of each file in the current directory to `root`, and the group owner to `bin`, type

```
chown -R root.bin *
```

System Services

When you're connected to the Internet and surf the Web using a browser program, it is perhaps not immediately obvious that your connection is a two-way conduit. If you can get out, others can get in!

This is not really a problem when using an operating system such as Windows 95/98 that has very few server features. With Linux it's different. Your system has the capability to run many service applications and is probably configured to run several of them already. It should be obvious that in order to prevent these applications from becoming security holes, they must be configured properly. But how do you know what services are configured to run on your system?

You can, of course, watch system messages scrolling by as the system boots, but this isn't exactly a foolproof method. Not only because you might miss some messages, but also because some services might not display any messages at startup. Moreover, many services are not started when the system boots, only when they are requested across the network.

System Startup

So how, exactly, does Linux start? After the initial boot, what actions does it perform? Or, to ask the question in a more pedestrian fashion, where is your `CONFIG.SYS` or `AUTOEXEC.BAT` file?

The filenames in Linux are different but their function is similar to the function of those two MS-DOS startup files.

This phase of the system boot process begins after the operating system's kernel has been loaded and initialized. The kernel starts the `init` process; `init`, reads its configuration file (`/etc/inittab`) to determine what needs to be done.

The `/etc/inittab` file determines the following:

- How to initialize the system under different runlevels
- What programs to run on different terminals
- How to respond to specific system conditions

Each `/etc/inittab` entry corresponds with a system event or a character terminal. For instance, consider the following:

```
pf::powerfail:/sbin/shutdown -h +5 "Power Failure; System Shutting Down"
```

PART

II

CH

4

This line tells init to run the /sbin/shutdown command if it receives a power fail signal (typically from a utility program that monitors an uninterruptible power supply).

In addition to specific system events, init also maintains the concept of a *runlevel*. The runlevel, typically a number between 0 and 6, determines the system's mode of operation. The meaning of the runlevel varies from one Linux distribution to the next, but runlevels almost always exist for the following operating modes:

- System halt
- System reboot
- Single user mode
- Multiuser mode
- Multiuser mode with graphical login prompt under X

The system's runlevel can be determined at startup, for example if you specify the single boot-time parameter. If no runlevel is specified, init determines the default runlevel from /etc/inittab by looking for a line similar to this:

```
id:3:initdefault:
```

Many entries in /etc/inittab refer to a specific character terminal. For instance, consider the following line:

```
1:12345:respawn:/sbin/getty tty1 VC linux
```

This /etc/inittab entry instructs init to run the /sbin/getty command (a program that initiates the user login process) on the first virtual console when the runlevel is between 1 and 5. The respawn keyword specifies that if all programs on this console are terminated, /sbin/getty should be restarted (so that on a console no longer in use, you can log on again).

The contents of /etc/inittab also determine what commands are run when the system is switched to a new runlevel (such as when the system is started). This typically is a script file usually contained somewhere in the /etc/rc.d directory. The exact name of this file varies from one Linux installation to the next, but the essence is the same: the file starts up various operating system services.

WARNING   Unless you know what you're doing, do not edit the startup files in /etc/rc.d. An invalid startup file can render your system completely unbootable.

Now you know where to check what system services are started when the system is initialized. Unfortunately, the scripts in /etc/rc.d are often quite complex and difficult to understand. The good news is that it is extremely rare that you ever need to edit these scripts directly. Most installations provide a means to configure your system without touching these scripts. It is also possible to specify additional startup actions by editing a script specifically reserved for site-specific customizations, typically /etc/rc.d/rc.local.

Another way to check what processes are running on your system at this very moment is by using the ps (process status) utility. Running ps ax gives a complete list of all running processes. This way you can verify that the set of running processes matches the desired set that you configured.

TEST SYSTEM

On Caldera OpenLinux, the startup scripts read configuration options from files under the /etc/sysconfig directory hierarchy. These configuration files are modified by the LISA utility. Starting LISA with the — system command-line option takes you directly to the system configuration menu (see Figure 4.2), where you can select the Configure Daemon/Server Autostart command.

FIGURE 4.2
LISA user administration module.

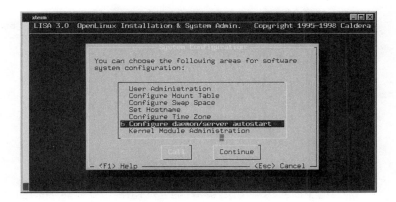

PART
II

CH
4

NOTE

The word daemon often occurs when talking about UNIX. This is not due to some medieval superstition (although quite a number of system administrators who had to deal with the quirks of UNIX had become superstitious as a result). It simply refers to system service processes that run in the background.

▼ During initial installation, I used this utility to specify that the following services be run:

- The atd batch server that lets users schedule a command for later execution

- The crond daemon that can be used to schedule recurring commands

- The Apache Web server

- The sendmail Mail Transfer Agent

- The named DNS server

- The Samba SMB server

- System log services

Typing **ps ax** lists all running processes:

```
PID TTY STAT TIME COMMAND
   1  ?   S    0:07 init
   2  ?   SW   0:00 (kflushd)
   3  ?   SW<  0:00 (kswapd)
  32  ?   S    0:00 update (bdflush)
 299  ?   S    0:00 inetd
 312  ?   S    0:00 syslogd
 315  ?   S    0:00 klogd -k /boot/System.map-2.0.35
 343  ?   S    0:00 xntpd
 349  ?   S    0:00 cron
 361  ?   S    0:00 sendmail: accepting connections on port 25
 377  ?   S    0:00 httpd -f /etc/httpd/apache/conf/httpd.conf
 450  2   S    0:00 /sbin/getty tty2 VC linux
 451  3   S    0:00 /sbin/getty tty3 VC linux
 452  4   S    0:00 /sbin/getty tty4 VC linux
 453  5   S    0:00 /sbin/getty tty5 VC linux
 454  6   S    0:00 /sbin/getty tty6 VC linux
 301  ?   S    0:00 rpc.portmap
 356  ?   S    0:00 atd
 449  1   S    0:00 login vttoth
 455  1   S    0:00 -bash
3655  1   R    0:00 ps axw
 381  ?   S    0:00 httpd -f /etc/httpd/apache/conf/httpd.conf
 382  ?   S    0:00 httpd -f /etc/httpd/apache/conf/httpd.conf
```

I took a careful look at this list and found that in addition to the services specified through LISA, a few extra services are also running. One of them is xntpd, which is not really a surprise because I added the Network Time Server service to the packages to be installed when I set up the system. Another is inetd, the Internet Superserver, which is covered in the following section.

Knowing what services run on your system is the first step toward establishing security. You need to also become familiar with the services themselves and ensure that they are configured properly and securely.

The Internet Superserver

Perhaps the most important service process or daemon that runs on a UNIX system is inetd, the Internet Superserver.

The idea is simple. An Internet-connected server is normally capable of performing dozens, perhaps hundreds, of different network functions. Running a service process for each of these functions would be incredibly wasteful. What happens instead is that the single service utility, inetd, is run. This utility monitors incoming network connection requests and starts up the desired services when requests arrive.

The inetd server obtains its configuration information from the file /etc/inetd.conf. This file contains a list of Internet port numbers and the names of service processes (more about this in the Chapter 5, "Internet Concepts").

For example, consider one of the most commonly used Internet utilities, the telnet program. This program lets you log on to a remote system via a facility called a *virtual terminal*. In order to accept a Telnet connection, the remote system must run a telnet daemon, the service process corresponding with the Telnet client program you run.

Rather than running several telnet daemons all the time (as many as the anticipated maximum number of simultaneous incoming Telnet connections) the server can have instead a single line in /etc/inetd.conf that reads like this:

```
23       stream  tcp     nowait  root    /usr/sbin/tcpd  in.telnetd
```

This tells the server's inetd daemon to start the telnet daemon every time an incoming connection attempt is detected on TCP port 23, the port used for Telnet connections by convention.

Examine, and if necessary, edit /etc/inetd.conf to remove services you do not need. For example, if you do not anticipate a need to support incoming Telnet connections, feel free to disable the preceding line by starting it with a pound sign (the standard comment line indicator in many UNIX configuration files).

PART

II

CH

4

TEST SYSTEM   Having examined `/etc/inetd.conf` on my test system, I found a few services that should be disabled. Here is the annotated version of my modified copy of this file (without the comment lines):

```
echo       stream  tcp     nowait   root      internal
echo       dgram   udp     wait     root      internal
discard    stream  tcp     nowait   root      internal
discard    dgram   udp     wait     root      internal
daytime    stream  tcp     nowait   root      internal
daytime    dgram   udp     wait     root      internal
chargen    stream  tcp     nowait   root      internal
chargen    dgram   udp     wait     root      internal
```

These built-in services are safe to run and consume virtually no resources on the server. However, you might consider turning them off on a server that is potentially exposed to an attack from the outside. Occasionally these services can be used to initiate a *denial of service* type attack on your system, consuming an excessive amount of network bandwidth and processor resources.

```
#time   stream  tcp     nowait   root      internal
#time   dgram   udp     wait     root      internal
```

Time services were turned off by default by the OpenLinux installer. Who am I to argue?

```
ftp       stream  tcp     nowait   root      /usr/sbin/tcpd in.ftpd -l -a
telnet    stream  tcp     nowait   root      /usr/sbin/tcpd  in.telnetd
#gopher stream  tcp     nowait   root      /usr/sbin/tcpd  gn
```

FTP and Telnet are services I intend to configure, but I have no plans to run a Gopher server. (*Gopher* is a method of delivering information content on the Internet, made practically obsolete by HTTP and the WWW.)

```
#shell  stream  tcp     nowait   root          /usr/sbin/tcpd  in.rshd
#login  stream  tcp     nowait   root          /usr/sbin/tcpd  in.rlogind
#exec   stream  tcp     nowait   root          /usr/sbin/tcpd  in.rexecd
#talk   dgram   udp     wait     nobody.tty    /usr/sbin/tcpd  in.talkd
#ntalk  dgram   udp     wait     nobody.tty    /usr/sbin/tcpd  in.ntalkd
```

These services allow a remote user to execute programs on this server or to communicate with users here. I have no practical use for these services on the system I am building, and they all represent potentially huge security holes. Out with them!

▼   `#dtalk  stream  tcp      waut     nobody.tty    /usr/sbin/tcpd  in.dtalkd`

▼   The dtalk service was off by default, which is just the way I like it.

```
#pop2    stream  tcp      nowait  root    /usr/sbin/tcpd ipop2d
pop3     stream  tcp      nowait  root    /usr/sbin/tcpd  ipop3d
#imap    stream  tcp      nowait  root    /usr/sbin/tcpd imapd
```

I plan to configure Internet mailboxes using the POP3 protocol; however, I turned off the other two mailbox services.

```
#uucp    stream  tcp      nowait  uucp    /usr/sbin/tcpd /usr/sbin/
                                   ↪uucico -l
```

I have no plans to offer incoming UUCP service over an Internet connection, so I turned this feature off as well.

```
#tftp  dgram   udp      wait    root    /usr/sbin/tcpd  in.tftpd
#bootps dgram  udp      wait    root    /usr/sbin/tcpd  bootpd
```

TFTP (tiny FTP) and bootps are services that allow this machine to act as a boot server for clients that boot the operating system over the network. I do not intend to configure such clients, so these two lines, commented out by default, remain the same.

```
#finger  stream  tcp      nowait  root    /usr/sbin/tcpd  in.fingerd
```

The finger service is actually a very useful service; unfortunately, it is also a very dangerous one because it reveals too much information to potential attackers. On any server exposed to the Internet, you should keep this service turned off.

```
#cfinger stream  tcp      nowait  root    /usr/sbin/tcpd  in.cfingerd
#systat  stream  tcp      nowait  nobody  /usr/sbin/tcpd  /bin/ps -auwwx
#netstat stream  tcp      nowait  nobody  /usr/sbin/tcpd  /bin/netstat
                                                          ↪—inet
```

Three more services that provide too much information to outsiders. Fortunately, these three were off by default.

```
auth     stream  tcp      wait    root    /usr/sbin/tcpd in.identd -w -t120
```

The authentication service is used by remote mail servers to verify that mail from this site comes from an authenticated source. It is okay to leave this service turned on.

Having completed my modifications to /etc/inetd.conf, I need to make the inetd server re-read its configuration file. Here is how to do it with the help of the killall command that sends a signal to all processes with the given name:

▼   killall -HUP inetd

▼

▲

Many system processes, `inetd` among them, respond to the hang-up (HUP) signal by reinitializing themselves. In terms of convenience and transparent system administration, this certainly beats rebooting the server every time a small configuration change is made.

Summary

Having completed your installation of Linux, it is time to secure the server.

Your first line of defense is user accounts and password security. Each user on the system has an account, the details of which are recorded in the file `/etc/passwd`. Usually, the contents of this file are updated through utilities designed to add, change, or remove users from the system. Each user's login is protected by a password; however, security is only as good as the passwords themselves, so care must be taken when choosing passwords. Easy to guess words or phrases should be avoided.

Users are organized into groups. All files and directories on the system are assigned an owner and a group owner. Permissions for each file or directory can be set on three levels: the user, the group, and everyone else. To change a file's ownership or permissions, use the `chown`, `chgrp`, or `chmod` utilities.

The superuser, or root, has unrestricted privileges. The root account should always be protected by a carefully chosen password. This account should not be used for routine tasks, only for administrative tasks that require superuser privileges.

After the operating system's kernel is started and initialized, it starts the `init` process which, in turn, reads configuration information from the file `/etc/inittab`. This file determines what commands are to be run at system startup, in response to specific system events, and on character terminals. The startup command scripts are usually stored in the `/etc/rc.d` subdirectory. These scripts are rarely modified by hand; Linux distributions provide utilities for this purpose. Make sure you only run the services you actually need. Unnecessary services, especially if not properly configured, can waste resources and represent a security hole.

Additional system services are started by the Internet Superserver, or `inetd`. Its configuration file, `/etc/inetd.conf`, contains a list of Internet service processes that are started in response to various requests. Carefully review this file and remove all services you don't need and do not intend to configure.

Internet Concepts

Isn't it obvious? **In order** to successfully install, configure, and manage a system that provides services on the Internet, you need to develop a basic understanding of the technology behind the network.

This chapter is a brief introduction to this complex subject, but it insufficient to help you understand basic Internet operations. If you want to have in-depth information about the IP family of protocols, a good book I recommend is *TCP/IP and Related Protocols*, by Uyless Black.

Internetworking

You've heard the term *Internet* so many times, you probably believe you know precisely what the word means. But do you?

Did you know, for instance, that the Internet is just one of many internets, that is, inter-networks, or networks of networks?

The name is also used to describe the core technology behind the Internet, the Internet Protocol (IP). IP is a mechanism used to connect computer networks together. To understand why this is necessary, you need to consider first how a local area network (LAN) works.

Local Area Networking

LANs, as the name implies, are used to connect together a cluster of computers that are in relative physical proximity. Regardless of the networking technology used, the basic concept is the same: the computers are connected to a shared conduit—*the* network, as in Figure 5.1—on which they transmit and receive data according to a commonly accepted protocol.

FIGURE 5.1
A local area network.

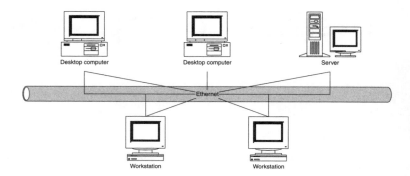

The most widely used LAN technology today is called *Ethernet*. When a computer is connected to an Ethernet LAN, all other computers *hear* its transmissions. The transmission itself contains the address of the computer that the transmission is intended for; other computers simply ignore the data.

Before a computer begins transmitting, it first checks to ensure that no other computer is using the network already. After it begins transmission, it checks to ensure that no other computer has interrupted. This mechanism is called *CSMA/CD* (Carrier Sense Multiple Access/Collision Detect), and it's the core of Ethernet technology. Fortunately, the rule "the longer the acronym, the less likely you need to worry about it" stands true here. CSMA/CD is implemented entirely in your network card's firmware.

Wide Area Networking

Connecting a small number of computers so that they can all hear each others' transmissions works well in practice. Doing so with a large number of computers would be an unmitigated disaster. Imagine thousands of computers all trying to talk using a single channel of communication. The sheer volume of data traffic would be so high, it would far exceed anything that can be reliably supported by this networking technology.

Physical distance is also a problem. Electrical or optical signals take time to travel over long stretches of cabling and therefore lose strength and quality.

Just like a city bus is not the ideal conveyance for cruising Interstate 80 across Nevada or Utah, LAN technology is not well suited for connecting remote sites. Wide area network (WAN) connections are typically *point-to-point* (see Figure 5.2), rather than being shared by many computers; a *conduit* is used for two remote systems to communicate with each other.

FIGURE 5.2
Wide area networking.

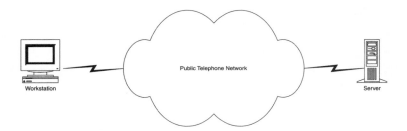

Another good way to think about is to consider the difference between a loudspeaker and a telephone. Loudspeakers are fine when addressing smaller crowds in your immediate vicinity; however, if you want to invite Aunt Selma from Australia over for Christmas it would not be very practical to use a huge PA system. You use a point-to-point connection instead, which only Aunt Selma can hear—you dial her telephone number.

Routes and Routers

The point-to-point connection provided by WANs can be used to connect a single computer with another at a remote location. How can you connect a networked set of computers, such as an office LAN, to another computer or network of computers?

The answer is simple: You create a point-to-point connection between a designated computer on one network and another designated computer on the other network (see Figure 5.3). These computers participate in their respective local networks and detect any data transmissions intended for the other network. They forward such transmissions over the WAN connection. Similarly, they take incoming data from the WAN and forward it to the local network. Computers dedicated to this purpose are called routers—that is, they route traffic from one network to another.

FIGURE 5.3
Connecting remote networks.

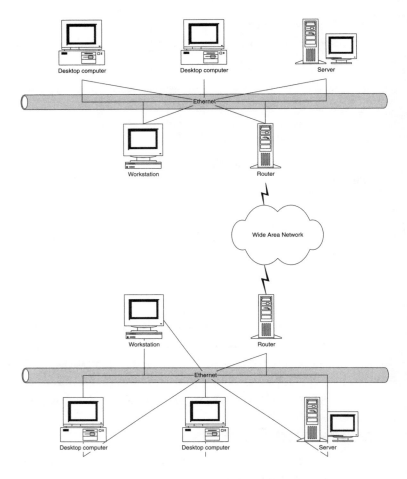

A router doesn't have to connect a LAN to a WAN. It can also provide a means to join two LANs together, as in Figure 5.4.

FIGURE 5.4
Routing between two LANs.

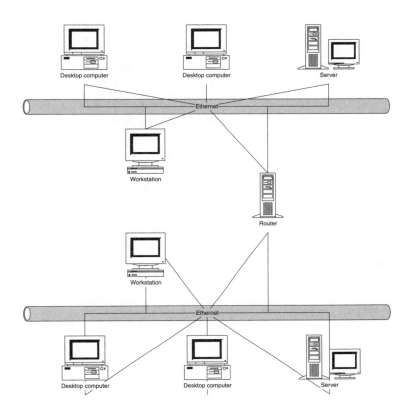

Internetworks

Of course there's more to this business of routing than merely exchanging data packets between two networks. There can be more than two networks involved, and in this case, finding the true destination of a transmission can become tricky.

One solution has been in use for over a century. Consider how the post office delivers a letter to a foreign country. Workers at the local sorting plant do not necessarily know where that country is, much less know street addresses within a foreign city, but they do know that such letters must be forwarded to designated postal facilities which, in turn, exchange letters with foreign post offices. When the letter arrives in the destination country, it is routed to the correct city and, in the end, arrives in the hands of a mail carrier who delivers it to the desired address. Only this mail carrier at the destination needs to know the physical whereabouts of the destination address. Nevertheless, all others involved in the process of delivery were able to route the letter correctly.

Routing data packets on the Internet is not really that different. When I send a packet to your Web server, for instance, my computer doesn't know where your Web server is, it simply knows that packets that are not on the local network must be forwarded to my ISDN router. That router doesn't know about your Web server either, but it forwards the packet to my ISP. My Canadian ISP might not know about your Web server either, but it forwards the packet to the correct international backbone router. That router knows a few things about your server's address, and forwards the packet, possibly through other back-bone routers, to your ISP. Your ISP in turn forwards the packet to the server that hosts your Web page. Throughout this process, only the final router actually knows which machine the Web address refers to; thanks to routing rules, the packet got there from my system anyway. Figure 5.5 shows how, as a packet nears its remote destination (192.168.1.1), more and more digits of its address are interpreted by routers.

FIGURE 5.5
Packet routing.

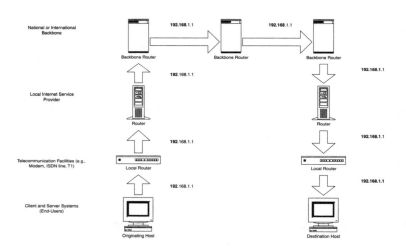

Speaking of backbones, this term usually refers to the high-capacity connections between remote locations provided by major Internet service providers (ISPs) such as MCI Worldcom. An Internet provider is typically considered a backbone provider if it

- Offers service at multiple geographic locations (has multiple *Points of Presence*, or POPs)
- Provides routing services for other ISPs

For instance, UUNet Canada wouldn't be a backbone provider simply because it has POPs in Ottawa, Toronto, or Montreal. However, because it also offers services to other, smaller ISPs as well as high-capacity channels carrying these ISPs' traffic to other U.S. providers, it qualifies as a backbone provider.

The Internet Protocol

Operating a worldwide, interconnected set of computer networks is a complex affair. What makes sense of this anarchy—and, incidentally, what makes it possible for otherwise incompatible computer systems to communicate with each other—is a family of network communication protocols, collectively referred to as the Internet family of protocols.

Of all the Internet protocols, the most fundamental is IP. This protocol is what makes it possible for data packets to reliably arrive at an arbitrary destination just about anywhere on the planet.

IP adds a block of information called a *header* to every packet of data. This header contains, among other things, the numerical address of the computer at the destination. This numerical address, or *IP address*, is a worldwide unique number, which identifies the destination interface.

Notice I said interface, not machine; that's because a machine can have multiple network interfaces and consequently, multiple IP addresses. For instance, a router connecting two LANs has a network interface on each LAN; both interfaces would have a unique IP number. So technically it's not correct to speak of a machine's IP address. However, in practice there's usually little confusion, as most machines that aren't routers only have a single network interface.

IP Numbers and Subnets

IP numbers are in the form of four *octets*—another word for byte, a collection of eight bits. Each octet represents a numerical value between 0–255. IP numbers are normally shown in *dotted notation* (also called *dotted decimal notation*). In this form, the four numbers are separated by a period, for example

```
192.168.1.1
```

IP numbers are not assigned at random. Rather, they are organized into *subnets*, which are assigned to organizations.

A subnet address consists of a fixed part and a variable part. To understand how these work, you must think of subnet addresses as binary, not decimal, numbers.

PART

II

CH

5

Take, for instance, the set of addresses between `192.168.1.0` and `192.168.1.255`. In binary notation, these two numbers look like this:

```
11000000 10101000 00000001 00000000

11000000 10101000 00000001 11111111
```

As you can see, the first 24 bits remain the same; only the last eight bits change. This subnet is therefore often written as follows:

```
192.168.1.0/24
```

Another way to describe subnets is through the concept of a *netmask*. The netmask is a 32-bit number with binary 1s representing fixed positions, and binary 0s representing the variable portion of the address. Sticking with the previous example, the binary netmask looks like this:

```
11111111 11111111 11111111 00000000
```

Or, in decimal notation it looks like this:

```
255.255.255.0
```

Whatever the size of your subnet, the first and last addresses within it are reserved. For instance, a /24 subnet contains 254 usable addresses (1–254, with 0 and 255 reserved.)

In the old days, the network address defined the subnet's size. Addresses that began with a number between 1 and 126 were Class A subnets with an 8-bit netmask; each such subnet had room for 256×256×256-2 = 16,777,214 computers. Class B subnets, with addresses that began with a number between 128 and 191, had a 16-bit netmask, and each contained 65,534 computers. Class C subnet addresses started with a number between 192 and 223, and had a 24-bit netmask, allowing for 254 computers in each subnet. Finally, addresses that began with a number between 224 and 254 (Class D) were reserved for special applications such as network multicasting (see Figure 5.6).

NOTE   The subnet address beginning with 127 is reserved for *loop-back*; by convention, addresses within this subnet (such as the often used address `127.0.0.1`) always refer to the local computer.

The maximum number of Class A subnets is 126; Class B, 16384; Class C, 2,097,152.

FIGURE 5.6
IP address classes.

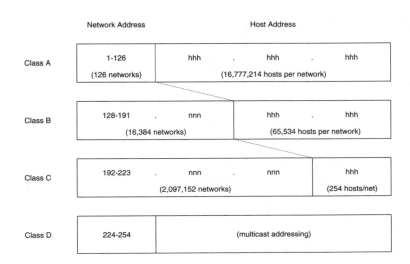

IP Address Assignment

The problem today is that what once seemed like an inexhaustible space of network addresses proved to be crowded a lot sooner than anyone expected, due to the unbelievable proliferation of the worldwide Internet. The addressing scheme that divided the network into Class A, B, and C subnets turned out to be incredibly wasteful; as the smallest unit of subnet allocation was a Class C subnet, organizations that only had a handful of computers were still assigned a Class C address space, leaving many addresses unused.

And if that weren't enough of a problem by itself, consider this: In order to deliver packets to their destination, core routers on the Internet must have information about each individual subnet. This wasn't a problem back in the days of the research Internet when the number of subnets ranged from a few dozen to a few hundred, perhaps a few thousand at most; nowadays, there are hundreds of thousands of subnets operating worldwide. Routers weren't equipped to deal with routing tables of this size.

These two problems required solutions that seemed contradictory at first. Keeping the size of routing tables manageable demanded that people use fewer subnets that were consequently larger in size. However, coping with the limitations of the address space was only possible if subnets were smaller, wasting fewer addresses.

PART
II

CH
5

The solution, adopted by Internet authorities and service providers worldwide, was to indeed use smaller subnets, but cluster subnet addresses into blocks. These blocks are assigned to ISPs and treated as a single subnet by everybody else. This kept the size of routing tables smaller because only a single routing entry was required for each block of subnets, as opposed to an entry for each individual subnet. ISPs are responsible for dividing up the blocks they receive efficiently as they assign individual subnet addresses to their customers.

What this means in practice is that when you sign up with an ISP these days, you might receive an address space for your network that looks similar to this:

    192.168.133.48/28

This means that you can use addresses in the range of 192.168.133.48–192.168.133.63; with the first and the last address reserved, you have room for 14 computers on your network.

On the other hand, your ISP might have allocated this range from the following address block:

    192.168.132.0/22

In other words, the ISP is free to use any addresses in the range 192.168.132.0–192.168.135.255. (If you're wondering how this range follows from a netmask of /22, work it out yourself by converting the numbers to binary first.)

This range gives the ISP control over an address space of 1,024 addresses. If all that space is used for subnets such as yours (with a netmask of /28), the ISP has address space for 64 subnet customers.

There is one drawback to this approach: Subnet addresses assigned under this numbering scheme are not portable because they cannot be individually routed. If you switch from one ISP to another, you cannot take your IP addresses with you; they must remain part of the block that was assigned to your old ISP. Portable IP addresses still exist, but due to the limitations of address space, they are rarely assigned.

Dynamic Address Assignment

The era of the dial-up Internet brought with it a new problem: Most ISPs have a much larger number of customers than phone lines. It would be wasteful to assign an IP number to each and every customer, including those who don't connect to the system for months at a time. Instead, most ISPs use a more limited pool of IP numbers, assigning them at random, or perhaps permanently assigning them to individual phone lines instead of doing so on a per customer basis.

If you are the customer of such an ISP, you have a potential problem. Every time you connect to the ISP, you are assigned a new IP number, rarely the same as before. This is not really an issue when only you initiate Internet connections, which is the case if you're viewing Web content with a browser. However, if you want to provide services for others to access, that is, accept incoming connections, a dynamic IP address is not an option; your system cannot be a moving target!

One workaround solves this problem by dynamically updating your address in the world-wide DNS (domain name system) database, which is covered in the Chapter 6, "The Domain Name System." This is not a perfect solution, however. If you want to provide professional quality services on the Internet—even if it's just a company Web page—a fixed IP address is a must.

Private Networks

These schemes of assigning IP numbers are all meant to be used for subnets directly connected to the Internet, but what happens if you're building an isolated network?

Well, you can of course use any addresses that suit your fancy. The real question is, should you? If there is the slightest chance that the network might one day be connected to the Internet one way or another, it pays to pick addresses from blocks specifically reserved for private networks. These blocks are as follows:

```
10.0.0.0/8

172.16.0.0/12

192.168.0.0/16
```

These blocks cover the address ranges `10.0.0.0–10.255.255.255`, `172.16.0.0–172.31.255.255`, and `192.168.0.0–192.168.255.255`.

What makes these addresses special is that they are *only* used for subnets that are not exposed directly to the Internet. Thus it is not a problem if you or I use `192.168.1.1` on a private network; because both of the networks are private, there is no conflict because packets cannot travel from one to the other.

PART

II

CH

5

Firewall Routers

A special kind of a private network is a network protected by a firewall. One frequently used firewall function is address translation, or *aliasing*. To the outside, your entire network appears under a single IP number, that of the firewall router. For outgoing packets, the firewall replaces the originating IP number in the packet with its own; for corresponding incoming packets, the destination address is replaced before the firewall router forwards the packet to the internal network (see Figure 5.7).

FIGURE 5.7
Data traffic through a firewall router.

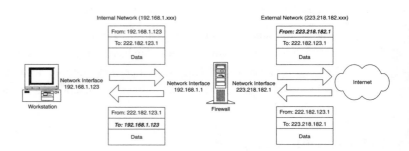

The main problem with this approach is that machines all appear under the same IP address to the outside, so there is no way to address them on an individual basis. Many firewalls offer a partial remedy; they can be configured, for instance, to deliver specific types of packets to specific internal hosts. For example, Web content requests might be routed to your Web server, whereas email connections are routed to your mail server. This is an imperfect solution because it doesn't allow an employee to fire up a Web server on his computer and expose it to the world, for example. Mind you, this is not necessarily a bad thing; preventing the appearance of ad-hoc Web servers on your company's network might be the reason the firewall was installed in the first place!

Other Internet Protocols

Although it is the most important protocol on the Internet, IP is by far not the only one. Protocols exist *beneath* IP, which make it possible to deliver IP packets over a medium other than a LAN. *Above* IP are higher level protocols that provide different types of connectivity; still higher up, application-specific protocols are used to deliver Web content, provide interactive connections, and more (see Figure 5.8).

FIGURE 5.8
Internet-related protocols.

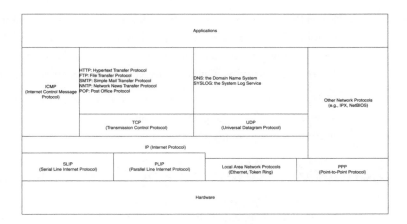

The set of Internet protocols is not immutable. Even established protocols can change occasionally, as new features are added; other, new protocols are also introduced regularly. The process of standardization of protocols, like many other aspects of managing the worldwide network, is a semi-formal process; protocol specifications are among the many documents that are published regularly in the form of RFCs (Request for Comments). (For more information, visit the Web site at `http://www.rfc-editor.org/`.)

Beneath IP: PPP, SLIP, and PLIP

On a LAN, IP packets are delivered by the Ethernet layer, which is implemented as a combination of network card drivers in your operating system, and network card firmware.

If you intend to establish an Internet connection over a modem line, the situation is different. Modems know nothing about packets; all they know is how to deliver data one character at a time, more or less reliably, to a remote destination. To cruise the Web using a telephone connection, some intermediate layer is required that allows IP packets to travel through this medium.

That layer is called either SLIP or PPP. SLIP, the Serial Line Internet Protocol, was the first attempt to make IP over telephone lines possible. Never a formal standard, SLIP was nevertheless adopted worldwide, no doubt due in part to its extreme simplicity.

Because SLIP is so simple, it doesn't always provide the right answer. For instance, SLIP provides no means to authenticate users. So in practice when you want to establish a SLIP connection, you must first *log on* to the ISP's server either manually or through the use of a log-on script. These log-on scripts are a major cause of frustration for many users of Windows 95's Dial-Up Networking.

PART
II

CH
5

Enter PPP, the Point-to-Point Protocol. PPP offers many features, including user authentication. There is no need to respond to login prompts by hand or send passwords in the clear without suitable encryption. PPP represents the state-of-the-art in serial line Internet connectivity, which is why you should use it whenever possible.

PLIP, the Parallel Line Internet Protocol, is a variant of SLIP that allows two computers to be connected via the parallel printer port. Given how cheap network adapters have become, PLIP has little practical utility these days.

Connection-oriented and Connectionless Protocols

The Internet Protocol can be used to deliver packets of data from one computer to another. But in practical situations, you want a bit more: you want packets delivered from one application to another. In other words, you don't want to connect your computer to my computer; you want to connect your Web browser application to my Web server application.

For application-level connectivity, two protocols are commonly used: TCP and UDP. TCP, the Transmission Control Protocol, is a connection-oriented protocol. A TCP connection is like a phone call; once it is established, data can travel through it in two directions until the connection is terminated. Furthermore, a TCP connection is reliable; drivers that implement this protocol ensure that all data transmitted is actually delivered, and delivered in the correct order.

UDP, the Universal Datagram Protocol, is used for sending individual packets of data without establishing a connection first. Delivery of UDP packets is not guaranteed; the protocol only guarantees that what does get delivered is error free.

So why would application designers use UDP if it's so limited? As it turns out, its apparent limitations are really the protocol's strengths. Because packet delivery is not guaranteed, the connection is not hung if a packet goes missing; subsequent packets continue to arrive.

UDP is ideal for use with streaming multimedia. When you're listening to a live radio station over the Internet using RealPlayer, you might not care if the sound is interrupted for a split second or its quality degrades briefly. But you'd be far more annoyed if playback were suspended for several seconds while the software requested retransmission of a missing packet and waited for it to arrive.

Both TCP and UDP make use of *port numbers*. The port number is usually a number between 0–65535. Server applications can *listen* to a port, awaiting incoming connections. Client applications can make a connection attempt (or send a UDP packet) to a specific port number on the destination machine. By using *well-known* port numbers for specific purposes, you can ensure that incoming client requests are processed by the appropriate application.

The list of known port numbers can be found on your system in the file /etc/services. This file is largely informational; a few applications use it to reference port numbers by symbolic name rather than by number.

For instance, TCP port 80 is dedicated for use by WWW servers. On machines that run a Web server, the server listens on port 80. Web clients connect to port 80 by default.

Port numbers between 0–1023 are reserved on Linux for use by processes owned by the root user; this prevents abuse. These low port numbers are commonly used for system services. Without this restriction, ordinary users on a multiuser system would be capable of running processes that mimic these services. For example, on a system with no running mail server, a user might be able to start a process that listens on port 25 (the port normally used for SMTP mail transfer) and pretends to act like a mail server, intercepting all incoming mail, including mail intended for other users.

ICMP

Practically all Internet applications use the TCP or UDP protocols. A third protocol type, the Internet Control Message Protocol (ICMP) is used mostly for network housekeeping. For instance, if you use the ping utility to verify connectivity to remote hosts, the utility sends ICMP *echo* packets to that host and displays the time it takes for the packet to return. ICMP is also used to inform a server of connection problems, deliver certain forms of routing information, and more.

PART
II

CH
5

Higher Level Protocols

Building on top of TCP or UDP, many higher level protocols exist. Thanks to these protocols, it is possible for applications made by different vendors to communicate with each other. For instance, Netscape's Navigator browser can read Web pages from a Microsoft IIS Web server because they both use the HTTP protocol for delivering Web content.

OPTIONS   Frequently used protocols include the following:

- *HTTP.* The Hypertext Transfer Protocol is used for communication between Web clients and servers.
- *FTP.* The File Transfer Protocol is an older protocol used to transfer files between two hosts.
- *TELNET.* A protocol that makes it possible to start an interactive session on a remote computer.
- *SMTP.* The Simple Mail Transfer Protocol is the primary means of delivering Internet mail between mail servers.
- *POP3.* The Post Office Protocol 3 is used by email client programs to read mail from a user's mailbox.
- *NNTP.* The Network News Transfer Protocol is used by newsgroup servers that exchange data with each other and by newsgroup readers that access these servers.

In the end, most network traffic goes through multiple protocol layers. For instance, when you connect with a Web browser to a Web site using a telephone connection, the following takes place:

1. The browser formulates a WWW request using the HTTP protocol.
2. The WWW request is sent to the server using the TCP protocol.
3. TCP packets are delivered using IP.
4. IP packets are delivered across the modem line via PPP.

This series of steps is repeated for every block of information that is passed between the client and server (see Figure 5.9). This figure shows you the result: an HTTP document inside an HTTP packet inside a TCP packet inside an IP packet inside a PPP packet, as transmitted over a modem line.

FIGURE 5.9
Encapsulation for data transfer
between client and server.

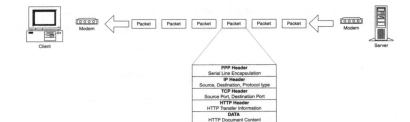

Tools

Under Linux, there are a handful of command-line tools that are used more often than
most to verify and troubleshoot network settings.

Configuration Tools

The `ifconfig` tool is used to check or change the status of network interfaces. Typing
`ifconfig` by itself lists all active interfaces, for instance

```
$ ifconfig
lo          Link encap:Local Loopback
            inet addr:127.0.0.1  Bcast:127.255.255.255  Mask:255.0.0.0
            UP BROADCAST LOOPBACK RUNNING  MTU:3584  Metric:1
            RX packets:229 errors:0 dropped:0 overruns:0
            TX packets:229 errors:0 dropped:0 overruns:0

eth0        Link encap:Ethernet  HWaddr 00:00:21:A5:36:09
            inet addr:192.168.1.1  Bcast:192.168.1.255  Mask:255.255.255.0
            UP BROADCAST RUNNING MULTICAST  MTU:1500  Metric:1
            RX packets:404514 errors:0 dropped:0 overruns:0
            TX packets:369931 errors:0 dropped:0 overruns:0
            Interrupt:11 Base address:0x340
```

The `ifconfig` command has many options to alter interface configuration. (Needless to
say, you need to run it as the root user to change a system setting.)

OPTIONS   Here are a few examples of using `ifconfig`:

`ifconfig eth0 down`   Disables the eth0 interface

▲   `ifconfig eth0 192.168.1.1`   Activates eth0 and assigns an address

PART
II

CH
5

The route tool can be used to view and manipulate the computer's internal routing table. Using route without parameters displays the current routing table. For instance

```
$ route
Kernel IP routing table
Destination     Gateway         Genmask         Flags Metric  Ref     Use
Iface
192.168.1.0     *               255.255.255.0   U     0       0       1
eth0
127.0.0.0       *               255.0.0.0       U     0       0       3 lo
```

OPTIONS   The route command can also be used to add new routes to the table or to delete existing routes. Here are a few useful examples:

route add 192.168.2.1 gw 192.168.1.1 To reach 192.168.2.1, use 192.168.1.1 as a router

route add -net 192.168.1.0 eth0   Network 192.168.1.0 is reachable via the eth0 interface

route add default gw 192.168.1.1   For all addresses for which specific routes don't exist, use this gateway

route del default   Delete the default gateway entry

route -n   List routes without trying to resolve addresses into symbolic names

▲

These commands are rarely issued by hand, however. They are usually invoked from system startup scripts. Other programs, such as programs that establish a PPP connection to your ISP, might also manipulate the routing table.

TEST SYSTEM   On my Caldera OpenLinux test system, scripts in /etc/rc.d set up the initial routing and interface configuration using data obtained from /etc/sysconfig/network-scripts. These files were created and updated automatically when I used the LISA utility to specify the computer's network address and other parameters.

▲

Diagnostic Tools

The netstat command can be used to view the network's current status. For instance, netstat -t can be used to list all active TCP connections. Typing netstat -r is equivalent to typing route; it displays the current routing table.

The ping tool can be used to verify accessibility to a remote host. The tool sends ICMP echo packets to the remote host specified on the command line and measures the time in milliseconds (ms) that it takes for an echo to arrive. For example:

```
$ ping -c 5 ns.uunet.ca
PING ns.uunet.ca (142.77.1.1): 56 data bytes
64 bytes from 142.77.1.1: icmp_seq=0 ttl=250 time=50.4 ms
64 bytes from 142.77.1.1: icmp_seq=1 ttl=250 time=47.1 ms
64 bytes from 142.77.1.1: icmp_seq=2 ttl=250 time=48.2 ms
64 bytes from 142.77.1.1: icmp_seq=3 ttl=250 time=48.0 ms
64 bytes from 142.77.1.1: icmp_seq=4 ttl=250 time=48.4 ms

--- ns.uunet.ca ping statistics ---
5 packets transmitted, 5 packets received, 0% packet loss
round-trip min/avg/max = 47.1/48.4/50.4 ms
```

Lastly, the traceroute command can be used to examine the route between the local host and a remote destination. Here is a real-life traceroute example:

```
$ traceroute ns.uunet.ca
traceroute to ns.uunet.ca (142.77.1.1), 30 hops max, 40 byte packets
 1  max1.ott1.uunet.ca (205.150.233.2)  26.49 ms  36.445 ms  30.16 ms
 2  e011.bb1.ott1.uunet.ca (205.150.233.1)  55.806 ms  62.596 ms
➥56.182 ms
 3  vl151.f000.bb1.tor1.uunet.ca (205.150.242.94)  37.307 ms
➥55.862 ms  39.374 ms
 4  ns.uunet.ca (142.77.1.1)  40.371 ms *  41.389 ms
```

Other Standards

PART

II

CH

5

In addition to standards directly related to the delivery of data packets between remote networks, other standards exist on the Internet that define various services and data formats. Here is a brief description of a few that you should know about.

Email Related Standards

One standard defines the format of email messages and message headers. Referenced only by its RFC number, RFC-822 defines the format of all those cryptic-looking header lines you see on top of email messages. These lines often help you track down the senders of offending email (and consequently, these lines that are often forged by scam artists to prevent you from succeeding).

MIME (Multipurpose Internet Mail Extension) addresses many of the shortcomings of RFC-822. RFC-822 messages are restricted to printable ASCII text. Over the years, a variety of ways were used to provide a means to send binary files, non-English text, and other content in email. MIME provides a flexible, and now widely accepted standard for this. Most modern email programs support MIME. As for email servers, they treat MIME messages like ordinary email messages; in other words, MIME messages can pass through all mail gateways, old and new.

Hypertext Documents

One of the most important formatting standards on the Internet is HTML. HTML is the format used for World Wide Web (WWW) documents. It is derived from SGML (Standard Generalized Markup Language) and provides many text-formatting capabilities. HTML documents can in fact be viewed as programs that are executed by the Web browser that renders the document.

Assigned Numbers

Many things are numbered on the Internet. There are IP addresses. There are the port numbers of TCP and UDP connections. Protocols themselves are often identified by a number when they travel inside IP packets (take a peek at `/etc/protocols` on your Linux system). In order for the global Internet to work, computers worldwide must agree on their use of these numbers, otherwise chaos reigns.

Many of these numbers are maintained by the IANA, the Internet Assigned Numbers Authority (`http://www.iana.org/`).

Batch Delivery

Email predates the Internet. Long before IP connectivity was widespread, email flowed between colleges and universities, institutions and modem bulletin boards. The conduit was often the telephone line, and the most widely used mechanism was UUCP: the UNIX to UNIX Copy standard.

UUCP is still very useful because it allows batch delivery of email and newsgroup messages. It is ideally suited for use on systems that don't have the benefit of a permanent Internet connection. With UUCP, you can run your own mail server on such systems and maintain individual mailboxes for your users, as opposed to having to rely on your ISP's mail server and pay for a limited number of mailboxes there. Unfortunately, UUCP is rarely supported by ISPs these days.

Summary

LANs join together computers in close proximity, using a shared conduit. Long distance, wide-area connections usually connect two remote computers. Internetworking allows many LANs to be connected together into an internet, the most prominent example of which is *the* Internet that spreads most of the globe.

Internetworking is made possible in part by the concept of routes and routers. Routers exchange traffic between different networks; traffic to remote networks is directed with the help of information stored in routing tables.

At the core of Internet technology is IP. IP numbers provide a means to uniquely identify a machine on the network. IP numbers are assigned through ISPs or for private networks, specific number ranges are reserved. IP numbers might also be assigned dynamically, such as when connecting to an ISP via a dial-up modem line.

Beneath IP exist protocols such as PPP or SLIP, which deliver IP data packets over modem lines. On top of IP, higher level protocols provide connection-oriented or connectionless conduits of data. On top of these, application-specific protocols are used for file transfer, Web content delivery, email messages, and more.

Other Internet-related standards specify, for instance, the format of email messages and message headers and the format used for Web content. Many numbers, such as reserved address ranges, connection port numbers, and protocol identifiers are agreed on by convention; these numbers are maintained by organizations such as the IANA.

PART

II

CH

5

The Domain Name System

If you read through the Chapter 5, "Internet Concepts," you probably thought to yourself that IP numbers, ports, and protocols are great, but what do they have to do with a Web address such as www.whitehouse.gov? SMTP and POP are probably great protocols, but how do email addresses such as president@whitehouse.gov enter the picture?

The answer isn't really a secret: it's called the Domain Name System, or DNS for short. This chapter provides you with enough information to get you started; for further reference, a very good book on the subject is *DNS and BIND*, by Paul Albitz and Cricket Liu. Some BIND documentation is also included with the OpenLinux 1.3 CD-ROM which accompanies this book; it is normally found in the /usr/doc/bind-8.1.1 directory. If it is missing, install the package called bind-doc-8.1.1-5 using LISA.

Domain Names and Name Servers

The idea behind domain names is simple: Rather than forcing people to memorize IP numbers, why not give them cryptic names to remember instead?

Bad jokes aside, the DNS has another important use: it makes a service independent of the server. Take the well known CNN Web server, for instance. At any given time, the name cnn.com translates into a list of servers that provide enough horsepower to maintain this popular service. The actual number of servers and their IP numbers can change at any time; what matters is that the symbolic name remains constant. You will always be able to reach http://cnn.com/ without having to keep track of changing numeric IP addresses.

The process through which symbolic names are translated into numeric IP addresses is called *address resolution*.

The /etc/hosts File

Long before the Internet turned into the many-tentacled worldwide monster that it is today, symbolic names were already in use. However, in those days, every computer on the Internet had its own copy of the list of all Internet machines. On UNIX systems, this list was stored in the file /etc/hosts.

Today, maintaining such a list is clearly an impossible task. Not only would it have to contain an entry for each of the tens of millions of computers on the network, it would also have to be updated continuously to reflect the changes that occur every second somewhere on the planet.

However, /etc/hosts still survives. No longer a list of all the computers on the Internet, it is still often used to list computers on your local network, or at least a few important systems that you want to be able to reach by name even if other means of name resolution are temporarily unavailable.

The structure of this file is simple and easy to understand. Each line contains an IP number followed by a list of names. The first of these is a *fully qualified hostname*, that is, the host's full name on the Internet; following that are nicknames, or alternative names by which the host is known.

TEST SYSTEM On my test system the LISA utility generated a /etc/hosts file after I specified a name for the newly configured machine during setup. The file has lots of comments (lines beginning with the # character) but only two lines of interest:

```
127.0.0.1 localhost
192.168.1.1 host.linux.sys host
```

The first line specifies a name for the loopback address. The second line assigns the name host.linux.sys to the IP address of the machine's Ethernet card, 192.168.1.1. It also contains a nickname so that programs on this machine can reference the machine by the word host instead of spelling out its fully qualified name.

One final note on /etc/hosts: Keep in mind that if this file is present, it is always consulted first, and entries in this file take precedence over data obtained from the network.

Name Service

The alternative to using /etc/hosts with an impossible number of hostnames is DNS. This is an amazing worldwide distributed database of domain and hostnames, IP addresses and more.

The idea behind DNS is to organize names into a hierarchy, with only a few top-level names. Assign root servers to top-level names, which in turn, know the servers for second level names. Repeat this if there are multiple levels in the hierarchy. At the lowest level, servers contain information about actual IP addresses (see Figure 6.1).

FIGURE 6.1
The hierarchy of domain names.

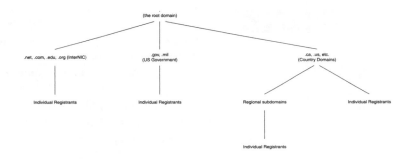

So what happens when you type www.cnn.com in your browser's address box? The browser connects to its local name server and asks for resolution of this name. Unless you're on CNN's private network, the name server has no information about this name, so it submits the query to one of the root servers. The root server won't have information about this specific address but it will give you the address of one of CNN's name servers. Your name server then contacts that server and obtains from it a list of IP addresses, which are returned to the Web browser. The browser picks one of the addresses and initiates a connection.

This mechanism is surprisingly robust. There are many root servers, and each organization can have multiple name servers. It is also common for organizations to provide name service for each other on a reciprocal basis. This ensures that even in the event an organization's name server is down, name service remains available.

Top-Level Domains

One of the secrets that make the domain name systems work is that you always know where to begin: the top-level of the naming hierarchy contains a set of fixed, well-known domains, such as .com or .ca. Top-level domain names are currently maintained by a commercial organization, Network Solutions, also known as the InterNIC. (NIC is an acronym for Network Information Center.)

There are, actually, two sets of top-level domains. The first set includes domain names such as .com, .mil, .gov, .edu, .net, and .org. These domain names are used primarily—but not exclusively—in North America and represent commercial entities, the U.S. military, the U.S. government, American educational institutions, sites related to managing the network itself, and other organizations. Domain names under .com, .edu, .net, and .org are maintained by the InterNIC. U.S. military and government domain names are maintained elsewhere.

> **NOTE**   The InterNIC obtained its mandate from the U.S. government several years ago. This mandate is subject to renewal and, therefore, the InterNIC might not remain the sole authority in charge of top-level domain names and the non-country, non-U.S. government top-level domains. There have also been attempts to establish alternative top-level registries, such as the ill-fated AlterNIC experiment that received prominent news coverage a while ago.

The other set of top-level domain names contains country domains. Although .com, .org, and .net domain names are used internationally, many countries have adopted another naming system, using the two-letter abbreviation of the country name as the top-level domain name. For instance, many Canadian organizations use a domain name that ends with .ca (for example, www.gov.ca). Country-level domain names are usually maintained by national organizations within that country. Some countries allow just about any name to be registered; in other countries, a strongly maintained hierarchy exists. For instance, in Canada domain names are organized by province; only businesses and organizations that are nationally registered or do business in more than one province are allowed to use a two-level domain name. Needless to say, when the rules are overly bureaucratic, many organizations opt to use domain names instead that they obtained from the InterNIC and ignore the country's own domain name system.

The `/etc/resolv.conf` File

Not every computer has a name server. You might be using multiple name servers for backup purposes or none at all, relying on your ISP's name server instead. But, how do applications know the whereabouts of the name server they need to query?

Under Linux, this information is stored in the file `/etc/resolv.conf`. This file can be edited by hand or using a configuration utility such as Caldera's LISA. Typically it is enough to have a file that contains only one line specifying your name server. If the name server is the local machine, you can use its loopback address, so `/etc/resolv.conf` might end up containing only the following line:

```
nameserver 127.0.0.1
```

Of course if your `/etc/resolv.conf` contains this line alone, you might as well not have it in the first place. That's because when this file is not present, the default behavior is to consult a name server on the local machine.

When an application on your system requests name service, the first thing that is consulted is this file. From this file, the system determines where to find a name server.

To obtain more information on the format of this file, type **man 5 resolver** to get the corresponding manual page. (You need to check section 5 because it contains information about file formats; I have no idea why you need to use the word `resolver` instead of `resolv.conf`!)

TEST SYSTEM   On my test system, `/etc/resolv.conf` was automatically generated by LISA during setup. Aside from comments including a dire warning about not editing this file by hand, the file contains three lines of relevance:

```
domain linux.sys
search linux.sys
nameserver 127.0.0.1
```

▲

DNS Tools

There are several command-line tools that help you query the DNS database or verify that your DNS configuration works correctly.

The `hostname` command can be used to retrieve the short name (`-s` command-line switch), full name (`-f`), or domain name (`-d`) of your computer.

The `nslookup` command can be used to query a name server. For instance, typing `nslookup mozilla.org` returns the address of `mozilla.org`, the server of the organization entrusted with the maintenance of the free, open Netscape source code. This command can also be used interactively and has extensive features for querying name servers, some of which are demonstrated later in this chapter.

The whois tool queries another database—the registration database for domain names. In other words, using whois you can find out who owns a specific domain name. For example

```
$ whois mozilla.org
[rs.internic.net]

Registrant:
Mozilla Dot Org (MOZILLA2-DOM)
    501 East Middlefield Road
    Mountain View, CA 94043

    Domain Name: MOZILLA.ORG

    Administrative Contact:
        Giannandrea, John  (JG62)  jg@MEER.NET
        650-317-2263 (FAX) 650-967-0689
    Technical Contact, Zone Contact:
        meer.net hostmaster  (MN85-ORG)  hostmaster@MEER.NET
        +1.650.317.2263
Fax- - +1.650.967.0689
    Billing Contact:
        meer.net paymaster  (DA3863-ORG)  billing@MEER.NET
        +1.415.317.2263Fax- +1.650.967.0689
Fax- - +1.650.967.0689

    Record last updated on 11-Jun-98.
    Database last updated on 14-Feb-99 05:25:21 EST.

    Domain servers in listed order:

    NS.MEER.NET                    140.174.164.2
    NS2.MEER.NET                   209.143.231.66


The InterNIC Registration Services database contains ONLY
non-military and non-US Government Domains and contacts.
Other associated whois servers:
    American Registry for Internet Numbers - whois.arin.net
    European IP Address Allocations        - whois.ripe.net
    Asia Pacific IP Address Allocations    - whois.apnic.net
    US Military                             - whois.nic.mil
    US Government                           - whois.nic.gov
```

Needless to say, in order for these tools to work and provide meaningful information, you need to have a valid name server configuration and a live Internet connection.

Domain Name Registration

The questions are simple. Do you require a domain name of your own? If so, how do you go about acquiring one? And what kind of a domain name do you want use?

The answer to the first question depends on your needs. Are you planning to expose a Web server to the world? Do you want to provide email addresses under your own domain name? Are you planning to provide any other service that users reach using a domain name? If the answer is yes to any of these questions, you probably need a domain name.

Picking a Domain Name

For most businesses, using a domain name in the .com top-level domain is an appropriate choice. One problem with this choice is that it is so popular and most of the meaningful domain names have already been snatched up. Recently I did a little experiment: I checked domain names such as aa.com, aaa.com, aaaa.com, to see how many A's I needed to type before I found a name that's not registered (.com domain names with only a single letter, such as a.com, are reserved.) The first unregistered domain name with all A's is aaaaaaaaaaaaaa.com. (Yes, 14 A's.) If this doesn't tell you something about a crowded namespace, I don't know what to say! In the somewhat less crowded space of .org domain names, the first unregistered all A's domain name is aaaaaa.org.

If you live outside the United States, (and even if you live in the United States; there *is* a .us country domain, after all!) you might want to consider picking a domain name within your country domain system.

Sometimes you don't need your own registered domain name. You might be able to use a domain name within your ISP's namespace, assigned to you by your ISP. So instead of myorg.org, you may be using a domain name such as myorg.myisp.net.

Regardless of what kind of a domain name you pick, it needs to be registered with the appropriate authority—the InterNIC, your country-level domain name registrar, or your ISP.

Checking Existing Domain Names

If you intend to pick a .com or .org domain name, you can use the whois tool to check whether the name you plan to obtain is already in use. You don't need to have a working copy of the whois program for this purpose; you can use any Web browser to connect to the InterNIC's server and use their graphical WHOIS interface (see Figure 6.2).

FIGURE 6.2
Using the InterNIC's WHOIS
service.

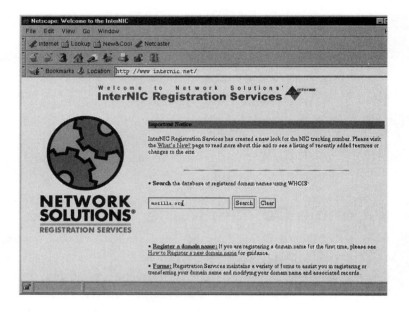

Checking domain names in country domains is more difficult. Many countries don't operate a WHOIS service. Others do, but might not provide a Web-based interface to the service, or the location of the interface might not be well known or easy to find.

Registering with the InterNIC

If you plan to pick a .com or .org domain name and you intend to provide your own name service, going to the InterNIC to register your own domain name is the appropriate choice.

The InterNIC allows you to register just about any domain name without regard to copyright or trademark restrictions. Their view is that it is the registrant's responsibility to ensure that a name doesn't violate other people's rights or the law. Registration has a fee; as of the time of this writing, first-time registrations, valid for two years, costs $70 U.S. dollars, with an annual renewal fee of $35 U.S. dollars applicable afterward.

Before you can register a domain name, you must have a name server for the domain. In fact, you must have two name servers, as per the InterNIC's registration agreement. For most organizations, this means their own name server is the primary server, with their ISP's name server acting as backup.

Domain names can be registered with the InterNIC through their Web page (`http://www.internic.net/`). You can follow the onscreen instructions and register a name through their Web-based forms.

Registration Through Your ISP

If you do not plan to run your own name service, domain name registration is best left to whoever does name service for you, typically your ISP. Some ISPs perform this function for no extra fee; others charge you a one-time fee for completing and submitting your registration. Some even charge a fee for processing each modification request to the registration.

If you are using a domain name within your ISP's name space, you don't need to register anything. Your ISP's domain name is already registered.

Country Domain Registrars

The procedures for registering a name within a two-letter country domain vary from one country to another. Sometimes even finding the registration authority can prove to be a challenge!

One helpful hint: Query the InterNIC's WHOIS database with the keyword *XX*-DOM, where *XX* represents the two-letter country code you're interested in (for example, US-DOM, or CA-DOM).

Information about the .us top-level domain can be found at `http://www.isi.edu/us-domain/`. For the Canadian top-level domain, .ca, visit `http://www.cdnnet.ca/`. In Europe, you might want to start your search with RIPE, the Regional Internet Registry of Europe (`http://www.ripe.net/`).

Running a Name Server

PART

II

CH

6

So why would you want to cope with the burden of running your own name server, especially when many ISPs would perform this service for you free of charge?

The key reasons are control and flexibility. Running your own name server means that you don't need to rely on your ISP when your network configuration changes. It also lets you perform functions that your ISP wouldn't do, such as providing name service for a private network behind a firewall.

Setting up name service for a small network isn't rocket science. You only need to create a few relatively simple files that contain information about the *zones* your name server will service.

The name of the Linux name server program is `named`. This is another example of a UNIX *daemon*, a process that runs in the background performing server functions. `named` is normally started automatically from the system startup scripts.

TEST SYSTEM   When setting up my test system with LISA, I configured `named` as a daemon to be run at system startup. However, typing `ps axuw` now shows no process with the name `named` running on the system. Poking around in `/etc/rc.d/init.d` I easily found the reason: The script `/etc/rc.d/init.d/named` only starts the daemon if its configuration file, `/etc/named.conf`, exists. Because that file has

▲   not yet been created, the daemon wasn't started when the system was last booted.

The named Configuration File

When `named` is started, it reads its configuration file, which in the past was called the boot file.

There are actually two widely used formats for this configuration file. Caldera OpenLinux 1.3 contains a new `named` distribution that uses the new file format; however, because the old format is still widely used, it deserves mention as well.

The new-style configuration file is usually named `/etc/named.conf` by default. The file's contents vaguely resemble the syntax of the C programming language. Blocks of option settings are enclosed by curly braces {}, and individual settings are terminated by a semicolon.

TEST SYSTEM   My test system uses the new version of `named` that came with Caldera OpenLinux. Consequently, the `named` configuration file is called `/etc/named.conf` and uses the new syntax.

The file begins with a section named `options`:

```
options {
        directory "/var/named";
};
```

The only option specified here is the name of the directory that contains additional `named` configuration files. On Caldera OpenLinux, an empty directory, `/var/named`, has been

▼   created by the installer for this purpose.

▼
```
zone "." {
        type hint;
        file "root.cache";
};
```

The domain name . is used to reference the *root domain*. The file root.cache contains information about name servers for this domain. The named program uses this file for initialization.

```
zone "linux.sys" {
        type master;
        file "named.hosts";
};
```

The domain linux.sys is the zone for which this server is responsible as a master server.

```
zone "168.192.IN-ADDR.ARPA" {
        type master;
        file "named.rev";
};
```

A name server can not only provide IP numbers that correspond with names; it can also perform a *reverse lookup*, finding the name that corresponds with an IP number. Without this reverse lookup capability, name service isn't complete. In fact, there are servers on the Internet that refuse connections from any machine whose address cannot be looked up this way.

By convention, for reverse lookup you use a pseudo domain name. This form always ends with IN-ADDR.ARPA and is preceded by the network's IP number in reverse order. Because I used private network numbers in the form 192.168.*xxx*.*yyy*, the pseudo domain name is therefore 168.192.IN-ADDR.ARPA.

```
zone "127.IN-ADDR.ARPA" {
        type master;
        file "named.local";
};
```

PART

II

CH

6

In order for the name server to work correctly, you also need to be able to perform reverse lookup on the localhost address, 127.0.0.1. This third file provides reverse
▲ lookup on this address family.

The old-style configuration file was usually called /etc/named.boot. Its format offered far less flexibility than the new format, although perhaps it was a bit easier to read and maintain by non-programmers. Each line in this file contained a keyword and parameters separated by spaces or tab characters.

An exact equivalent to the `/etc/named.conf` file of my test system in the old-style format would look like this:

```
directory                                 /var/named
cache           .                         root.cache
primary         linux.sys                 named.hosts
primary         168.192.IN-ADDR.ARPA      named.rev
primary         127.IN-ADDR.ARPA          named.local
```

The Root Cache

Next to the configuration file, the most important file `named` uses is the root cache, usually named `root.cache`. Basically, this file lists those name servers that `named` contacts first when resolving a domain name.

The root cache should be periodically (for example, once every few months) refreshed by the system's administrator to ensure that it contains up-to-date information. A good source for a recent `root.cache` file is `ftp://rs.internic.net/domain/named.root`.

Here is the `root.cache` file I am using on the test system, with comment lines removed.

```
.                           3600000   IN   NS    A.ROOT-SERVERS.NET.
A.ROOT-SERVERS.NET.         3600000        A     198.41.0.4
.                           3600000        NS    B.ROOT-SERVERS.NET.
B.ROOT-SERVERS.NET.         3600000        A     128.9.0.107
.                           3600000        NS    C.ROOT-SERVERS.NET.
C.ROOT-SERVERS.NET.         3600000        A     192.33.4.12
.                           3600000        NS    D.ROOT-SERVERS.NET.
D.ROOT-SERVERS.NET.         3600000        A     128.8.10.90
.                           3600000        NS    E.ROOT-SERVERS.NET.
E.ROOT-SERVERS.NET.         3600000        A     192.203.230.10
.                           3600000        NS    F.ROOT-SERVERS.NET.
F.ROOT-SERVERS.NET.         3600000        A     192.5.5.241
.                           3600000        NS    G.ROOT-SERVERS.NET.
G.ROOT-SERVERS.NET.         3600000        A     192.112.36.4
.                           3600000        NS    H.ROOT-SERVERS.NET.
H.ROOT-SERVERS.NET.         3600000        A     128.63.2.53
.                           3600000        NS    I.ROOT-SERVERS.NET.
I.ROOT-SERVERS.NET.         3600000        A     192.36.148.17
.                           3600000        NS    J.ROOT-SERVERS.NET.
J.ROOT-SERVERS.NET.         3600000        A     198.41.0.10
.                           3600000        NS    K.ROOT-SERVERS.NET.
K.ROOT-SERVERS.NET.         3600000        A     193.0.14.129
.                           3600000        NS    L.ROOT-SERVERS.NET.
L.ROOT-SERVERS.NET.         3600000        A     198.32.64.12
.                           3600000        NS    M.ROOT-SERVERS.NET.
M.ROOT-SERVERS.NET.         3600000        A     202.12.27.33
```

Zone Files

Zone files contain actual information about specific domains for which the name server provides service as a primary or master server.

Each zone file contains one or more *records*. Each record consists of several fields, some of which are optional.

The first field specifies the name that the record describes. It always must start at the beginning of the line. The name can be a single @ character, which is a substitute for the name of the zone that the file describes; or it can be an ordinary name which is interpreted as a name within the domain that the zone file describes. For instance, if you have a zone file for the domain `linux.sys`, the @ character in a zone file would be a substitute for this domain name; the word `host` would be taken to mean `host.linux.sys`, that is, a name within the `linux.sys` domain. The first field can be omitted when multiple records are present that all refer to the same name.

The second field is the record's class; almost always, it is set to `IN`, which signifies an Internet record.

The third field describes the record's type. Under ordinary circumstances, you'll encounter five, perhaps six different record types, although a lot more exist. These frequently used record types are:

- `SOA`. The Statement of Authority record provides information about the zone. Three fields follow the SOA keyword:
  - *Originating Host.* The fully qualified name with a period at the end of the host where this data was created.
  - *Administrator email.* The email address of the zone's maintainer with the @ character replaced by a period and another period appended at the end.
  - *Parameters.* A list enclosed between parentheses that contains five numerical values:
    1. *Serial Number.* An arbitrary number that should be incremented every time the file's contents change, which is how name servers know that the file needs to be reloaded.
    2. *Refresh.* How often (in seconds) *slave* (secondary) name servers check if the data is still up to date.
    3. *Retry.* How often slave servers should attempt to retry if they fail to contact the primary host.

PART

II

CH

6

4. *Expire.* How long the data remains valid on a secondary server without refresh.

5. *TTL (Time-to-live).* How long data is considered valid by other name servers that cache this information.

- NS. Name Server records specify the name of the master name server for this zone. Following this keyword is the name of that server, with a period appended at the end.

- MX. Mail Exchanger records specify the systems that handle mail for this zone. Following the keyword are two fields: the preference value is a number, followed by the mail server's name. Mail exchangers with a lower preference are contacted first; thus you can use MX records to specify primary mail servers and backups (with a higher preference) that are used in case the primary mail server is unreachable.

- A. Address records identify the IP address for the specified name.

- PTR. Pointer records provide address-to-name mappings and are used for *reverse lookup* (matching a host name to an IP number).

- CNAME. Canonical name records let you create aliases. For instance, if www.mydomain, ftp.mydomain, and mail.mydomain are really all aliases for the single computer known as myhost.mydomain, you can use CNAME records for this purpose.

TEST SYSTEM   On my test system, I created three zone files, all in the /var/named directory. The first, named.hosts describes the linux.sys domain and contains the following text:

```
@   IN    SOA     host.linux.sys. root.host.linux.sys. (
                  1                 ; Serial number
                  10800             ; Refresh after 3 hours
                  3600              ; Retry hourly
                  604800            ; Expire after a week
                  10800             ; Time to live is 3 hours
                  )

                  IN    NS    host.linux.sys.
                  IN    MX    10 host.linux.sys.
localhost         IN    A     127.0.0.1
host              IN    A     192.168.1.1
```

The Refresh, Retry, Expire, and TTL values are a result of experience. Setting them too short results in excessive queries. Setting them too long causes another problem: if you make a system change, it will be a while before the changes are propagated, during which time many remote machines will still attempt to reach your site using the wrong information.

▼

▼   The second file, `named.rev`, contains address-to-name mappings for `linux.sys`:

```
@   IN   SOA     host.linux.sys. root.host.linux.sys. (
                 1                      ; Serial number
                 10800                  ; Refresh after 3 hours
                 3600                   ; Retry hourly
                 604800                 ; Expire after a week
                 10800                  ; Time to live is 3 hours
            )

                 IN      NS      host.linux.sys.
     1.1         IN      PTR     host.linux.sys.
```

This file contains an `SOA` record and `NS` record identical to those in `named.hosts`. The `PTR` record is for the name `1.1`; when the zone's name, `168.192.IN-ADDR.ARPA` (from `/etc/named.conf`) is appended, I get the correct `IN-ADDR.ARPA` form of the numeric address `192.168.1.1`: `1.1.168.192.IN-ADDR.ARPA`.

Lastly, the `named.local` file provides address-to-name mappings for the `localhost` address:

```
@   IN   SOA     host.linux.sys. root.host.linux.sys. (
                 1                      ; Serial number
                 10800                  ; Refresh after 3 hours
                 3600                   ; Retry hourly
                 604800                 ; Expire after a week
                 10800                  ; Time to live is 3 hours
            )

                 IN      NS      host.linux.sys.
     1.0.0       IN      PTR     localhost.
```

▲   As before, the `SOA` and `NS` records are unchanged; the `PTR` record describes `127.0.0.1`.

Checking Your Configuration

The configuration files for `named` aren't simple to understand, and errors are often made even by experienced administrators. How can you tell if this is the case? How do you verify that your configuration files are valid and accurate?

When you are done with a configuration change, the first thing to do is to restart the name server. If a name server is already running, this can be done using the hang-up signal:

```
killall -HUP named
```

If no name server is running, start the `named` program, which will take care of moving itself to the background. The program is typically found in the `/sbin` or `/usr/sbin` directories.

The `named` server sends error messages and warnings to the system log. You need to have the `syslogd` daemon running in order to intercept these messages and store them in log files. The log files might contain entries like this:

```
host named[6400]: /etc/named.conf:1: syntax error near directory
host named[6401]: No root nameservers for class IN
```

If you see messages like these, which indicate an error condition, try to correct that condition and restart the server.

TEST SYSTEM

On my test system, `named` messages appear in the system log file `/var/log/messages`. After I managed to establish a working configuration, I checked the last few entries in this file using the `tail` command:

```
$ tail -5 /var/log/messages
host named[6794]: cache zone "" (IN) loaded (serial 0)
host named[6794]: master zone "linux.sys" (IN) loaded
➡(serial 1)
host named[6794]: master zone "168.192.IN-ADDR.ARPA" (IN) loaded
➡(serial 1)
host named[6794]: master zone "127.IN-ADDR.ARPA" (IN) loaded
➡(serial 1)
```

After system restart, these messages appeared on the console instead; the reason for this behavior is that Caldera's standard startup scripts start `named` before starting the system log service.

▲

To verify that the data supplied by `named` is accurate, use the `nslookup` tool in interactive mode. Typing `nslookup` reveals the presence of a working name server as specified by `/etc/resolv.conf`. For instance, before I had a zone file for `127.IN-ADDR.ARPA` on my test system, attempts to start `nslookup` resulted in an error:

```
$ nslookup
*** Can't find server name for address 127.0.0.1: Server failed
*** Default servers are not available
```

In interactive mode, you type the name that you want to resolve, and `nslookup` prints the result. There are also specific commands you can use, most prominently the `set type` command, that lets you look for specific record types.

TEST SYSTEM   Without further comment, here is the transcript of a brief `nslookup` session that helped me verify that my `named` configuration is correct:

```
$ nslookup
Default Server:  localhost
Address:  127.0.0.1

> host
Server:  localhost
Address:  127.0.0.1

Name:     host.linux.sys
Address:  192.168.1.1

> host.linux.sys.
Server:  localhost
Address:  127.0.0.1

Name:     host.linux.sys
Address:  192.168.1.1

> 192.168.1.1
Server:  localhost
Address:  127.0.0.1

Name:     host.linux.sys
Address:  192.168.1.1

> linux.sys.
Server:  localhost
Address:  127.0.0.1

Name:     linux.sys

> set type=MX
> linux.sys.
Server:  localhost
Address:  127.0.0.1

linux.sys  preference = 10, mail exchanger = host.linux.sys
linux.sys  nameserver = host.linux.sys
host.linux.sys     internet address = 192.168.1.1
> set type=NS
> linux.sys.
Server:  localhost
Address:  127.0.0.1

linux.sys  nameserver = host.linux.sys
host.linux.sys     internet address = 192.168.1.1
> set type=ANY
> linux.sys.
Server:  localhost
```

▼

▼
```
Address:  127.0.0.1

linux.sys
        origin = host.linux.sys
        mail addr = root.host.linux.sys
        serial = 1
        refresh = 10800 (3H)
        retry   = 3600  (1H)
        expire  = 604800 (1W)
        minimum ttl = 10800 (3H)
linux.sys  preference = 10, mail exchanger = host.linux.sys
linux.sys  nameserver = host.linux.sys
linux.sys  nameserver = host.linux.sys
host.linux.sys     internet address = 192.168.1.1
> 168.192.IN-ADDR.ARPA.
Server:  localhost
Address:  127.0.0.1

168.192.IN-ADDR.ARPA
        origin = host.linux.sys
        mail addr = root.host.linux.sys
        serial = 1
        refresh = 10800 (3H)
        retry   = 3600  (1H)
        expire  = 604800 (1W)
        minimum ttl = 10800 (3H)
168.192.IN-ADDR.ARPA    nameserver = host.linux.sys
168.192.IN-ADDR.ARPA    nameserver = host.linux.sys
host.linux.sys     internet address = 192.168.1.1
```
▲

Summary

IP numbers are translated into easy-to-remember names with the help of DNS.

The simplest way to map host names to addresses is by using the /etc/hosts file. Because this file has to be updated by hand, and because a copy has to be maintained on each computer participating in the network, use of this file is only practical with a small number of hosts, such as those on a small local network. For anything larger and certainly for resolving names on the global Internet, a name server should be used.

The global name service is a hierarchical, distributed database. Root servers provide information on top-level domains such as .com, .org, or .ca. They also provide the names of name servers for second-level domains which, in turn, provide specific information about those domains.

On a Linux computer, the file /etc/resolv.conf determines the name servers that programs on this machine must query.

Useful DNS tools include hostname, nslookup, and whois.

Domain names can be obtained from the InterNIC or national registrars either directly or through your ISP. You can also consider using a domain name within your ISP's name space if such names are offered.

If you want to operate your own name server, you need to create a configuration file, obtain a recent copy of the root cache, and create zone files for each domain you intend to service.

Checking your name server configuration can be done by checking for named-related error messages in the system logs and by querying the server using the nslookup tool.

PART

II

CH

6

Making the Connection

So how do you go about establishing a cost-effective, reliable connection for your network to the global Internet? Here are the basic steps:

1. Understand what you're doing (by reading the preceding chapters, for instance) and prepare your systems for the connection

2. Find the right Internet service provider (ISP)

3. Establish IP connectivity using, for instance, PPP over a modem line

4. Configure routing for your network if necessary

Preparing for the Connection

All the discussion in the preceding chapters about the basics of Internet networking is meant to serve one purpose: to help you make an informed decision when it comes to shopping for an ISP and getting your network connected. You want to obtain the services you need, at the best possible price; you do not want to pay for services you don't require. Most ISPs also appreciate it when they can deal with a "knowledgeable user," one who can provide a coherent response to questions such as "how many addresses do you need in your subnet?" or "do you have a firewall that performs IP aliasing?"

Finding the Right ISP

How do you pick an ISP for your business? How can you tell good ones from bad ones? How can you provide the best connectivity for your network at a moderate price?

Picking an ISP is hard. Most service providers serve the mass market; their idea of an Internet user is a teenager with a Windows 95 machine, browsing the Web, wasting time in chat rooms, and exchanging silly emails. With rare exceptions, the service these ISPs provide is totally inadequate when connecting a server of any sort. Some even explicitly state in their service contract that no such connections are allowed. In other words, don't expect to be able to connect your company's local area network (LAN) to the Internet for $20 a month!

Before you choose a provider, list your needs. Here is a simple set of questions you'll need to be able to answer when shopping for the service:

1. Do you require IP connectivity for your network?

   For instance, if you plan to provide Web access to users on your network, run your own Web or FTP server, the answer is yes.

   1.1   Do you require a high-speed connection?

   A high-speed connection is essential if you have many users, or if you are offering services such as a Web server to the Internet public.

   1.2   Do you require a dedicated (full-time) connection?

   1.3   Do you require a fixed IP number?

   If you will be offering services on the Internet, such as a Web or FTP server, a dedicated connection and a fixed IP number are a must.

   1.4   Do you need more than one IP number?

   More than one IP number is needed if you're connecting a network of more than one computer to the Internet, unless you're using your Linux system as a masquerading firewall (see Chapter 11, "Firewalls," for more information on this topic.)

   1.5   Do you require routing for a network or just an individual host or firewall gateway?

   If you are using more than one IP number, routing is required.

2. Do you require mail services?

   2.1   Will you run your own mail server?

   Running your own mail server frees you from having to rely on your ISP for managing user mailboxes, and it also allows you to easily implement intra-office email.

2.2 Do you require batch delivery of mail?

Batch email delivery is not essential but very helpful if you are running your own mail server and don't have a full-time Internet connection.

2.3 Do you want the ISP to act as your backup mail server?

If you're running your own mail server, naming your ISP as your backup server helps you avoid losing messages in case your server is down.

2.4 Do you require mailboxes at your ISP? (How many?)

If you aren't going to run a mail server, you must have mailboxes somewhere else, such as a public freemail service or your ISP.

3. Do you need a domain name?

3.1 Do you want the ISP to register the domain name for you?

If you're registering a domain name in the .com *domain, it's probably cheaper to do it yourself, unless your ISP offers this service as part of a package deal.*

3.2 Do you want the ISP to act as your primary or secondary name service?

Even if you will run your own mail server, a secondary server (in case yours is down) is useful.

4. Do you plan to have a Web site?

4.1 Do you want the ISP to provide Web hosting services?

Having your ISP host your Web site frees your Internet connection from the added load of incoming Web traffic. It also provides faster download speeds for your visitors, at the cost of more cumbersome Web site management procedures and added expenses.

4.2 Do you need secure transaction capability?

Secure transaction processing is important if you plan to offer online shopping services or deal with confidential information.

5. Do you want to have a local news server?

5.1 Do you want to exchange Usenet newsgroups with your ISP?

Some news servers are used to host only private newsgroups; however, you may opt to host a few public newsgroups as well, if they're viewed often by users on your network. See Chapter 9, "Mailing Lists and Newsgroups," for more information.

If you can answer these questions, you can present a shopping list to prospective ISPs. For instance, a few years ago, when I switched to a new service provider, I was able to ask them for a quote for the following services:

1. I need dial-up PPP (not dedicated) at 28.8Kbps. I have my own portable set of IP numbers (a Class C subnet) for which I require routing.

2. I need two-way batched mail delivery via UUCP.

3. I need two-way batched delivery of a specific set of about 100 Usenet newsgroups.

4. I have my registered domain name, for which I require primary and secondary name service.

5. I need to be able to establish a Web site on the provider's host (no secure transactions required).

As I began shopping around, I found that some ISPs had no idea what I was talking about when I mentioned things such as UUCP. Others did not provide certain services I needed or quoted an exorbitant price. Eventually, I found a local ISP that was able to provide all the services I asked for, and I remained their happy customer for several years thereafter, even today maintaining a backup account with them.

In addition to checking whether the ISP delivers the services you need at a competitive price, you also want to ensure that it's an ISP you can rely on for your Internet connectivity. You don't want to be stranded without an Internet connection when your modem loses carrier during the evening peak hours and isn't capable of reconnecting for several hours afterward because all lines are busy. You don't want an ISP that has plenty of modems and offers all the services you need, but has limited outgoing data capacity, causing extreme lag during peak periods of usage. Lastly, you don't want an ISP that goes out of business or gets locked up in an ownership dispute while you remain disconnected. Switching to another ISP in an emergency can be done, but I assure you that it's no fun at all!

TEST SYSTEM   For my test system, I have the following shopping list:

1. I need dedicated dial-up PPP service.

2. I need a single, fixed IP number for my server.

3. I need the option of batched UUCP mail delivery for test purposes.

4. I need a domain name that can be one from the ISP's namespace. I want to provide primary name service for this subdomain.

▼

▼   5. I will run my Web server, newsgroup server, and other servers locally.

Picking the ISP is easy: I am going to provide these services for myself, using other
▲   existing systems.

Setting Up Your Modem

Before you can establish a dial-up connection over a telephone line, you obviously need
a working modem.

Under Linux, it is not necessary to *install* a modem. Unless you managed to compile a
kernel for yourself with no serial line support, your system already has everything it
needs to "talk to" and utilize an internal or external modem.

The easiest way to test the modem is by using a communication program. minicom is a
robust, simple, but versatile communication program is included with most Linux distributions.

When you run minicom for the first time, do so as the root user, and use the -s command-line switch. This invokes a menu through which you can set the program's initial
configuration (see Figure 7.1). The actual settings are, of course, dependent on your
system configuration, modem type, etc. Save the configuration as df1, the default
configuration.

FIGURE 7.1
Configuring minicom.

If minicom is successfully configured, you should be able to interact with your modem. For instance, typing **AT** and pressing Enter should cause the modem to respond with OK.

One odd feature of Linux serial line handling is that the standard interface that many applications use to configure the line allows only 38400bps as the maximum speed of the line. Higher speeds can be achieved by setting a special flag, which minicom knows about, but other applications may not. This flag can be set at system boot time using the setserial utility. For instance, to set up /dev/ttyS1 so that a speed setting of 38400bps actually means 115200bps, you'd use the following:

```
setserial /dev/ttyS1 spd_vhi
```

Using PPP

Had I written this book a few years ago, it would have featured SLIP (Serial Line Internet Protocol) prominently. Times change, however; most (if not all) ISPs nowadays offer dial-up connections using (only) PPP.

This was meant to happen of course. Whereas SLIP was a quick-and-dirty solution that provided just the barest essentials for delivering IP traffic over a serial connection, PPP is a full-featured beast; in addition to IP, it can also be used to deliver packets using Novell's NetWare and other protocols, it supports user authentication, password encryption, and more.

PPP Components

So what, exactly, does PPP look like under Linux?

In the strictest sense, PPP is a feature of the Linux kernel. In order for the PPP interface to exist, the kernel must be compiled with this feature enabled. (Don't worry if you haven't recompiled your kernel; if you're using the Caldera OpenLinux distribution from the attached CD-ROM, PPP is configured as a loadable module. Nearly all other Linux distributions also include a kernel that supports PPP. For more information about recompiling the kernel, please refer to Appendix A, "Configuring the Kernel.")

Of course no kernel features exist by themselves; programs are needed to enable or disable them or to control their behavior. PPP is no different. The program that sets up and maintains a PPP connection is pppd, the PPP daemon. This program usually runs in the background, and it is responsible for configuring the PPP interface, setting up routing when the interface is enabled, providing authentication information, and more. The daemon can also be run from the command-line; for instance, you may log on to a remote system, run pppd there, and then enable the PPP interface on your machine to establish an IP connection.

The Dial-Up Process

Before you can run pppd, you need to have an established connection. The PPP daemon knows nothing about modems, and certainly cannot dial a phone number.

There is, fortunately, a small utility usually distributed along with pppd. The chat utility is used to perform a simple *conversation* with your modem. This term is commonly used in UNIX-land to describe simple command-response scripts that look somewhat like this:

Wait for this	Then send this
	ATDT5551212<CR>
CONNECT	<CR>
Host Name:	CIS
User ID:	70000,1111/go:pppconnect<CR>
Password:	SECRET*WORD<CR>
One moment please	

You get the idea. This, incidentally, is a valid, *live* script that I use to connect a Linux machine to CompuServe if my primary Internet connection fails for some reason. The actual syntax is different; the conversation strings are passed to the chat program in a file as follows:

```
"" ATDT5551212 CONNECT "" "Host Name:" CIS "User ID:" \
"70000,1111/go:pppconnect" "Password: " "SECRET*WORD" "One moment please"
```

Auto-Dialing

Okay, so pppd knows how to establish an IP connection, whereas it lets chat take care of the actual dialing process. But who determines when the connection must be established in the first place?

For a single-user workstation, the easy answer is to let the user invoke pppd, perhaps from a simple command-line script to make his life easier. Not an elegant solution, to be sure, but it works. It would be so much nicer though if you could make the dialing happen automatically instead, so that the connection comes *up* when the user starts using a Web browser, for instance, and it's automatically terminated when no data traffic occurs for a set period of time.

What's merely a useful feature on a workstation becomes an essential one on a server. For servers not permanently connected to the Internet, the *demand-dial* capability ensures that the system's users can access the Internet seamlessly (that is, without having to log on to the server and invoke pppd manually, and then forgetting to shut it down afterward!) Even on systems with a permanent connection over a dial-up line, it's necessary to be able to re-establish a connection automatically in case it's terminated due to bad phone line quality, for example.

All this and more can be established by a very useful tool: diald, the dialer daemon. Developed by Eric Schenk, this utility works with a complex set of rules that determine when a connection should be established or torn down.

The rules can say something as simple as "keep this connection up at all times," or "keep this system connected between 9 a.m. and 5 p.m. on weekdays, otherwise connect when there's outgoing traffic, and disconnect after five minutes of inactivity." Or they can be more complex, ignoring specific types of packets for instance, or adjusting the dialer's behavior to match the metering rules of phone companies in countries where local calls are metered.

A version of the diald daemon is available on the attached Caldera OpenLinux CD-ROM. If you're interested in obtaining the latest version of diald or just want to find out more about it, (at the time of this writing) the diald home page was available at http://www.loonie.net/~eschenk/diald.html.

Routing and Forwarding

When the IP connection is up and running, the system must be configured to use the connection for traffic that is sent to destinations outside the local network. This is accomplished by setting up the *default route*, that is, the route used for any data packet for which no other known route exists. This can be done automatically; pppd under Linux can set up the default route when the physical connection is established and remove the route once the connection is broken.

Setting up the default route, however, is not sufficient by itself to turn the system into a *router*, that is, a host that acts as an interface between other machines on your local network and the external connection. For this, packet forwarding (IP forwarding) must also be supported by the kernel and enabled. (If you are using a recompiled kernel, make sure it contains IP forwarding support.)

TEST SYSTEM   If you're using the stock Caldera kernel from the attached CD-ROM, IP forwarding support is already present. Caldera OpenLinux, however, disables the IP forwarding feature by default and it must be enabled through the LISA utility.

To do so, start LISA with the -system parameter, and select the Configure server/daemon Autostart option from the menu. In the subsequent screen, one of the options is labeled IP forwarding (normally disabled!). Enable this option (see Figure 7.2).

FIGURE 7.2
Enabling IP forwarding.

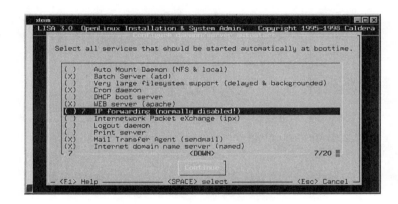

For the new setting to take effect, you need to restart the kernel. Alternatively, you can manually enable IP forwarding using the following command (issued as the root user):

```
echo 1 >/proc/sys/net/ipv4/ip_forward
```

Obtaining IP Numbers for Your Network

Turning on IP forwarding is still not by itself sufficient to allow other computers on your network to connect to the Internet via your Linux system. The problem is that those other computers all have IP numbers that might not be recognized by any system outside your local network. Therefore, even though those machines will be capable of sending data packets out, no return packets can reach them and, therefore, no IP connections can be successfully established.

PART
II

CH
7

There are two solutions to this problem. First, you can enable firewall gateway capability (specifically, IP aliasing, also known as IP masquerading) on your Linux server. This enables your entire network to appear under a single IP number to the outside world. The use of Linux as a firewall gateway is covered in detail in Chapter 11, "Firewalls." The disadvantage of this solution is that a firewall gateway doesn't support all types of Internet connections.

Another solution is to obtain an address range from your ISP. The main advantage of this solution is simplicity and compatibility; once the addresses are properly configured, all computers on your network will have full Internet access with no restrictions. One important disadvantage is that if your IP numbers change, you need to reconfigure all systems on the network; another is that since all machines are directly accessible from the Internet, you are not taking advantage of the full protection that a firewall gateway can offer.

Regardless of which solution is used, the address of your Linux machine must be specified on all participating workstations on your network as the default router address.

Incoming Connections

Modems on servers are often used not only to dial out to a remote host, but also to accept incoming connections. For instance, you might want to be able to dial in to the system when its Internet connection is down for some reason. Or you might want to maintain a second modem to accept incoming connections from the system's regular users, who may be on the road, dialing in for their email from home, etc.

A Linux server can also be turned into a receive-only fax server with a modest effort. Incoming fax pages can be packaged as email attachments and sent to a mail recipient (for example, your company receptionist).

Incoming Data Calls

When it comes to accepting incoming connections over serial lines, UNIX systems have a distinct advantage. Unlike MS-DOS, UNIX has been designed from the beginning to support multiple users connecting via serial terminals. Consequently, it's practically second nature for a UNIX system to allow a user to connect and log in via a serial port. This feature lets remote users log on using any terminal emulation program in combination with their modem.

The secret to this capability is the getty program and its variants. If you list running processes on your system (using `ps axu`, for instance), you'll notice a number of copies of this program running, one for each virtual console in fact. It is the getty program that displays the initial login prompt, and after accepting the user's identifier, calls the `login` command for password validation and to start the user's shell.

Now getty works just as well on serial lines as on virtual consoles. The trick to using it with a modem is to place the modem in auto-answer mode. On many external modems this can be accomplished by setting a switch. On internal modems, you can configure and store this setting in the modem's non-volatile memory (NVRAM) to ensure that the modem comes up in the proper configuration after it's powered up. Please refer to your modem's manual for more information.

To ensure that the modem operates properly you might also want to enable the Hangup on DTR and Carrier Detect settings. The first ensures that the modem correctly drops the phone line connection when the user's work is finished. The second setting allows the modem to inform the computer if the line was disconnected.

> **NOTE**
>
> Once you enable your modem's auto-answer setting, it will *always* answer the phone line when powered on, unless explicitly disabled by software. If you have a dual-use phone line, you might want to adjust the number of rings that the modem waits before answering (see your modem's manual for details).

So how do you ensure that getty is started every time the system is powered on and that it monitors the modem line? Why, by putting it in `/etc/inittab` of course! If you recall from Chapter 4, "Internet Configuration and Basic Security," it is `/etc/inittab` where you specify what programs are run at startup. If you look at this file, you will already see entries containing the `getty` command; these entries initiate getty on virtual consoles. What you need is another entry, one that initiates getty on a serial line with a modem attached.

TEST SYSTEM

▼

My test system contains an external U.S. Robotics Sportster 33.6 modem. This modem has a row of DIP switches in the back that can be used to adjust the modem's default behavior. I set switch 1 to the Off position (dropping DTR terminates the call), and switch 5 also to the Off position (Auto Answer).

PART

II

CH

7

▼   My /etc/inittab file contained six getty lines for the six virtual consoles, but no entry
      for the modem. My modem is on /dev/ttyS1, so I added the following line:

      s1:3:respawn:/sbin/getty ttyS1 38400 vt100

      It is interesting to note that the 38400 parameter isn't really a line speed parameter; it is a
      label that identifies an entry in /etc/gettydefs. This file contains terminal configura-
      tions for consoles (VC) and serial lines, one of which (38400) is the correct configuration
      line for most modern high-speed modems.

      The last parameter, vt100, is what getty initially sets the terminal type to (the TERM envi-
      ronment variable.) This setting is compatible with most terminal emulation programs.

      Once I made the change, I forced the init program to re-read /etc/inittab by typing the
      following:

      kill -1 1

      that is, I sent a hangup (HUP) signal to the init program, which always runs under process
      ID 1.

      With this setting made, I was able to dial in to the test system from another computer
      and phone line. I also tested how the system responds to a disconnect during a session; it
      correctly terminated all running applications on the now orphaned serial line and
▲   restarted the getty program which, in turn, reset the modem.

      Using plain old getty has a major drawback: it does not permit the *sharing* of the modem
      line between applications. If you are using the same modem line for incoming and out-
      going connections, getty just won't do.

      Fortunately, another version of getty comes to the rescue: *uugetty*. This program received
      its name from UUCP, the system from which it inherited its locking mechanism. The
      idea is simple: When a process wants to use the serial line, it first checks for the pres-
      ence of a *lock file* at a known location. If a lock file is present, the process doesn't access
      the serial line; otherwise, it creates its own lock file before doing so. The lock file con-
      tains the process ID, so if a process dies without releasing its lock, other processes can
      make note of this fact and delete the stale lock file.

      This simple mechanism allows cooperating applications to share a modem. The minicom
      application, uugetty, and pppd are all capable of using compatible lock files. The one
      problem is that several conventions exist for the location and format of these lock files;
      fortunately, most decent Linux distributions contain binary versions of important pro-
      grams that are compatible with each other.

TEST SYSTEM   On my test system, all I needed to do to enable uugetty was to change the recently added line in /etc/inittab to the following:

```
s1:3:respawn:/sbin/uugetty -d /etc/getty.ttyS1 ttyS1 38400 vt100
```

The file /etc/getty.ttyS1 contained a single line:

```
ALTLOCK=cua1
```

Use of this line ensures that the locking mechanism works properly if you are using /dev/cua1 as the device name with other programs that access the modem, such as minicom.

After this, I once again sent a hangup signal to init (kill -HUP 1). Because I already had a getty running on the serial line, I also had to remove it. I located the process using the ps command and killed it with a HUP signal. In response to this, init spawned a copy of uugetty on the serial port. I then tested the system by once again dialing in to it from
▲   another computer.

PPP for Incoming Calls

Now this is all very good that you can log on from remote machines using terminal emulation but how can remote machines establish an IP connection?

By starting the pppd daemon, of course. This is a bit more complicated than it sounds, for the following reasons:

- You cannot start pppd from a terminal emulator[md]all you would get is garbage characters on the emulator's screen. The system you connect from must run its own version of pppd and chat or their equivalent.

- You need to start pppd with the proper command-line switches, which can get quite complicated.

The first problem is solved on most desktop operating systems through the use of logon scripts. For instance, under the Dial-Up Networking (DUN) facility of Windows 95/98, scripts with the .SCP filename extension are (typically) stored in the Program Files\Accessories directory.

The answer to the second problem is a properly formulated pppd command line. This command line could be typed manually, but far more likely, you'll make it part of a logon script, such as the scripts used with Windows 95 DUN. The command line, in many cases, will look like this:

```
exec /usr/sbin/pppd passive silent modem crtscts 192.168.1.1:192.168.1.128
```

PART
II

CH
7

pppd has many more options, but this line is typical when handling incoming connections. The use of the `exec` command is a simple way to save a little bit of memory and system resources. Instead of launching `pppd` as a separate process, `exec` causes the shell to transform into the new process. That means one less entry in the list of processes and a little bit of memory and system resources saved.

The `passive` and `silent` options tell the `pppd` daemon to sit there and wait for the user's workstation to initiate PPP negotiation.

The `crtscts` and `modem` options ensure that `pppd` uses hardware handshaking to communicate with the modem, and they monitor the Carrier Detect signal to detect when a connection is dropped.

The final part of the command line specifies the local and remote IP addresses. The local address can be the machine's primary address (in this case, it actually doesn't represent a problem if you use the same IP address that's normally used for the Ethernet interface).

As for the remote address, it can be anything as long as the workstation that connects to your system doesn't expect to connect via your system to other computers. If, however, such routing is desired, the address assigned to the remote workstation must be a valid address for which you can provide routing. Depending on what IP address range you use, it might make sense to reserve a portion of it for incoming dial-up connections. For instance, if you have a full Class C address space of 256 addresses, you might want to reserve the upper 128 addresses for incoming PPP connections and other uses, and use the lower 128 for your LAN (with a netmask of /25, or `255.255.255.128`).

As you will see, Chapter 19, "Configuring Workstations," contains more information on setting up workstations to connect to your server.

Running a FAX Server

In a small office or home office, you might not want to maintain separate phone lines for incoming data and fax connections. One solution is to use Linux itself as a fax server.

The tool to use is called *mgetty+sendfax*. As the name implies, this package actually consists of two parts: mgetty is a smart version of the getty program specifically designed to work with FAX modems, and sendfax is a fax-processing module.

Configuring mgetty isn't always easy. The package is usually distributed in source form, and you need to make adjustments to parameters in a C language source file and recompile the package before it can be used. It's worth the effort, however, if you use a modem extensively for dial-in purposes.

One of the features of mgetty is its capability to call an external program after a fax is received. Utility programs are also available that convert raw *group 3* fax files into a more recognizable format, such as TIFF. Using a combination of these tools and features, it is possible to have mgetty invoke a simple shell script that, in turn, creates a mail message with a properly formatted multipage TIFF attachment. Indeed, newer mgetty distributions already come with a sample implementation of this capability.

TEST SYSTEM Connecting the Test System

To demonstrate these principles in practice, I have set up my test system to connect to a "service provider"—a regular Linux system in my home office that accepts dial-in data calls.

My goal is to configure my system to connect on demand, and disconnect when idle, so as to allow incoming calls.

Dial-up Instructions

The "service provider" gave the following instructions for establishing a PPP connection:

1. Dial the server.
2. Connect as usual, typing your user ID and password when prompted.
3. Start the PPP daemon on the server by sending it the following command line:
   ```
   exec /usr/sbin/pppd passive silent modem crtscts
   192.168.2.1:192.168.2.132
   ```

4. Start your local copy of the PPP daemon.

I was told that my local IP address will be 192.168.2.132, and my gateway is 192.168.2.1. I can also get name service from this system if I need to, and it runs a mail server as well. My user ID on the remote system is vttoth, and my password is SECRET.

Testing the Login Procedure

Before fiddling with PPP, I wanted to test whether my password worked. I also needed to see what responses I got from the system so that I could build a properly functioning chat script.

▼

PART

II

CH

7

▼   Using minicom, I dialed the number provided and logged on. Here is a transcript of my session:

```
atdt5551212
CONNECT 28800/ARQ/V34/LAPM/V42BIS
You have reached a private computer system. Calls to this system are
logged
using calling party identification (caller ID). Unauthorized calls violate
my privacy, not to mention the law! If you have not been specifically
authorized by me to access this system, now would be a great time to
terminate your connection.

Viktor

Welcome to Linux 2.0.30.


vtt1!login: vttoth
Password:
Last login: Thu Feb 25 04:12:49 on ttyS0
Linux 2.0.30.

Liar, n.:
        A lawyer with a roving commission.
                — Ambrose Bierce, "The Devil's Dictionary"

vtt1:~$ exit
NO CARRIER
```

Running pppd

Having assured myself that I can log on to the provider's system, I now need to build a chat script that defines the *conversation* for login. I named the file /etc/connect.chat; its contents are based on the transcript of my test session and the instructions of my *provider*:

```
"" ATDT5551212 CONNECT "" "ogin:" vttoth "assword:" SECRET "vtt1:~$"
"exec /usr/sbin/pppd passive silent modem crtscts
➥192.168.2.1:192.168.2.132"
```

It is now time to test fire PPP. As root, I invoked PPP using the following command line on my local machine. (Don't be confused by the fact that we invoke use of the pppd command on both my local machine, which does the dialing, and the server that accepts incoming calls):

```
/usr/sbin/pppd -d ttyS1 38400 connect '/usr/sbin/chat -f
➥/etc/connect.chat' \
modem crtscts lock defaultroute
```

▼

▼ The result? It worked! I heard the modem dial, and after a few seconds, my system was connected to the Internet. I could verify this a number of ways.

First, I looked at the file /var/log/messages. After invoking PPP, it contained messages similar to the following:

```
Feb 25 04:25:31 host pppd[18539]: pppd 2.2.0 started by root, uid 0
Feb 25 04:26:01 host pppd[18539]: Serial connection established.
Feb 25 04:26:02 host pppd[18539]: Using interface ppp0
Feb 25 04:26:02 host pppd[18539]: Connect: ppp0 <—> /dev/ttyS1
Feb 25 04:26:03 host pppd[18539]: local  IP address 192.168.2.132
Feb 25 04:26:03 host pppd[18539]: remote IP address 192.168.2.1
```

Next, I typed /**sbin**/**ifconfig**. If the PPP interface is functioning, this command shows an entry like the following:

```
ppp0      Link encap:Point-to-Point Protocol
          inet addr:192.168.2.132  P-t-P:192.168.2.1  Mask:255.255.255.0
          UP POINTOPOINT RUNNING  MTU:1500  Metric:1
          RX packets:6 errors:0 dropped:0 overruns:0
          TX packets:6 errors:0 dropped:0 overruns:0
```

Then there is the routing table; typing /**sbin**/**route** showed the newly established default route:

```
# /sbin/route
Kernel IP routing table
Destination   Gateway        Genmask          Flags Metric  Ref  Use Iface
192.168.2.1   *              255.255.255.255  UH    0       0      0 ppp0
192.168.1.0   *              255.255.255.0    U     0       0     28 eth0
127.0.0.0     *              255.0.0.0        U     0       0     12 lo
default       192.168.2.1    0.0.0.0          UG    0       0      1 ppp0
```

But most importantly, I was now able to use the ping and traceroute commands to reach remote destinations. For instance

```
traceroute to www.mcp.com (198.70.146.70), 30 hops max, 40 byte packets
 1   192.168.2.1 (192.168.2.1)   164.715 ms   187.385 ms   169.697 ms
 2   192.168.2.126 (192.168.2.126)   139.576 ms   187.577 ms   149.699 ms
 3   max1.ott1.uunet.ca (205.150.233.2)   169.497 ms   198.209 ms   169.679 ms
 4   e011.bb1.ott1.uunet.ca (205.150.233.1)   189.530 ms   168.225 ms   189.68
➥1 ms
 5   a10-0-0.102.bb1.ott1.a10-0-0.102.bb1.tor2.uunet.ca (205.150.242.89)   2
➥19.522 ms   207.993 ms   189.675 ms
 6   224.ATM10-0-0.GW1.CHI6.Alter.Net (137.39.75.17)   219.519 ms   218.574 m
➥s   209.684 ms
 7   111.ATM2-0.XR2.CHI6.ALTER.NET (146.188.208.78)   229.518 ms   208.602 ms
➥209.684 ms
 8   190.ATM8-0-0.GW2.IND1.ALTER.NET (146.188.208.97)   239.524 ms   208.631
➥ms   219.674 ms
```
▼

PART
II

CH
7

▼
```
 9  iquest-gw.customer.alter.net (157.130.103.94)  219.527 ms   248.690 ms
➥219.650 ms
10  iq-ind-core1.iquest.net (206.53.249.1)  219.534 ms  218.615 ms
➥219.66
1 ms
11  iq-ss2.iquest.net (206.246.190.161)  219.541 ms  219.840 ms  218.672 m
s
```

Running `diald`

Having proven that I can run `pppd` manually, all I needed to do now was to automate the process using `diald`.

First, `diald` needed a configuration file. This file is normally called `/etc/diald.conf`. One of the simplest `diald` configurations allows the link to come alive when there is traffic, and it shuts down the link after some time of inactivity. Here is a `diald` configuration file that accomplishes this:

```
accept any 300 any
```

Not a difficult one, is it? In human language, this line simply tells `diald` to accept any kind of a packet as a trigger to activate the link or keep an inactive link alive. The connection will only be terminated if no packets are sent or received for five minutes.

The problem with this script is that it's a bit too simplistic; with many ISPs you will find that with a script like this, the link stays alive all the time. The reason is that even on an otherwise idle link, routing packets are transmitted occasionally. You can prevent these types of packets from activating the link by using a `diald` configuration file as follows:

```
ignore udp udp.dest=udp.route
ignore udp udp.source=udp.route
accept any 300 any
```

Next, `diald` itself had to be started. I created a small script file named `rc.diald` that contained the following:

```
#!/bin/sh
/usr/sbin/diald /dev/ttyS1 -m ppp connect '/usr/sbin/chat -f
/etc/vttoth.chat' modem crtscts lock defaultroute \
local 192.168.2.132 remote 192.168.2.1
```
▼

▼   This script can be invoked from the command line, or it can be integrated into /etc/rc.d to ensure that diald is activated every time the system is booted. Don't be surprised if a newly booted system dials right away; the culprit is probably your name server as it initializes itself. Depending on what service applications you run, it may occur at other times as well that a seemingly idle system suddenly dials and activates the connection.

To make diald start every time the system is booted, I created the file /etc/rc.d/init.d/diald with the following content:

```
#!/bin/sh
NAME=diald
DAEMON=/usr/sbin/diald
PIDF=/var/run/$NAME.pid

. /etc/sysconfig/network

case "$1" in
 start)

   [ -x $DAEMON ] ¦¦ exit 0
   [ ${NETWORKING} != "no" ] ¦¦ exit 0

   echo "Startind $NAME"
   if [ -f /etc/diald.conf ]; then
     $DAEMON /dev/ttyS1 -m ppp connect '/usr/sbin/chat -f \
     /etc/vttoth.chat' modem crtscts lock defaultroute local \
     199.166.252.132 remote 199.166.252.1
   fi
   ;;

 stop)
   [ -f $PIDF ] ¦¦ exit 1
   echo "Stopping $NAME"
   kill `cat $PIDF`
   ;;

esac
exit 0
```

This is essentially a somewhat modified version of the standard Caldera OpenLinux startup scripts. The name /etc/rc.d/init.d/diald is already known to the Caldera OpenLinux startup process, so creating this file (and ensuring that it has execute permissions!) is sufficient.

After I installed and tested diald, I had a system that provided seamless support for outgoing *and* incoming IP connections over a single modem line.

▲

PART

II

CH

7

Using External Routers

The preceding sections explained how you can use a Linux machine with a built-in modem to connect to the Internet. The instructions also apply if your built-in modem is actually an ISDN device that acts like a modem. But what if you are using an external ISDN or higher speed router?

It turns out that (at least inasmuch as the Linux box is concerned) an external router greatly simplifies things. You no longer need to worry about modem configurations, auto-dialer daemons, and such. If your router is properly configured, you just need to set the default route on your Linux system to point to the router.

In this case, the routing function and other server functions are no longer performed by the same box. Client workstations on your network will use the external router for IP data traffic, but they will continue to use your Linux machine as the mail server, for instance. (See Figure 7.3.)

FIGURE 7.3
Using an external router.

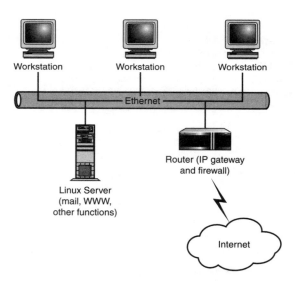

The topic of using external routers is explored in more detail in Chapter 12, "Using External Routers."

Summary

The steps you need to take to successfully establish an Internet connection include finding the right ISP, establishing the connection using PPP, and setting up routing.

In order to choose the best ISP, you need to know your needs—the speed of the connection you want to use, whether it is a dedicated connection, whether you need IP addresses for your network, and so on.

To establish the connection, you need to first set up your modem. Linux supports modems on serial ports by default, so you can verify whether your modem is working properly by using a telecommunication program such as minicom.

With the modem up and running, you need to configure PPP. The `pppd` daemon uses another program, chat, to execute simple connection scripts. The connection script you use should reflect the logon instructions you received from your ISP.

To ensure that the PPP connection is activated (and optionally terminated) automatically based on usage, you can utilize the `diald` daemon. This program monitors IP traffic in the background, and establishes the PPP connection as and when needed, based on the rules stored in its configuration file.

You can also use a Linux server in conjunction with an external router. In this case, the Linux server will continue to perform many server functions (such as, mail and name service) while the router will take over IP forwarding and, optionally, firewall gateway functions.

Manual Pages

For additional information on topics discussed in this chapter, please refer to the following manual pages.

```
man chat

man getty

man gettydefs

man inittab

man minicom

man pppd

man setserial

man 7 signal
```

PART
II

CH
7

Part III

Basic Services

8 Running a Mail Server

9 Mailing Lists and Newsgroups

10 Web Service

Running a Mail Server

Email is the most popular application on the Internet today. The most popular email server in use by ISPs and other organizations is the free server sendmail. This package is extremely robust and very powerful; unfortunately, it is also notoriously difficult to configure.

The reason for this difficulty is not conceptual complexity; mail transfer and delivery are relatively straightforward processes. The main reason is the convoluted syntax of sendmail's infamous configuration file, `sendmail.cf`.

Just to illustrate: the *definitive reference* on sendmail, a book from Bryan Costales and Eric Allman (*sendmail*, 2nd edition) is a densely written tome of over 1,000 pages!

There is reason behind this apparent madness; sendmail is a tool designed to deal with a multitude of email systems in diverse networking environments. Only recently have mailing systems become largely uniform, making a lot of this flexibility unnecessary; and even today, many *weird* environments exist that cannot be served by a simpler program.

Needless to say, compressing the information contained in a 1,000-page tome into a 20–30 page chapter is an impossible task. The best you can hope for is a reasonably coherent explanation of the fundamentals, which is what I am providing here.

The Mail Delivery Process

You probably send and receive dozens of email messages every day. But do you know what happens to your words after you click the Send button in your email application?

As the first step, your mail client contacts your outgoing mail server (the Mail Transfer Agent, or MTA) via a protocol called SMTP (Simple Mail Transfer Protocol.) The mail server at the receiving end of the SMTP conversation is a program (for example, send-mail, smail, Microsoft Exchange Server) that accepts the message body, along with any headers that your email client added to the message.

Next, the server processes the sender and recipient addresses and the headers. Based on the information collected, the server decides what to do with the message. The message may be delivered locally to a mailbox; it may be stored temporarily in a queue, awaiting delivery; or it may be passed on to another server. The rules that govern delivery can be elaborate, and a message can travel a complex route before arriving at the desired destination.

In the end, though, unless the address is incorrect or some other delivery problem occurs, a server somewhere will eventually accept the message as a locally deliverable one. It then deposits the message into the recipient's mailbox. Mailboxes come in many shapes and forms; on UNIX systems, a user's mailbox is typically a file (`/var/spool/mail/`*`username`*) that contains all the user's unread messages.

Finally, the message is picked up from the mailbox by the user's email client program (or Mail User Agent, MUA.) Locally run clients can access the mailboxes directly; if the client runs across the network (for example, if you run your client on your home computer, but access your mailbox on your ISP's mail server) a network protocol such as POP3 (the Post Office Protocol) is used.

This process is demonstrated graphically in Figure 8.1.

Notice that the last step of the delivery process is different from the rest. Up to this point, all messages were *pushed*; that is, it was always the sender who initiated the transaction that moved the message one step closer to its intended destination. During the last step, the process is reversed; it is the client that *pulls* the message by querying the server for available messages.

FIGURE 8.1
The mail delivery process.

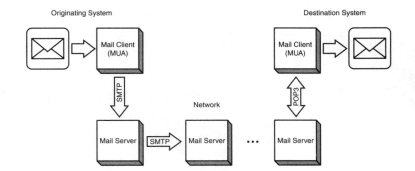

Mail User Agents

MUAs are the client programs that users use to communicate with the mail system.

The simplest MUA under Linux is the `mail` command. This is a very bare bones mail client; because it doesn't even use a network protocol such as POP3 for accessing mail, it can only read messages in your local mailbox. Nevertheless, `mail` is more than sufficient to test your mail system. If invoked without command-line arguments, the program checks the local mail spool to see whether you have any mail:

```
$ mail
No mail for vttoth
$ mail
Mail version 8.1 6/6/93.  Type ? for help.
"/var/spool/mail/vttoth": 1 message 1 new
>N  1 vttoth@linux.sys  Thu Feb 25 16:22  13/425    "Test"
& 1
Message 1:
From vttoth  Thu Feb 25 16:22:21 1999
Return-Path: <vttoth>
Received: (from root@localhost)
        by linux.sys (8.8.7/8.8.7) id QAA00666
        for vttoth; Thu, 25 Feb 1999 16:22:20 -0500
Date: Thu, 25 Feb 1999 16:22:20 -0500
From: "Viktor T. Toth" <vttoth@linux.sys>
Message-Id: <199902252122.QAA00666@linux.sys>
To: vttoth@linux.sys
Subject: Test
Status: R

Test Message

& x
$
```

One of the most popular UNIX email clients is the pine program. Unlike mail, pine presents a full-screen interface (see Figure 8.2). It is also capable of decoding and saving MIME-compatible file attachments.

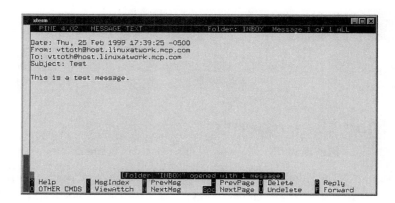

Of course, most people these days don't use UNIX-based MUAs to access their mailboxes, even if the mailboxes themselves reside on UNIX (Linux) systems. The most widely used email clients are those that are distributed with popular Web browsers: Netscape's Messenger, Microsoft's Outlook Express. A high-end email client for Windows PCs is Microsoft Outlook; this MUA can access, in addition to UNIX-style email systems, many other mail server types, including the Microsoft Exchange Server or CompuServe Mail, for instance.

Mail Transport Agents

MTAs, or mail servers, come in many flavors, but the sendmail server stands out as by far the most widely used server on the Internet. This excellent tool is the Cadillac of Internet mail servers; it does everything you ever wanted a mail server to do and more. It has been around for many years, and the current versions are exceptionally stable and robust. About the only bad thing you can say about sendmail is that because of its widespread popularity, it is a frequent target of attempted security breaks. On the other hand, due to the program's robustness, most of these attempts are unsuccessful, at least when sendmail has been configured properly!

Another UNIX mail server is the smail program. Although it provides many of the functions of sendmail, it's somewhat easier to configure. Moreover, I find it easier to set up smail on systems that use demand dialing to connect to the Internet and use batch delivery for email.

Outside the world of UNIX, popular mail servers include the Microsoft Exchange Server or Domino from IBM-Lotus, for instance. The sendmail server also has non-UNIX implementations, including one for Windows NT.

Mailboxes and Protocols

With this many MTAs and MUAs around running on different operating systems, you might rightfully wonder how these programs manage to operate together.

The secret is standardization. All Internet mail programs use a common set of protocols. All UNIX mail agents use commonly known file locations, formats, and access mechanisms. Thus, even though up to half a dozen different programs might process a mail message as it travels from the sender to the destination, the result is a seamless, reliable (at least most of the time) mail system.

SMTP: The Simple Mail Transfer Protocol

All Internet mail servers accept messages using a common mechanism: SMTP. Whether it is your mail client or another mail server forwarding a message, the method is the same: the sending system connects to the receiving server using this protocol, specifies the sender and recipient of the message, and then transfers the message itself.

The use of the word *simple* in the name SMTP is not a euphemism. The protocol is actually so simple that you can perform the transactions by hand. Here is an example that speaks for itself:

```
$ telnet localhost smtp
Trying 127.0.0.1...
Connected to localhost.
Escape character is '^]'.
220 linux.sys ESMTP Sendmail 8.8.7/8.8.7; Thu, 25 Feb 1999 17:38:55 -0500
HELO linux.sys
250 linux.sys Hello vttoth@localhost [127.0.0.1], pleased to meet you
MAIL FROM: vttoth@linux.sys
250 vttoth@linux.sys... Sender ok
RCPT TO: vttoth@linux.sys
250 vttoth@linux.sys... Recipient ok
DATA
354 Enter mail, end with "." on a line by itself
From: vttoth@linux.sys
To: vttoth@linux.sys
Subject: Test

This is a test message.
.
```

```
250 RAA00760 Message accepted for delivery
QUIT
221 linux.sys closing connection
Connection closed by foreign host.
```

It's worthy to note that the actual delivery address is not the address contained in the To: line in the message header; it is defined in the RCPT TO: SMTP command. This is how it is possible to send *blind copy* messages or messages to large distribution lists without showing the true recipient address(es) in the message header. Sadly, it is also a feature frequently abused by email advertisers who use it to hide their real identity, sending out messages with forged headers.

UNIX-Style Mailboxes

Your *mailbox* on a UNIX system is normally a file that resides in the /var/spool/mail directory and has your user ID as its name.

Every message in the mailbox file begins with a From line. This line has a well-defined format, which helps mail programs recognize where one message ends and another begins. (In case you're wondering, yes, it's possible to confuse mailer programs. If a message contains a properly formatted From line, a mailer program might interpret that as the beginning of the next message.)

Following the From: line are message headers, which are explained in the next section. After the last message header there is a blank line, followed by the message body. For instance

```
$ cat /var/spool/mail/vttoth
From vttoth@linux.sys   Thu Feb 25 17:39:37 1999
Return-Path: <vttoth@linux.sys>
Received: from linux.sys (vttoth@localhost [127.0.0.1])
        by linux.sys (8.8.7/8.8.7) with SMTP id RAA00760
        for vttoth@linux.sys; Thu, 25 Feb 1999 17:39:25 -0500
Date: Thu, 25 Feb 1999 17:39:25 -0500
From: vttoth@linux.sys
To: vttoth@linux.sys
Subject: Test
Message-Id: <199902252239.RAA00760@linux.sys>

This is a test message.
```

Message Headers and Formats

As the preceding example shows, all email messages have headers that identify the sender, recipient, delivery path, and more. These headers are not arbitrary; their format and content are defined in an Internet Request for Comment (RFC) document, RFC-822. Some headers are created by the sender's mail client program, while others are added en route by servers that process the message.

Here are a few of the most frequently used header lines you might encounter:

The `To:` line specifies the recipient(s). The line can contain a single email address, multiple email addresses separated by commas, or pairs of *display names* and email addresses, in which case the email address portion is enclosed in angle brackets. If the display name contains punctuation marks, it should be enclosed in double quotes.

The `From:` line specifies the sender(s). The syntax is the same as for the `To:` line. Occasionally, a message might have a `Reply-To:` header as well, which specifies the return address for the message, if it is different from the address shown in the `From:` line.

Most messages also have a `Date:` and a `Subject:` header. Dates are typically in the form of `DDD, dd MMM yyyy hh:mm:ss tzone`. (Just to confuse everyone, dates in the `From:` line that separate messages in a UNIX-style mailbox file are in the form `DDD MMM dd hh:mm:ss yyyy`.)

Other header lines include `Comment`, `Cc`, `Bcc`, `Sender`, `Message-ID`, or `X-special-header:` lines, where the `special-header` part is a placeholder for application-specific keywords.

The so-called MIME (Multipurpose Internet Mail Extensions) standard extends RFC-822 in a variety of ways. First, it adds a new header, Content-Type. Second, it defines several content types, among them the *multipart* content type, which allows the creation of messages that consist of multiple parts. Third, it defines a mechanism for encoding binary data, such as compressed data files, executable programs, images, or audio, in a form suitable for transmission over a text-only mail system. MIME messages are fully compatible with RFC-822, so they can easily be transmitted over existing networks, even via old mail servers. To decode a MIME message, you need a mail client that recognizes MIME headers and formats. Most modern mail clients can deal with MIME formats with no difficulty.

POP3: The Post Office Protocol

The SMTP protocol makes it possible to forward a message to a mail server, or MTA. It does not provide a means to deliver the message to its final destination, that is, the client program (MUA) running on the recipient's workstation. In other words, you can *send* a message to a server via SMTP, but you cannot *request* a message this way. For reading messages stored in a mailbox, another protocol is used; most often, this protocol is POP3.

POP3 is easy to understand. Like SMTP, this protocol can also be used by hand, connecting to a server:

```
$ telnet localhost pop3
Trying 127.0.0.1...
Connected to localhost.
Escape character is '^]'.
+OK POP3 localhost v4.47 server ready
USER vttoth
+OK User name accepted, password please
PASS Secret
+OK Mailbox open, 1 messages
LIST
+OK Mailbox scan listing follows
1 473
.
RETR 1
+OK 473 octets
Return-Path: <vttoth@linux.sys>
Received: from linux.sys (vttoth@localhost [127.0.0.1])
        by linux.sys (8.8.7/8.8.7) with SMTP id RAA00760
        for vttoth@linux.sys; Thu, 25 Feb 1999 17:39:25 -0500
Date: Thu, 25 Feb 1999 17:39:25 -0500
From: "Viktor T. Toth" <vttoth@linux.sys>
Message-Id: <199902252239.RAA00760@linux.sys>
Status:

This is a test message.
.
DELE 1
+OK Message deleted
QUIT
+OK Sayonara
Connection closed by foreign host.
```

Conversations like this are precisely what mail client programs perform when retrieving your mail to a server.

On the Linux side, the POP3 service is implemented by a server application that goes by the name of `ipop3d` or `in.pop3d`, depending on the naming conventions of the Linux distribution used. This server is usually invoked by the Internet superserver, `inetd`; the POP3 server is specified in `/etc/inetd.conf` as the handler for TCP port 110, the standard POP3 port.

POP3 is not the only protocol for accessing mailboxes. Another popular protocol is IMAP, supported by an increasing number of email applications.

Mail Forwarding and Aliases

Often it is necessary to forward mail. For instance, a user might be temporarily away and want to have his mail delivered to a mobile address.

Individual users on Linux can set up mail forwarding by creating a file named `.forward` in their home directory. This file usually consists of a single line that contains the forwarding address.

Another common method for forwarding mail is through the global alias file, usually `/etc/aliases`. This file contains lines such as the following:

```
postmaster:    root
```

This line ensures that any incoming mail addressed to `postmaster` will actually be delivered to the root user's mailbox. The destination does not need to be on the local system, for instance:

```
webmaster:     webmaster@headoffice.org
```

If you change the `/etc/aliases` file, you need to run the command `/usr/bin/newaliases` for the changes to take effect.

UUCP: UNIX to UNIX Copy for Batch Delivery

When you run a sendmail server, it is usually assumed that you have a permanent Internet connection so other sendmail servers can connect to yours to deliver mail, and your server can connect to them to send out outgoing messages.

In many cases in a small office environment, a permanent Internet connection is not practical or cost-effective. However, operating a sendmail server might be desirable because it is reliable, it can act as a mail server for internal email, and it frees you from being dependent on the ISP for the creation and management of mailboxes.

This presents a dilemma. How can a mail server, designed primarily to exchange messages interactively with other servers using the SMTP protocol, operate well in an isolated environment?

First, you can utilize sendmail's capability to pass any messages it cannot locally deliver to a *smart host*. It is so named because it is presumed to be *smarter* than your host, in that it knows how to deliver messages that your copy of sendmail cannot handle.

Second, you can tell sendmail to deliver messages to this smart host via UUCP.

UUCP is a simple mechanism to deliver a batch of files from one host to another. Files are passed to UUCP via uux command, and they usually end up in a spool directory until the uucico command is activated. The actual delivery is performed by uucico, which can dial a remote system via a modem, log on, and communicate with a remote copy of uucico there. After files are transferred, they are processed by the uuxqt program on the destination system (see Figure 8.3).

FIGURE 8.3
File exchange via UUCP.

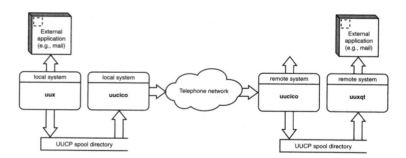

UUCP is not specific to email. It can be used to copy any kind of a file and execute any command on the remote system (as long as the remote system's security settings permit such execution.) When it is mail that is being processed, the rmail command is invoked on the target system; this companion command to UUCP is designed to process remote mail.

The uucico program is usually scheduled to be executed at regular intervals, such as hourly, for example. Delivery of a handful of mail messages usually takes only seconds, leaving the modem line free the rest of the time.

It is also possible to configure UUCP to operate over an existing IP connection. This is especially useful if the modem normally used for UUCP mail delivery is also used to establish an Internet connection. If the Internet connection is up for a long period of time, that would normally prevent the regular flow of mail because uucico would never have a chance to take control of the modem. The capability to operate over an IP connection overcomes this difficulty.

PART

III

CH

8

Configuring sendmail

Mailboxes, protocols, mail client programs; in the center of all this is the sendmail program.

The role of sendmail is simple:

1. Accept incoming mail

2. Process headers and delivery addresses

3. Deliver the message locally, if possible, or

4. Forward the message to a host that can process it

Rulesets

The sendmail program accomplishes these steps by processing a series of *rulesets*. Each ruleset is invoked at a specific stage of message delivery, and each contains a set of rules that tell sendmail how addresses of different types should be handled.

Several rulesets are defined by sendmail internally, and are used for the processing of all mail messages. These are illustrated in Figure 8.4. Their purpose is threefold: processing sender and recipient addresses and selecting a method for delivery.

Each rule in a ruleset performs a specific action. First, sendmail checks whether the address that is being processed matches the current rule. If that is the case, it then performs the action prescribed by the rule. The action can cause the address to be rewritten; it can also select a delivery agent or trigger an error condition.

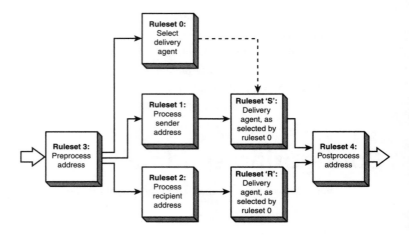

FIGURE 8.4
The core rulesets of sendmail.

The `sendmail.cf` File

Rules are stored in the file `/etc/sendmail.cf`. Rather than creating this file from scratch, you will usually use a copy that was installed along with sendmail as a starting point. Alternatively, sendmail has tools that are used to generate different versions of `/etc/sendmail.cf` using a set of relatively simple macros.

Rules in `sendmail.cf` are written using a syntax that is very powerful but extremely difficult to remember. For instance, here is a rule that causes all addresses from the domain `whitehouse.gov` to be rejected:

```
R$* @ $* . whitehouse . gov   $#error $: "550 Spam Forbidden"
```

Needless to say, each character in the preceding line is significant; even a difference between an invisible space and tab character can completely change the meaning of the rule.

The reason why you should bother to have at least a superficial understanding of rules and rulesets is simple: the `sendmail.cf` file is your best defense against that growing menace on the Internet—unwanted email, or spam.

Using Macro Tools

The `sendmail.cf` file is usually an incomprehensible monster, containing more than a thousand lines of cryptic rules, impossible to understand macro definitions. No one in his right mind would attempt to write this from scratch.

Coming to the rescue is a general-purpose macro language called *m4*. This macro language is available on most UNIX systems (including the Caldera OpenLinux distribution on the attached CD). The purpose of a macro language is very simple: It interprets definitions associated with symbols, and later, whenever a previously defined symbol is encountered, it replaces it with the definition. Here is a simple m4 example:

```
define(text,replacement)
This is some text.
```

Let's feed this file (named `test.m4`) to the m4 program:

```
$ m4 <test.m4

This is some replacement.
```

As you see, the word *text* was replaced with the word *replacement* in the output. It's also possible to eliminate the extra blank line (a placeholder for the line that used to contain the `define` command) in the output by appending the keyword `dnl` (delete through new line):

```
define(text,replacement)dnl
This is some text.
```

This apparent simplicity of the m4 tool is deceptive. All new distributions of sendmail come with a complex set of m4 macro files, many of them several hundred lines in length, which help you automate the creation of large chunks of the `sendmail.cf` file. A fully functional `sendmail.cf` file can in fact be created using only a few lines of macro code. For example, one of the simplest sendmail configurations—a setup for a system that does no local delivery and merely forwards all mail to another host—can be created using only two lines:

```
OSTYPE(`linux')
FEATURE(`nullclient',`mail.provider.net')
```

(The address `mail.provider.net` should of course be replaced with the actual address of the mail host that handles forwarded mail.) To use this file to create a `sendmail.cf` file, type the following:

```
m4 /usr/share/sendmail/cf/m4/cf.m4 null.mc >sendmail.cf
```

This line invokes the m4 macro processor with `cf.m4` and `null.mc` as inputs; the output is sent to `sendmail.cf`. Note that the actual location of `cf.m4` (a macro file that contains all the definitions necessary to build a `sendmail.cf` file) may vary; the location used here is standard for Caldera OpenLinux 1.3.

While using an m4 macro file is still not exactly simple, it's far less baffling than the raw `sendmail.cf` syntax. Distributions of sendmail also contain many sample m4 macro files (usually identifiable by the `.mc` extension) that can be used as a starting point for creating your own file.

Message Filtering

As mentioned earlier, one of the key reasons why you should bother with customizing `sendmail.cf` is to control unwanted email.

Why control spam in the first place? Above and beyond the annoyance factor, and arguments about the right to free speech notwithstanding, there are several very important reasons to curtail spam if your system enjoys a permanent connection to the Internet.

First, spam can represent a significant load on your system. Depending on the number of users you have and the amount of email they usually get, even a relatively small system can be the target of several hundred spam messages a day.

The second reason is far more serious. The sendmail program and the underlying SMTP protocol offer no built-in security model; a sendmail server by default accepts mail from anyone and delivers mail to arbitrary addresses without restriction.

This feature is used by spam artists on a daily basis. Rather than operating a powerful mail server of their own along with a high-speed Internet connection, they connect to *your* unsecured mail server, pass to it a *single* copy of the message they want to send out along with a delivery list containing thousands, even hundreds of thousands of recipients, and then leave. Your poor little mail server will then spend the next several hours, possibly days, resolving thousands of addresses and delivering copies of the message to thousands of remote hosts. It'll then continue with the processing of thousands of rejection messages that are returned because of bad addresses, spam-rejecting hosts, or other reasons. If it happens on a Friday evening, by the time the problem catches your attention, your mail server is hopelessly overloaded, legitimate mail not only isn't delivered but may become lost altogether, and you won't even be able to resolve the problem by logging in from a remote machine—the mail server's Internet connection is overloaded as well.

And yes, in case you were wondering, spam artists do know that your server is out there. They may not know much about computers, the Internet, or SMTP, but they know how to operate programs that search the global DNS database and contact mail servers around the world to check for hosts that can *relay* messages.

So rather than having a ticking time bomb sitting in your server, why not prevent spam in the first place?

Newer versions of sendmail actually offer a neat way to accomplish this. These versions define two special rulesets: check_mail and check_rcpt. These rules are invoked when a remote host connects to your sendmail server and sends its MAIL FROM: and RCPT TO: commands. In other words, these rules can be used to prevent spam *before* it occurs, as opposed to moving spam messages to a discard folder after the fact.

Utilizing these rulesets, it is possible to define rules that perform the following:

1. Reject messages coming from a known spam host
2. Reject messages coming from a known spam sender
3. Reject messages relayed through a known spam relay host
4. Reject messages coming from an outside host if the recipient is outside of the local system as well (relaying)

These rules, if properly implemented, can save you a lot of trouble later on. In fact, in this day and age anyone running an unprotected sendmail server on a permanent Internet connection is inviting disaster; it's not a question of if, but a question of when. The next section contains, among other things, sample additions to sendmail.cf that implement minimal filtering behavior.

> **NOTE**   The latest versions of sendmail (version 8.9 or later, not included on the attached CD-ROM) further simplify relay filtering. For more information, visit the following Web page: http://www.sendmail.org/tips/relaying.html.

TEST SYSTEM   Configuring the Test System

When I installed sendmail along with other components using the Caldera OpenLinux installer, a usable sendmail.cf file was installed along with it as /etc/sendmail.cf. *As is*, this file already provided for a sendmail configuration that was capable of delivering mail locally and exchanging mail with remote servers. However, I was not satisfied with this result; I wanted a sendmail configuration that also provided protection against the most dangerous form of spamming, the relaying of unwanted mail.

▼

▼   The test system was configured to operate even when not permanently connected to the Internet. For this reason, I wanted a sendmail configuration that allowed delivery via UUCP.

With these goals in mind, I began by activating the sendmail server.

Activating sendmail

When the Caldera OpenLinux installation program installs sendmail, you might not have configured it to start automatically. (In fact, it's probably a good idea not to let it start automatically before it is fully configured in order to avoid a potential security risk.) To configure auto-starting sendmail, you need to use the LISA utility. Make sure you're the root user, and type the following:

```
lisa —system
```

This takes you directly to the LISA System Configuration menu, where you can select the Configure daemon/server Autostart option. The next screen lists all system services that can be started automatically; make sure that there's an X next to the Mail Transfer Agent (sendmail) option (see Figure 8.5).

FIGURE 8.5
Selecting sendmail for automatic start.

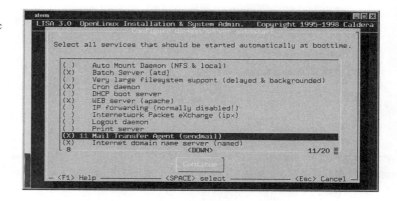

The new setting will take effect after the system is rebooted. Alternatively, you can start sendmail manually using the following command line (as the root user, of course):

```
/usr/sbin/sendmail -bd -q5m
```

If sendmail is operating, it should show up in the process list, for example

```
$ ps axu ¦ grep sendmail
root    1831  0.0  1.1  1272  720  ?   S   23:22  0:00 sendmail: accepting c
```
▼

▼ I was also able test sendmail by connecting to the SMTP port on the local machine using telnet, as shown earlier in this chapter.

Creating `sendmail.cf`

Having proven that sendmail works, I set out to create my own version of the configuration file, `sendmail.cf`, or rather, an m4 macro file from which the `sendmail.cf` file can be automatically generated. Here is the result of some experimentation:

```
OSTYPE(linux)dnl
define(`HELP_FILE',`/usr/share/sendmail/sendmail.hf')
define(`STATUS_FILE',`/var/log/sendmail.st')
define(`SMART_HOST',uucp-dom:mcp)
MASQUERADE_AS(`linux.sys')
FEATURE(always_add_domain)
FEATURE(local_procmail, `/usr/bin/procmail')
FEATURE(masquerade_envelope)
FEATURE(nocanonify)
FEATURE(nodns)
FEATURE(smrsh,`/usr/sbin/smrsh')
MAILER(local)
MAILER(smtp)
MAILER(uucp)
```

The first line is mandatory; the OSTYPE macro defines the basic characteristic of the operating system on which this configuration file will be used. The next two lines define file locations as per the standard Caldera OpenLinux distribution.

The fourth line is very important: it defines a *smart host*—a host to which all email that cannot be delivered locally will be forwarded. In effect, this fourth line tells sendmail that when processing an incoming message, it should attempt to deliver the message locally. If that cannot be done, regardless of the identity of the recipient, sendmail should forward the message to the system named mcp using UUCP, and let that system deal with it. Note that such a smart host is only required because I connect via UUCP. If you're running a server with a full-time Internet connection, no smart host is needed.

The fifth line is also an important configuration option. It tells sendmail to *masquerade* as linux.sys for all messages that originate on the local network, even if they come from different machines. So for instance, if Gary the receptionist sits in front of a machine named reception.linux.sys, his email will appear to come from gary@linux.sys, and not gary@reception.linux.sys.

▼

▼   The next several lines turn on a variety of features. Here is a brief description of each:

always_add_domain. When an address doesn't contain the full domain name (for example, vttoth@host instead of vttoth@host.linux.sys), it will be added, even if the message containing the address is delivered locally.

local_procmail. Messages will be delivered locally using the procmail program, a very useful and highly configurable utility that users can use to automate the processing of incoming mail (see man procmail for details).

masquerade_envelope. Normally, the MASQUERADE_AS option (see earlier in this section) masquerades addresses that appear in message headers (the From: field) but not during the actual mail delivery (for example, in the MAIL FROM: command during the SMTP conversation, shown earlier in this chapter). This option ensures that masquerading takes place even during delivery.

Nocanonify. This option is sometimes useful to prevent sendmail from adding an incorrect domain name part to a hostname in an address.

Nodns. This option prevents sendmail from looking up hostnames using DNS (Domain Name System). On the test system, this is important because the system has no permanent Internet connection. Instead, connection is established when needed by the diald auto-dialer daemon. Attempts by sendmail to perform DNS lookup would trigger the auto-dialer every time an outgoing message is processed, just so that the recipient's address can be resolved.

Smrsh. Sometimes, sendmail can *deliver* a message by passing it to an executable program for processing. This option ensures that when this happens, sendmail invokes the *sendmail restricted shell*, or smrsh, instead of the default shell program. This is a highly recommended security feature.

This file, which I named linuxsys.mc, can be used to generate a fresh copy of sendmail.cf using the following command:

```
m4 /usr/share/sendmail/cf/m4/cf.m4 linuxsys.mc >/etc/sendmail.cf
```

Needless to say, before doing this I first created a backup copy of the original version of /etc/sendmail.cf, just in case.

If the file was processed by m4 without problems, sendmail can be restarted:

```
$ killall sendmail
$ /usr/sbin/sendmail -bd -q5m
```

The sendmail program also posts messages to the system log. On Caldera OpenLinux systems, these appear in /var/log/mail. After restarting sendmail, I found the following line appearing at the end of this file:

```
Mar  7 21:59:43 host sendmail[1344]: starting daemon (8.8.7):
SMTP+ququein
g@00:05:00
```
▼

▼   This is yet another indication that sendmail has been capable of processing `/etc/send-mail.cf` and runs healthy.

Adding Rules to Prevent Spam

Although I have replaced the default `sendmail.cf` file with one of my own creation, I have not yet achieved either of my objectives. UUCP delivery doesn't work because I haven't configured UUCP yet. I also haven't added any rules to prevent spam. I decided to deal with this problem first. (Incidentally, the solution presented here is more appropriate on systems that do not use UUCP at all; when delivery is made via UUCP, these spam filtering rules will not work very well.)

As it turns out, although I am adding actual rules to my sendmail configuration, there's still no need to edit `/etc/sendmail.cf` directly. These rules can be appended to my m4 configuration file. Starting with the file developed in the previous section, I added the following lines:

```
LOCAL_CONFIG

Scheck_rcpt

# Anything terminating locally is OK
R< $* >                      $1
R$*                          $: $>3 $1
R$* < @ $+ . > $*            $1 <@ $2> $3
R$+ < @ $=w >                $@ OK
# Anything originating locally is OK
R$*                          $: $(dequote "" $&{client_name} $)
R$=w                         $@ OK
R$@                          $@ OK
# Anything else is bogus
R$*                          $#error $: "550 Relaying Denied"
```

The `LOCAL_CONFIG` symbol tells the macro processor that any lines that follow must be added to the output file without change.

The `Scheck_rcpt` command is a sendmail configuration command used to define a rule. The `check_rcpt` rule is invoked by sendmail immediately after it receives the `RCPT TO:` command during an SMTP session, allowing it to not simply reject a message, but to prevent its delivery altogether.

The actual rules transform the address to a standard format and compare it with the address from which the sender is connecting to you. If the recipient address is on your
▼   local system, you accept the mail. If the sender system is on your local network, you

▼   accept the mail. However, if both are outside of your network, this is likely an illegal *relaying* attempt, someone trying to use your mail server to send mail to third-party recipients; such messages will be rejected with the Relaying Denied error message.

Similar rules can be built to reject messages from specific hosts or senders, for instance. It is possible to maintain a simple database of known violators and reject any messages originating from them or from systems under their control. However, these you can live without; on the other hand, if your system has a permanent Internet connection, you simply cannot live without a filter configuration that prevents mail relaying. If you do, it's only a matter of time before you're discovered by a spammer; one morning you're liable to find a severely overloaded server processing a junk mail message with a recipient list containing thousands of addresses, and also thousands of angry replies from offended recipients around the world who think that the message originated on your system.

Needless to say, it is also possible to modify the rules so that relaying is accepted for specific hosts for whom you intend to provide a third-party mail delivery service. For more information on this complex subject, visit the sendmail Web site (http://www.sendmail.org). It contains information on the latest sendmail distribution and many ideas on adjusting your configuration files to make your system as robust and flexible as possible.

Configuring UUCP Delivery

When I installed Caldera OpenLinux, I specified UUCP as one of the components. Consequently, I found a working copy of the so-called *Taylor UUCP* package on my test system. What I needed is a set of configuration files to make this copy of UUCP functional. On Caldera OpenLinux, the location of these files is the /etc/uucp directory.

The first configuration file is named config, and it contains a single line:

```
nodename linuxsys
```

This line defines the *UUCP name* of my test system.

The second file is called sys, and it contains a description of each remote system that my copy of UUCP knows about. In my case, it contains a definition for a single system named mcp:

```
system mcp
time Any 1
speed 38400
port modem
phone *70,,5551212
```
▼

▼
```
chat "" \p\p\p\r\c ogin: \p\L word: \P :~$ /usr/lib/uucp/uucico
chat-timeout 90
chat-fail BUSY
call-login vttoth
call-password Secret
max-retries 999
```

These lines tell UUCP that the system mcp is available on telephone number 555-1212, using a port named modem. They provide a chat transcript for logging on to the system and starting UUCP there; and they provide the login name, password, and other parameters.

The port parameter is actually a pointer into the third file, unsurprisingly named port:

```
port modem
device cua1
dialer modem
port modem
type pipe
command /usr/bin/rlogin -E -8 -l vttoth mcp.com
```

The first three lines are fairly straightforward. They specify that the port we called modem is actually on device cua1. The dialer parameter is a pointer into the fourth configuration file, named (surprise) dialer. But before we get to that, let's take a closer look at the second set of three lines.

These lines together implement the capability to perform UUCP delivery even when the modem is in use, maintaining an Internet connection. In that case, dialing out on the modem will fail because the modem is busy. That's when UUCP will turn to the alternative connection, which simply uses the rlogin program to log on to the remote system (mcp.com, the same system we can reach using the telephone number 555-1212) and perform UUCP delivery over the Internet connection.

There are other ways to accomplish UUCP over an Internet connection; the beauty of this otherwise kludgy solution is that it requires little cooperation on behalf of the service provider. As long as they provide UUCP, and as long as the login sequence on their system is the same whether you're using a dial-up connection or connecting via telnet/rlogin, this solution will likely work.

The last configuration file is called dialer and it contains instructions for dialing over a modem:

```
dialer modem
chat "" ATZ OK ATE0 OK ATDT\D CONNECT
chat-timeout 60
```
▼

▼   The first line defines the name of this dialing sequence (modem); this is the name by which the sequence was referred to in the port file. The second line defines the actual dialing sequence; the third line defines a timeout value, which will cause the dialing to fail if no connection is established after this many seconds have elapsed.

Before this configuration became useful I needed to perform one additional small change to my system:

```
chmod 6555 /usr/sbin/uucico
chown root.uucp /dev/cua1
chmod 0660 /etc/cua1
```

Together, these commands ensure that the uucico command runs under the uucp group identifier, and that the port /dev/cua1 is owned by this group. This guarantees that uucico will actually be able to take control of the port.

Time to test this configuration. To do so, I first created a mail message addressed to an outside recipient. Then I was able to verify with the uustat command that the mail was spooled properly:

```
$ mail vttoth@mcp.com
Subject: Test
Test message.
.
EOT
$ uustat -a
vttoth.CIowFyfAABKU vttoth bin 03-08 04:14 Executing rmail vttoth@mcp.com
(sending 389 bytes)
```

Next, the actual delivery. I invoked UUCP as follows:

```
/usr/sbin/uucico -Smcp
```

Subsequently I heard the modem dial, and within a few seconds, the UUCP queue was empty; soon after, I was able to verify that the message arrived at the destination.

One question remains. Obviously, I don't want to invoke UUCP by hand every time I want to have a message delivered or check for messages on the remote system. How can this be automated?

The answer lies with the crontab utility. This utility allows you to schedule the execution of commands at configurable times. As root, you can edit the UUCP crontab by typing the following:

▼
```
crontab -e -u uucp
```

▼ This opens the vi editor with the existing crontab for UUCP or a new blank file, if no
such crontab existed.

The crontab I used contained the following lines:

```
MAILTO=postmaster
5,20,35,50 * * * * /usr/sbin/uucico -r1
19 * * * * /usr/sbin/touch /var/spool/uucp/vttoth/C./C.vttothA0000
```

The first of these lines specifies that if any errors are encountered during execution of the
scheduled commands, mail is sent to `postmaster` (usually an alias that points to the system administrator's email address). The second line ensures that `uucico` is invoked four
times an hour to check if there's anything that needs to be delivered. However, with this
line alone, `uucico` will not dial unless there's outgoing mail; in other words, it won't
check for incoming mail all by itself. That is forced by the third line, which creates a *poll
file* once an hour; when uucico finds such a poll file, it will check for incoming mail
▲ even if no outgoing messages are waiting to be processed.

Summary

Because email is the most popular Internet service today, running a mail server is one of
the primary tasks of the system administrator. The most popular mail server is the widely
used sendmail program, which is powerful and robust but difficult to configure.

Email is created using a Mail User Agent (MUA). It is transferred to one or more Mail
Transfer Agents (MTAs) and in the end, it is viewed using another MUA. Throughout
this process, a variety of standards are used that provide common file and message formats, delivery protocols, and more.

The most important of these standards include SMTP (the Simple Mail Transfer
Protocol), which is used to deliver a message to an MTA; POP3, used by MUAs to
retrieve messages; and RFC-822 and MIME, which defines common message formats.

For systems not permanently connected to the Internet, use of the standard protocol used
for mail delivery, SMTP, might not be practical. An alternative is UUCP (UNIX to UNIX
copy) that allows for the batched background delivery of mail messages. UUCP delivery
can be performed over modem lines or over Internet connections, which makes it possible to use the same modem for both. If the Internet connection is active, UUCP delivery
will take place over that connection; otherwise UUCP will use the modem to connect
directly to the server.

The sendmail server can be configured using the `sendmail.cf` file. This file is a container for rulesets, which govern mail processing and delivery. However, rulesets are notoriously difficult to write and maintain; for this reason, helper tools are provided that make it possible to create rulesets using a small set of relatively simple macros.

The `sendmail.cf` file can be used to define custom rules used to prevent delivery of unwanted email. On systems with a permanent Internet connection, it is essential to block unwanted *mail relaying*, because junk mail operators often hijack unprotected mail servers for the delivery of their messages to a large number of recipients.

Manual Pages

For additional information on topics discussed in this chapter, please refer to the following manual pages.

```
man aliases

man makemap

man procmail

man sendmail

man uucico

man uucp

man uustat

man uux

man uuxqt
```

Mailing Lists and Newsgroups

Regular email allows users to communicate one on one with each other. Often, another method of communication is desired, such as a discussion group.

Two of the most widely used methods for implementing discussion groups are mailing lists and newsgroups. Mailing lists work like regular email; a special email address is used as an alias for members of the group, and any mail sent to this address is distributed to all group members. Newsgroup messages, however, are usually not copied for each user, but stored on a server that authorized users can access with appropriate client software.

Both methods have advantages and pitfalls; and both can be configured with relative ease on a Linux server.

NOTE	Another increasingly popular method to maintain discussion groups is to do so through a Web-based interface. To use this method, you must be operating a Web server or, alternatively, have access to a Web server that allows you to run server-side scripts. Also popular are chat facilities, but these, too, require dedicated server software.

Mailing Lists

The purpose of a mailing list is to provide a list address as a valid email address, and ensure that all mail sent to this address is rerouted to every member of the list.

The apparent simplicity of this task is deceptive. Except for the smallest of private mailing lists, many added requirements exist to ensure that the mailing list can be managed securely and efficiently.

Some of the most commonly found requirements are

1. The capability for users to "sign up" automatically
2. Verification of a user's identity (by sending him email and requiring a response) before adding the address to the list
3. Approval of new users by the list administrator prior to adding them to the mailing lists
4. The capability to "moderate" the list (that is, approve messages prior to distribution)

Mailing lists can be set up in a variety of ways, satisfying different needs. It should come as no surprise that the simplest solutions are also the least flexible ones, with the most serious potential security problems.

Using the .forward File

Every UNIX user can have a file, named .forward, in his home directory. If it exists, this file controls how mail to that user is delivered. The .forward file is typically used to maintain a forwarding address for users that are temporarily away and want to receive mail on another system.

> **NOTE**   The .forward file, like all files with names that begin with a period, is *hidden*, in that it does not appear in normal directory listings. To view all files, including hidden files, in your directory, use the ls -a command.

That said, the contents of the `.forward` file are not restricted to a single email address. It can contain an arbitrary number of text lines, each containing a valid address, providing an instant method for the creation of a mailing list. The `.forward` address can reside in the home directory of a valid user (turning his email address into a list address), or you can create a fictitious user just for this purpose.

Unfortunately, this approach has several shortcomings. First, the list must be managed by hand; users need to be added or removed by editing the `.forward` file. Second, it is not possible to "moderate" the list; messages sent to the list address are forwarded unconditionally. Third, this method is very inefficient, and may cause a severe load on your system if the list is large, or if several mailing lists are managed. Lastly, the method offers no security; anyone who's aware of the list address can send mail to the list, including unsolicited junk mail and other unwanted messages.

Using `/etc/aliases`

Using the global alias file, `/etc/aliases`, is a variant of the method presented in the previous section. Rather than forwarding a specific user's mail to a list of addresses, you can create an alias name for the list by placing a line similar to the following in `/etc/aliases`:

```
bigguys: president@whitehouse.gov,linus@linux.org,billg@microsoft.com
```

> **NOTE** When you edit `/etc/aliases`, you must run the `newaliases` command for the changes to take effect.

If you are using this method, the mailing list can only be changed by the administrator(s) who has write access to `/etc/aliases`. Depending on your circumstances, this may be a good thing. The `/etc/aliases` file is also processed a bit more efficiently than the `.forward` files of individual users. Beyond that, this method retains the same shortcomings as using the `.forward` file—it has no means to moderate the list or automate the adding or removal of list members.

List Manager Programs

When a mailing list is large, or when specific security or list management requirements exist, it might be appropriate to use software developed specifically for this purpose, such as mailing list managers.

PART
III

CH
9

One of the most widely used mailing list manager programs is called *Majordomo*. Developed by Great Circle Associates, this excellent package can be downloaded free of charge from the Internet. A recent version of it is also available on the CD-ROM attached to this book.

The idea behind Majordomo, like the idea behind all list manager programs, is simple. For each known mailing list, the list manager maintains a list of subscribers. Incoming messages are distributed to the list subscribers, and certain administrative features are provided.

These administrative features include the following:

- Changing of message headers, for instance hiding certain header fields to protect the identity of senders, or adding a Reply To field to make it easier to send replies to the list

- Providing a means to subscribe to or unsubscribe from the list automatically (with or without list operator approval)

- Providing a means to moderate the list by sending all incoming messages to designated moderator addresses

- Optionally restricting the list to accept incoming messages only from its members, or only from designated users (for example, an announcement list.)

Configuring a list server package is a moderately difficult task. The main steps include

1. Unpacking and setting up the list server software

2. Creating a configuration file

3. Updating and changing the main mail server's (sendmail's) configuration if necessary

4. Creating lists and list aliases

5. Editing and testing list configurations

The relative complexity of these steps is offset by the advantages of using a separate software-based mailing list, such as its capability to automatically manage subscriptions or its improved security.

Newsgroups

Mailing lists have many advantages but also one key shortcoming: each and every message is delivered to each and every list user in its entirety. When the list is small or messages are few, this is rarely a problem. With large, popular lists, however, thousands of messages can be generated daily, causing a significant drain on the resources of the system processing the list, not to mention the list users' mailboxes!

With such large lists, it doesn't make sense to deliver all messages to all users. After all, chances are that most users won't read the majority of the messages, they'll probably only skim the headers. So even if your server has the capacity to process the list, why overload their mailboxes?

The alternative to mailing lists is the use of newsgroups. This is actually old technology; newsgroups were popular long before the advent of the World Wide Web. Usenet is a global collection of 20,000-plus newsgroups, and is in constant use today, generating several gigabytes worth of daily traffic. Many other privately maintained newsgroups exist, some used internally and others offered by companies as a means of customer support.

Basic Concepts

One way to look at a newsgroup is to treat it as a "community mailbox." When regular email is delivered to your account, it is deposited into your mailbox and later retrieved by your mail client program. If only you could make your mailbox readable by others, you wouldn't need a mailing list; you'd just tell others how to access the mailbox, and presto! Everybody would be able to read its contents.

Of course, a mailbox isn't exactly suitable for this purpose because, for instance, it allows anyone with access to it to delete messages. For a community mailbox, or bulletin board, you don't want that capability. Even if erasing messages is permitted, it should only be possible by the author of the message and, perhaps, by the administrator.

Newsgroups have been invented precisely to overcome these limitations of mailboxes.

Next to email, newsgroups are the oldest service on the Internet. In fact, just like email, newsgroup technology predates the modern Internet. Also just like email, newsgroups can be delivered using alternative delivery methods, such as UUCP, to remote sites. That's why Usenet newsgroups find their way even to remotely located universities and organizations (for instance, in the third world), which still do not enjoy full Internet access.

A Guided Tour

To the end user, newsgroup messages don't look very different from email. The main difference is that newsgroup messages are addressed not to individuals, but to newsgroups (in this sense, the newsgroup name operates like a mailing list name). Often the same client program is used to access mailboxes and newsgroups (for example, Microsoft Outlook Express for Windows users).

Newsgroups are typically organized into hierarchies, with a naming convention similar to Internet host and domain names. The main difference in appearance is that in newsgroup names, the highest level of the hierarchy, come first; Internet names are the other way around. For instance, the Linux newsgroup under the operating system hierarchy under the general computing section of Usenet is called `comp.os.linux.name`, not `name.linux.os.comp`.

When you run a news program, it usually starts by downloading the list of newsgroups available on the server to which you are connecting. This procedure, however, is not repeated every time for a very obvious reason: Servers that carry a reasonably complete set of the Usenet newsgroups used worldwide might have as many as 30,000 newsgroups, so even the list of newsgroups can be several megabytes in length. Rather than downloading the entire list, the news program checks whether any new newsgroups have appeared on the server.

When you select one of the newsgroups, your news client program downloads a list of messages in that group from the server. When you select an individual message, the client downloads and displays the entire message. Most client programs maintain a local *cache* of downloaded messages to avoid downloading the same message repeatedly.

A message can appear in multiple newsgroups. This is called *cross-posting*. (Note that it is considered bad form—bad *netiquette*—to post a message to an excessive number of newsgroups.) It is very important to understand that cross-posting is not the same as placing a separate copy of the same message to several newsgroups! When you cross-post, only one copy of your message exists on the server, it is merely cross-referenced from multiple groups. This allows intelligent news clients to mark a message as read even if the user only reads it in another newsgroup, thereby saving readers the trouble and annoyance of having to read the same message multiple times, as they browse different newsgroups.

Public newsgroups should be used for their intended purpose. For instance, comp.os.linux.hardware exists for the exchange of information or asking questions about hardware, not for advertising your new Web site dedicated to the care and feeding of Siberian tigers. This is true no matter how important the message might be or what your thoughts are about the constitutionally protected right of free speech! After all, free speech doesn't mean you're allowed to interfere with a public television signal, for instance, even if the message you broadcast, overriding a local channel, is of great public importance. Sadly, not everyone realizes this, and many public newsgroups are littered with irrelevant messages, offensive advertising, and worse.

Servers and Messages

Newsgroup messages *propagate* around the world because participating servers exchange messages continuously. When you configure a news server, you specify which other servers it is in contact with and what kinds of messages are exchanged. For instance, if you run a local server with all Usenet newsgroups in the comp.os hierarchy, you'd specify comp.os.* as the set of newsgroups that you would exchange with your Internet service provider (ISP). On the other hand, you might specifically want to exclude all local.* newsgroups to avoid private newsgroups from being sent out to the Internet. However, if your company has a branch office, and that office has its own news server, you'd want to exchange local newsgroups with them (see Figure 9.1). The possibilities are endless.

FIGURE 9.1
Newsgroup propagation.

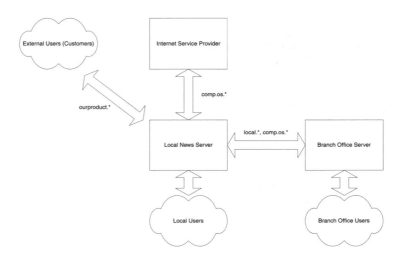

Public Versus Private Newsgroups

Given the sheer volume of messages on Usenet, nowadays it makes little sense to operate a large news server with many Usenet newsgroups, unless you're an ISP, or operate a large corporate site with hundreds or thousands of users. The traffic alone (several gigabytes a day) would require an Internet connection that's faster than what most of us can afford.

Sometimes, however, you might still want to maintain a small set of Usenet newsgroups on your server. For instance, if your site doesn't have a permanent Internet connection and your users have a very focused set of needs, you may want to maintain a local copy of a few hundred newsgroups. For example, a company that works in the fields of Web application development might maintain its local copy of the newsgroups in the comp.infosystems.www hierarchy.

That said, the main reason why you would want to operate your own news server is likely not to become part of Usenet, but to provide newsgroups either internally or externally (for example, for product support).

Examples abound. For instance, InstallShield Corporation, the maker of a well-known Windows software installation tool, has a news server at news.installshield.com with several dozen support newsgroups. Microsoft Corporation also operates public newsgroups, as well as private groups utilized by its products' beta testers. Although many privately maintained online discussion groups are now Web-based, newsgroup technology remains a popular choice.

Servers, Clients, and NNTP

News clients must be capable of communicating with news servers, which, in turn, must also be capable of communicating with each other to exchange newsgroup messages. As it turns out, a single protocol is used for both purposes: NNTP, the Network News Transfer Protocol.

Like many other Internet protocols, NNTP uses human-readable commands and responses. Therefore, it is possible to use the Telnet utility to connect to an NNTP server, and perform an NNTP conversation manually to get an idea what NNTP is like:

```
$ telnet nntp.uunet.ca nntp
Trying 142.77.1.198...
Connected to demon.uunet.ca.
Escape character is '^]'.
200 nntp.uunet.ca InterNetNews NNRP server INN 1.5.1 17-Dec-1996 ready
(posting ok).
```

```
mode reader
200 nntp.uunet.ca InterNetNews NNRP server INN 1.5.1 17-Dec-1996 ready
(posting ok).
group comp.os.linux.announce
211 87 12998 13084 comp.os.linux.announce
article 13084
220 13084 <pycola.922833764.10248@revelation.bak.helsinki.fi> article
    article body appeared here
.
quit
205 .
Connection closed by foreign host.
```

PART

III

CH

9

Notice the use of the `mode reader` command; this is how a news client tells the server that it's a client, not another news server that exchanges messages with this one in bulk.

Knowledge of the NNTP protocol is not required when you're setting up, configuring, or using a news server. This information can be helpful, however, if you're trying to troubleshoot a configuration. You may be able to verify whether a server is working by connecting to it with Telnet and executing simple commands.

Newsgroups and Articles

Under most UNIX news servers, newsgroups are represented by subdirectories under a directory specifically reserved for this purpose. For instance, the newsgroups `comp.os.linux.announce` would be represented by the directory `/var/spool/news/articles/comp/os/linux/announce`. Each individual news message is stored in a separate file under the directory of the group to which it belongs.

News articles can be cross-posted. Modern UNIX news servers do not store multiple copies of a message that is posted to multiple groups. Instead, they use the UNIX file system's capability to *link* a file (that is, have more than one directory entry point to the same file). This is a space-saving measure that can make a significant difference on large servers.

News Server Configuration

One of the best and most popular news server packages for Linux is INN, the InterNetNews server. This server is also widely used by ISPs.

Obviously, the first step to setting up a news server is installing the software. If you're using Caldera OpenLinux from the CD-ROM that accompanies this book, the INN package can be installed along with other components during setup. If your Linux distribution doesn't contain a copy of INN, or if you want to install a more recent version, you might need to download the package from the Internet. The Internet home of INN is at the Internet Software Consortium Web site, located at `http://www.isc.org/`.

The next step involves creating or modifying configuration files. The files that absolutely must be edited are as follows:

`inn.conf`	General configuration options
`nnrp.access`	Who gets to read or post what
`newsfeeds`	Where news is coming from and going to

Depending on how your system is set up, these files may be found in `/etc/news`, `/usr/lib/news`, or `/var/lib/news`.

You must also create two special newsgroups. The `control` newsgroup contains special messages related to newsgroup management (for example, messages that instruct the server to create a newsgroup or delete an article), whereas the `junk` newsgroup is a depository for erroneous or rejected messages.

Lastly, you must use the appropriate tools to create the `active` and `history` files. The former lists all newsgroups that this server manages; the latter contains information about messages posted to this server.

TEST SYSTEM   Test System Example

On my test system, I set up the INN news server with two local newsgroups, one of which was made accessible to external sites (`linux.news`). This simulates a real-life situation where an organization would operate a news server for both internal discussions groups and for groups used to disseminate information to external users.

The INN package was already installed on my test system because I selected this package during initial setup. Thus I was able to immediately proceed and configure the package. (If you're using Caldera OpenLinux from the attached CD-ROM but haven't installed INN during setup, you can run `lisa —pkginstall` to install additional components.)

First, I located the INN configuration files. On Caldera OpenLinux, these are placed into the `/etc/news` directory. Here, I first created `inn.conf`:

▼
```
cp inn.conf.sample inn.conf
```

▼ I then edited the file and modified the following entries in it:

```
organization:          A Linux test site
server:                 host.linux.sys
pathhost:
domain:                 linux.sys
mailcmd:                /usr/libexec/inn/innmail
pathnews:               /var/spool/news
pathbin:                /usr/libexec/inn
pathfilter:             /usr/libexec/inn/filter
pathdb:                 /etc/news
```

All other entries remained at their default setting.

I also edited the `nnrp.access` file (first creating a backup copy, which I named `nnrp.access-orig`.) My version only contained three lines:

```
*:: -no- : -no- :!*
*.linux.sys:RP:::*
*:RP:::linux.news
```

The first line specifies that by default, no one has read or write access to articles on this server. The second line ensures that hosts within the (local) domain `linux.sys` can access all newsgroups on the server. The last line identifies the newsgroup `linux.news` as a public newsgroup, that is, one that can be accessed for both reading and writing from any host on the Internet.

I also created a `newsfeeds` file:

```
ME:*::
myisp:*,!local.*,!linux.*,!junk*:Tf,Wnb:
```

The first line defines the local site. The second line identifies the set of newsgroups that I exchange with the (hypothetical) ISP named `myisp`. This line *excludes* the newsgroups `local.*`, `linux.*`, and `junk`. The first two are excluded because they are local to this site and should not be propagated to the ISP; the third one is an administrative group that is local by definition.

In effect, this means that, if I set up other newsgroups on my server (for example, `comp.os.linux.announce`), messages posted to these groups would be forwarded to my ISP. Because I am configuring this system to exchange mail and news articles using UUCP, the actual act of forwarding would be performed by the `send-uucp` command

▼ invoked at regular intervals.

▼   Then I actually create the newsgroups themselves:

```
cd /var/spool/news/articles
mkdir linux
mkdir linux/news
mkdir local
mkdir local/news
mkdir junk
mkdir control
```

Note that the only newsgroups that you absolutely *must* create are the control and junk groups; everything else is subject to your local configuration needs.

Before proceeding any further, I made sure that all the newly created/modified files were owned by the news account and group:

```
chown news.news /etc/news/inn.conf
chown news.news /etc/news/nnrp.access
chown news.news /etc/news/newsfeeds
chown -R news.news /var/spool/news/articles
```

The next step was to create the active file. The makeactive tool locates all subdirectories in the designated newsgroup directory hierarchy and uses them to create a list in the required format:

```
makeactive >/etc/news/active
```

It was also necessary to modify this file by hand because makeactive assumes that every subdirectory it finds actually represents a newsgroup. In reality, some directories are merely the parent directories for other newsgroups; for instance, on this server, I have a linux.news newsgroup, but no linux newsgroup. Hence, I had to edit the active file to read as follows:

```
linux 0000000000 0000000001 n
linux.news 0000000000 0000000001 y
local 0000000000 0000000001 n
local.news 0000000000 0000000001 y
junk 0000000000 0000000001 y
control 0000000000 0000000001 y
```

Notice that I changed the flag (the last character on the line) for the linux and local newsgroup lines. An alternative would have been to remove these lines from the active file.

The last step was to create the history file:

▼   `makehistory -f history`

▼   Again, it's a good idea to ensure that these new files are owned by the news account:

```
chown news.news /etc/news/active
chown news.news /etc/news/history*
```

Next, I started the server. If all goes well, the following command will do the trick:

```
/usr/libexec/inn/rc.news
```

This command might take several minutes to execute, mainly because it waits periods of time in excess of 60 seconds to ensure that all news server components have started up successfully.

When rc.news returns, there should be a process named innd running (to verify, type ps axu ¦ grep inn.) Also, check whether the server is running by attempting to telnet to the NNTP port. If the server is working fine, I should see something like this:

```
# telnet localhost nntp
Trying 127.0.0.1...
Connected to localhost.
Escape character is '^]'.
200 host.linux.sys InterNetNews server INN 2.1 24-Jul-1998 ready
```

If the server did *not* start correctly, examine the log file /var/log/news.all. This file may indicate the cause of the problem.

If all is well, configure INN to start automatically. To do so, I invoked the LISA utility with the -system command-line switch, selected the Configure daemon/server autostart, and made sure that the News Server item is checked (see Figure 9.2). This ensured that after reboot the news server would be fired up automatically.

FIGURE 9.2
Configuring INN for auto-start.

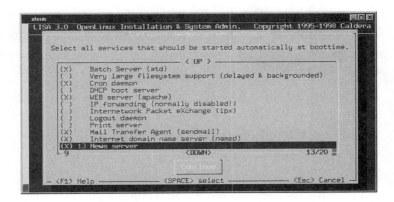

▲

Managing the Server

Once the server is up and running, you rarely need to modify its configuration. Sometimes, however, it may be necessary to make some changes.

The most important tool used for managing INN is the ctlinnd program. With this program, you can start and stop the server, or perform many server management tasks.

It is very important to remember that INN does not like it when you edit its configuration files while it is running. For instance, editing the active file while the server is running guarantees a near certain disaster. The reason is that the server does not reload the contents of this file automatically, rather, it actually writes to the file at character positions it remembers. If the file's layout changes (for instance, if you insert a new newsgroup), the next time INN updates the file, entries will appear at the wrong position, rendering the file dysfunctional.

To edit these files, you must temporarily suspend, or throttle, the server:

```
ctlinnd throttle reason
```

The *reason* parameter is an arbitrary text string. Newsreader programs may display this text when they're unable to access a throttled server. You can restart a throttled server by typing

```
ctlinnd go reason
```

where the *reason* parameter matches the text string that was provided when the server was throttled.

Fortunately it is not necessary to throttle the server for many administrative tasks. For instance, you can add a newsgroup using the newgroup option of the ctlinnd command without throttling the server first.

OPTIONS

To get a complete list of the options supported by ctlinnd, type

```
ctlinnd -h
```

Summary

Personal email is not always the optimal medium for exchanging messages. When a discussion group is desired, better alternatives are available, such as mailing lists and newsgroups.

Mailing lists make it possible for email messages sent to the list address to be relayed to multiple recipients. Mailing lists can be implemented in many ways. Simple lists can be created using the UNIX `.forward` file or the `/etc/aliases` file. Advanced mailing list programs exist that automate many aspects of list management and also provide protection against abuse. One of the most popular mailing list programs is Majordomo (developed by Great Circle Associates). This free utility is also available on the CD-ROM accompanying this book.

An alternative to mailing lists is newsgroups. Newsgroups are one of the oldest features of the Internet, having been around in the form of the global Usenet hierarchy for many years. The main advantage of newsgroups is economy: with mailing lists, a copy of each message is generated for each recipient, with newsgroups, messages reside on dedicated news servers. News servers exchange messages with each other on a regular basis using NNTP, the Network News Transfer Protocol; this protocol is also used by news client programs to retrieve messages from a news server.

The most widely used UNIX-based news server is the InterNetNews server (INN). With INN, it's possible to configure a large site that carries most or all of the nearly 30,000 Usenet newsgroups. It is also possible to configure a small server that carries only a few internal newsgroups or supports newsgroups accessed by external users. INN is also available on the CD-ROM that accompanies this book. Configuring the software consists of creating, or modifying, several configuration files and setting up the server for automatic start at system boot time.

Manual Pages

For additional information on topics discussed in this chapter, please refer to the following manual pages.

```
man active

man aliases

man ctlinnd
```

```
man inn.conf

man innd

man newsfeeds

man nnrp.access
```

> **NOTE**
>
> Keep in mind that if you're using Caldera OpenLinux from the CD-ROM attached to this book, INN manual pages may not be available unless you first configure the man page path as follows:
>
> ```
> export MANPATH=\:/usr/share/inn/man
> ```

Web Service

If you're planning to establish a permanent connection to the Internet for your Linux server, chances are that the main reason (or one of the main reasons anyway) is so that you can provide your own Web pages. Depending on your circumstances, this may be more advantageous than renting space on your ISP's Web server.

Often, however, you might want to do more than merely provide a means for users to retrieve Web pages from your server. You may want to be able to provide a file library service, advanced server features, or support for SSL, the Secure Sockets Layer.

Basic Concepts

Web browsers these days are complicated pieces of software. This should come as no surprise, given the complex tasks that these applications are expected to perform. Web browsers interpret pages written using HTML, the Hypertext Markup Language. They also include an engine that renders these pages on the screen, complete with support for fonts, color, embedded images, and more.

In contrast, Web servers are relatively simple. In the first approximation, a Web server needs to do nothing but provide a file download service for HTML files and embedded images. To such a server, the files are opaque—the server delivers the contents of the files without interpreting them.

A modern Web server has many advanced features. However, even such an advanced server does not need to render a document graphically, and it can safely ignore parts of an HTML file that it does not understand, so the server can remain lean and efficient. This is of great importance for high-capacity sites that may serve thousands of Web pages every minute.

Formats and Protocols

Web pages are written using a special language: HTML. This language is derived from an older standard (SGML, the Structured Generalized Markup Language.) The HTML syntax is not complicated, but it is not exactly self-explanatory either.

OPTIONS   By way of example, here is a part of the first paragraph of this chapter in HTML format:

```
<HTML>
<BODY>
<H2>Web Service</H2>
<P>If you're planning to establish a permanent connection
to the Internet for your Linux server,</P>
</BODY>
</HTML>
```

When a Web browser receives this block of text, it renders it by interpreting the directives contained within. For instance, the <H2> directive (header, second-level) instructs the browser to show the text that follows in using a highlighted style (typically a large, bold font). The end of the highlighted text is marked by the </H2> directive.

HTML is not hard to write, but it's easier if you have a WYSIWYG (What-You-See-Is-What-You-Get) tool. One such editor that many Windows users are familiar with is Microsoft FrontPage.

HTML is not the only format used by Web browsers. For graphical images, the two commonly used file formats are GIF (the Graphical Interchange Format developed by CompuServe, and based on the Lempel-Ziv compression method patent of Unisys) and JPEG (the Joint Photography Experts Group). GIF is a lossless compression best used for line art, diagrams, and screen shots; the pixels of a GIF file are exactly preserved. JPG is a more efficient, but lossy compression technique (that is, the restored images do not exactly match the original), which is more appropriate for photographs. Most Web browsers can also interpret and display plain ASCII text files.

File formats are not to be confused with the method used for delivering them. The preferred method of delivery for Web content is HTTP, the Hypertext Transfer Protocol. However, HTTP is often used to deliver files other than HTML files; and HTML files can be delivered using other methods. The second most commonly used method for file transfer is the venerable FTP, or File Transfer Protocol.

Uniform Resource Locators

To request Web content on your desktop, you provide a URL, or Uniform Resource Locator, to your browser. For instance

```
http://www.mcp.com/index.html
```

Each URL consists of three parts. The part that precedes the colon defines the protocol that is to be used for delivering the content. The remainder of the URL contains the name of the server where the desired content is located, and the content's filename or identifier.

In the case of the preceding example, the protocol is defined by the keywords `http`; the file that the browser is asked to show is `index.html`, located on the server `www.mcp.com`.

If Macmillan Publishing had a suitably configured FTP service running on the same server, it would be possible to request the same page using the following URL:

```
ftp://www.mcp.com/index.html
```

PART

III

CH

10

The File Transfer Protocol

One of the oldest and simplest methods used for transferring files on the Internet is FTP. This protocol has been around many years before the first Web page was created.

OPTIONS

Although most Web browsers can access FTP servers, FTP is typically used with ftp client software, such as the Linux `ftp` command:

```
$ ftp ftp.mcp.com
Connected to ftp.mcp.com.
220 iq-mcp FTP server (Version wu-2.4(4) Sun Dec 21 13:01:32 EST 1997)
rea
dy.
Name (ftp.mcp.com:vttoth): ftp
331 Guest login ok, send your complete e-mail address as password.
Password: vttoth@linux.sys
230-Please read the file README
230-  it was last modified on Wed Apr  8 22:26:36 1998 - 360 days ago
230 Guest login ok, access restrictions apply.
ftp> ls
200 PORT command successful.
```

```
▼        150 Opening ASCII mode data connection for /bin/ls.
         total 18
         drwxr-xr-x   7 root      other        512 Apr 26   1998 .
         drwxr-xr-x   7 root      other        512 Apr 26   1998 ..
         -r--------   1 root      other          0 Dec 30   1997 .forward
         -r--------   1 root      other          0 Dec 30   1997 .qmail
         -r--------   1 root      other          0 Dec 30   1997 .rhosts
         lrwxrwxrwx   1 root      other          6 Apr 26   1998
         Files_are_in_pub_dir
          -> README
         -rw-r--r--   1 root      other         54 Apr  9   1998 README
         d--x--x--x   3 root      other        512 Apr 26   1998 bin
         dr-xr-xr-x   2 root      other        512 Apr 26   1998 dev
         d--x--x--x   2 root      other        512 Apr 26   1998 etc
         drwxr-xr-x  54 672       anon-ftp    1024 Feb 24 20:59 pub
         dr-xr-xr-x   3 root      other        512 Apr 26   1998 usr
         226 Transfer complete.
         ftp> get README
         200 PORT command successful.
         150 Opening ASCII mode data connection for README (54 bytes).
         226 Transfer complete.
         57 bytes received in 0.0039 secs (14 Kbytes/sec)
         ftp> bye
         221 Goodbye.
```

Many FTP servers, such as the one shown in the preceding example, allow *anonymous* access without a password, if you supply the word anonymous as your username. Often, ftp is a synonym for anonymous. In either case, you're asked to supply your email address in place of a password. The password is usually not echoed (indicated by the use

▲   of italics in this listing.)

Behind the scenes, your FTP client program connects to the remote server and sends simple commands to it. When the time comes to actually begin transferring files, a secondary channel of communication is opened, through which file content is transmitted.

You may wonder why another protocol was developed for Web documents. Among the reasons are added features that pertain to Web content and a more efficient delivery mechanism.

The Hypertext Transfer Protocol

So what, exactly, happens when you throw a URL such as http://www.mcp.com/ index.html at your Web browser?

First, the browser takes the initial part of the URL that defines the protocol to be used. It also extracts the name of the server from the second part—in this case, www.mcp.com.

Next, the browser actually establishes an Internet connection to that host, specifically to the appropriate server (for example, the HTTP server) on that host. Your browser knows that when the HTTP protocol is specified on the URL, it must connect to the standard HTTP port, port 80, on the destination machine using the TCP protocol.

OPTIONS Because the HTTP protocol uses human-readable command strings, it is actually possible to simulate by hand what your browser does, using the telnet utility from the Linux command line:

```
$ telnet www.mcp.com http
Trying 198.70.146.70...
Connected to www.mcp.com.
Escape character is '^]'.
GET /index.html
<HEAD>YP<LINK rel="stylesheet" href="/includes/stylesheets/maize_corporate
.css"><BODY text="#000000" bgcolor="#FFFFFF">
...
```

This is almost embarrassingly simple. Of course there's more to the HTTP protocol than the GET command, but this transcript illustrates the idea well.

Once it has successfully transmitted HTTP commands to the server, the browser receives the files it requested and renders them on the screen. It may also copy the files to its temporary (*cache*) directory, so if the same file is requested later on, it will not need to be retrieved from the network again.

PART
III

CH
10

Secure Sockets

Sometimes, you access Web pages through a URL that begins with https://. This keyword indicates to your browser that an SSL connection must be used.

In practice, this means two things. First, your browser connects to a different TCP port on the server. Instead of the standard port number associated with HTTP, port 80, it connects to port 443, which is associated with secure HTTP connections. Second, all information packets transmitted back and forth between your browser and the server will be encrypted using a complex encryption mechanism that provides protection against eavesdropping, and also authenticates the server to protect you against impostors.

The SSL is not unique to HTTP. However, other servers (for example, FTP) do not routinely support SSL transactions.

Setting Up an FTP Server

The FTP service is simple to use and administer, which is why it is a good idea to begin with this step when configuring an Internet server. Chances are that your Linux installation already contains a functioning copy of an FTP server.

The main steps of setting up an FTP server are as follows:

- Installing the software
- Configuring the Internet superserver
- Configuring the FTP directories
- Managing the server

Server Installation

FTP servers usually come in the form of a single executable program, one that goes by names such as `ftpd`, `in.ftpd`, or something similar. It is typically located in the `/sbin` or `/usr/sbin` directory.

TEST SYSTEM
On my test system, the FTP server was one of the components installed during the initial system setup. Caldera OpenLinux comes with one of the most commonly used FTP servers, developed at the University of Washington. This server's executable file is named `in.ftpd` and it is located in `/usr/sbin/`.

Once installed, the FTP server provides access to files by users who have an account on your system. These users will be able to access the same files that they normally have access to, for instance when they log on to the system interactively. In other words, if you log on to a remote system via FTP using your username and password on that system, you'll be able to access files in your home directory for reading and writing. You might also be able to read (download) other files that you normally have read access to on that system.

Configuring the Internet Superserver

Placing the FTP server executable on your computer is not sufficient by itself to provide FTP access. For this, you must also ensure that the FTP server is invoked when an incoming request arrives.

Such incoming requests come in the form of connections to TCP port 21, the port reserved for FTP access. The standard method for invoking a server is through `inetd`, the Internet superserver. This server, introduced in Chapter 4, "Internet Configuration and Basic Security," is configured through the file `/etc/inetd.conf`.

TEST SYSTEM   On my test system, the Caldera OpenLinux installer placed the following entry in `/etc/inetd.conf`:

```
ftp      stream  tcp     nowait  root    /usr/sbin/tcpd in.ftpd -l -a
```

The two command-line switches used install the server to log entries to the system log (`-l`) and to use the `ftpaccess` file. This file is optional; if it exists, the FTP server uses it to establish configuration options. For more information, read the manual page (`man ftpaccess`.)

▲

Configuring Anonymous Access

When a regular user logs on to the system via FTP, all the access privileges that normally apply to this user ID remain in effect throughout the FTP session. The user can retrieve any file or execute arbitrary commands on the system.

In contrast, anonymous users cannot be allowed such a privilege. Unlike regular users who are trusted (why else would they have a password on your system?), anonymous users could turn out to be hostile intruders. As a result, their access must be limited to the downloading of publicly accessible files and optionally uploading files to public directories.

> **WARNING**   It's usually a bad idea to offer a directory in which both anonymous uploading and downloading are permitted, because it allows third parties to use your server as a location for exchanging files without your knowledge. FTP servers with such publicly accessible directories are frequently abused by peddlers of *warez*—illicit copies of copyrighted software.

In order for an FTP server to provide anonymous access, it is necessary to have a user account named `ftp` on your system. This user account is never used for interactive login, and does not require a valid password. However, when an anonymous FTP user connects to your system, the FTP server will use this account's access permissions for accessing files. Furthermore, anonymous users only see files that are located in the home directory associated with the `ftp` user ID.

In addition to files anonymous users can download, this directory also contains special versions of commands such as `ls`, and a special copy of the `etc` directory. During an anonymous session, the FTP server uses the `ftp` home directory as its root directory; in other words, it can *only* see these copies of executable commands and files from `/etc`, not the originals. This prevents an anonymous user from accessing the real version of `/etc/passwd` (conceivably obtaining a copy of all your encrypted passwords if you're not using the shadow password suite; see Chapter 4, for more information) or executing other commands and exploiting them for security leaks.

Most Linux distributions establish the `ftp` user ID and create its home directory during initial system installation.

TEST SYSTEM My test system is no exception: The `ftp` user ID and home directory were created by the Caldera OpenLinux installer. The file `/etc/passwd` contains the following entry:

```
ftp:x:14:50:FTP User:/home/ftp:
```

In `/home/ftp`, I found the following files and directories:

```
/home/ftp/bin/
/home/ftp/bin/gzip
/home/ftp/bin/ls
/home/ftp/bin/tar
/home/ftp/bin/zcat  -> gzip
/home/ftp/etc/
/home/ftp/etc/group
/home/ftp/etc/passwd
/home/ftp/pub/
```

The presence of the tar and gzip utilities allows the FTP server to provide the contents of an entire directory in a single transaction. With the `tar` command the files are combined into an archive, and then optionally compressed using `gzip`. These commands are explained in detail in Chapter 17, "Backups."

As you can see, the `pub` directory is currently empty. Usually, files that can be down-loaded by anyone are placed in this directory.

Server Management

Once your FTP server is up and running, it requires very little attention. However, you may still want to monitor it from time to time to ensure proper operation and prevent abuse attempts.

The principal means of monitoring server activity is through the transfer log file. This file, usually `/var/log/xferlog`, contains an entry for each successfully completed file transfer.

The server also logs important messages to the standard system log. On most systems, these entries will end up in `/var/log/messages`.

Running Apache

In the simplest case, Web service involves running a copy of a Web server program. By far the most popular Web server program under Linux (indeed, according to some, the most popular Web server program, period) is Apache, a free, high-quality server application.

Running Apache is not difficult, but things can get tricky. For instance, you might want to set up multiple *virtual hosts* on your server. Or you might want to provide areas that are password-protected. But before we get into that, let's start with the basics.

Starting Apache

Before you start the Apache server, it obviously needs to be installed. If you are using a distribution such as the one found on the CD-ROM that accompanies this book, you're lucky because a copy of Apache is provided on the CD and can be installed along with the operating system (or anytime afterward). You can also download and install a copy from the Internet. If you need to resort to this alternative, the latest version of Apache is available at `http://www.apache.org/`.

Just like the FTP server, a Web server usually comes in the form of a single executable file, typically named `httpd`. Running a Web server means running a copy of this program.

Unlike an FTP server, a Web server is configured to run all the time, as opposed to being started on demand by the Internet superserver, `inetd`. The disadvantage of this method is that the server consumes system resources (for example, memory) even when it isn't being used. The advantage is that the overhead associated with starting the server application every time a request arrives is avoided.

A running Web server awaits incoming connections on the HTTP port, TCP port 80. When such a request arrives, the server begins processing it, possibly spawning extra copies of itself, if necessary, in order to handle multiple requests simultaneously. Thus, you should not be surprised to see even dozens of copies of httpd running on a heavily loaded server.

So how does a Web server start up when you boot your server? Through the system initialization files of course, along with other service applications. Depending on the distribution you use, your system startup files might already contain the necessary entries for starting up the server.

TEST SYSTEM On my test system, I installed Apache along with other system components during initial setup. As a result, the Web server is already up and running as evidenced by the following:

```
$ ps axu ¦ grep http
nobody     409   0.0   1.2   1380    816  ?   S    Mar 28    0:00  httpd -f
/etc/h
nobody     410   0.0   1.2   1380    816  ?   S    Mar 28    0:00  httpd -f
/etc/h
root       405   0.0   1.1   1332    696  ?   S    Mar 28    0:00  httpd -f
/etc/h
```

Poking around in the /etc directory, I easily discovered how the Web server is started up when the system is booted. In /etc/rc.d/init.d, the file httpd contains the startup script for the server. This file, in turn, references settings from the file /etc/sysconfig/daemons/httpd. The actual name of the server executable is /usr/sbin/httpd.apache.

To verify that the Web server is indeed functional, I connected to it through a Web client running on another computer (see Figure 10.1). This showed the default Web page supplied with Caldera OpenLinux. (Note that many of the options on this page only work if your Web client runs on the same machine as the server; since I haven't installed X on the test system, I cannot run a graphical program, such as a Web client, on it.)

It is possible to use the LISA utility to control whether the Web server is started when the system is booted. Starting LISA with the --system command-line switch and selecting the Configure Daemon/Server Autostart command brings up the screen shown in Figure 10.2, where the Web server can be selected or deselected.

FIGURE 10.1
The Caldera OpenLinux default
Web page.

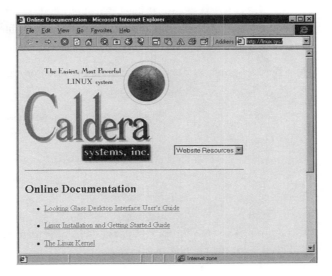

FIGURE 10.2
Configuring the Apache server
for autostart.

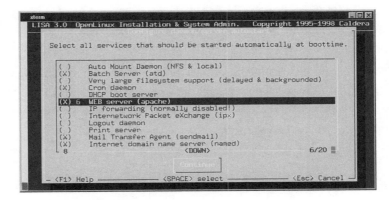

Server Configuration

Unless you are using a preconfigured Web server such as that supplied with Caldera
OpenLinux, starting the server executable from your system startup script is not likely to
be sufficient to start the Web server. The reason for this is simple: Web servers such as
Apache need several configuration files before they can run.

These configuration files are often found in subdirectories under the `/var/lib/httpd` or `/etc/httpd` directory. Typically at least two subdirectories can be found here: `conf` and `logs`. As the names imply, the latter contains server access logs, whereas the former contains the configuration files themselves.

The Apache configuration files that reside in this directory are as follows:

`access.conf`	Web content directories and access rights
`httpd.conf`	General server configuration settings
`mime.types`	List of known file types
`srm.conf`	Directory names and formatting directives

The file `mime.types` lists file types known to Apache. You may be wondering what, if anything, a Web server might have to do with the MIME standard for Internet email. The reason is simple: The HTTP protocol uses headers borrowed from the MIME protocol to identify the type of the content that follows.

The three `.conf` files, as it turns out, are not treated differently from each other. (The use of three separate files is largely a convention.) They are simply read in the order of `httpd.conf`, `srm.conf`, and `access.conf`. The complete set of directives that these files can contain is listed at `http://www.apache.org/docs/mod/directives.html`.

Apache installations contain default versions of these configurations that you can modify. These default versions are named `access.conf-dist`, `httpd.conf-dist`, and `srm.conf-dist`, where `dist` stands for the word *distribution*.

So why would you change the defaults in these configuration files? The main reasons are customization, security, and setting up the location of Web files on your system.

To start with a meaningful server configuration, it is sufficient to edit only `httpd.conf` at first. This file contains entries that identify your server (`ServerName`) and its administrator's email address (`ServerAdmin`.) Either this file or the file `srm.conf` defines the starting location for Web content files (`DocumentRoot`.)

TEST SYSTEM

▼

On my test system, I edited the file `/etc/httpd/apache/conf/httpd.conf`. I modified two entries in this file as follows:

```
ServerName linux.sys
ServerAdmin webmaster@linux.sys
```

▼   I set up the traditional Web site administrator address, `webmaster`, under the
`ServerAdmin` entry, but I also had to ensure that this was a valid email address. For this, I
had to edit `/etc/aliases` and add the following line:

`webmaster: vttoth`

After I ran the `newaliases` command, I was able to verify, by sending email to it, that
▲   the address is now valid.

Setting Up Web Pages

Let me state the obvious: A Web server is of little use without Web content. Once your
server is properly configured and up and running, you will probably want to use it to
publish Web documents.

So where do these documents go? The obvious place is the location specified by the
`DocumentRoot` entry in the `httpd.conf` configuration file. Files that you copy to this
directory will immediately become visible as Web content.

Many Web servers host Web pages that are maintained by multiple users. The situation
would be chaotic if these Web pages had to reside in a common directory and could be
overwritten by all users. Fortunately, this is not the case. In its default configuration, the
Apache Web server also allows *personal* Web pages to be created in each user's home
directory.

The location of these personal Web pages is defined by the `UserDir` directive in the file
`srm.conf`. This is set by convention to `public_html`; changing it is rarely necessary.
Because of this option, users who have a home directory on your system can create a
subdirectory named `public_html`, and publish individual Web content there.

These individual user Web pages can be accessed using a special URL syntax:
`http://server.domain/~username/`. The tilde (~) character indicates to the Web server
that what follows is a user ID that must be expanded to the pathname of the `public_html`
directory under the user's home directory.

Often when you access a Web page, you do not specify the name of an individual file.
For instance, to access the popular Internet news service of CNN, you'd type
http://cnn.com/ as the URL. The reason why this works is simple: Most Web servers,
when presented with a directory name only, will respond with a *default document*. With

PART
III

CH
10

Apache, the name of the default document is defined by the `DirectoryIndex` configuration entry in `srm.conf`. (As originally envisioned, the default document provides an index for the directory in which it resides; you are, of course, free to use it for any purpose that suits your needs.)

> **NOTE**
>
> Notice the trailing slash at the end of a URL such as `http://cnn.com/`. This is the syntactically correct URL for representing a directory (as opposed to a file). Most Web browsers will also accept the form `http://cnn.com`. However, a few won't, so it's always best to use the complete form when specifying a URL, whether it is in a hot link to another document or on your business card.

TEST SYSTEM   To test whether Apache functions correctly, I created a `public_html` directory under my home directory on the test system. In it, I placed a file named `index.html` that reads as follows:

```
<HTML>
<HEAD>
<TITLE>
Viktor's Web page
</TITLE>
</HEAD>
<BODY>
<H1>Viktor's new Web page.</H1>
This is my brand new Web page.<P>
</BODY>
</HTML>
```

When I attempted to access this file through the URL `http://linux.sys/~vttoth/`, I got what I expected, as seen in Figure 10.3.

FIGURE 10.3
A new personal Web page.

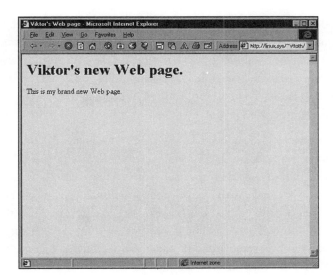

▲

Advanced Web Server Features

Being able to publish Web pages is great, but there's more to Web servers than providing access to HTML files. For instance, even if you aren't an ISP, you might want to host Web pages for multiple organizations, each with its own domain name. You also might want to restrict access to certain content to registered users. Or you may wish to provide SSL support for financial transactions. The possibilities are nearly limitless and clearly, this book can only skim the surface.

Virtual Hosts

Simply put, the virtual host mechanism allows a Web server to act as a server for multiple domains and host multiple Web sites. This technique is often used by ISPs who want to avoid maintaining a separate server for each of the hundreds of domains for which they provide Web hosting. But even in such a low-end environment as your home office, virtual hosts can be useful. For example, you might want to use the same Web server to host Web pages for your personal (family) domain and your home-based business.

So how does the virtual host mechanism work? When a Web server receives an information request, it has no way of knowing what domain name was used in the request—whether, for instance, it was a request for the page `http://www.myfamily.sys/index.html` or `http://www.mycompany.sys/index.html`. In both cases, all the Web server knows is that a request arrived for the file `index.html`. This is clearly a problem that has no obvious solution.

However, we're not helpless! Recall (from Chapter 5, "Internet Concepts") that an IP number is associated with each *network interface* (a network card—a modem used for SLIP/PPP.) What if, for instance, you use two network cards, each with its own unique IP number, and associate one of the two domain names with each? When a user requests `http://www.myfamily.sys/index.html`, the request will arrive through the first network card. The Web server, while it may not know the domain name part of a document request, always knows the IP number of the interface through which the request arrived, so it can distinguish between the two.

Clearly, this is a solution, but with limitations. It might be a little difficult (not to mention expensive) if an ISP, for instance, tried to install 200 network cards on a single server in order to provide Web hosting for 200 individual domain names.

As it turns out, there's a simpler solution. It is possible to associate multiple IP numbers with a single interface, so there's no need for multiple network cards. To use this feature, you might need to recompile the Linux kernel (see Appendix A, "Configuring the Kernel") and enable this feature (*IP aliasing.*)

With multiple IP number support enabled, you can configure additional IP numbers for a network interface using the `ifconfig` command. For example, to add a new IP number to the `eth0` interface (the first Ethernet card on your system), type

```
# /sbin/ifconfig eth0:1 192.168.1.64
```

Needless to say, you need to be accessing the system as the root user in order for this to work. Here is how you can verify the result:

```
# /sbin/ifconfig eth0:1
eth0:1    Link encap:Ethernet   HWaddr 00:00:21:A5:36:09
          inet addr:192.168.1.64  Bcast:192.168.1.255   Mask:255.255.255.0
          UP RUNNING  MTU:1500  Metric:1
          RX packets:0 errors:0 dropped:0 overruns:0
          TX packets:0 errors:0 dropped:0 overruns:0
```

Setting up multiple IP numbers is just the first step. You must also make sure that these IP numbers are associated with valid domain names.

When all this is finished, you can verify that the new domain is alive and accessible by using the ping utility, for instance. If all is well, you can proceed with configuring the Web server itself to host multiple virtual hosts. This is accomplished by editing `httpd.conf` and adding a `VirtualHost` entry that contains, at a minimum, a `DocumentRoot` directive.

TEST SYSTEM   On my test system, I decided to set up a personal domain, `vttoth.sys`. Setting up this domain in the form of a virtual host began by adding a new IP number to my Ethernet interface:

```
# /sbin/ifconfig eth0:1 192.168.1.64
```

This IP number also needed to be associated with a symbolic domain name. This required editing my name server configuration files (see chapter 6, "The Domain Name System"). When all this was done, I was able to verify that the new domain name was indeed functional:

```
# ping 192.168.1.64
PING 192.168.1.64 (192.168.1.64): 56 data bytes
64 bytes from 192.168.1.64: icmp_seq=0 ttl=64 time=0.4 ms
64 bytes from 192.168.1.64: icmp_seq=1 ttl=64 time=0.3 ms
64 bytes from 192.168.1.64: icmp_seq=2 ttl=64 time=0.3 ms
64 bytes from 192.168.1.64: icmp_seq=3 ttl=64 time=0.3 ms
64 bytes from 192.168.1.64: icmp_seq=4 ttl=64 time=0.3 ms
```

Note that some kernel configurations may require you to explicitly add the new IP address to the kernel routing table before it can be made to work:

```
# /sbin/route add 192.168.1.64 eth0:1
```

Next, I edited `/etc/httpd/apache/conf/httpd.conf`. I added the following lines at the end of this file:

```
<VirtualHost vttoth.sys>
DocumentRoot /home/vttoth/public_html
ServerAdmin vttoth@linux.sys
</VirtualHost>
```

Finally, I had to restart the Web server in order for these settings to take effect. Using the command `ps axuw ¦ grep httpd`, I located the process identifier of the copy of the Web server that runs under the `root` user ID, and killed it using the `kill` command. This terminated all running copies of `httpd`. I then restarted the server using `/usr/sbin/httpd.apache -f /etc/httpd/apache/conf/httpd.conf`.

With the server up and running, I was able to test the new settings. As expected, I could now retrieve my personal Web page using the URL `http://vttoth.sys/`.

Restricted Access

Web technology is designed primarily for disseminating information to the general public. That said, often it is desirable to restrict access to some of your Web content to specific users.

Access restrictions can be configured individually for each directory by creating a file named .htaccess. Directives in this file specify what kind of access is permitted to the directory's contents.

For example, your organization might have a Web server with content offered for public viewing as well as a directory that contains information only employees should have access to. To restrict access to this directory, create an .htaccess file in the directory with the following content:

```
<Limit GET POST>
order deny,allow
deny from all
allow from mycompany.sys
</Limit>
<Limit PUT DELETE>
order deny,allow
deny from all
</Limit>
```

In order for the .htaccess file to work as expected, you may also need to further modify httpd.conf (see the Apache documentation for the AllowOverride directive).

Adding SSL Support

The development of secure transactions over the Internet has been hampered by two factors: patented technologies and the U.S. government's reluctance to allow the export of data encryption technology. It is because of these reasons that a free Web server such as Apache does not include SSL support.

That said, there are several ways to obtain SSL support for your system.

First, you can opt to use one of the commercial implementations. One of the commercial Apache-derivatives that supports SSL is Stronghold; see their Web page at http://www.c2.net/. Another commercial product is Raven, which is a cryptographic upgrade module to Apache (see http://www.covalent.net/raven/ssl/).

If you are outside the United States, or if you are not using SSL for a commercial purpose, it might be possible to use a free SSL implementation. My recommendation in this case is to use Apache-SSL (http://www.apache-ssl.org/).

> **WARNING** Before you use a free SSL implementation, you're strongly advised to read all available information to determine whether you can legally make use of this software due to patent, export licensing, and cryptography restrictions that may be applicable in your geographic area.

Installing SSL support is *not* a simple task. In addition to installing the software and modifying configuration settings, you must also obtain a *certificate* from a known Certification Authority (CA). The reason for this lies in the security model employed by SSL. In this model, a server provides proof of this identity by supplying a certificate issued to it by a trusted issuer. The certificate is encrypted in such a way so that counterfeits cannot be produced unless the certification authority's systems are compromised. The certificate contains the name of the system for which it is issued, so unauthorized use is not possible. The idea is that when you're using SSL, you are assured that the credit card number you type will indeed be sent to, say, amazon.com and not an impostor site.

This certificate is basically just a small block of data that is transmitted at the beginning of an SSL transaction. Along with this data, the client and the server also exchange keys that are used to encrypt all data transmission between them. The key exchange itself is also protected by a different encryption mechanism. In the end, all transmission is encrypted and protected both against eavesdropping and forgery.

Forms Processing

Probably the most important server-side feature that you might want to utilize is the capability to process *forms*.

Forms allow Web pages to contain fields in which the user can enter information. Creating forms is easy, even if you're writing HTML code manually. For instance, here's a simple Web page that collects a single field of information:

```
<HTML>
<HEAD>
<TITLE>Form</TITLE>
</HEAD>
<BODY>
<FORM METHOD="GET" ACTION="mailto:cgi-bin/form.cgi">
  <P>Enter value:<INPUT TYPE="text" NAME="Value">
  <INPUT TYPE="submit" VALUE="Submit"></P>
</FORM>
</BODY>
</HTML>
```

Writing a form isn't difficult—deciding what to do with the information you collect is the tricky part!

Specifically, it is the ACTION parameter of the FORM tag that determines where the information goes. This parameter must be a URL that can accept form data. The URL usually points to an executable program.

These executable programs are invoked by the Web server using a mechanism called *CGI*, the Common Gateway Interface. The executable can be a program you received from another source; more often, though, it is a simple script that you write yourself. Yes indeed, this means programming.

Fortunately we're not talking about the programming of complex applications consisting of hundreds of thousands of lines of source code, only a few lines of a shell script or, more commonly, a few lines written in the Perl language.

Perl is used often because it has powerful text processing capabilities. Indeed, if you're serious about creating interactive Web content, some familiarity with this language is essential. That said, many simple tasks can be accomplished without Perl; instead, you can use simple shell scripts.

For example, the value submitted through the Web form presented earlier could be processed by a script such as this:

```
#!/bin/sh
echo
echo $QUERY_STRING
```

This script returns the submitted value to the user, and thus it is of no practical value, but it demonstrates the basics.

CGI scripts cannot be placed at arbitrary locations. They must reside in directories specifically designated in the HTTP server's configuration file as containing executable programs. It is also possible to associate CGI script directories with virtual hosts.

TEST SYSTEM   To test CGI scripting capability, I added the two files shown earlier in this section to my personal Web page. I placed form.html into my public_html directory. For the CGI script (which I named form.cgi), I created a new directory named cgi-bin under public_html, so the file went to public_html/cgi-bin/form.cgi.

▼ To enable this new directory as a CGI directory, I needed to modify `httpd.conf`. Recall that I added a `VirtualHost` entry to this file when I set up a Web page for the `vttoth.sys` domain. This time, while logged on as the root user, I inserted a new line just before `</VirtualHost>` that read as follows:

```
ScriptAlias /cgi-bin/ /home/vttoth/public_html/cgi-bin/
```

Once again, I had to restart the HTTP server for the new setting to take effect. Figure 10.4 shows the result: The first window contains the form from `form.html`, whereas the second shows the Web page that appears after the `form.cgi` script was run.

FIGURE 10.4
Processing a Web form.

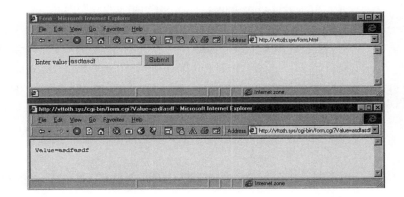

▲

Chances are that if you intend to maintain professionally designed Web forms, you'll need more information than this simple introduction could provide. A very good reference I use is *HTML 3.2 & CGI Unleashed*, by John December and Mark Ginsburg. As for the Perl language, the best reference is *Programming perl* by Larry Wall (Perl's creator) and Randal L. Schwartz.

Logs

As the Web server does its job, it logs its activities to one or more log files. These files can (or should) be examined regularly for indications of configuration errors, network problems, and hostile attempts to access your server.

By default, the Apache Web server creates two log files: `access_log` and `error_log`. The former of these two contains an entry for each document request that was sent to your server. The latter contains information about any errors the server might have encountered during execution.

If you are administering multiple virtual hosts, it may be desirable to direct their log entries to alternative files. This is possible if you specify additional `ErrorLog` and `TransferLog` entries in the `VirtualHost` entry in `httpd.conf`.

Summary

One of the main reasons for a permanent Internet connection is to maintain a Web site. For this, Web server software is used, the most popular of which is the free Apache server. Apache can be downloaded from the Web; it is also available on the CD-ROM accompanying this book, as part of the Caldera OpenLinux distribution.

Web pages are created using HTML, the Hypertext Markup Language, and delivered through HTTP, the Hypertext Transfer Protocol. They can also be delivered through an older protocol, FTP, the File Transfer Protocol. Neither of these protocols is restricted to HTML files; they can deliver files of any type, including text and binary content.

A Web page is identified using a URL, the Uniform Resource Locator. The URL specifies the protocol used to deliver the page, the server on which the page is located, and the name of the file that contains the page.

Some Web servers also support secure transactions using SSL, the Secure Sockets Layer.

To set up your own FTP server, you need to install the software first (if it isn't already installed as part of your Linux distribution). Next, you need to change `/etc/inetd.conf` to ensure that incoming FTP requests invoke the server. You must also configure anonymous access. Many, if not all, of these steps might have been performed automatically during the initial installation of Linux on your system.

The Apache Web server is invoked through system startup scripts. Configuration for the server is contained within several configuration files, which contain a large number of directives. These files are used to specify the Web directories, set up access control, enumerate file types, and more. Individual Web pages can be placed at the standard document root directory or in HTML directories maintained by individual users. Additional directories can be specified by modifying the configuration files. The Web server also maintains a series of logs that can be used to track server activity and view error conditions.

The Apache Web server also supports many advanced features. Multiple Web sites can be hosted on a single computer using its virtual host feature. Forms processing and other advanced services can be implemented using CGI scripts. Access to certain Web content can be restricted using access control files (.htaccess). Extensions are also available that add SSL support, although depending on your geographic location and the commercial nature of your server, you might need to pay a license fee.

Manual Pages

For additional information on topics discussed in this chapter, please refer to the following manual pages.

```
man ftp

man ftpaccess

man ftpd

man httpd

man ifconfig

man inetd

man lynx

man ping

man route

man xferlog
```

Part **IV**

Advanced Networking

11 Firewalls

12 Using External Routers

13 File Services For Windows: Samba

14 Time Services

Firewalls

Dedicated firewall systems can cost many thousands of dollars. Yet a free copy of Linux, running on antiquated hardware, can accomplish many of the same tasks that these expensive boxes do—often better than the dedicated systems.

The role of a firewall is to protect your internal network from outside intrusion. As long as you remain connected to the Internet, the chance of an intrusion can never be fully eliminated, only reduced. This is where a firewall can help. However—and this must be emphasized—no firewall system is a substitute for proper system management and monitoring. In other words, your best line of defense against intrusion is a thorough knowledge of your systems; firewalls can only help, but they will not do the job for you.

What Firewalls Do

What, exactly, are the functions performed by a firewall? Exactly what does a firewall protect you against? And how is this protection accomplished?

Basically, a firewall system separates your internal network from your external network connection. Systems behind the firewall will be invisible to systems on the outside. Only the firewall exists, inasmuch as the outside network is concerned. All outgoing traffic originates from the firewall, and all incoming traffic is sent to the firewall. To the outside, your network appears as a single computer (see Figure 11.1). This differs from a network connected via an ordinary router gateway, which provides a transparent connection between machines on the local network and hosts on the Internet.

FIGURE 11.1
A firewall gateway.

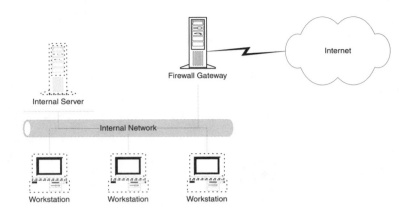

A firewall gateway accomplishes its task using a combination of two techniques: packet filtering and masquerading. In addition to hiding your internal network this way, the firewall can also offer network-monitoring features that let you detect intrusions.

Packet Filtering

Packet filtering is the most obvious method for protecting a network. A filtering gateway compares each packet that it forwards against a specific set of rules, in order to determine what to do with the packet.

Any data packet that arrives via a network interface has a header, which contains information identifying the type of the packet, its originating host, and its intended destination. When a firewall gateway that is configured for packet filtering receives a packet, it may check any of the following (see Figure 11.2):

- The interface through which the packet arrived (for example, Ethernet card and PPP modem connection)
- The originating host
- The destination host
- The packet's type (for example, TCP and UDP)
- The originating/destination port number (for TCP and UDP packets)

FIGURE 11.2
Packet filtering criteria.

Depending on what it finds, the firewall gateway may decide to

- Reject the packet (sending back error information to the originating host)
- Ignore the packet (do nothing)
- Forward the packet to its destination

For instance, suppose you're configuring a server that is used for email only. That server accepts incoming connections on TCP port 25 (the SMTP port reserved for mail servers); it may also originate connections to that port number on remote systems. To protect this server, you could configure a firewall to accept connections to port 25 when either the originating or destination host is the mail server, and reject all other packets sent to, or originating, from this server.

There are two different strategies of packet filtering that you can adopt. You may elect to filter certain packet types that are known to cause trouble (for instance, you might decide to disallow incoming Telnet connections from outside your local network). Or, a more restrictive strategy is to filter everything by default, and only enable packet types you know you will need to use.

PART
IV
CH
11

IP Masquerading

Packet filtering may prevent many types of attack against your system, but a would-be intruder still enjoys the advantage of being able to access each computer on your network individually. Thus, your network is only as secure as the least secure system on it; once that machine is compromised, the intruder may be able to gain access to other network resources and attack other systems.

A solution to this problem is to hide machines on your network behind the firewall gateway. This concept, already discussed in Chapter 5, "Internet Concepts," (see Figure 5.7, for instance) allows a server to masquerade as the originating host for all outgoing connections. So for instance, when a user originates a WWW request on one of the machines on your network and this request is transmitted to the firewall gateway, the gateway replaces the originating address with its own. When a response appears, the gateway changes the destination address to that of the user's computer, and forwards the packet to the user.

In this configuration, only a single computer is visible to the external network: the firewall gateway itself. It is not possible to reach machines behind the firewall from outside your network; the firewall gateway only forwards packets that are in response to a request originating from such a machine.

Hiding behind a masquerading firewall has another advantage: Because only one machine is visible to the external network, you only need a single IP address. All other machines behind the firewall can have private IP addresses, as discussed in Chapter 5.

Accounting

Even when you don't need packet filtering or masquerading capabilities, a firewall gateway can be of great service as a monitoring tool. Rules similar to those used for packet filtering can also be used to selectively log traffic.

For instance, a well-known bug in many operating systems is the so-called Ping of Death bug. Without going into details, this bug allows an attacker to send an intentionally malformed packet to your computer that might cause your system to crash. If you have installed the latest updates and fixes, your system may no longer be vulnerable to this type of attack. Nevertheless, you might still want to log incoming packets of this type, to be notified of an attempted attack.

This is precisely what IP accounting can do for you. Once again, you can select packets based on criteria such as

- The interface through which the packet arrived (for example, Ethernet card or PPP modem connection)
- The originating host
- The destination host
- The packet's type (for example, TCP and UDP)
- The originating/destination port number (for TCP and UDP packets

The level of log detail is also selectable. You can collect statistical information, have a log entry made for each packet that arrives, or even log the packets' contents.

> **WARNING** Network accounting and logging features should be used with care. Depending on the logging detail selected, you might end up with many kilobytes of log data collected every second, severely impacting the performance of your system (potentially making it unresponsive).

Application Support

Some applications use network resources in a way that is incompatible with the way firewalls work. A typical example is the popular streaming media application RealPlayer. When you connect to a server with this application, the server, in addition to sending responses over the communications channel that was initiated by your computer, also establishes separate connections to your machine for streaming audio and video. If your computer is hidden behind a firewall, this attempt will not succeed. Your machine may send to the server its own IP address, but this address is meaningless outside of the firewall. Furthermore, even if the remote server was to use your firewall gateway's external address, the data packet would not be routed to the originating computer, because the firewall has no way of knowing that this data is intended for a machine on the inside network (see Figure 11.3).

FIGURE 11.3
When firewalls do not work.

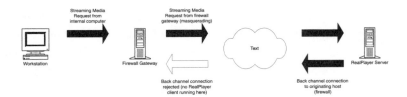

Some modern firewalls provide application-level support. In essence, these firewalls monitor traffic and analyze known types of data packets. Connection information is extracted from these packets and, if necessary, the firewall routes incoming connections to the correct computer on the internal network.

In the case of the RealPlayer example, a RealPlayer-aware firewall would recognize an outgoing RealPlayer request. It would also adjust the outgoing packet, replacing any internal network addresses in it with its own external address, just as it does in the standardized headers. When the remote server makes an attempt to connect back to the originating computer, the firewall would know, from previously collected information, which computer on the local network should receive the data, and route it accordingly (see Figure 11.4).

FIGURE 11.4
Application-level support in a
firewall.

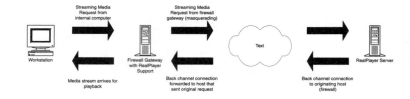

Unfortunately, Linux provides limited application-specific support, so if you need this firewall capability, you might have to obtain third-party software or purchase a dedicated firewall system.

Do You Need a Firewall?

Having read through all this discussion about the various ways in which a firewall protects your network against intrusion, you may wonder why everybody isn't using a firewall already.

Aside from the costs associated with setting up and maintaining a firewall system, there are a few less obvious reasons why a firewall isn't always a meaningful solution.

Firewalls and Dial-Up Systems

If your system is not permanently connected to the Internet, chances are that installing any kind of a firewall is a waste of your time and money. The reason is simple: Most of the time your system will not be physically connected to the network, so intrusions are not possible. Furthermore, the times when you are connected are unpredictable and on top of that, your IP address will probably be assigned dynamically, so it will be different every time, making life even harder for a would-be intruder. And, chances are that when you're connected, you're using most of the bandwidth of your modem connection (for example, downloading files), making it even more difficult for an intruder to communicate with your system interactively.

What a Firewall Doesn't Do

Let me start by relating something from personal experience: Recently, I've been working on a development project for a major customer. What I developed was a client-server application, and while I had an experimental server running in my office, I often made new versions of the client available to my customer. On one occasion, when he had problems on his test system, I asked him to connect to my server instead. Then I waited in vain for his connection request to show up in my server's log; the request never came. After we wasted several minutes, getting increasingly more frustrated in the process, it occurred to me to ask: "Are you behind a firewall?"

The morale of this story is that a firewall not only prevents intruders from accessing your system, it often blocks legitimate traffic as well. As a result, the decision to install a firewall always represents a compromise between security and productivity.

Why Firewalls Make Life Harder

When a firewall performs packet filtering, it may be configured to filter only specific packets or to filter all but known and approved packet types. In the latter case, when a user wants to make use of a new network feature or service, the network administrator must first enable the new packet types to pass through the filtering firewall. This may be a cumbersome, bureaucratic process at some organizations.

If the firewall is a masquerading firewall, the situation is even worse. Essentially network services that require a remote server to connect back to the client workstation will always fail, unless they are specifically supported by the firewall software. Even known applications can suddenly fail, for instance, after a version upgrade or after a configuration change at the remote server site. More often than not, there is simply no solution to this problem. Users must accept the network administrator's statement that the requested type of service is not accessible from their workstations.

What to Protect Against

Perhaps my opinion about firewalls is already clear: I rarely consider a full-featured firewall necessary, and often find them harmful. Firewalls might help you improve your network's security, but they are not the ultimate answer to all your security concerns. Far more important than firewalls is your knowledge of your systems and continuous monitoring.

That said, it is not necessarily a good idea to place a completely unprotected network on the Internet either. You may not need a masquerading firewall, but protecting against a few of the most obvious methods of intrusion can be helpful and provide a real improvement in security, with little or no loss of functionality.

Forged IP Numbers

Perhaps the most obvious form of attack uses forged headers in an IP packet sent to your system. Typically, headers are forged to pretend that the packet originated from within your network. The reason why this has a good chance at succeeding is quite simple: Many security settings on Linux and other systems are host-specific, that is, features are enabled when a request arrives from a predetermined set of IP addresses. For instance, you may be running a graphical X server on your desktop, and want programs running on other machines on your network to be capable of appearing on this display. However, you definitely don't want an intruder from, say, China, to be able to make windows appear on your desktop (or worse) do so without your permission!

Fortunately, this form of intrusion can be prevented easily. What you need to do is to configure your gateway to reject any packets that arrive via an external interface (that is, from your modem or network router) if their originating address matches an address on your network. Note that this should also include the localhost family of addresses (127.*nnn*.*nnn*.*nnn*.).

NetBIOS Connections

The commonly used MS-DOS/Windows networking protocol, NetBIOS, can also be made to work over TCP/IP connections. This very helpful feature can also become a security problem if intruders make attempts to connect to machines on your network using the NetBIOS protocol.

Another related problem is that ill-configured Windows machines often send out NetBIOS packets with destination addresses outside your local network. These packets may carry information such as weakly encrypted passwords, which is not a good idea to send to random destinations on the worldwide Internet.

The good news is that unless you have remote users who use shared DOS or Windows directories or printers, there is no need to allow NetBIOS traffic to flow between your local network and the Internet.

NetBIOS traffic may use any combination of TCP and UDP ports 137, 138, and 139. To block all NetBIOS traffic, you must block both incoming and outgoing traffic to these port numbers.

Setting Up a Linux Firewall

As mentioned in the introduction to this chapter, a Linux system makes an excellent fire-wall. You can use a Linux box as a dedicated firewall gateway (see Figure 11.5), or, more commonly, you can combine firewall and router functions in a Linux box that contains a modem or ISDN card, for instance (see Figure 11.6.)

FIGURE 11.5
A firewall with an external router.

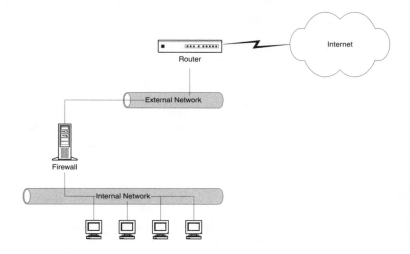

FIGURE 11.6
Combining firewall and router functions.

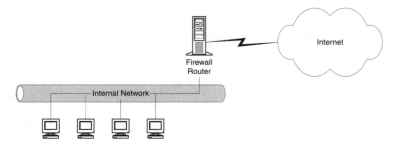

Support for core firewall functionality is supported in the Linux kernel itself. If set up properly, the kernel can monitor data packets, alter headers, and collect statistics. The only firewall function that Linux does not support "out of the box" is application-specific support, such as for RealPlayer.

Kernel Support

In order to support firewall functions, the Linux kernel must be properly configured. Depending on the distribution you use, these features may already be present in the kernel on your system. Most currently shipping Linux distributions are firewall-ready. (This is the case if you're using the modular kernel from Caldera OpenLinux, as supplied on the CD-ROM that accompanies this book.) Otherwise, you may need to reconfigure the kernel yourself through the process called recompiling, as outlined in Appendix A, "Configuring the Kernel."

The firewall functions in the Linux kernel are as follows:

IP: Forwarding/Gatewaying. While not strictly a firewall function, if your system is to act as a router gateway (firewall or not), this feature is required.

IP: Firewalling. Support for packet filtering and accounting.

IP: Firewall Packet Logging. Verbose (per packet) logging support.

IP: Masquerading. Support for altering IP headers to hide a local network behind the firewall host.

It is safe to turn all these features on and use them as and when needed.

Certain versions of the Linux kernel also contain experimental protocol-specific firewalling features. Due to their nature, these features are best left turned off on a production server, unless you understand and absolutely need a particular feature.

The `ipfwadm` Command

Once you have a kernel that supports firewall functions, you can use the `ipfwadm` command to selectively turn on or off these features. The command can be used to configure the kernel for accounting, packet forwarding, filtering, and masquerading.

OPTIONS

The functions of the `ipfwadm` command are simple, but its syntax is arcane. It requires several confusing options to be specified on the command line.

The first of these options specifies the firewall gateway function category that the command is to apply to:

-A	Accounting (logging)
-I	Incoming packet filtering
-O	Outgoing packet filtering

▼

▼

-F	Forwarding gateway filtering and masquerading rules
-M	Masquerading

The next option specifies the firewall administration command. Some possible values for this option are as follows:

-a	Append a rule at the end of the list
-i	Insert a rule at the beginning of the list
-d	Delete a rule
-l	List all rules in this category

For rules in the incoming, outgoing, and forwarding categories, the command must be followed by a policy keyword, which may have one of the following values: `accept` (allow the packet to be processed), `deny` (drop the packet), and `reject` (drop the packet, returning an error to the sender).

Within each of the function categories, the system maintains an ordered list of rules. When a packet arrives, it is matched against the rules; when a matching rule is found, the packet is processed. For instance, consider the following command:

```
# ipfwadm -I -a reject -P tcp -D 0.0.0.0/0 137
```

This command sets up the kernel to reject any incoming packets when the destination is the TCP port 137 (used for NetBIOS name service). It is possible to list previously established rules in the -I category as follows:

```
# ipfwadm -I -l
IP firewall input rules, default policy: accept
type  prot source                destination          ports
rej   tcp  anywhere              anywhere             any -> netbios-ns
```

If there are several rules within a category, they are evaluated in the order in which they are listed by the -l command. So for instance, adding the following rule to the preceding one (shown) will have no effect:

```
# ipfwadm -I -a accept -P tcp -D 0.0.0.0/0 137
```

The reason is that the previously appended rule, which specifies that packets of this type must be rejected, precedes the new rule in the list:

```
# ipfwadm -I -l
IP firewall input rules, default policy: accept
type  prot source                destination          ports
rej   tcp  anywhere              anywhere             any -> netbios-ns
acc   tcp  anywhere              anywhere             any -> netbios-ns
```

▼

▼   However, if you use the `-i` command, inserting the new rule before existing rules, the situation is different:

```
# ipfwadm -I -l
IP firewall input rules, default policy: accept
type  prot source                    destination            ports
acc   tcp  anywhere                  anywhere               any -> netbios-ns
rej   tcp  anywhere                  anywhere               any -> netbios-ns
```

In this case, the `accept` rule precedes the `reject` rule, so packets of the specified type will be accepted.

Rules can be deleted using the `-d` command. The rest of the command line must exactly match the syntax used for creating the rule in the first place:

```
# ipfwadm -I -d accept -P tcp -D 0.0.0.0/0 137
# ipfwadm -I -d reject -P tcp -D 0.0.0.0/0 137
# ipfwadm -I -l
IP firewall input rules, default policy: accept
```

A compact summary of `ipfwadm` options can be obtained by typing `ipfwadm -h`. For more detailed information on how this command works, use the manual page
▲   (`man ipfwadm`).

The `ipfwadm` command can be used interactively, or it can be placed into your system startup files. For instance, if you intend to always block NetBIOS traffic from being forwarded by your Linux server, you'd place commands such as this one in your system startup file:

```
/sbin/ipfwadm -I -a reject -W ppp0 -P tcp -D 0.0.0.0/0 137
```

On Caldera OpenLinux systems like that found on the CD-ROM accompanying this book, custom startup commands like this one are best placed into the file `/etc/rc.d/rc.local`.

TEST SYSTEM   On my test system, I am using a customized kernel. When I compiled this kernel (see Appendix A), I made sure that firewall features were enabled. Therefore, I could use all firewall gateway services. (Note that this would also be the case if I had elected to use the modular kernel that came on the Caldera OpenLinux CD-ROM.)

Following my own advice, I decided to add filtering rules to prevent NetBIOS traffic from reaching this host from the outside or from escaping to the outside by accident. I also blocked packets with headers that are forged to make it appear that they originated
▼   on my internal network.

▼   Additionally, I also decided to log all ICMP packets. This helps me quickly identify any hosts that may be probing my network using the ping, traceroute, or similar commands.

To accomplish all this, I added the following lines to my /etc/rc.d/rc.local file:

```
/sbin/ipfwadm -I -a reject -W ppp0 -P tcp -D 0.0.0.0/0 137
/sbin/ipfwadm -I -a reject -W ppp0 -P tcp -D 0.0.0.0/0 138
/sbin/ipfwadm -I -a reject -W ppp0 -P tcp -D 0.0.0.0/0 139
/sbin/ipfwadm -I -a reject -W ppp0 -P udp -D 0.0.0.0/0 137
/sbin/ipfwadm -I -a reject -W ppp0 -P udp -D 0.0.0.0/0 138
/sbin/ipfwadm -I -a reject -W ppp0 -P udp -D 0.0.0.0/0 139
/sbin/ipfwadm -O -a reject -W ppp0 -P tcp -D 0.0.0.0/0 137
/sbin/ipfwadm -O -a reject -W ppp0 -P tcp -D 0.0.0.0/0 138
/sbin/ipfwadm -O -a reject -W ppp0 -P tcp -D 0.0.0.0/0 139
/sbin/ipfwadm -O -a reject -W ppp0 -P udp -D 0.0.0.0/0 137
/sbin/ipfwadm -O -a reject -W ppp0 -P udp -D 0.0.0.0/0 138
/sbin/ipfwadm -O -a reject -W ppp0 -P udp -D 0.0.0.0/0 139
/sbin/ipfwadm -I -a deny -W ppp0 -S 127.0.0.0/8
/sbin/ipfwadm -I -a deny -W ppp0 -S 192.168.0.0/16
/sbin/ipfwadm -A -a -P icmp -o
```

The first 12 lines implement the blocking of TCP and UDP traffic to and from the known NetBIOS ports. These and the next two lines, which block forged packets, all use the -W ppp0 option, which specify that the rules apply only to packets that arrive or are transmitted via the PPP interface (that is, through my modem). The final line turns on accounting for all ICMP packets, regardless of their type, origin, or the interface through which they arrive.

When IP accounting is configured with the -o flag, an entry is created in the system log for each packet that matches the accounting rule. Thus my final ipfwadm command caused lines like this to appear in /var/log/messages:

```
# tail -2 /var/log/messages
Apr  8 09:34:47 host kernel: IP acct out eth0 ICMP/8 192.168.1.1
192.168.1.2 L=84 S=0x00 I=57961 F=0x0000 T=64
Apr  8 09:34:47 host kernel: IP acct in eth0 ICMP/0 192.168.1.2
192.168.1.1 L=84 S=0x00 I=41304 F=0x0000 T=128
```

▲

PART

IV

CH

11

Summary

Firewall gateways can protect your Internet-connected network from many types of intrusions. Rather than purchasing a dedicated firewall costing thousands of dollars, you can configure your Linux server to act as a firewall gateway.

A firewall gateway can perform many protective functions. These include packet accounting and logging, filtering, masquerading, and application-specific support. Logging features let you monitor traffic between your network and the Internet. Filtering allows you to block certain types of data. Masquerading makes it possible to hide your internal network behind the firewall gateway. And, application-specific features make it possible to use certain applications that would otherwise be incompatible with a masquerading firewall.

Do you need a firewall? The answer is probably no if you do not have a permanent connection to the Internet. Even if you are permanently connected, you may not require a full-featured firewall, although filtering certain types of packets can greatly improve your system's security. The most dangerous types of packets include those with forged header information, and packets used to access DOS/Windows shared resources, such as NetBIOS packets.

Firewalls can also make life harder. When a workstation is hidden behind a firewall gateway, many Internet applications will fail to function, while others may require upgrades to the gateway itself.

To use Linux as a firewall gateway, two tools are required: a properly configured kernel and the `ipfwadm` command. The modular kernel found on the CD-ROM that accompanies this book is configured to support firewall gateway functions. The `ipfwadm` command can be used to add, delete, or examine rules used for accounting, filtering, and masquerading.

Manual Pages

For additional information on topics discussed in this chapter, please refer to the following manual pages.

```
man ipfwadm

man route

man services

man traceroute
```

Using External Routers

As more and more people and businesses are beginning to use high-speed or permanent Internet connections, it is increasingly likely that you will encounter a situation where the router function is separated from other server functions. You might be using separate systems to improve performance. You might be using a firewall gateway to isolate your internal network from the Internet. Or you might be using a dedicated router device for a high-speed Internet connection. Whatever the reason, when your Linux system is behind a router, as opposed to performing routing functions itself, a few different rules apply.

Routing Revisited

If you recall from Chapter 5, "Internet Concepts," the function of routing is to connect separate networks together. A computer that contains network interfaces for two or more networks is called a *router*, if it relays information from one network to another.

Routing with Linux

In typical small office or home office applications, one of these two networks is your Ethernet LAN; the other "network" is a point-to-point connection to your Internet Service Provider (ISP) using a modem, ISDN, or leased line (see Figure 12.1.)

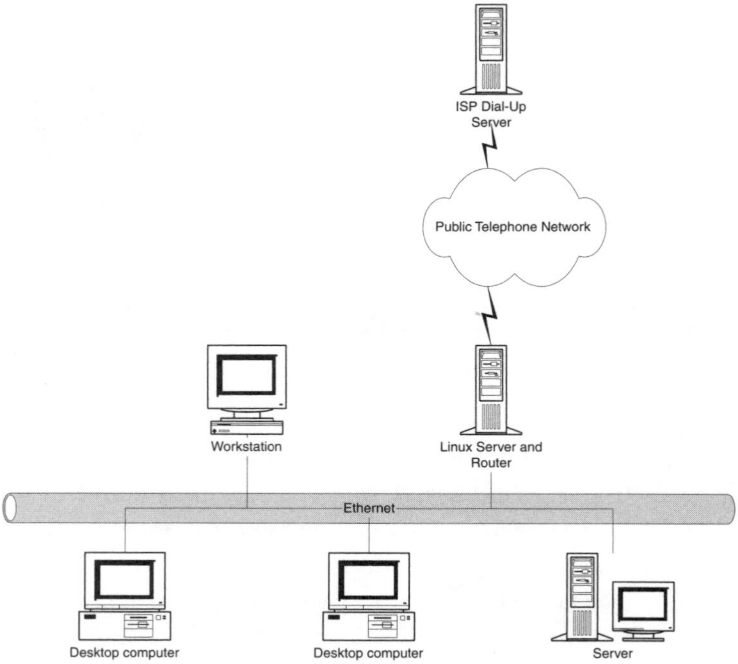

FIGURE 12.1
Routing to your ISP.

One of the most practical uses of a Linux computer is to make it serve as a router for your office. As shown in Chapter 7, "Making the Connection," the Linux machine can be easily configured to use your modem either as a means of permanently connecting your LAN to the Internet or to establish the connection only when needed, using demand-dial software.

Routing Externally

Regardless of Linux's capability as a router, it is sometimes necessary to separate routing from other server functions. Usually, this occurs because you are using a dedicated router device for high-speed connections.

In this scenario, your Linux server no longer plays a special role inasmuch as routing is concerned. However, it retains the role of acting, for instance, as your Web or mail server (see Figure 12.2). The router may be a special purpose hardware device or a dedicated computer that exists as a separate entity on your network, equipped with its own IP number.

FIGURE 12.2
Using an external router.

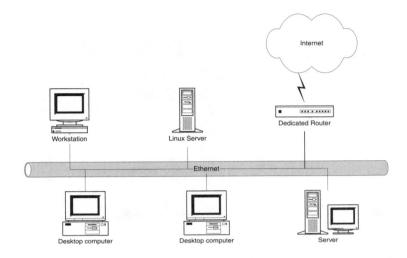

When you change your configuration from one using the Linux server as a router to one with an external router, you need to perform a series of steps.

First, make sure that the router has the correct IP number. Often, your ISP expects you to use the same IP number as before; however, until now, that IP number belonged to your Linux machine. You need to assign that old IP number to the router, and assign a new IP number to your Linux machine. This may also necessitate configuration changes on other systems that rely on your Linux machine's IP number (as opposed to its host name.) All this can be avoided, of course, if your ISP can be persuaded to alter your connection profile.

Second, you must turn off packet forwarding on your Linux machine because it no longer performs a routing function.

OPTIONS

Packet forwarding can be turned off in a variety of ways. Perhaps the easiest is to type the following command as root:

```
echo 0 >/proc/sys/net/ipv4/ip_forward
```

This method does not permanently turn off IP forwarding. To do that, you need to modify your system startup files. Under Caldera OpenLinux, this can be accomplished using the LISA utility. Oddly, the corresponding item cannot be found under LISA's network configuration settings; it is displayed if you invoke LISA with the −system command-line option and select the Configure Daemon/Server Autostart command. Here, make sure that the IP forwarding option is turned off (see Figure 12.3).

FIGURE 12.3
Turning off routing.

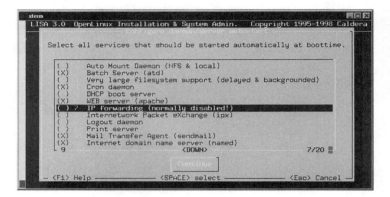

If it was necessary to change your Linux machine's IP number, you should also make sure that all DNS entries are properly updated. For instance, if your Linux machine's IP number was 192.168.1.1 and is now changed to 192.168.1.32, any old entry that identified, say, www.linux.sys with the old IP number needs to be updated. If your ISP maintains DNS for you, ask them to make the necessary changes. If you're running your own name server, you must update the database yourself. (See Chapter 6, "The Domain Name System," for details.)

Segmented Networks

Sometimes it's useful to add an external router in another configuration. Rather than replacing your Linux machine as a router for your network, the device may assume the role of the modem instead. In other words, your Linux machine would continue to act as your network's main router, but rather than using a modem, the machine would use your new router device as its interface to the outside world.

This is accomplished by installing another network segment that connects the Linux machine and the router (as indicated in Figure 12.4). This configuration has one disadvantage: If either the dedicated router device or your Linux server is down, your Internet connection is disabled.

FIGURE 12.4
A segmented network.

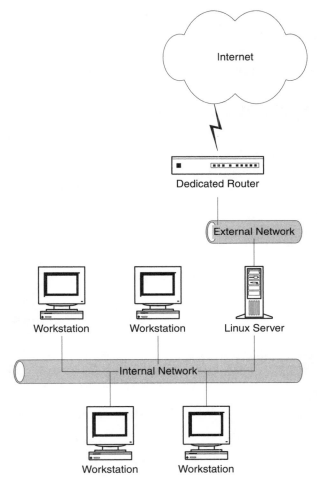

Despite this disadvantage, a segmented configuration is often used when the Linux machine performs a firewall gateway function.

When you have two separate network segments, assigning IP numbers becomes a more complicated issue. The two network segments must each have their own range of IP numbers.

If the gateway linking the two segments performs a firewall masquerading function, one of the segments would need to be assigned numbers from the pool reserved for internal networks, for example, 192.168.nnn.nnn (see Chapter 5). When no such firewall gateway functionality is used, your IP number pool must be divided into two halves.

Other number schemes are, of course, also possible. For example, if you have a three-segment network and a Class C block of 256 host addresses, you can assign one half to one segment (allowing up to 128-2=126 computers), and divide the remaining half between the other two (allowing up to 62 computers in each).

Multisegment Routing

In a segmented network configuration, each network segment has a router that connects it to the outside world (possibly via other segments). Routing information must be configured accordingly on each computer; an example is shown in Figure 12.5.

FIGURE 12.5
Routing on a multisegment network.

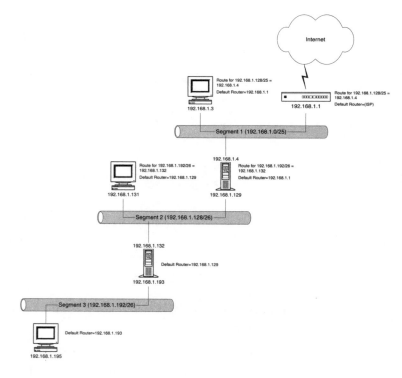

In this example, a Class C network address space of 256 addresses (192.168.1.0 - 192.168.1.255) is divided into three segments. The first segment is 192.168.1.0/25 (this notation specifies that the network portion of the address occupies the first 25 bits, leaving 7 bits, or 128 possible combinations, for the host address). The default router for this segment is 192.168.1.1, which is the dedicated router that connects the network to the Internet.

However, when a packet is sent to host `192.168.1.131`, for example, you don't want that packet to be sent out to the Internet, but sent to the second segment instead, via `192.168.1.4`. Therefore, extra routing information must be added to hosts on the first segment; this extra information will be used to direct all packets with an address in `192.168.1.128/25` to be routed via `192.168.1.4`. This address is that of an interface card on a computer (possibly a Linux server), which acts as a router between the two segments and sports two network interfaces.

On the second segment, the default route is no longer `192.168.1.1`, as that router cannot be reached on this segment directly. Instead, packets are routed to `192.168.1.129`, which is the address of the second interface card of the machine connecting segments 1 and 2. This machine, in turn, routes packets to `192.168.1.1` as its default destination. The same logic is repeated for segment 3.

So, for instance, let's examine what happens when a machine on segment 3 sends a packet to an address that is external to the network, say, `1.2.3.4`. First, because the address is not on this Ethernet segment, the workstation sends it to its default router, `192.168.1.193`. This router finds that the packet cannot be delivered on either of the network segments that it has an interface on, so it forwards the packet to its default router, `192.168.1.129`. That router, connecting segments 1 and 2, also cannot deliver the packet directly, so it forwards the packet to its own designated default router, `192.168.1.1`. This router connects the network to the Internet and correctly forwards the packet to the ISP's connecting host.

Had the packet been sent to `192.168.1.3` instead, the router between segments 1 and 2 would have been capable of delivering it directly to that host on segment 1.

OPTIONS To change the routing on a Linux machine, you need to use the `route` command. For instance, to set up routing for the server connecting segments 1 and 2 in Figure 12.5, you would need to enter the following commands:

```
/sbin/route add -net 192.168.1.192 netmask 255.255.255.192 gw
➥192.168.1.132
/sbin/route add default gw 192.168.1.1
```

Entering these commands from the command line will not make the settings permanent; for that, you need to copy the commands to your system initialization files. The second of these commands is added automatically by the LISA utility when you configure your network settings. The first one can be inserted, for instance, into your `/etc/rc.d/rc.local` file.

External Routers and Firewalls

So what if you are using an external router and want to protect your network using a firewall gateway?

First, many external router devices support firewall features. These range from simple packet filters to advanced features such as IP masquerading or application-specific firewall support. Unfortunately, often these software features are only available as costly optional add-ons.

Alternatively, you can retain your Linux machine as a firewall gateway by placing it between the external router and your local network, as shown previously in Figure 12.4. As described in Chapter 11, "Firewalls," in this case in addition to performing a routing function between the two segments, your Linux server might also act as a masquerading server and translate IP addresses.

Special Router Devices

The two most commonly used external routers in small office or home office environments are ISDN routers and cable modems.

Using an External ISDN Router

ISDN (Integrated Services Digital Network) operates on a digital telephone line and is capable of delivering data at a speed of 64 or 128 kilobits per second. There exist modems (internal or external) that connect to an ISDN telephone line, but the preferred method for connecting to an ISDN line is through an ISDN router, which provides better performance and more flexible features. This type of device usually has an Ethernet connector to connect to your LAN, and another RJ-45 plug for connecting the ISDN line. (Because the plugs are similar, care should be taken not to accidentally connect the ISDN line to the 10BaseT Ethernet port on the device or vice versa.)

The first step when installing an ISDN router is ordering ISDN service from your local phone company. You cannot connect an ISDN router to an ordinary telephone line. Once ISDN service has been established, it's time to connect the router. Most newer routers connect directly to the ISDN wall connector, but some require a terminal adapter, which has to be purchased separately, or may be supplied by the telephone company.

Setting up the ISDN router usually requires that you first configure the telephone line side by entering your ISDN "SPID" (Service Profile Identifier) numbers and specifying the exact type of ISDN service. On the Ethernet side, you must configure the router with a proper IP number for your network and routing information obtained from your ISP. You must also enter the account identifier and password for your ISP account, as well as configure network protocol settings as specified by the ISP.

Many ISPs perform these steps for you and deliver you a fully configured and tested ISDN router.

On the Linux server side, using an ISDN router is no different from the use of any other router device. In particular, you do *not* need to turn on any ISDN-specific features in the Linux kernel. These are only required if you use certain types of internal (expansion card) ISDN devices.

The Trouble with Cable Modems

A special type of an external router is a cable modem. These devices allow high-speed Internet connections via the cable-TV network's coaxial cabling. Cable modems are typically devices that attach to your LAN. They work in a way that's very similar to a regular router's operations, but there is a crucial difference: Many cable modems reflect *all* LAN traffic between your Ethernet LAN and the local cable loop. In effect, these cable modems extend your LAN to include the local cable loop.

So why is this a problem? There is a simple reason: LANs are broadcast-type networks, meaning that the transmission of any computer on the network can be seen by all other computers connected to the same network. But when a cable modem is used, your LAN is extended to include all your neighbors' computers. If you have more than one computer on your LAN, every time they communicate with each other, that traffic will be visible to all your neighbors who have cable modems on the same local cable loop.

In other words, when you send an email, even if it's an internal message transmitted from one of the computers on your network to another, your neighbor will be able to see its contents. When you save your financial records to a shared file over the network, your neighbor will be able to obtain a copy. When you create a backup over your LAN, your neighbor will have a chance to see the contents of every backed up file. Chances are that most of your neighbors are friendly, and few have the software tools needed for this type of network monitoring. Still, is this a chance you want to take?

Fortunately, the solution is simple. When you use a cable modem that is affected by this problem, you should make sure that it is on an Ethernet segment which is separate from your main LAN segment (see Figure 12.6). In effect, you are isolating your network from the cable modem through a firewall technique, even if the firewall in this case doesn't perform any of the functions normally associated with network firewalls and merely provides physical separation of the two network segments.

FIGURE 12.6
A cable modem and your neighbors.

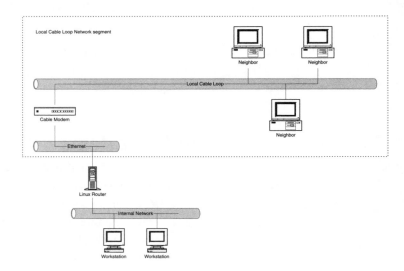

This method also provides a solution to another problem: namely, that cable modem services intended for home use usually allow you to use only one IP number (or charge a fee for extra IP numbers). If your Linux server is configured for IP masquerading, you'll be able to connect your entire network through that single IP number.

Keep in mind, however, that many cable companies do not assign a permanent IP number, but use techniques such as DHCP (Dynamic Host Configuration Protocol). While configuring DHCP is a topic beyond the scope of this book, it's important to know that techniques like this assign, or *lease*, IP numbers on a temporary basis, and so your IP number is subject to change. Consequently, if you want to be able to offer services (such as a Web site) over the Internet, a home-grade cable modem service might not be appropriate.

Summary

Although a Linux server makes an excellent router, sometimes it is necessary to use an external routing device. Typically this occurs because you use a dedicated router for high-speed Internet connections. In this case, even if you continue using the Linux host as a server, routing and other server functions become separated, and the system and your network must be configured accordingly.

Sometimes, an external router is used in combination with a segmented network. In this case the Linux server can be retained as a router between the two segments, while the outer segment is routed to the Internet via the dedicated device. This configuration is often used when the Linux server is configured with firewall gateway functionality.

When an external router is used, the network needs to be reconfigured. This is especially true if a segmented network is created, because new routing rules must be added.

The most frequently used external router devices in small office or home office environments are ISDN routers and cable modems. Configuring ISDN modems is fairly straight-forward if you have the requisite information from your telephone company (which installed the ISDN telephone line) and your ISP. Cable modems, however, deserve special attention, because many of these devices represent a serious security risk.

To prevent a cable modem from reflecting confidential traffic from your LAN to the local cable loop (and consequently, to your neighbors) it is best to isolate the cable modem from your LAN using a segmented network technique. Linux can serve you well as a router between your internal network and the cable modem. In addition, the firewall capabilities of a Linux server not only enhance your network's security, but also allow you to access the Internet from multiple hosts using a single IP number assigned to you by the cable company.

PART
IV

CH
12

Manual Pages

For additional information on topics discussed in this chapter, please refer to the following manual pages.

```
man ifconfig
```

```
man proc
```

```
man route
```

```
man traceroute
```

File Services for Windows: Samba

To most mortals on planet Earth, Samba is the name of a pleasant dancing rhythm of Brazilian origin. To Linuxers and other UNIX users the word has a completely different meaning: Samba is a software package, developed originally by Australian Andrew Tridgell, which adds Windows-style file and printer sharing capability to a Linux server.

What Can Samba Do?

It was possible even before Samba to view the contents of a Linux disk drive over the network and print to a printer connected to your Linux server. All you needed was some third-party software that was capable of communicating with NFS (Network File System) servers or printing to UNIX-style network printers. No problem… except that these packages were notoriously unreliable, slow, and expensive.

Samba approaches the problem from the other way around. Rather than teaching Windows how to talk to a UNIX server, it teaches the UNIX server to act like a Windows host sharing its resources. The result is a fast, highly reliable, commercial grade implementation that is recommended for everyone. Best of all, Samba is free! (But this really isn't news in the world of Linux, is it?)

Resource Sharing in Windows

You know the routine: You right-click on a drive or directory in Windows Explorer and make it a shared resource. This permits others to access the contents found here, with or without using a password, at your discretion.

If you're old-fashioned, or using a DOS machine, you can still do the same thing: if network drivers are installed, you use the `net use` and `net share` commands to access, or make accessible, resources on a network computer.

In either case, the magic behind the scenes is performed by SMB, the Server Message Block protocol. This protocol is used by Microsoft operating systems to implement most network functionality.

Samba and SMB

Samba is a UNIX implementation of the SMB protocol. The basic Samba package provides the tools necessary to share UNIX directories and printers for use by DOS and Windows machines across the network. It also contain utilities that allow you to access shared DOS and Windows resources from a UNIX machine.

In practical terms, Samba allows you to turn a Linux machine into a file and printer server on a Windows network.

> **NOTE**   Samba uses TCP/IP networking. Because of this, on any DOS or Windows machine that you intend to use with Samba, TCP/IP networking must be installed, and NetBIOS over TCP/IP must be enabled. On Windows machines that also have a modem-based Internet connection, you might want to enable NetBIOS over TCP/IP on the local area network (LAN) interface. But, you should disable NetBIOS over TCP/IP on the serial (PPP) interface to improve security.

Samba Components

Samba is a suite of several programs. The two key program files are `smbd` and `nmbd`. The first of these, `smbd`, implements the most of the SMB services that Samba provides. The other key component, `nmbd`, provides NetBIOS name service; it allows other computers to browse the resources provided by the Samba server.

The most useful supplementary component of the Samba suite is `smbclient`. This program provides an interface similar to that of an FTP client for accessing shared resources on other computers in an SMB network. The suite also contains other components such as monitoring and configuration tools.

By default, Samba executable files are installed in the `/usr/local/samba/bin` directory. However, in specific distributions, the location may be different. If Samba is installed from the CD-ROM included with this book, these executables are deposited in `/usr/bin`.

Setting Up Samba

As usual, with software packages, the first step of Samba installation is obtaining a copy of the software.

Where Can Samba Be Obtained?

If you're installing Linux from a CD-ROM, chances are that a copy of Samba is already available on that distribution. (This is certainly the case if you are using the CD-ROM that accompanies this book.)

If you do not have a copy of Samba, or if you want to install the latest version, the best place to look is the Web site: `http://www.samba.org/`. Here you'll be able to find links to an FTP download site that is near you.

Samba is usually distributed in source code form. If you obtained a copy of Samba from the Internet, it might be necessary to follow the instructions in the readme files contained within to compile and install the package.

The Samba Configuration File

Most Samba settings are contained in a configuration file, `smb.conf`. By default, this file is under `/usr/local/samba/lib`. However, specific distributions may place the file in other locations; most notably, the version of Caldera OpenLinux that is found on the CD-ROM attached to this book places this file in `/etc/samba.d`.

The general format of this file should be familiar to those of you who have edited Windows `.INI` files. The file is divided into sections, and each section contains one or more parameters. Sections are identified by the section name, which is in square brackets; parameters appear on separate lines, with the parameter's name and value separated by the equal sign:

```
[section1]
parameter1=value1
parameter2=value2
[section2]
...
```

PART
IV

CH

13

Another similarity with Windows .INI files is that lines beginning with a semicolon are treated as *comment* lines; that is, these lines are ignored when the configuration file is parsed.

The Samba configuration file contains three special sections: global, homes, and printers. All other sections identify individual shared resources, with the section header serving as the resource's name.

Global Configuration Settings

The only mandatory section of the Samba configuration file is the global section. This section, as its name implies, contains general configuration parameters that govern the behavior of Samba. These settings are critical for the correct operation of Samba. They are also used to ensure that Samba operates securely, allowing access to shared resources only by authorized users.

In the rest of this section, some of the most important global parameters are described. For a more complete description, please refer to the Samba documentation (in particular, the smb.conf manual page is very informative).

System Identification

The workgroup parameter specifies the name of the Windows workgroup that this computer will be a member of. The server string parameter specifies the machine's human readable name; this string will appear as the computer's name when you browse the network from other workstations.

Note that it is also possible to make a Linux Samba server a member of a Windows NT domain.

Basic Security

When you run a Samba server, obviously you don't want the whole world to access the files that it has. This problem was less prominent on Windows networks, which traditionally didn't use TCP/IP as the underlying network transport for SMB transactions. With Samba and TCP/IP, restricting access to your server becomes a real concern because, in principle, anybody in the world can interrogate your Samba server if it is connected to the Internet.

As a matter of fact, Samba implements the password security found in Windows networks. However, the degree of security offered by this feature is weak; moreover, shared resources are often not password protected on an internal network. Let's examine Samba parameters and their roles:

- `hosts allow` *parameter.* Used to restrict access to the SMB server to specific hosts or subnets. This parameter can be set to a full IP number or the network portion of one. It can also contain a list of IP numbers or IP number ranges.

- `interfaces` *parameter.* Used to further restrict access to Samba. For instance, on a Linux computer that doubles as a router or firewall, you may be able to restrict Samba access to the internal network using this parameter.

- `security` *parameter.* Specifies whether Samba should adhere to the user-level or share-level security model of Windows networking.

- `guest account` *parameter.* Identifies the guest account that is used for guest logins. This parameter is used when you allow anonymous (guest) logins to the server. The value of the parameter must be a valid account identifier on your system (usually the `nobody` account.)

Logging

Samba can log many events. The `log file` parameter specifies the name of the file where these log entries are placed. The size of the file can be limited using the `max log size` parameter.

Encrypted Passwords

Samba can send and receive passwords (used for logging on to Samba or to another server and access resources) in encrypted form. This feature is used in one of two cases: Either you're using Windows NT and having trouble logging in (more about this situation in a moment) or you don't want anyone equipped with the right software tools on your LAN to be able to snoop passwords.

Password encryption is turned on using the `encrypt password` parameter. Samba maintains its own password file where passwords can be set using the smbpasswd utility. The password file's name is specified using the `smb passwd file` parameter.

Oftentimes user identifiers differ on Windows and Linux systems. The obvious example is the root user of UNIX; the system administrator account is called Administrator on Windows NT. To resolve such differences, Samba can make use of an auxiliary file that maps usernames. The name of this file is specified through the `username map` parameter.

PART

IV

CH

13

Printing

On most UNIX systems (Linux is no exception) the printers attached to the computer are enumerated in the file /etc/printcap. With the load printers parameter, Samba can be instructed to make the printers listed in this file automatically available to authorized users. The printcap name parameter specifies the name of the printcap file (if different from the default, usually /etc/printcap). Other printer-related parameters such as print command and printing specify how printers will be accessed.

Test System Example

TEST SYSTEM   On my test system, the smb.conf file is located in the /etc/samba.d directory. Its global section contains the following settings:

```
[global]
   workgroup = VTTOTH
   server string = Caldera Samba Server
   hosts allow = 192.168.1. 127.
   printing = bsd
   printcap name = /etc/printcap
   print command = /usr/bin/lpr -h -r -s -P%p %s
   load printers = yes
   guest account = nobody
   log file = /var/log/samba.d/smb.%m
   max log size = 50
   security = user
   encrypt passwords = yes
   smb passwd file = /etc/samba.d/smbpasswd
   username map = /etc/samba.d/smbusers
   interfaces = 192.168.1.1/24
```

The workgroup name happens to be the workgroup name in use on the LAN to which the test machine is attached. The hosts allow parameter lists, in addition to the network address in use for the LAN, the loopback address as well. Also, note the format of the log file parameter; the %m part at the end instructs Samba to append the connecting machine's name to the log filename. This way, accesses from different computers are logged to different files.

I also enabled encryption, which allows me to access the Samba server from recent versions of Windows NT without difficulty. More about this in the following sections.

Configuring Shared Directories

So how do you make shared directories available through a Samba server?

First, Samba can make users' home directories available automatically. Second, you can specify individual shared directories by adding the appropriate entries to the Samba configuration file.

Sharing Users' Home Directories

Users can access their own home directories via Samba if the `homes` section is present in the Samba configuration file. On larger systems, this saves you the trouble of having to explicitly share each individual user's directory in the Samba configuration file.

The `homes` section should contain at least four parameters. The `public` parameter determines whether the directories can be accessed anonymously. Except for rare circumstances, you'd want to set this parameter to `no`; otherwise, everybody will be able to read everybody else's files on the server.

The `read only` parameter determines whether files can be written to. Again, set it to `no` unless you don't want users to be able to modify files in their Linux directory via Samba.

The `create mode` parameter specifies the file permissions that Samba will use on files it creates. The format is identical to the numeric format used with the `chmod` command (see `man chmod` for more). Setting this parameter to `0700` ensures that any newly created files will only be readable or writable by the file's owner.

Finally, the `map archive` parameter determines how Samba handles the DOS/Windows "archive" bit. DOS and Windows mark files that have been written to with this flag; the flag is usually cleared when a backup program creates a copy of the file. UNIX has no similar flag, so Samba has the capability to map it to the UNIX executable flag (which has no equivalent under DOS). The downside is that a file written to a Samba shared directory will automatically become marked as an executable program, so it's best to leave this option turned off.

Other Shared Directories

To share a directory over the network, create a new section in the Samba configuration file. The section's name will be the name of the share on the network. The actual location of the shared directory is determined by the `path` parameter.

PART

IV

CH

13

The type of access to the shared directory is determined by a set of parameters. These include public (when set to yes, it allows anonymous access to the share), writable (when set to no, disallows write access to the directory), printable (set to no unless the shared resource is a printer), and map archive (as described earlier).

Test System Example

TEST SYSTEM   On my test system, I allow access to users' home directories (given that I am the only user on this system, it was an easy choice to make). Additionally, I also share the test system's CD-ROM drive. To do this, I have the following sections in my Samba configuration file:

```
[homes]
    public = no
    read only = no
    create mode = 0700
    map archive = no

[cdrom]
    path = /mount/cdrom
    public = no
    writable = no
    printable = no
    map archive = no
```

Configuring Shared Printers

There are two ways to share a printer on a Samba-equipped Linux server. You can instruct the server to share any printers it finds in the /etc/printcap file automatically; or, you can explicitly share individual printers by adding sections to the Samba configuration file.

Background Printing under Linux

Linux, like most versions of UNIX, has an advanced background printing facility. At the core of this facility is lpd, the line printer daemon. This program is usually started when the system boots and runs in the background monitoring print spool directories.

The file /etc/printcap describes all the printers attached to your Linux machine. This file can get quite complicated if advanced features are used, but for a single general-purpose printer, a single line can suffice. For instance

```
lp:lp=/dev/lp1:sd=/usr/spool/lp1
```

This entry describes a line printer attached to the /dev/lp1. (What is known as LPT1 under MS-DOS appears as either lp0 or lp1 under Linux systems, depending on your actual hardware configuration.) It also assigns the spool directory /sr/spool/lp1 to this printer; when files are being printed, this directory is used for temporary storage.

> **NOTE**   If the Linux distribution you use has a graphical configuration tool, you might want to use that tool to set up printers instead of editing /etc/printcap by hand. For instance, if you installed Caldera OpenLinux from the attached CD-ROM along with the X Window System, you may be able to use the Caldera's configuration tool for printer setup.

Once a printer is properly configured, you can send print jobs to the print spooler using the lpr command. For example, to print your /etc/inittab file you'd type

```
lpr /etc/inittab
```

The lpq command can be used to examine the current contents of the print queue. Typing lpq will list all pending print jobs.

Sharing a Printer

Typically, printers on a Samba server are shared by adding a [printers] section to the Samba configuration file. This allows any printers listed in /etc/printcap to be shared via Samba.

Settings in this section are similar to those used when sharing directories. Most importantly, make sure that you include printable = yes. The path parameter specifies the temporary location of the files being spooled to the printer.

To share printers this way, you may also need several settings in the global section of the Samba configuration file, as discussed earlier.

It is also possible to share printers by creating individual sections in the Samba configuration file. However, this method is rarely used and isn't recommended.

Test System Example

TEST SYSTEM   First a confession: My test system has no printer attached. The following example is real enough, but it is from a "production" Linux machine that I use as a server on my network. This machine

PART
IV

CH
13

uses an older version of Linux from a Slackware distribution. However, the version of Samba in use is fairly recent, and is almost identical to the version on the CD-ROM included with this book.

The printer attached to this server is an HP LaserJet 6L. I have installed the appropriate printer drivers on my Windows machines, so ideally, Samba and the Linux line printer daemon will pass through print data without any change. To make sure that this is the case, my `/etc/printcap` file contains the following entry:

```
lp:lp=/dev/lp1:sd=/usr/spool/lp1:sh:ff=
```

> **NOTE**
>
> While on this subject, I'd like to bring to your attention a peculiarity. I've been using a shared printer via Samba for ages; ever since, I've had a problem of an extra blank page being printed at the end of each print run. This was quite annoying, and I could not find a solution. Fortunately, since I print very little, I wasn't bothered by this issue too much.
>
> Now, as I was preparing to write this chapter, I revisited this problem. What I found was an apparent bug in the version of the line printer daemon on this server, which caused a form feed character to be added at the end of each print run even when the file was specified as one that requires no form feed. Therefore, no matter how I configured Samba, when Windows sent a print job to the server, an extra form feed was added in addition to the form feed added at the end of a print job by Windows. This caused the extra blank page to be ejected. Because I was unable to turn off the extra form feed, I had to find another solution: I set the value of the form feed string to an empty value. This is the explanation behind the last element of the printer definition line shown above (`ff=`).

This printer on this test system is shared on my Windows network via Samba. The `global` section of my Samba configuration file contains the following entry:

```
print command = /usr/bin/lpr -h -r -s -P%p %s
```

This entry differs from the default in one key aspect: The `-s` flag instructs the line printer daemon to *not* create a copy of the file being printed but use a UNIX-style soft link instead. The `-r` file tells the daemon to delete the original file when printing is finished. Together, these two settings eliminate an extra copying phase and also make it possible to have print jobs of arbitrary length.

The printers section on this system looks like this:

```
[printers]
    path = /tmp
    public = no
    writable = no
    printable = yes
    create mask = 0700
```

No surprises here. Temporary files are placed in the /tmp directory, the share is marked with the printable flag, and it is only accessible to authorized users (public = no). Note that shared printers do not need to be made writable.

Samba and Encryption

As mentioned earlier in this chapter, Samba supports encrypted Windows passwords. This feature becomes especially important if your network has machines running Windows NT Service Pack 3 or later from which you are trying to access a Samba server.

The Problem with Windows NT

Starting with Windows NT Service Pack 3, Microsoft modified the behavior of Windows NT systems on a LAN. Previously, when a Windows NT system accessed a shared resource across the network, it attempted to communicate password information in encrypted form first, but if failed, it re-sent the password without encryption. Beginning with the Service Pack 3, Windows NT no longer behaves this way; instead, it reports an authentication failure if the encrypted password cannot be used to access the desired resource. The reason for this change was improved security, preventing passwords from being transmitted in cleartext form without the user's knowledge.

Unfortunately, this was bad news for Samba users. Until recently, Samba did not support encrypted passwords unless you acquired an extension module and recompiled the software yourself. In essence, this meant that it was no longer possible to access a Samba shared resource from Windows NT without reconfiguring Windows NT or going through the non-trivial process of compiling your own patched version of Samba.

As it turns out, changing the behavior of Windows NT is fairly easy; all you need to do is to set the Registry value `EnablePlainTextPassword` under the Registry key `HKEY_LOCAL_MACHINE\CurrentControlSet\Services\Rdr\Parameters` to a value of 1 (a `DWORD` value). However, you might want to take advantage of the encrypted password facility instead. After all, it is never a bad idea to protect passwords in any way you can!

SMB Passwords

Enabling encryption is easy with newer versions of Samba. These versions support encrypted passwords "out of the box," with no need for patching or recompiling the software. All you need to do is change a few settings in the configuration file and create a Samba password file.

Here are, once again, the settings that are used to enable encrypted passwords:

```
encrypt passwords = yes
smb passwd file = location of password file
username map = location of user name map file
```

The password and username map files require a special format.

The password file contains one line for each user who can access Samba resources using a password. Although some versions of the smbpasswd utility program can create entries in the password file, most of the time it is still the case that entries must be added by hand initially. A typical blank password file entry will look like this:

`user:uid:NO PASSWORD:NO PASSWORD:::`

The `user` field contains the name that the user will use to log on to the Samba server. The `uid` field must correspond with a valid numeric user identifier as found in the `/etc/passwd` file.

Immediately after these entries are created, you should use the smbpasswd utility to set the new users' passwords to some meaningful initial value. Without this step, the new accounts will remain *passwordless*, allowing access by anyone. The smbpasswd utility replaces the two occurrences of the `NO PASSWORD` string with 32-digit numeric values that represent the password using two different forms of encryption.

> **WARNING**   Unauthorized access to the Samba password file must not be allowed; once the password file is obtained, the encrypted passwords found within are immediately usable with the proper software tools. For this reason, always make sure that this file is readable to the root user only! (Use `chmod 0700 smbpasswd` and `chown root.root smbpasswd` to set this file's permissions.)

The username map file can be used to create aliases for any user identifier on the system. As mentioned earlier, this file can be used to resolve differences in usernames on Linux and Windows systems. The format of the file is simple: Each line contains a Linux user identifier, followed by the equal sign, and a list of Windows usernames separated by spaces:

```
userid = username1 username2 ...
```

> **TEST SYSTEM**   On my test system, the Samba password file, located at `/etc/samba.d/smbpasswd`, contains the following:
>
> ```
> # Samba SMB password file
> vttoth:100:00000000000000000000000000000000:00000000000000000000000000000000
> ➥00:::
> ```
>
> The first line, beginning with the pound sign (#), is a comment line that will be ignored by Samba. The second line contains my user identifier and password.
>
> The username map file, `/etc/samba.d/smbusers`, on this system looks like this:
>
> ```
> # Unix_name = SMB_name1 SMB_name2 ...
> vttoth = administrator admin
> nobody = guest pcguest smbguest
> ```
>
> Once again, the first line is a comment. The second line allows me to log on using my own user identifier, even when I am connecting from a Windows NT system on which I am the administrator. The third line identifies the designated guest user identifier (nobody) with guest usernames that are often used under Windows networking.

▲

Using Samba

You've set up a Samba server and it functions beautifully. So how do you access it from Windows machines? What are the instructions that you need to provide to other users of the network in order to let them access your Samba shared resources?

Accessing Shared Drives from Windows

When everything is properly configured on your Samba server, the server should show up as part of your "Network Neighborhood" on Windows systems. For instance, Figure 13.1 shows a Samba server as it appears on a Windows NT computer.

FIGURE 13.1
Browsing Samba from
Windows NT.

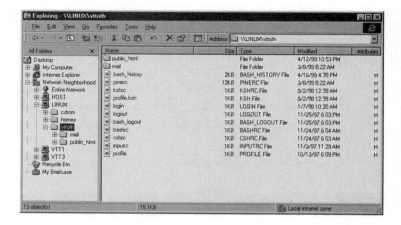

You can also connect to Samba shares or examine the contents of a Samba server from the DOS command line. The advantage of this method is that command-line commands can also be included in DOS batch files, in case you want to automate tasks. To examine the contents of a Samba server, use the `net view` command; to connect to a specific share, type `net use`.

TEST SYSTEM   To access my test system from my Windows NT workstation and see the shared resources there, I use the following command:

```
C:\>net view \\linux
Shared resources at \\linux

Caldera Samba Server

Share name    Type          Used as  Comment

----------------------------------------------------------------------
cdrom         Disk
homes         Disk
printers      Print
vttoth        Disk                   Home directory of vttoth
▼     The command completed successfully.
```

▼   To connect to the shared `cdrom` directory as drive Q: under MS-DOS, I type the following:

```
C:\>net use Q: \\linux\vttoth
The command completed successfully.


C:\>dir q:
 Volume in drive Q is vttoth
 Volume Serial Number is 052E-0876

 Directory of Q:\

03/08/99  06:22a       <DIR>          mail
04/12/99  10:53p       <DIR>          public_html
             2 File(s)               0 bytes
                          676,708,352 bytes free
```

Finally, here is how I view existing connections and delete an established network connection:

```
C:\>net use
New connections will be remembered.


Status      Local     Remote                  Network

-------------------------------------------------------------------------
OK          Q:        \\linux\vttoth          Microsoft Windows
Network
The command completed successfully.


C:\>net use q: /del
q: was deleted successfully.
```

▲

Setting Up a Network Printer in Windows

When you share a Samba printer over the network, you can add it as a Windows printer on any Windows computer that is connected to the network. What is important to keep in mind is that many advanced printer drivers that require bidirectional communication will not work with a network printer. Since most of these printers come with alternative drivers that can be used when the printer is being networked, this is not usually a problem. However, some printers exist that cannot be shared this way (or indeed, may not be usable with Linux at all!)

PART

IV

CH

13

You can set up a shared printer on a Windows computer using the Add Printer Wizard, or alternatively, using the `net use` command. The latter method is also available on networked DOS machines. You can also identify the shared printer with an `LPT` printer port, making it possible to print from older (16-bit) DOS and Windows applications.

TEST SYSTEM On my test system, the printer in use is an HP LaserJet 6L. To add support for this printer on my Windows NT workstation, it was first necessary to install HP's Windows NT drivers on this computer from floppy disks supplied with the printer. (This is the case regardless of the fact that the printer is physically connected to the Linux machine, not to the Windows NT workstation.)

When the proper driver is installed, you can add the specific printer using the Add Printer Wizard. Figure 13.2 shows a snapshot of the Add Printer Wizard under Windows NT.

FIGURE 13.2
Adding a Samba printer under Windows NT.

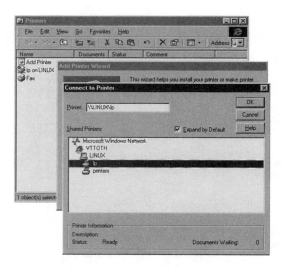

I was also able to add this printer from the Windows command line:

```
C:\>net use lpt1: \\linux\lp
The command completed successfully.


C:\>net use
New connections will be remembered.


▼      Status        Local        Remote                        Network
```

▼

```
OK              LPT1        \\LINUX\lp                  Microsoft Windows
Network
The command completed successfully.
```

▲   `C:\>`

Accessing Shared Resources from Linux

In addition to being able to provide shared resources on a Linux server, it is also possible
to access shared resources found on a DOS/Windows network from a Linux server. There
are two methods available for this: the smbclient tool and the SMB file system.

Using smbclient

The smbclient utility is a command-line tool that can be used to transfer files to or from
a DOS/Windows network share and perform a few other simple functions. In appearance,
this utility is very similar to the FTP program.

TEST SYSTEM   To connect to a Samba share on my test system with smbclient and
list the files there, I used the following commands:

```
$ smbclient \\\\192.168.1.1\\vttoth
Server time is Sat Apr 17 16:32:40 1999
Timezone is UTC-4.0
Password:
Domain=[VTTOTH] OS=[Unix] Server=[Samba 1.9.18p8]
smb: \> ls
  .kshrc                        H         186  Wed Sep   2 00:39:30
1998
  .profile.ksh                  H         182  Wed Sep   2 00:39:30
1998
  .bash_logout                  H          49  Tue Nov  25 18:03:05
1997
  .bashrc                       H         913  Mon Nov  24 06:04:32
1997
  .cshrc                        H         650  Mon Nov  24 06:03:03
1997
  .inputrc                      H         111  Mon Nov   3 11:29:05
1997
  .login                        H         392  Wed Jan   7 10:20:15
1998
  .logout                       H          51  Tue Nov  25 18:03:11
1997
  .profile                      H         341  Mon Oct  13 18:08:59
```

▼

PART
IV

CH
13

▼
```
     1997
       .bash_history                      H       1199   Fri Apr 16 16:39:10
     1999
       mail                               D          0   Mon Mar  8 06:22:34
     1999
       .pinerc                            H      11427   Mon Mar  8 06:22:34
     1999
       public_html                        D          0   Mon Apr 12 22:53:54
     1999

                       55748 blocks of size 16384. 41303 blocks available
     smb: \> exit
```

Note the extra number of backslash characters in the smbclient command line. These are necessary because the backslash character is interpreted by the Linux shell as a special character; two backslashes, however, are passed on as a single backslash. If you find so many backslash characters confusing, you can enclose the string in quotes instead.

That said, newer versions of smbclient also accept the forward slash character in the place of a backslash. When using the forward slash, it is no longer necessary to type it twice:

▲   smbclient //192.168.1.1/vttoth

The SMB File System

While not part of the Samba suite itself, the SMB file system deserves mention here. Simply put, this extension to the Linux kernel makes it possible to mount a shared directory over a Windows network as though it was just another UNIX-compatible file system.

The SMB file system is a capability that is compiled into the Linux kernel. Many Linux distributions contain precompiled kernels that already support this option. (The modular kernel found on the CD-ROM that accompanies this book is one such example.) If your kernel does not support the SMB file system, you might need to recompile it; for more information, please refer to Appendix A, "Configuring the Kernel."

If kernel support for the SMB file system is present, remote shares can be mounted using the smbmount command. This command is usually distributed with Samba, even though it is not actually considered a part of the Samba suite.

A Windows share can be mounted as a file system using the smbmount command. To unmount, use smbumount.

TEST SYSTEM   To mount a Samba share as a file system on my test machine, list the files there, and then unmount the share, I used the following commands:

```
# smbmount //192.168.1.1/vttoth /mnt/smb
Password:
# ls /mnt/smb
mail                  public_html
# smbumount /mnt/smb
```

▲

Summary

Samba is a set of software tools that make it possible to share Linux directories and printers over a DOS or Windows network. The name of the package is derived from SMB, the Server Message Block protocol, which is used by Windows networking.

Samba is available as part of most Linux distributions. The package's two main components are smbd and nmbd, which implement SMB services and NetBIOS name service, respectively. The latter is used to announce a Samba server over the Windows network and handle NetBIOS name resolution requests.

Samba operates over the TCP/IP protocol. Therefore, NetBIOS over TCP/IP must be installed on Windows machines from which you intend to access Samba servers.

The most important step of configuring Samba is setting up its main configuration file, smb.conf. This file contains global setup parameters as well as sections that control individual shared resources.

Samba can be configured to automatically share users' home directories. It can also share all UNIX printers that have been configured to work with the line printer daemon, lpd.

Samba can utilize encrypted Windows passwords. This not only improves network security, but also makes Samba interoperate better with later versions of Windows NT.

It is possible to access shared Windows resources from a Linux computer using the smbclient utility, which is an FTP-like command-line tool. An alternative is the SMB file system; when compiled with the Linux kernel, it makes it possible to mount shared Windows directories as UNIX-style file systems.

PART
IV
CH
13

Manual Pages

For additional information on topics discussed in this chapter, please refer to the following manual pages.

```
apropos smb

man lpd

man lpq

man lpr

man samba

man smb.conf

man smbd

man nmbd

man smbclient

man smbmount

man smbpasswd

man smbumount
```

Time Services

The **built-in clocks of** most personal computers are notoriously inaccurate. Even newer models run fast or slow by several seconds, sometimes whole minutes each day. Yet for quite some time now, I've been used to my computers always displaying the time, accurate to the second. Cool, you say, the author is a mad perfectionist; but what's the point? Is there a practical use, or need, for keeping your computers' clocks accurate?

The Need for Synchronization

When all you have is a simple computer that you use to browse the Web occasionally, it is indeed irrelevant whether your computer's clock shows the proper time. However, when you have several computers interacting via a network, synchronization becomes important. When you save a file to a network file server, you want the file's time and date stamp to mean the same thing on both systems. Even more importantly, some cooperative software packages actually depend on the assumption that all participating computers have the same time.

Synchronizing Hosts

To solve this problem, you need to synchronize all the computers on the network to a single host. This can be accomplished in a variety of ways, depending on the operating systems in use and the software packages installed. It doesn't matter if the computers don't actually display an accurate time; what is important is that they always display the *same* time, and shared network services will operate properly.

Synchronizing to an External Service

Going one step further, it is also possible to synchronize your computers to an accurate external time source. For many years, software packages have been available that use your modem to connect to a well-known time service (for example, the time service of the U.S. Naval Observatory) to get the current time. Now it is also possible to do this via the Internet. The most comprehensive solution for this is provided by the Network Time Protocol (NTP).

UNIX, the Internet, and Timekeeping

Accurate timekeeping has been an important function ever since the dawn of Internet software development. Therefore, in addition to the deluxe solution represented by NTP, several other solutions exist on UNIX systems that provide certain types of timekeeping functionality.

Your Computer and Its Clock

As you surely know (who doesn't, in the year of the infamous Y2K problem?) PC-compatible computers have an internal *CMOS clock*. This is a battery-powered, low-power consumption clock device that keeps the time (and, incidentally, many other permanent BIOS configuration settings) when the computer is turned off. When the computer is turned on, the computer's operating system reads the time from the CMOS clock and sets the clock if necessary (for instance, in response to user commands).

Under MS-DOS, the CMOS clock is updated if you set the time with the `date` or `time` commands, or through the Windows Control Panel or clock utility.

Under Linux, the situation is different. The operating system maintains its own *system time*. The initial date and time is loaded from the CMOS clock when the operating system boots. The date and time can be set together using the `date` command. For example, to set the date and time to April 18, 1999, 01:20:20, you'd type (as the root user):

```
# date 041801201999.20
Sun Apr 18 01:20:20 EDT 1999
```

The CMOS Clock

An important difference between MS-DOS and Linux is that the `date` command does *not* set the CMOS clock! To do so, you must use the `hwclock` command. (Note that on many distributions, especially older versions, the command is called `clock`.)

The `hwclock` command, in addition to being capable of setting and querying the CMOS clock, can also perform translations between local time and Universal Coordinated Time (Greenwich Mean Time). Customarily on UNIX systems, the hardware clock runs on UTC. However, if your computer can dual boot Linux and DOS (or another operating system) you might want to use local time on the hardware clock, because that's what DOS understands.

A particularly useful function of the hwclock utility is its capability to periodically update the hardware clock to compensate for drift. When you set the clock using `hwclock`, the program can save a calibration value to a special file. When it is later invoked with the appropriate command-line options, it can use the value found in this file to adjust the clock. The reason why this function is so useful is that although PC clocks are rarely accurate, their inaccuracy is systematic and predictable.

Simple Time Services

All UNIX systems provide simple Internet time services that can be used by other computers to update their clocks. To see for yourself, try the following:

```
$ telnet localhost daytime
Trying 127.0.0.1...
Connected to localhost.
Escape character is '^]'.
Sun Apr 18 01:10:19 1999
Connection closed by foreign host.
```

In addition to responding on the `daytime` port (port 13), some systems also provide a time service on port 37, the `time` port. When you connect to this port (if a server is available) you receive a binary response consisting of four binary bytes; these represent the current time and date in a compact, machine-readable format.

The Network Time Protocol (NTP)

The NTP is a protocol specifically developed for synchronizing computer clocks across an unreliable network such as the Internet. Synchronization is accomplished by connecting to NTP servers that serve the correct time. These servers, in turn, connect to other servers until you reach *stratum 1* servers, which have their own high-precision clock hardware (for example, atomic clocks or GPS receivers). Such stratum 1 servers are operated by many entities that also provide stratum 2 NTP servers as a public service, including government agencies in the United States, Canada, and elsewhere (see Figure 14.1.)

FIGURE 14.1
The NTP server hierarchy.

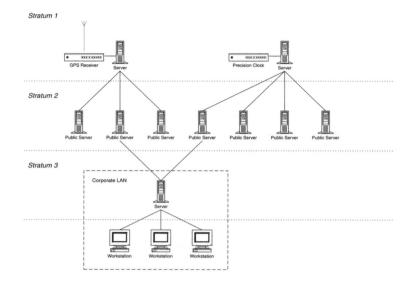

It is also possible to use the NTP on a system that is not permanently connected to the Internet. An NTP server can be installed even on a computer that has no special clock hardware. Other computers can then be synchronized to this server. The server's clock can be kept accurate using the hwclock command or the NTP server's own capability to periodically adjust the clock for drift.

Installing and Using NTP Software

The software tool that is the de facto standard used for implementing NTP services is the NTP daemon and associated tools. This tool can be used to synchronize a computer using a high-precision clock or external servers; it can also be used on standalone systems with no such time reference and still keep accurate time.

Installing the NTP Server

The NTP server (usually under the name xntp) is found on the CD-ROMs of many a Linux distribution. This is certainly the case if you're using the CD-ROM attached to this book. However, if you do not have a copy, or if you want to install the latest version, it can be obtained via the Web (http://www.ntp.org/). The software is distributed in source form, so it will be necessary to recompile and install the code before it becomes usable.

After the NTP software is installed, you'll have to ensure that it is started when the system is booted. This is accomplished by modifying your system startup files.

TEST SYSTEM

On my test system, the NTP daemon has been installed along with other Caldera OpenLinux components. This daemon does not need to be set up for autostart via LISA; when I rebooted the system, xntpd was one of the daemons already running in the background.

NTP Servers on the Internet

The most common mode of operation of the NTP daemon is when it's used to synchronize your server to other servers on the Internet and let other machines on your network, in turn, synchronize themselves to your server.

This is accomplished by preparing the appropriate configuration file for NTP. This file, usually located in /etc/ntp.conf, defines how the NTP daemon will behave, what other servers it will contact during its operation, and what computers it will accept incoming connection requests from.

The NTP daemon has a very large number of complex configuration options; however, for simple operation, all you really need are server and restrict lines in the configuration file. A server line defines a system that your NTP server can contact for accurate time. A restrict line defines what privileges other hosts have when connecting to your server.

That said, you cannot arbitrarily name a server in your NTP configuration file and expect it to work. First, and most obvious, the server you name must actually be running an NTP server, and it must be a system you can reach via the Internet. Second, it must be a server that you have permission to access! Most stratum 1 servers are not publicly accessible; however, many stratum 2 servers are, and it is best to find two or more such servers for synchronizing your clocks. Third, the server you pick should be one that is relatively nearby in terms of network hops, so as to minimize network latency, which may affect the accuracy of your clock settings.

The NTP Web page contains links to many public NTP servers. Note that the operators of some of these servers expect that you send them a courtesy email when you begin using their service.

TEST SYSTEM   I set up my test system to synchronize with two external NTP servers. Both of these servers are stratum 2 servers that are relatively "close" to my LAN. The first server is operated by Environment Canada in Montreal, and it is nine network hops from here. The second server, operated by Wang in the United States, is a bit further away, about 12 network hops.

My NTP configuration file, /etc/ntp.conf, contains the following entries:

```
server www1.cmc.ec.gc.ca
server ticktock.wang.com
restrict     default              notrust lowpriotrap nopeer nomodify
restrict     199.212.17.48    mask 255.255.255.255    nopeer nomodify
restrict     150.124.4.13     mask 255.255.255.255    nopeer nomodify
restrict     192.168.1.0      mask 255.255.255.0      # local hosts
restrict     127.0.0.1        mask 255.255.255.255    # local config
```

The two server lines identify the two NTP servers. The restrict lines that follow ensure that only authorized hosts can access my NTP server. In particular, the first line sets the default policy, namely that no unauthorized host is allowed to connect to my server for any NTP function. Next, the two remote servers are listed, in order to enable synchronizing my server's clock from them. The last two restrict lines allow local machines on my network to connect to the server and perform any function.

As is common with UNIX-style configuration files, the pound sign (#) marks the beginning of a comment; anything after the pound sign up to the end of the line is ignored when the configuration file is being processed.

▲   To ensure that these new settings take effect, I killed the xntpd server and restarted it by typing xntpd on the command line (while logged on as the root user of course).

Setting Up a Standalone Server

Perhaps you don't have a permanent Internet connection and you're not about to invest a considerable sum just to keep your computers' clocks synchronized. Fortunately this is not necessary. You can run an NTP server without an external connection and still use it as a time reference for other machines on your network.

This mode of operation is possible because the NTP software contains several drivers for different hardware clocks. These include a driver for the local system clock. Setting up a driver for a local hardware clock is accomplished through a *hack*—a phony network address is used to identify the hardware device as an NTP "server." These phony addresses are in the form of $127.127.t.u$ where t identifies the type of the device, and u is a serial number between 0 and 3, which is used to distinguish multiple devices of identical type from one another.

The type identifier for your local system clock is 1. Therefore, the server address for the local system clock will be $127.127.1.0$.

TEST SYSTEM   To set up my test system for operation with the local system clock, I modified my /etc/ntp.conf file to read as follows:

```
server 127.127.1.0
restrict        default         notrust lowpriotrap nopeer nomodify
restrict        192.168.1.0     mask 255.255.255.0      # local hosts
restrict        127.0.0.1       mask 255.0.0.0          # local config
```

▲   To make sure these settings take effect, once again I had to restart the xntpd server.

Synchronizing Other Linux Machines with `ntpdate`

Although installing the NTP server isn't terribly difficult, sometimes an even simpler solution is available. You can use the ntpdate command for synchronizing your Linux machine if the following conditions are true:

- The machine can access an NTP server over the network (either on the LAN or via a permanent Internet connection)
- The machine is not expected to be used as an NTP server itself by other computers

Note that the second of these two conditions doesn't mean that the machine cannot be accessed for synchronization purposes; it simply means that it will not be accessed using the NTP protocol. Other methods (such as connecting to the daytime port, as shown earlier in this chapter) will still work.

The ntpdate command accepts an Internet hostname on its command line. For instance, typing **ntpdate host.ntp.sys** would synchronize your system clock from a host named host.ntp.sys if such a host existed and was equipped with a publicly accessible NTP server.

PART

IV

CH

14

The best way to use the ntpdate command is to invoke it periodically. Chapter 18, "Scheduled Tasks, Scripts, and Programming," contains more information on the use of the crontab facility for this purpose. When you run ntpdate this way, it is a good idea to use the -s command-line switch, which directs all ntpdate output to the system log (instead of being displayed interactively).

Synchronizing Windows Hosts

Once you have a Linux system that keeps accurate time, you can synchronize other hosts with it. If those other hosts are running versions of Microsoft Windows, there are several methods available for this purpose.

One time-honored synchronization method under DOS and Windows is the net time command. This, however, requires that the server you use for synchronization be a participant in Windows networking. This isn't necessarily the case if your server is a Linux computer. However, if you are using the Samba suite (see Chapter 13, "File Services for Windows: Samba") you can synchronize a Windows machine using the following command:

```
C:\>net time \\linux /set
Current time at \\linux is 4/18/99 3:45 PM

The current local clock is 4/18/99 3:45 PM
Do you want to set the local computer's time to match the
time at \\linux? (Y/N) [Y]: y
The command completed successfully.
```

Needless to say, you should substitute the Samba name (NetBIOS name) of the actual server that you're using for synchronization in place of \\linux, which is the Samba name I assigned to my test Linux system.

When you're using this command from a batch file, for instance, you can also append the /y command-line switch, in order to avoid the confirmation question.

Note that using the net time command does not require an NTP server on the other end; you can synchronize your workstation's clock to any computer that participates in Windows networking.

On Windows NT systems, there's another tool available for accurate timekeeping. The *TimeServ* time service is a freely available tool, also distributed as part of the Windows NT Resource Kit. This tool implements a Windows NT service that runs in the background, much like xntpd on Linux systems. It can synchronize your Windows NT computer to many types of sources, including NTP servers.

Other third-party tools also exist that can be used on DOS or Windows systems to synchronize your system clock to a remote UNIX server.

Summary

Keeping system clocks accurately synchronized on your network is not merely a perfectionist's mad dream; many software packages expect that networked computers keep more or less the same time when they interoperate.

Linux maintains a system clock that is separate from your computer's hardware CMOS clock. Often, the hardware clock is set to UTC, although in order to maintain compatibility with other operating systems on a multiboot computer, setting it to the local time is also possible.

The system clock can be set using the `date` command. The hardware clock can be set or queried using `hwclock`. This command can also be used to periodically adjust the hardware clock in order to compensate for drift.

A more sophisticated solution is to use NTP, the Network Time Protocol. With NTP server software, it is possible to synchronize your Linux system to timekeeping hosts over the Internet. It is also possible to run your Linux system as a server to which other hosts can synchronize themselves. You can run NTP server software even without a permanent Internet connection; in this case, the time source is your computer's local clock or special time hardware.

If your Linux host is not expected to operate as an NTP server, but has access to another (local or remote) NTP server, you can use the `ntpdate` command for synchronization instead of installing the full NTP server.

Windows workstations on your network can be synchronized with a Linux host in a variety of ways. These include the `net time` command (which requires a NetBIOS compatible server on the other end, such as Samba for Linux), the *TimeServ* service for Windows NT, and other third-party tools.

PART
IV

CH
14

Manual Pages

For additional information on topics discussed in this chapter, please refer to the following manual pages.

```
man date
```

```
man hwclock
```

NTP Documentation:

```
/usr/doc/xntp-3.5.91/html
```

Part V

Managing Your System

15 User Accounts

16 Logs

17 Backups

18 Scheduled Tasks, Scripts, and Programming

19 Configuring Workstations

20 Security Revisited

User Accounts

When you run a Linux server for an organization such as a small business, one of the recurring tasks is administering user accounts. This subject is touched on briefly in Chapter 4, "Internet Configuration and Basic Security." However, there's more to user account management than simply setting up a user identifier.

What Is a User Account?

So what, really, is a user account? The answer depends on how you look at it.

To the programmer, the user account is merely a two-byte number between 0 and 65,535 that identifies the owner of a resource such as a file or a running process.

To the administrator, the user account is a one word identifier—a symbolic name that's used by the user to log on to the system.

To the user, his account is a collection of many things, such as his identifier and password, his home directory, and his email address.

In any case, the user's existence is controlled by entries in the main password file, /etc/passwd. This is where the user's symbolic and numeric ID, full name, home directory, and other parameters are recorded.

User Identifiers

For most users, their identity on a UNIX system is simply represented by their respective user IDs.

Several schools of thought exist regarding the choosing of a user ID. Some organizations assign user IDs at random (for example, ab123). Others use the users' first or last names; this has the disadvantage that if several users share the same first or last name, they must be distinguished somehow, usually by appending a number (for example, joe23). Still others use a combination of users' first and last names; for instance, I've been using the identifier vttoth on UNIX systems for many years. Regardless of the method you choose, it's a good idea to remain consistent and assign IDs to all users via the same method.

That said, the symbolic identifier is *not* really a true representation of the user's identity. Internally, the user is identified by a numeric value. Any files the user owns, for instance, are marked by this numeric value, not the user's symbolic ID.

Therefore, if you remove a user from the system and later create a new account with the same numeric ID as that of the user recently removed, you should not be surprised to find that any files or directories owned by the recently removed user are now owned by the user you just added. For this reason, it's important to avoid recycling numeric user identifiers.

The Home Directory

Simply put, a user's home directory is the place where the user keeps his files. That, of course, is only part of the picture. The home directory is a holder of files explicitly created by the user as well as files used by the programs the user runs. For instance, when the user logs on and a shell program starts under his name, this program takes its initial parameters from a file located in the home directory. Similarly, when the user receives an email message, the mail server consults the .forward file in the user's home directory to find out whether the message needs to be forwarded.

Not all users need to have a home directory. For instance, if a user is never expected to log on to the system interactively, a home directory may be an unnecessary luxury. In this case, you may want to set the home directory to point to /tmp, the standard location for temporary files.

Email Addresses

Usually, a user's email address is his user ID, with the name of your system appended. For instance, my email address on my test system is vttoth@linux.sys.

Sometimes it's necessary to assign alternate email addresses to users. For instance, if your company has a software product for which it offers email support, you may want to have an address in the form of support@*system.domain* on your system. As explained in Chapter 8, "Running a Mail Server," this is easily accomplished using the /etc/aliases file.

The Shell

When a user logs on to the system interactively, a shell program is started. This shell program is what provides an interactive text-based interface for the user to work with. Although the shell program can be customized for individual users, it must be one of the programs listed in /etc/shells.

You should resist the temptation to add arbitrary program names to /etc/shells. This should list only those programs that are suitable to act as a user's startup shell.

If the user's shell, as specified in /etc/passwd, points to a program file not listed in /etc/shells, the user will not be able to log on interactively. This would be a nice way to prevent users from logging on to the system in interactive mode, except there's a catch: Other forms of accessing the system (for example, via FTP) may also become impossible as a result! For this reason, I often find myself using a small dummy shell program I've added to the list in /etc/shells; this program does nothing more than print a message informing the user that he has no shell access; however, its mere presence enables other services to run properly.

TEST SYSTEM In order to make it possible to create accounts on my test system with no interactive access, I've added a "no shell" shell to the list of shells in /etc/shells. This "no shell" shell has to be created first, of course. Even if you aren't a programmer, you should have no problem copying the following few lines to a file you name nosh.c:

```
#include <stdio.h>

int main(void)
{
        printf("Sorry, you are not permitted to have shell access.\n");
        sleep(1);
}
```

▼

▼   If the C compiler and associated tools are installed on your system (if they aren't, they
       should be, because many software packages for Linux are distributed in source form and
       must be compiled before use), these lines can be compiled using the following com-
       mand:

```
cc -o nosh nosh.c
```

If all goes well, this command creates a file named nosh. I copied this file to the directory /usr/local/bin and then added the following line to /etc/shells:

```
/usr/local/bin/nosh
```

After this step, I could create user accounts with /usr/local/bin/nosh as the name of
the shell command; these users are able to access the system via FTP, a mail client, or
some other ways, but they aren't able to access the system interactively (for instance, via
▲   telnet).

Managing User Accounts

User account management entails creating, changing, and removing accounts when necessary. Accounts can only be created or removed by the root user. However, many
aspects of a user account can be changed by users themselves.

The /etc/passwd File

A user account is said to exist when a corresponding entry is present in the file
/etc/passwd. This file is introduced in Chapter 4.

One would think that the easiest way to create a user account is by editing this file.
Manually editing /etc/passwd is, however, not recommended. If you make an error
while editing this file, you can render the system completely unusable. Instead, you
should use software tools for adding and removing accounts. This is especially true when
the shadow password suite is used and you need to edit both /etc/passwd and
/etc/shadow in order to create, modify, or remove an account.

Creating and Removing Accounts

On most systems, two utilities exist for adding a new user: useradd and adduser. The former is a utility distributed with the shadow password suite. The latter is a nonstandard
tool that might not be shadow password compatible. For instance, on the CD-ROM

accompanying this book, adduser is a simple but functional shell script that can make use of shadow passwords. However, on another Linux system I use, adduser is a binary program that stops with an error if shadow passwords are installed.

Another shadow password utility is userdel; it can be used to remove an existing user.

The useradd utility does not create a home directory for the user. This directory can be created by hand, after a new user has been added. Typically, you would populate this directory with standard startup files, which on most systems are located in /etc/skel. These startup files will ensure standard behavior for shells and other common tools for the new user.

Many Linux distributions provide full-screen and/or graphical tools for user administration. The copy of Caldera OpenLinux that's found on this book's CD-ROM also has such a tool. If a tool like this is available, it can greatly ease the task of managing user accounts.

TEST SYSTEM   I tried all the aforementioned user administration utilities on my test system. First, I used the utilities from the shadow password suite to add a user account. After the account was added, I used the grep command to verify that it appeared in /etc/passwd and /etc/shadow as expected. I then removed the account using the userdel command; a second attempt to use this command showed that the account was already absent:

```
# useradd -d /home/juser juser
# grep juser /etc/passwd
juser:x:500:100:Caldera OpenLinux User:/home/juser:/bin/sh
# grep juser /etc/shadow
juser:*not set*:10700:0:-1:7:-1:-1:
# userdel juser
# userdel juser
A user with name juser does not exist.
```

Next, I tried the adduser utility:

```
# adduser juser

Looking for first available UID... 500
Looking for first available GID... 502

Adding login: juser...done.
Creating home directory: /home/juser...done.
Creating mailbox: /var/spool/mail/juser...done.
```

PART
V

CH
15

▼   Don't forget to set the password.

```
# ls -al ~juser
total 11
drwxrwxr-x   2 juser     juser        1024 Apr 19 05:46 .
drwxr-xr-x   7 root      root         1024 Apr 19 05:46 ..
-rw-r--r--   1 juser     juser          49 Nov 25  1997 .bash_logout
-rw-r--r--   1 juser     juser         913 Nov 24  1997 .bashrc
-rw-r--r--   1 juser     juser         650 Nov 24  1997 .cshrc
-rw-r--r--   1 juser     juser         111 Nov  3  1997 .inputrc
-rwxr-xr-x   1 juser     juser         186 Sep  2  1998 .kshrc
-rw-r--r--   1 juser     juser         392 Jan  7  1998 .login
-rw-r--r--   1 juser     juser          51 Nov 25  1997 .logout
-rw-r--r--   1 juser     juser         341 Oct 13  1997 .profile
-rwxr-xr-x   1 juser     juser         182 Sep  2  1998 .profile.ksh
# userdel juser
# rm -r /home/juser/
# rm /var/spool/mail/juser
```

Note that this utility actually created a new group, juser, along with the new user ID. This is not necessarily what I wanted, so I don't think I'll personally be using this utility in the future.

Fortunately, the Caldera OpenLinux system administration tool, LISA, also has a graphical user administration utility that actually works very well. This tool, shown in Figure 15.1, can be invoked by typing **lisa – useradm** on the command line.

FIGURE 15.1
The Caldera OpenLinux user administration module.

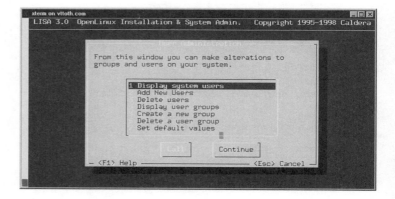

Shadow Passwords

As explained in Chapter 4, the shadow password suite is designed to overcome a weakness in basic UNIX password security: namely, that anyone who can log on to the system has the ability to obtain, and decrypt, the password file. The following sections briefly explain passwords so that you might improve the security of your system.

Password Encryption

If you examine the file `/etc/passwd` on a computer that has no shadow passwords installed, you'll find lines similar to the following:

```
juser:aseb23hfAQ12B:501:100:Joe User:/home/juser:/bin/sh
```

The gibberish immediately following the user's symbolic identifier is the user's password in encrypted form.

The encryption method in use is fairly secure. First, it's a *one-way* encryption, meaning that it isn't possible to recover the original password from the encrypted text. The reason is that many different passwords can be mapped to the same encrypted text, so if only the encrypted text is known, there's no way to find out which of the many possibilities is the original password (see Figure 15.2).

FIGURE 15.2
One-way password encryption.

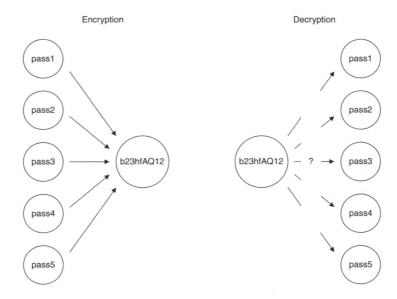

So, how is this password file used if passwords cannot be decrypted? It's simple: When a password is entered (for instance, in response to the `login:` prompt), it's encrypted again. Then, the result of the encryption is compared against the text found in `/etc/passwd`.

An added security feature of UNIX passwords is *salting*. The password is said to be *salted* with a random value, which changes the result of the encryption. Therefore, even if two users use an identical password, the encrypted text will likely remain different; therefore, attacks based on comparing the encrypted password against known values are destined to fail.

That said, even this encryption method is no match for today's powerful computers. A common method of attack, if encrypted passwords are known, is the so-called *vocabulary attack*, in which values from a list (the vocabulary) are encrypted using the same salt value found in the password file and compared against the encrypted password there. Despite widespread concerns about system security, surprisingly many users use simple words containing no mixed-case letters or numbers, so these attacks are often successful. However, even cleverly chosen passwords provide no guarantee against a determined attacker; on a high-end workstation, even a *brute force* attack (sequentially trying all combinations of letters and numbers until one works) has a decent chance of succeeding within a finite amount of time.

The Shadow File

The reason why UNIX password encryption has this weakness is that the file containing passwords, `/etc/passwd`, is by necessity readable by anyone who has an account on your system. Once a copy of this file is obtained, the attacker can use whatever tools are at his disposal to obtain a cracked password. The solution to this problem, as explained in Chapter 4, is to move passwords to a separate file—the *shadow password file*. This file is set to be readable only by the system administrator—in effect closing the security hole represented by `/etc/passwd`.

Password Policies

The shadow password suite does more than merely relocate encrypted passwords to a different file. It also provides tools to implement a *password policy*.

The password policy, in this case, determines when users can and must change their passwords. It's widely believed that password security is improved if users are forced to change their passwords regularly. (Personally, I do not subscribe to this religion.)

The shadow password file, in addition to user identifiers and encrypted passwords, also contains a series of numeric fields that together implement the password policy of your choice. These fields, separated by colons, contain values that determine the following:

- When the password was last changed
- Minimum number of days between subsequent password changes
- Maximum number of days after which the password must be changed
- Number of days before expiry when the user is warned
- Number of days after expiry when the account is disabled
- When the account was disabled

TEST SYSTEM　　The shadow password suite was installed by default when I installed Caldera OpenLinux from this book's CD-ROM. The /etc/shadow file on my test system contains the following line for my personal account:

```
vttoth:123h235isdjrlk:10647:0::7:7::
```

The first and second fields contain my user ID and encrypted password.

The third field contains the date when my password was last changed, expressed as the number of days since January 1, 1970 (10647 equals February 25, 1999).

The fourth field contains 0, indicating that I can change my password anytime. The fifth field is blank, which means my password never expires.

The sixth and seventh fields, both set to 7, specify that I will be warned seven days before my password expires, and that seven days after it has expired, I will no longer be able to log on to the system. Of course, because my password is set to never expire in the first place, this is irrelevant.

▲ The eighth field is nonblank only for expired passwords; for these, it contains the date (again expressed as the number of days since January 1, 1970) when the password expired.

Obtaining and Installing the Shadow Password Suite

Unlike many other software packages, the shadow password suite is not simply a set of programs that you install on your computer. The reason is that in addition to installing the shadow password file and converting your existing passwords to the new format, you need to replace a number of programs and utilities on your system that utilize password information.

Because of this, installing the shadow password suite is not for the faint hearted! Not only do you need to obtain and install core utilities such as a shadow-compatible version of login or passwd, you must also obtain shadow-compatible versions of anything that might ever access the password file—including the FTP server, the POP3 mail server, and the X Windows System authentication program xdm, to name only a few examples. Therefore, the best advice is to install instead a Linux distribution that already has shadow password support, such as the version of Caldera OpenLinux found on the CD-ROM included with this book. If, despite this advice, you decide to install the shadow password suite separately (for instance, you already have a running Linux system that you do not want to reinstall), a recent version of the shadow password suite, along with many shadow-compatible utilities, can be found at the Sunsite FTP site. Connect to sunsite.unc.edu via FTP and switch to the /pub/Linux/system/admin directory.

User Quotas

On a multiuser system, disk space is at a premium. Even with today's large hard drives, it's easy to run out of space if you have many users who use your Linux system regularly.

One solution to this problem comes in the form of *quota support*. This solution makes it possible to define an upper limit of disk space each individual user can use. When this space is exhausted, the disk will, in effect, appear full to the user, even though there may remain plenty of disk space available for use by others.

Quotas and the Kernel

The bulk of quota support is implemented as part of the Linux kernel. Therefore, in order to add quota support to your system, you may need to recompile the kernel and enable quota support. (The Caldera OpenLinux version found on the CD-ROM accompanying this book already has quota support.) For more information about compiling the Linux kernel and the CONFIG_QUOTA kernel compilation option, refer to Appendix A, "Configuring the Kernel."

Quota Support Tools

To actually make use of quota support in the Linux kernel, you need administration tools. These tools include command-line utilities such as quota (to check your file system quota), edquota (to edit a user's quotas), and repquota (to report on quota usage).

These tools are not part of the Linux kernel, and they aren't available in many Linux distributions. Instead, they must be obtained separately. For instance, you may be able to obtain a recent copy of the quota tools from the Sunsite Web site at the `sunsite.unc.edu` FTP address (switch to `/pub/Linux/system/admin/diskusage` directory). Installation of the tools requires them to be compiled and configured.

Summary

Some of the most common tasks a Linux administrator must perform are creating, managing, and deleting user accounts. A user account consists of an entry in the `/etc/passwd` file, the user's home directory, and the user's mailbox.

Internally, users are identified by a number between 0 and 65,535. A user knows his account by its symbolic name, which is also known as the user ID. In addition to a user ID, a user usually has a home directory, where most of the user's files are stored. The user's startup shell is the interactive program that's activated when the user logs on to the system.

To add a user, as a minimum, a new entry must be created in `/etc/passwd`. This is best performed using software tools such as useradd or the user administration module of the Caldera OpenLinux system administration utility LISA.

Because of security problems with `/etc/passwd`, many systems store encrypted passwords in a separate file, `/etc/shadow`. The set of tools that implement this are collectively called the *shadow password suite*. This suite, although it can be installed separately, is best installed along with a Linux distribution, because installing after the fact is a complex task.

It's also possible to limit the amount of disk space individual users can use on your system. To do so, you need to install quota support. Quota support requires an appropriately compiled Linux kernel and the installation of quota tools, which can be obtained from many Linux archives on the Internet.

Manual Pages

For additional information on the topics discussed in this chapter, refer to the following manual pages:

- `man 5 shadow`
- `man passwd`
- `man chfn`
- `man chsh`

Logs

Whether you're trying to diagnose a problem, catch an attacker trying to gain access to your system, or just monitor your system's health, the primary tools you'll use are the various system logs. Their importance cannot be overstated. In order to manage a Linux server effectively and with confidence, it's important that you become thoroughly familiar with the logs generated on your system and are able to read them so as to locate messages of importance with ease.

The System Log

Most UNIX systems provide a general-purpose log facility that can be used by the operating system itself as well as by application programs. This facility is called the *system log*. In Linux, the system log is under the control of a special-purpose server program—the syslog daemon, `syslogd`.

Log Messages

By convention, most log messages are placed in the file `/var/log/messages`. This file contains lines similar to these:

```
Apr 12 22:25:03 host syslogd 1.3-3: restart.
Apr 12 22:25:05 host kernel: klogd 1.3-3, log source = /proc/kmsg
started.
Apr 12 22:25:06 host xntpd[347]: xntpd 3-5.91 Wed Aug 19 06:20:55 MST
1998
Apr 12 22:25:06 host cron[353]: (CRON) STARTUP (fork ok)
```

As you can see, every line in the log file begins with a date and time stamp. The next field is the name of the computer where the log message originated. Most of the time, this will simply be the name of your Linux system; however, if you permit logging over the network, other computer names may show up here as well.

The computer name is followed by the name of the application that generated the log message. The application's numeric process identifier is also shown in square brackets. Finally, the actual message is printed.

Running syslogd

The Linux system log server program is called syslogd, and it's usually started along with other system daemons at boot time. The function of syslogd is simple: It listens for incoming messages and places these messages in the appropriate file.

If your system doesn't have a running copy of syslogd, you can start it by typing **syslogd** as the root user. (Since syslogd might not be on your default path, it might be necessary to precede it with a full path name, for instance /usr/sbin/syslogd.) This command can be added to your system initialization files in /etc/rc.d to ensure that syslogd is started when the system boots.

Logging over the Network

In addition to logging local events, the system log facility can also log events from across the network. Because this capability clearly provides a means to abuse your system (if a malicious hacker or malfunctioning computer begins sending massive amounts of syslog messages to your system, you have a problem), it's turned off by default. You can turn it on by changing the way syslogd starts; simply add the -r command-line switch to the syslogd startup command.

This command-line switch instructs syslog to not only listen to local messages, but also to messages that come in across the network through UDP port 514. (See Chapter 5, "Internet Concepts," for more information about TCP and UDP ports.)

> **WARNING**   Before using the -r switch with the syslogd command, you must understand that there's no way to make syslogd selectively listen only to messages coming in from certain computers. Any computer on the network can send log messages to a server that runs the syslog utility with this switch.

Therefore, if your system is connected to the Internet (especially if it's permanently connected), you should filter any incoming data that's coming from an outside source and is directed at UDP port 514. For more information about packet filtering, see Chapter 11, "Firewalls."

Configuring syslogd

The fact that `syslogd` listens for incoming log messages is obviously only one part of the equation. Where do the received messages go?

The answer is simple: The behavior of `syslogd` is controlled by the contents of the file `/etc/syslog.conf`. This configuration determines how incoming messages are processed and into which log files they'll be deposited.

Log messages can be selectively processed because, in addition to what you see in the log file, each log message has two additional attributes: a facility identifier (see Table 16.1) and a priority level (Table 16.2).

TABLE 16.1   Syslog Facility Identifiers

Facility	Description
auth	Security/authorization messages
authpriv	Security/authorization messages (private)
cron	Clock daemon
daemon	System daemons
kern	Kernel messages
lpr	Line printer subsystem
mail	Mail system
mark	Reserved for internal use
news	Network news subsystem
syslog	Messages generated internally by `syslogd`
user	Random user-level messages
uucp	UUCP subsystem
local0 through local7	Locally defined use

Table 16.2   Syslog Priority Identifiers

Priority	Description
debug	Debug-level messages.
info	Informational.
notice	Normal but significant conditions.
warning	Warning conditions.
err	Error conditions.
crit	Critical conditions.
alert	Action must be taken immediately.
emerg	System is unusable.

These identifiers in the two tables are used in /etc/syslog.conf to specify how specific message types are to be processed. Each line in /etc/syslog.conf looks like this:

```
facility.priority      action
```

The *facility* and *priority* fields contain keywords from Tables 16.1 and 16.2, respectively. The *action* field determines how messages of the selected type will be processed.

It's possible to specify multiple facilities, separated by commas, or to use a single asterisk to mean *all facilities*. In the *priority* field, a single keyword means *all messages of the specified priority and above*. However, you can precede priority keywords with an equal sign (meaning only the specified priority). The priority (with or without the equal sign) can also be preceded by an exclamation mark, which negates its meaning. For instance, !warning means only priorities lower than warning, and !=emerg means all priorities except emerg.

The *action* field can contain any one of the following:

- A full pathname, in which case messages of the specified type are written to the file specified by this path
- An "at" sign (@) followed by the network address of a machine that's configured to receive syslog messages
- A user or list of users (separated by commas) or all currently logged on users (*)
- The name of a device such as a console or a named pipe

WARNING The *action* field must be separated from the *facility.priority* part using tab characters (space characters will not work on most systems)!

NOTE In order to guarantee the integrity of log files in case of a system crash, syslogd always flushes the contents of a log file to disk every time the file is written to. This ensures that no data remains cached in memory in case of a crash; however, this behavior incurs a performance penalty. To prevent syslogd from flushing a particular log file, precede the file's name with a minus sign in /etc/syslog.conf.

TEST SYSTEM Caldera OpenLinux, as installed on my test system, comes with a preconfigured syslog.conf file that contains the following configuration lines:

```
*.info;news,mail,authpriv,auth.none    -/var/log/messages
authpriv.*;auth.*                       /var/log/secure
mail.*                                  /var/log/mail
news.*                                  /var/log/news.all
uucp,news.err                           /var/log/spooler
*.emerg                                 *
```

This configuration is fine; it works well for most purposes. However, I decided to add one line to ensure that error messages are logged to another host on my network as well:

```
*.err                                  @192.168.1.2
```

Needless to say, the host specified here is also equipped with a running copy of syslogd—one that has been configured to accept log messages over a network connection.

Kernel Logging

A special category of log messages is reserved for those generated by the Linux kernel. By default, these messages are printed on the console, which can be quite disturbing when they pop up while you're editing a critical file, for instance. There isn't a need to see most kernel messages immediately; quite a few of them are just informational messages, such as those telling you that the CD in your CD-ROM drive has been changed.

Kernel log messages can be redirected to the system log using the kernel log daemon, klogd. This daemon is usually started along with syslogd at system boot time. When this daemon is running, all kernel messages except "panics" (messages indicating a catastrophic system failure) will be redirected to the system log instead of being displayed on the console.

The most recent kernel messages can also be viewed at any time using the dmesg command. The kernel keeps a fixed-size internal buffer in which it stores the messages it generates; when the buffer becomes full, it's reused from the beginning in a circular fashion (which is why it's called a *ring buffer*). The dmesg command simply lists the contents of this buffer. Optionally, it can also be used to clear the contents of the buffer. (Note that it will not remove any messages that have been sent to the system log.)

Boot Notification

One highly practical use of the dmesg command is to create an informational email message every time the system boots. This not only informs you of an unexpected system boot, it may also give you advance notification in case there's a hardware problem with your system.

One way to create such a notification message is by adding the following command to the file /etc/rc.d/rc.local (which, with most Linux distributions, is the file that contains local customizations to the system boot process):

```
/bin/dmesg ¦ /bin/mail -s "System boot: `/bin/date +%y%m%d`" root
```

Note the use of the back quote character (`) in this line; it enables the output of the quoted command (in this case, the /bin/date command) to appear as a parameter to another command (/bin/mail.)

This command creates a mail message with the following text in the Subject line:

```
System boot: yymmdd
```

The body of the message will contain all kernel messages collected since the system booted. The message is mailed to the root user. Needless to say, you're free to customize this line to fit your needs—for example, you may want to alter the format of the output of the date command to show a four-digit year (a Y2K requirement at many organizations) or change the addressee of the message.

Reading the Log Files

Depending on its level of utilization the way its log files are configured, a Linux system can generate tens, even hundreds of kilobytes of log messages a day. System log files can look quite intimidating at first; fortunately, they can be easily tamed if you're armed with a little knowledge and a few common UNIX text-processing tools.

The Meaning of Log Entries

PART

V

CH

16

It's important to remember that just because something appears in the log file doesn't mean it requires your immediate attention. In fact, the vast majority of log messages are simply informational and can be safely ignored, unless you're looking for signs of a specific event or occurrence.

TEST SYSTEM   Because my test system is rather sterile, its logs tend to be uninteresting. Instead, I've picked a few log entries from a real "live" Linux system to serve as examples:

```
Apr  1 00:01:49 host1 sendmail[5025]: XAA05023: to=some.user@spectraweb.ch
➥, delay=00:04:50, xdelay=00:03:45, mailer=esmtp, relay=smtp.plusnet.ch.,
s
➥tat=Deferred: Name server: smtp.plusnet.ch.: host name lookup failure
Apr  1 00:04:03 host1 in.pop3d[5061]: connect from 192.168.1.3
Apr  1 00:10:01 host2 ntpdate[9175]: adjust time server 192.168.1.1 off-
set
➥  -0.354835 sec
Apr  1 00:12:17 host1 sendmail[5064]: XAA05023: to=some.user@spectraweb.ch
➥, delay=00:15:18, xdelay=00:02:55, mailer=esmtp, relay=smtp.plusnet.ch.
[1
➥94.158.230.8], stat=Sent (HAA31396 Message accepted for delivery)
Apr  1 00:55:38 host2 named[57]: NSTATS 922946138 920191184 A=5063
PTR=777
➥86 MX=42 ANY=84
Apr  1 01:26:20 host1 xntpd[97]: synchronisation lost
Apr  1 01:27:24 host1 xntpd[97]: synchronized to 150.124.4.13, stratum=2
```

All kinds of messages appear here, but none of them are critical. Indeed, none of them require any attention unless in connection with another problem.

The first message in this list (`sendmail`) informs us that the mail server failed to deliver a message due to a name server problem. Nothing to be concerned about; the mail server will retry later, and if it continues to fail, it will eventually notify the sender anyway.

▼
The second message (pop3) simply tells us that a mail client logged on, checking for messages. This should only be of concern if the logon attempt is made from an unknown Internet address; however, that is not the case here.

The third message (ntpdate) is a notification made by the ntpdate command when it updated the system clock (see Chapter 14, "Time Services").

The fourth message tells us that sendmail was finally able to deliver the previously undeliverable message. The fifth message is a routine statistic logged by the name server. The sixth and seventh messages are status reports by the Network Time Protocol server. This is all routine stuff that's of no interest to you unless you're looking for notifications related to a specific problem.

A little bit more worrisome is a message like this one:

```
Apr  1 02:32:46 host1 su: FAILED SU vttoth on /dev/ttyp1
```

This message means that a user attempted to gain superuser privileges and failed (presumably because he didn't know the correct root password). It so happens that, in this case, the user in question was yours truly, and the failure was due to stubby fingers. However, messages like this can be of potential concern.

Even more bothersome are messages like this one:

```
Apr  1 04:49:04 host2 kernel: scsi : aborting command due to timeout :
pid
➥4224928, scsi0, channel 0, id 6, lun 0 0x28 00 00 30 22 22 00 00 80 00
```

This message indicates a potential hardware failure. A failure of the SCSI controller can be of grave concern, because it can cause file system corruption or worse. Fortunately, on the system that generated this message, the SCSI adapter is known to act up under heavy load and then recover without further problems, but messages like this should not
▲
be ignored without investigating their cause and possible consequences.

As you gain experience with reading logs, it will become easier to distinguish messages of importance from recurring log entries of no significance. You may also find it convenient to customize your copy of syslog.conf, directing messages to different files to improve readability.

Logs and Text-Processing Commands

So how do you find the "interesting" lines in the system log? Clearly, reading through a file that's several hundred kilobytes or even several megabytes in length can be time consuming. Fortunately, UNIX text-processing commands can be of great assistance here. Four commands are particularly useful when you're dealing with log files.

The `tac` command (observant readers might notice that this is just the reverse of `cat`) lists the contents of a file backwards. In combination with `more` (or `less`), this command can be used to list log files one page at a time, showing the most recently added messages first.

The `head` command can be used to list the first few lines of a file. By default, `head` lists the first 10 lines of a file. By adding a numeric argument in the form of `-#` before the filename, you can specify how many lines you want to see listed.

The `tail` command works similarly to `head`, except that it lists the last few lines (10, by default) of the file specified on the command line.

Finally, one of the most useful UNIX commands, `grep`, can be used to search for all occurrences of specific text in a file.

These commands, when combined, can make your use of system logs very efficient.

TEST SYSTEM   As an example, I decided to view all NTP (Network Time Protocol) messages in my test system's log. To list only NTP messages, list them in reverse time order, and show them one page at a time on the screen, I used the following command:

▲   `tac /var/log/messages ¦ grep ntp ¦ less`

Continuous Monitoring

The `tail` command can also be used to monitor log files on a continuous basis. This is made possible by the `–f` command-line parameter. For instance, try the following command:

`tail –f /var/log/messages`

As you'll notice, the command prints the last few lines of the named file, but it does not return a command prompt. Instead, additional lines will appear on the screen as they are written to the specified file. You can use this command on a virtual console, or you can use it in a window if you use a graphical interface or connect to your Linux system remotely and keep your system's log files under constant watch.

Other Log Files

Not all applications use the system log exclusively for logging important messages. This section provides a review of some other important log files that may appear on your system.

Login Records

Two binary files, utmp and wtmp, are used to discover users who are currently logged on to the system and to record logins and logouts. These files are not human readable; they're parsed by special utility programs.

The who command shows all users currently logged on. This list is generated from the contents of utmp.

The last command shows all past logins for which records exist. It essentially displays the contents of wtmp in reverse order. An optional parameter in the form of -#, where the pound sign represents an arbitrary number, can be used to limit the number of lines displayed by this command.

The size of utmp is limited to a few hundred bytes for each logged-on user. The size of wtmp, however, can grow beyond limit, because a new entry is added to it every time a user logs on or logs off the system.

TEST SYSTEM   Here's the output produced by the who and last commands on my test system:

```
$ who
vttoth     ttyp2     Apr 16 16:39 (vtt1.vttoth.com)
$ last -5
vttoth     ttyp2          192.168.1.2        Fri Apr 16 16:39     still logged
in
root       tty1                              Fri Apr 16 16:28 - 16:41
(00:13)
vttoth     ttyp1          192.168.1.2        Tue Apr 13 17:09 - 15:50
(2+22:41)
```

```
reboot    system boot                Tue Apr 13 16:56
ftp       ftp            localhost   Sat Apr 13 09:26 - 09:26
(00:00)
```

▲   Notice that in addition to normal logins and logouts, the list also contains logins via FTP and system boot events.

A third binary file, `lastlog`, also contains information about user logins. From this file, you can determine the last login time for each user on your system. The file can be read using the `lastlog` command, available with some Linux distributions.

Transfer Logs

When users access your system via the File Transfer Protocol (FTP), entries are generated in the transfer log file. This file—normally called `xferlog` and placed in the `/var/log` directory—contains an entry for each file transfer completed.

Web Server Logs

The Apache Web server normally generates two log files. The access log contains an entry for each access to your server; the error log contains an entry for every Web server error that occurred.

If your Web server hosts multiple virtual hosts, you may see multiple copies of the access and error logs, one for each virtual host on your system.

The location of these log files is specified in your Web server configuration file. In Caldera OpenLinux, these files are normally stored in `/var/log/httpd/apache/`.

UUCP Logs

If you use UUCP for mail or news transfer, the UUCP system also creates its own log files. These log files contain information about incoming and outgoing calls and files transmitted or received. Depending on how your copy of UUCP is configured, these log messages may be deposited in a single file or multiple files, one for each UUCP system with which you exchange information.

News System Logs

The INN news server generates several log files as it operates. These files are normally deposited in the /var/log/news or /var/log/news.d directory.

Log Maintenance

No doubt you've been wondering, "If log files can grow beyond limit, how can I prevent them from gobbling up all the disk space on my Linux system?"

The solution, of course, is to create new log files periodically. This procedure is called *rotating the logs* (for reasons that will become obvious in a moment).

Rotating Logs

Why wouldn't you simply erase log files periodically to free up disk space? For two reasons, actually. First, by erasing files, you erase traces of recent activity. Erasing files that contain month-old messages shouldn't be a problem, but erasing files that contain entries up to the present moment isn't such a hot idea.

The second reason is that when you erase a log file that's in use, often the programs generating the log messages will fail to create new files. Instead, no log entries will be made.

The solution to both of these problems is *log rotation*. This procedure entails the following steps:

1. Remove old log files.
2. Rename existing log files.
3. Inform server programs to start using new log files.

These steps can be performed either by hand, using simple script files, or under program control.

The first two steps are easy. For instance, you may decide to save the most recent copy of /var/log/messages as /var/log/messages.old. To rotate the log, you would use the following commands:

```
rm /var/log/messages.old
mv /var/log/messages /var/log/messages.old
```

So how will the system log daemon be told to create a new copy of /var/log/messages? Simple, all you need to do is to send it a hang-up signal:

```
killall -HUP syslogd
```

In addition to syslogd, other programs are designed to respond to the hang-up signal by rereading their configuration files and reinitializing; this also includes reopening an existing log file or creating a new one if necessary. However, this behavior is by no means universal; before sending a hang-up signal to your favorite system daemon, you should consult its manual page!

On many distributions, including the version of Caldera OpenLinux found on the CD-ROM that accompanies this book, programs already exist that automate this procedure.

TEST SYSTEM   **Test System Log Files**

On my test system, the following log files are generated by the system log daemon and other server applications:

```
/var/log/lastlog
/var/log/mail
/var/log/messages
/var/log/news.all
/var/log/secure
/var/log/spooler
/var/log/wtmp
/var/log/xferlog
/var/log/httpd/apache/access_log
/var/log/httpd/apache/error_log
/var/log/news.d/errlog
/var/log/news.d/news
/var/log/samba.d/nmbd
/var/log/samba.d/smb.smb
/var/log/samba.d/smb.hostname
/var/log/samba.d/smbd
/var/log/uucp/Log
/var/log/uucp/Stats
```

Many of these log files have multiple copies because of the log rotation scheme used by Caldera OpenLinux. This scheme is implemented by the program /usr/sbin/logrotate and its associated configuration files in /etc/logrotate.d. For the log files this tool is configured to process, old copies are saved with a numeric extension added to the filename (for example, messages.01, messages.02, and so on). As it comes "out of the box," logrotate is set to compress some old log files; these have an additional .gz extension (for example, spooler.01.gz). These compressed files can be displayed without decompression using the zcat command (or displayed one page at a time using zless).

Summary

Like any decent UNIX system, Linux produces copious amounts of logs during daily use. Understanding the log files your system produces is the key to maintaining a healthy system.

The central logging facility under Linux is the system log. When the `syslogd` daemon is running, server applications can send log messages to it. The files where these messages are deposited are defined in the system log configuration file, `/etc/syslog.conf`. It's possible to direct certain types of log messages to other computers on the network. It's also possible to configure the `syslogd` daemon to accept such log messages over the network from other systems.

A specific category exists for messages generated by the Linux kernel. These messages normally appear on the console, but with the help of the `klogd` daemon, it's possible to redirect them to the system log. Recent kernel messages are temporarily buffered and can be viewed using the `dmesg` command.

Log files can be viewed efficiently using simple text-processing commands. The `head`, `tail`, `tac`, and `grep` commands are particularly useful when viewing the beginning of log files, viewing the end of log files, viewing log files in reverse order, and searching for specific text within a log file, respectively.

In addition to the main system log, other log files are generated by various applications. These logs include login records, Web and FTP server transfer logs, and UUCP and news system logs.

To prevent log files from filling up your system's hard disk, you need to rotate these files. Rotation can be accomplished using a few simple commands or by using utility programs such as logrotate that have been specifically developed for this purpose.

Manual Pages

For additional information on the topics discussed in this chapter, refer to the following manual pages:

- man syslogd
- man klogd
- man syslog.conf
- man dmesg
- man wtmp
- man who
- man last
- man xferlog

Backups

You've heard it enough from system gurus: Always have an up-to-date backup of all data on your computer! When it comes to servers, maintaining backups is even more important; if the system goes down and data is lost, many users might be affected.

But what, exactly, is a meaningful backup strategy for a Linux server? And on the practical side, what's the best way to create backups?

Backup Strategies

Creating a backup should be simple, right? All you need to do is to make a copy of all the files on the hard drives of your system. Then, when disaster strikes, you simply restore the files from backup, and—Presto!—everything is ready to go. Or is it?

Backing Up Is Not Enough

The trouble with this simplistic backup strategy is that although it does ensure that all your data has backup copies, it fails to take into account the procedure of restoring the data.

Consider the following example: You've created a full backup to tape using the Linux `tar` command (we'll talk more about this command later) on a tape drive you purchased recently at an auction, and this tape drive has been giving you trouble-free service ever since. A compressed, encrypted archive is stored on a tape that, for added safety, you decided to store offsite. Then, one morning, you enter your office, only to find that your Linux machine has been stolen or destroyed by a short circuit in its power supply. What now?

Obtaining another machine should present no great difficulty, especially considering that a Linux server that's not heavily loaded runs on just about everything that deserves to be called a computer these days. Getting a hold of your dad's old 486 is not a problem, but it's not going to solve your dilemma. The first puzzle you'll face will be fairly obvious as soon as you notice the lack of a suitable receptacle into which your backup tape, just retrieved from off-site storage, would be inserted. Ouch!

So, you spend the next 24 hours in a mad search for a compatible tape drive. If you're lucky, you at least know the model number. Later, you eventually find an online surplus store on the Internet that's willing to ship you the correct unit, at a huge markup, from a warehouse somewhere in Alaska or Hawaii. Eventually the unit arrives; you install it and turn on the system. You're greeted with the prompt of an obsolete DOS version still on dad's computer, and you have no clue as to how your perfectly functional Linux system can be retrieved from your tape. DOS has no `tar` command, nor does it recognize tape drives without third-party software.

Eventually, you realize that in order to run tar to read your tape, you must have a working copy of Linux first, and so you proceed with the installation of a fresh copy. You install a minimum system, access the tape, find to your delight that the tape is perfectly readable, and start the process of restoring files. When you're finished, you attempt reboot the system; however, the system fails to boot.

After some head-scratching, you realize why: The system you just brought back from the tape is incompatible with your dad's old hardware. So, you proceed with a fresh Linux installation, setting up a more complete system this time, and then you begin the painful process of restoring files and directories selectively. You take great care to ensure that you restore your critical data and system settings but that you don't overwrite the new operating system configuration, which would render Linux unbootable on this computer.

How many hours, how many days have passed? How long was your Web site unavailable, your colleagues without email, your office without an Internet connection? All these problems could have been avoided, of course, if instead of following a textbook backup strategy, you had planned for restoring your system.

Planning for Restores

The term *backup strategy* is a misnomer. Anyone should be able to issue a `tar` command to copy his system's contents to tape or use one of those fancy window-based backup programs that are so fashionable these days. Rotating tapes and doing backups on a scheduled basis is not much of a strategy.

No, the real planning should be about what to do after disaster has struck. How are you going to bring the system back online with backup hardware? What files should be backed up in the first place? What hardware should you use for backup purposes?

Chapter 22, "Moving to Backup Hardware," tells you what needs to be done when your Linux system fails and it's necessary to install a backup system. The focus of this chapter is on creating suitable backups that will make your job easier as well as on recovery from less severe failures.

Backing Up Files

When you back up a system, what you really do is create a copy of the files found on that system. Obviously, it's not necessary to copy files that can be easily located elsewhere; however, it is essential to create backup copies of files that cannot otherwise be recovered. So, exactly what are the files that need to be backed up?

First, and most obvious, are user or data files. Next, you also must make a copy of your system configuration settings. Last, you also want to create backup copies of any customizations, including software packages you downloaded that are not part of the standard Linux distribution you installed. There's no need to create a backup copy of system files; these can be restored from the distribution CD-ROM from which you installed the system in the first place. Furthermore, if you need to reinstall the system, by the time you get to the point of being able to access your tape drive, system files will presumably be installed already anyway.

Note that I am not advocating that you should not create a full backup of your system, including a backup of application programs and other system files. However, keep in mind that such a backup has limited use; if you're trying to rebuild a system using a different hardware configuration, simply restoring from a full backup may not be a viable option.

Backing Up Data

As mentioned previously, the most important candidates for backup are user data files. Note that I'm using the term *data* from the system administrator's perspective; in this context, user programs that aren't part of the operating system are also seen as data. Indeed, any file is data if it didn't come from the installation CD-ROM or isn't a configuration file. If the system experiences a failure and it's restored from backup, users rightfully expect to find the contents of their directories intact and their files readable.

Keep in mind, though, that user files exist outside of home directories. For instance, user mailboxes are located in /var/spool/mail on most systems, and these must be backed up as well—otherwise, if the system fails, important mail messages could get lost.

Other user files are located in common directories. Examples include Web files (which may be located in /home/httpd/html or /var/lib/html/htdocs) and the contents of the public FTP directory (/home/ftp).

Configuration Files

In order to reinstall your system quickly and efficiently, you should always have an up-to-date backup of your system configuration files. These, however, are probably best stored separately from data files. Indeed, because these files are small, it's a good idea to create a copy of them on a floppy disk. That way, if and when you need to reinstall your system, you'll be able to make use of these files right away, without having to restore them from a large archive first.

Here's another reason why a copy on a floppy disk is a good idea: It lets you restore these files selectively. When you install Linux on backup hardware that's not identical to the hardware originally used, many of your configuration files will not be applicable without change. With the files on a floppy disk, you're able to easily access them one at a time, compare them with installation defaults, or just move parts of these files to their "live" counterparts on the system.

Customizations

After a system has been in use for several months, its configuration may no longer resemble the configuration installed from the CD-ROM months earlier. In particular, you may have downloaded new versions of software packages and compiled and installed them with custom configuration options. Obviously, in addition to the configuration files mentioned previously, downloaded source archives also must be saved if you want to be able to restore your system to a working state. This is particularly important because months after the fact, you may no longer even remember what your customizations were—and if the job of understanding the downloaded package, combing through its various documentation files, and creating an installation that suits your needs took days when you did it the first time, you can expect it to take nearly as long when you're forced to do it again.

For this reason, when you download a software package, it's best to experiment with it first using a regular user account (and not as the root account, to avoid damage). When you're satisfied that the package works as intended, you should install the executables as well as move the downloaded source archive to a common location, such as /usr/src. When you prepare your backup, make sure this directory is backed up. That way, during disaster recovery you'll be able to quickly rebuild these packages as they were before.

The Tools of Backup

Now that you know what needs to be backed up, the next question is obvious: How do you accomplish it? What are the tools and procedures for backing up your system under Linux?

PART

V

CH

17

Choosing Your Backup Hardware

First, you have to decide which target device you'll use for backup purposes. In the old days, there really was no question about it—unless you wanted to mess with dozens of floppies (a good enough method for a hobbyist's system but certainly not one you intend to use as a server in your office, for instance), you needed to invest in a tape drive.

In many cases, tapes still represent the solution of choice for reliable backups. High-capacity tape drives can be obtained for a reasonable price and will give you years of trouble-free service. However, these days many *removable media* alternatives exist. Most popular among these are CD-R, CD-RW devices and removable hard disks.

CD-R, or *CD-Recordable*, is a technology that lets you create CD-ROMs using low-cost devices. The CDs you create are *write once*—that is, once written, they cannot be erased. It is, however, possible to write to a disk multiple times, adding data to whatever exists on the disk already. Due to its nature, CD-R is best used for creating a permanent or semipermanent archive. The use of CD-Rs may also present a problem on more heavily loaded systems because of strict timing requirements; if the computer cannot maintain the required writing speed, the resulting CD-R may be a useless coaster.

CD-RW is a similar optical technology, but it uses rewritable media. Due to the recent price drop in CD-RW devices, and due to the fact that most CD-RW devices can create CD-R media as well, a CD-RW drive is probably a very good investment. You can use a few CD-RW disks (which are relatively expensive) to create regular backups, and you can use CD-R disks to create occasional "one-shot" backups to store offsite.

Increasingly popular these days are removable cartridge drives. Perhaps the best known among these are Iomega's ZIP drives, which offer 100MB of capacity (some now offer 250MB), and the larger JAZ drives, offering 1 or 2GB of storage. The advantage of these devices is that they offer the convenience of floppy disks; the disadvantage is their price and less-than perfect record of reliability.

Whichever device you choose for backup, make sure it's commonly available. A backup tape or cartridge is of little use if you cannot find a system that can read its contents!

Using Backup Hardware

Backup devices can be internal or external; they can connect to your computer's IDE or SCSI bus or the floppy controller. They may also come with their own controller cards. Whatever the case, the backup device you choose must have drivers for Linux. Unfortunately, many manufacturers target only the mass market, represented by Windows 95/98 computers; drivers for other operating systems, including not just Linux but even Windows NT, are not always trivial to come by.

That said, there often are no special drivers needed in order to use a device. This is certainly the case if you're using a tape device or removable cartridge drive that's connected to a SCSI controller inside your computer, because Linux has generic drivers for these types of devices. Linux also has generic drivers for tape units that are connected to your computer's floppy disk controller.

However, if you're using a CD-R or CD-RW drive, or any other backup hardware not recognized by Linux, you may need to obtain third-party software, at the very least, for writing to the media. Also keep in mind that although CD-R and CD-RW CDs are readable on almost any computer equipped with a CD-ROM drive, the same cannot be said about other types of backup media. This can be a problem; after all, you're supposed to be devising a strategy for restoring your system, remember? How do you plan to restore a system from backup if the only copy of the software required to perform the restore is, itself, on that backup disk or tape?

As a rule of thumb, if a device cannot be readily accessed from a freshly installed Linux system using standard Linux commands, it's probably not suitable for backup purposes. Back in my student days, we often joked about "write-only memory," which is, of course, an eminently useless device. A write-only backup is just as useless a thing to have!

Tapes and File Systems

When you're backing up files to a floppy disk or removable disk cartridge, you're really just copying files from one file system to another. You might as well be copying files between two directories on your hard disk or from one hard disk to another; inasmuch as the commands go, there's really very little difference.

One particular difference between removable media and hard disks is that removable media cannot be used right away. This is not the case under MS-DOS, where you're probably used to simply popping in that CD-ROM or floppy disk and reading its contents without the need to issue any special commands first for the system to recognize the disk.

As shown first in Chapter 3, "System Installation," under Linux, a file system must be mounted before use. This is true of file systems on your hard disk, just as it's true of floppy disks, CD-ROMs, and any other media that contains a file system.

With tapes, the situation is different. Tapes do not contain a file system; for all practical intents and purposes, a tape looks like one large file that can only be accessed sequentially. In fact, the most commonly used tool for tape archives, tar, can be used just as readily with any file serving as its input or output just as if it were another tape device. Tapes are usually accessed through reserved device names such as `/dev/rmt0`.

Backup Commands

It's time to get to the practicalities of creating backups under Linux. What are the commands you should use?

The most common backup command is the `tar` (tape archive) command. As its name implies, this command is designed to create an archive on magnetic tape. However, tar is both more and less than a simple tape backup utility.

It's more than a simple tape backup utility because it can be used with an ordinary file (or indeed, any file-like device) in place of a tape. In fact, archives created with tar represent one of the most commonly used formats for distributing UNIX files over the Internet.

> **WARNING** Do not use tar with the name of a hard disk device (for example, `/etc/sda1`) as its archive parameter, unless you're sure that's what you mean to do. This will destroy any file system you may have on the specified drive, wiping out all files there.

However, tar is also less than a true tape archiver, because it does not offer any tape-management commands. It has no facilities to rewind, retension, or format a tape, or even locate specific spots on the tape. These functions are incorporated into another utility, mt.

Archives created with tar are not compressed. To save space, you may want to perform compression. The most popular compression utility under Linux is *gzip*, short for *GNU ZIP*. GNU versions of tar, such as the versions found with most Linux distributions, can create gzip-compatible compressed archives with a simple command-line switch.

> **NOTE** Despite its name, gzip does not create an archive of multiple files like the well-known PK-ZIP utility under DOS or Windows. The gzip utility merely creates compressed versions of individual files. This is why gzip is used in conjunction with tar—to create a compressed archive containing multiple files.

Another compression utility is *compress*, which uses a somewhat less efficient compression method (but one that is, or at least has been, compatible with a greater variety of UNIX systems than gzip.)

TEST SYSTEM My test system doesn't have a dedicated backup device. However, it does have two hard disks. Linux is installed on /dev/sda, which is a removable device. The other drive, /dev/sdb, is an internal hard drive that's formatted with a single DOS partition. Because this drive has lots of free space, I can use it as the destination for my backup. Or, to correct myself here quickly, I'd be using a *file* on this drive as backup. Using the disk's device name as the backup destination would destroy all data on that drive!

In its simplest form, the `tar` command can create an archive of selected files on the default device. For example, to back up all files on your drive, you type this:

```
tar c /
```

Unfortunately, this is not good enough. Depending on the version of tar you use, this may produce an output on the tape device /dev/rmt0 (which I don't have on the test system) or on standard output (that is, listed onscreen), which is not exactly what I had in mind for a backup.

▼   Instead, I must specify the output file or device. But first, I must mount that second hard
disk on which I want to create a backup file:

```
mount /dev/sdb1 /mnt/sdb1
tar cf /mnt/sdb1/backup.tar /
```

The directory /mnt/sdb1 is simply an empty directory used as the mount point for
/dev/sdb1 (see Chapter 3).

This form of invoking tar is still not satisfactory, however. It would back up all files
indiscriminately. That includes, in addition to data and configuration files, all system
files, pseudo-files in the /proc directory (possibly locking up the backup process), device
nodes in the /dev directory, and so on. Worse yet, it will also attempt to back up
/mnt/sdb1, which is the mount point of the second hard disk, and through this mount
point, all the contents of that second hard disk as well!

What I really need is a more selective way of invoking tar. Consider the following command line:

```
tar clvf /mnt/sdb1/backup.tar /etc /var /home
```

In this form, the command will back up the contents of the /etc, /var, and /home directories. It will not back up files from another file system due to the 1 flag; however, it will
display a verbose listing of the files it processed due to the v flag. The /etc directory
contains mostly configuration files. The /var directory contains many transient files,
including user mailboxes, and /home, of course, is the location of all home directories,
including the home directories of FTP and the Apache Web server.

I also have another Linux system that does happen to have a tape drive. On this system,
backups are performed weekly using the following command:

```
tar clvf —atime-preserve /dev/rmt0 /etc /usr/local/samba
➥/usr/local/majordomo /home /root /var/adm /usr2/src
```

This command causes tar to use /dev/rmt0 as the backup device. The directories include
all home directories as well as directories containing configuration settings and customizations. The —atime-preserve flag ensures that tar doesn't change the last access
▼   time of files that it backs up.

PART
V

CH

17

▼

> **NOTE**　　Each tape drive on a Linux system can be accessed through two device names: rmt*n* and nrmt*n* (the names rst*n* and nrst*n* may be used on some SCSI systems.) When accessed via the first form, the tape will be rewound at the end of the operation (which is precisely how I want it to behave). When accessed through the second form, the tape will remain positioned at the location where the operation ended.

▲

TEST SYSTEM　　Yet another command often used for backup purposes is cpio. This command can be used to create and maintain archives in many different formats, including the tar format.

Both the tar and cpio commands can also be used to copy entire directory trees from one place to another. The tar command is invoked twice using an intermediate archive; cpio can do this in one pass, without the use of such an archive. In the past, this capability of these commands was highly useful because older versions of the cp command

▲　could not copy directories recursively, nor could they preserve file ownership and flags.

OPTIONS　　For reference, here's how you can copy the contents of /dir1 to /dir2 recursively (preserving file ownership and excluding files located on another file system), using all three of the commands mentioned.

First, the cp command:

```
cp -ax /dir1 /dir2
```

Use of this command will not preserve the access time on the original files as they are copied. For example, by typing **ls — time=atime**, you'll be able to see that the files were recently accessed by cp.

The tar command needs to be invoked twice, and it also requires that you create the destination directory first:

```
mkdir /dir2; tar clf - —atime-preserve -C /dir1 . ¦ tar xpf - -C /dir2
```

As you can see, the output of the first tar command (an archive) is never saved to a file; instead, it's reused as the input of the second invocation of tar, which unpacks this archive in the destination directory. In the form used here, tar will accurately preserve creation and access times on the original files. It will also copy any empty directories

▼　used as mount points without actually copying the mounted file system.

▼   The `cpio` command needs to be invoked in combination with `find`, which is used to generate a list of files to be copied:

```
cd /dir1; find . -xdev -print ¦ cpio -admp /dir2
```

If you're using the `tar` command to create a file or tape archive, you can also add the `z` command-line flag to create a compressed archive in gzip format. The command `tar czf - /dir1` is equivalent to `tar cf - /dir1 ¦ gzip`. The `z` flag is not necessary (in fact, it'll slow down operations) if you're using tar to copy the contents of one directory to another, as shown previously.

> **WARNING**   Due to the nature of the compression algorithm employed by gzip, a single error in a compressed archive can render the rest of the archive unreadable. For instance, if you're backing up to tape using the `tar` command with the z option, a read error at the start of the tape might render the entire tape useless. Because of this problem, you may want to avoid using data compression on critical backups.

▲   If you create a tar archive that's a file, it's customary to add the `.tar` extension to the filename. For archives compressed with gzip, use `.tar.gz` or `.tgz`.

So, which program should you use for creating your backups? Over the years, I've found tar entirely satisfactory for my backup needs. It may not be the most state-of-the-art utility, but it does its task well, and it's compatible across different Linux distributions. (Indeed, it's compatible with just about any operating system in existence, because versions of `tar` exist on every system from the Macintosh to MS-DOS, from Windows to OS/2.) Your Linux distribution may contain an elegant backup program with a full-screen user interface, but when you're in trouble—trying to restore files to an ailing system after booting a minimal system from a floppy disk—you'll bless the day you decided to use the lowly tar utility as your backup tool.

Restore Commands

Because the focus of this chapter is on your ability to restore files from backup after a disaster, it would be a severe omission if the chapter contained no instructions for performing the restore.

Of course, if your backup is in the form of files copied (to another directory, hard drive, cartridge, or CD-ROM), there's not much to say. Restoring simply means copying the files back to your original location, either one at a time or in bulk. The commands used are the exact same commands used for creating the backup in the first place, because the operation is symmetric; whether it's a backup copy you're creating from the original or the original you're restoring from backup, you're simply copying files while preserving file ownership and permissions.

If the file has been created using an archive format, the program that created the archive must be invoked with the appropriate flags to read the archive and restore files from it.

OPTIONS

Specifically, the `tar` command must be invoked with the x command-line flag to perform a restore. This flag can be combined with other flags to ensure that files are restored with the correct permissions.

For instance, to restore files created earlier on a tape device, `/dev/rmt0`, you type this:

```
tar xpf /dev/rmt0
```

The p flag ensures that all ownership and permission information is properly preserved when the files are extracted. The files and directory trees from the archive will be extracted in the current directory, so you should `switch` to the desired destination directory first (creating it if necessary.)

The `tar` command can also be used to extract from a compressed archive. For instance, if you have a compressed archive file named `dir1.tgz`, you can extract its contents by typing this:

```
tar xzpf dir1.tgz
```

Of course, quite often, you won't want to restore all the files from backup, only selected ones. You can do this by appending the filename to the extraction command. For instance, to extract only `file1` from the archive `dir1.tgz`, you can type the following:

▲   ```
tar xzpf dir1.tgz file1
```

# Advanced Topics

So, when would you perform a backup? How many backup copies should you maintain? Can you use your LAN to perform a backup between two computers?
```

Backup Scheduling and Media Rotation

How often you need to perform a backup of your system depends on the typical uses of the system. Obviously, the backup needs of a system that processes large amounts of information on a daily basis are quite different from those of a system that acts, say, as an Internet router and stores no data. For the former, a daily backup may be necessary; for the latter, a backup after every significant configuration change may be sufficient, with no need to perform scheduled backups at all.

Another question concerns the backup media you use. Should you just use a single tape, cartridge, or CD-RW CD over and over again? Obviously, this is not such a hot idea. What if your system fails right in the middle of the backup process, leaving you with an incomplete and unreadable backup? What if an error occurs before the backup takes place, corrupting the backup?

On systems used as moderately loaded Internet servers (including a Web server, news server, and mail server) that contain little or no user data, I've found a weekly backup schedule satisfactory. I'm using two pieces of backup media (two tapes or two removable disks), which I rotate when the backup is complete. One of them is left in the computer to allow it to perform the backup in the background on a scheduled basis, whereas the other one is stored offsite.

PART

V

CH

17

> **WARNING** With many removable media devices you're advised not to leave media (tape, disk cartridges) in the drive when the drive is not in use. Make sure you read the drive's documentation before making a decision on how the drive will be used.

The next chapter, "Scheduled Tasks, Scripts, and Programming," provides information on how you can actually schedule backups to be run in the background, at a time when the system is under the least amount of use.

Incremental Backups

Sometimes it's not necessary to copy all files during a backup, but only files that have changed since the last backup. This type of a backup is called an *incremental* backup.

In my personal opinion, incremental backups are more trouble than they're worth, at least on smaller Linux servers. As usual, the problems come when you're trying to restore the system. Rather than restoring from a single source (your latest backup tape, cartridge, or file), you may have to iterate through several incremental backups in order to restore the correct version of all files. This procedure can be complex and error prone, and you also increase your exposure to the danger of losing data due to a corrupted archive.

Needless to say, if your system contains vast amounts of data, incremental backups can be a money saver. However, on most Linux servers, doing a full backup on a scheduled basis while implementing a media rotation schedule is probably the best option.

Using Encryption

Backups are meant to serve one purpose: to be able to restore your system quickly and easily in case of a disaster. At first sight, making that task harder by encrypting your backup appears counterintuitive.

Encrypting backups may nevertheless be necessary if, for instance, you're storing back-ups offsite. For years now, I've been following the practice of keeping a backup set in my car's glove compartment. This way, even if my home office is destroyed in, say, a fire, my years of work will not be lost. However, cars get broken into and stolen, and although I certainly wouldn't weep over the loss of an old tape or disk cartridge, letting gigabytes of data fall into the wrong hands would trouble me deeply. This is why I use encryption with these backups.

TEST SYSTEM   An encryption program that's reasonably secure and can be readily used to encrypt files and data streams (such as the stream of data written to a magnetic tape) is the `des` command, which implements the well-known Data Encryption Standard. This command is available on many UNIX systems. Unfortunately, due to concerns about U.S. export controls, the makers of most Linux distributions elected not to include this command with their systems. The program is easily obtainable through the Internet, however. For instance, I obtained my copy of `des`, along with other components of the "libdes" library, from its Australian FTP home: `ftp.psy.uq.oz.au` (from the directory `pub/Crypto/DES`). This package can be compiled according to the instructions included within. If all goes well, you'll end up with a `des` command that you

▼   can install, for instance, in the `/usr/local/bin` directory.

▼   I use the des command on one of my Linux systems for creating encrypted backups on
tape. The actual command I use is a variation of the backup command shown in the previous section:

```
tar -clf - /etc /usr/local/samba /usr/local/majordomo /home /root /var/adm
➥/usr2/src ¦ /usr/local/bin/des -E -k PassWord > /dev/rmt0
```

Using a minus sign (-) after the f flag in the tar command instructs tar to generate the
archive on its standard output. That output is redirected as the input of the des command.
The output of that command, in turn, is redirected to the tape drive.

If you're using this command or a variation of it, you should replace *PassWord* with a
suitable password of your own choosing. Just make sure it's something you can remember; after all, when your system fails and you need to restore it from backups, the last
thing you want to do is to hunt for that missing piece of paper containing the long-for-
▲   gotten secret word!

Backups Over the Network

If you have more than one computer on a network and have sufficient storage, an obvious place for a backup is another machine across the network. This type of a backup
won't protect you from a major catastrophe, but it will protect you from single-machine
failures, such as a hard disk crash.

There are many ways to perform a backup over the network. On some systems, dedicated
commands exist for accessing remote tape devices. To backup to a remote disk directory,
however, the simplest method is probably to mount that remote directory using a method
such as Samba (see Chapter 13, "File Services for Windows: Samba") or the Network
File System (NFS).

TEST SYSTEM   I actually back up over the network not with my test system but
with another Linux machine that's host to the online game MUD2.
Every day, early morning, when the system is the least used, all the server's critical
directories are copied across the network to another machine.

In order for this to work, the remote file system must be mounted first. I've created a
mount point, an empty directory by the name of /backup. When needed, the file system
can be mounted using the following command:

▼   ```
mount host1:/home/backup /backup
```

**PART**

**V**

CH

**17**
```

▼ In this line, host1 is the name of the system that's the backup's destination, and /home/backup is the directory where backup files are deposited.

Needless to say, you can't just mount a directory from a remote computer as a file system on yours and expect it to work. NFS must be enabled on the remote computer. On the system in question, this is accomplished by making sure that the required daemons run and allowing access from the computer on which the backup is being performed by entering a line to /etc/exports, similar to the following:

```
/home/backup   host2(rw,no_root_squash)
```

Because this book is about using Linux as a server in a predominantly non-Linux network environment, NFS is not covered. If you have two or more Linux machines and want to learn more about this feature, you can start by reading the manual pages for
▲ nfsd, mountd, portmap, and exports.

Summary

Creating frequent backups is your best protection against disasters. However, people tend to forget that rather than establishing a backup strategy, the focus should be on the ease of restoring a system.

The files that you need to back up include user data, system configuration settings, and customizations, such as extra utilities that you downloaded and installed on your system. It's rarely necessary, or even useful, to create a backup of your entire system; in most cases, in order to begin a restore, you'd need to install a minimal system anyway. Furthermore, if you're restoring files to a different computer, those system files may not even be appropriate.

When choosing backup hardware and software, ease of recovery should be your primary concern. Whether it's a tape drive, removable cartridge, or optical disk you use, make sure that you're using a common format. This way, when disaster strikes (and perhaps the device on which the archive was created is completely destroyed), you'll be able to restore your system from the backup.

The most commonly used Linux backup command is the tar command. It's designed to create archives on tape. However, it can also be used to create archive files (optionally compressed) or copy files between directories. Another frequently used backup command is cpio. The ordinary UNIX copy command, cp, can also be used to perform simple backups across directories.

When planning your backups, make sure you're using more than one piece of media and rotate it regularly. That way, you'll never be left without a usable backup, even if the system fails during a backup operation and your backup media is destroyed.

Sometimes it's necessary to encrypt backups. This is especially important if you store your backups offsite and the storage facility is not secure.

You can also create a backup over the network. The simplest method to use is to mount a remote directory via NFS or Samba and copy files using `cp` or `tar`.

Manual Pages

For additional information on the topics discussed in this chapter, please refer to the following manual pages:

- `man cp`
- `man tar`
- `man cpio`
- `man gzip`
- `man compress`
- `man mt`
- `man des`
- `man nfsd`
- `man mountd`
- `man portmap`
- `man exports`

Scheduled Tasks, Scripts, and Programming

Under Linux, many system administration tasks can be greatly simplified through automation. The tools you use include a UNIX daemon that runs scheduled tasks in the background (crond) and simple programming utilities.

No, I'm not planning to tell you that you need to become a programmer in order to manage a Linux server effectively. However, it's always a good idea to know at least a little bit about this subject. Just as DOS and Windows "power users" are able to automate many simple tasks using batch files—although it's a little bit of a stretch calling MS-DOS batch files a form of programming—you'll be able to do tasks more efficiently under Linux if you know how to create simple shell scripts to automate your work.

First, let's see how you can automate the execution of scheduled tasks.

Scheduling Program Execution

Many system administration tasks are recurring. Whether it's the rotation of log files, the creation of weekly backups, or other daily, weekly, or monthly tasks, you can make your life much easier if you have these programs execute automatically.

Linux (and indeed, most UNIXes) offer two tools for the scheduled execution of tasks. The cron daemon lets you schedule recurring tasks; the at command lets you schedule the execution of a specific task at a given time.

The `cron` Daemon

The `cron` daemon runs in the background. It regularly checks the contents of the `/var/spool/cron` directory (`/var/spool/cron/crontabs` on some systems), rereading any files that have been changed. These files have names that coincide with user identifiers, and they contain schedules of programs that are to be executed under those users' names.

For instance, if I want to run a program named myprog, located in my home directory, once every hour, I could have a `crontab` line like this one:

```
0 * * * * /home/vttoth/myprog
```

OPTIONS

The `cron` daemon uses a simple, yet powerful format for schedules. Each line in a `crontab` file looks like this:

```
min hour day mon wday command
```

The *min*, *hour*, and *day* arguments represent the minutes, hours, and day of month, respectively. Each of these arguments can be a single numeric value, a list of values following a special syntax, or a single asterisk (meaning *any value*).

The aforementioned special syntax is easier to demonstrate via a few examples than to explain. For instance, you may have the following values in place of the *min* field:

`0`	At the top of the hour
`30`	At the bottom of the hour
`0,30`	At the top and bottom of the hour
`7,25,42`	At 7, 25, and 42 minutes after the hour
`*/15`	Every 15 minutes
`*/30,10-25/5`	Every 30 minutes, plus every 5 minutes between the 10th and 25th minutes of the hour

The *hour* and *day* fields follow a similar logic.

The *mon* field represents the month. Three-letter abbreviations are used—for example, `jan`, `feb`, and so on.

▼   The *wday* field represents the day of the week. Again, three-letter abbreviations are used, and ranges can be specified. For example, `mon-fri` means the five workdays of the week.

▼   If you specify both a day of the month and a day of the week, the scheduled task will be executed on both dates. Suppose, for example, you have a `crontab` entry like this:

`0 0 13 * fri /home/vttoth/badday`

▲   The program `badday` will be executed on both the 13th of the month and every Friday, even if a particular Friday doesn't fall on the 13th.

Your `crontab` entry can be edited or viewed using the `crontab` command. To bring up your `crontab` entry for editing, type **crontab -e**. This will open a copy of your `crontab` file using the dreaded vi editor. Note that the file may contain lines that begin with the pound sign (#). These lines are considered comment lines and are ignored by the `cron` daemon.

When you're finished editing the file, the `crontab` command will install your new `crontab` file automatically.

You can also use `crontab` to simply list the contents of your `crontab` file: `crontab .l`. Lastly, as the root user, you can edit other users' `crontab` files using the `.u` parameter. For instance, you may want to edit the `crontab` file that belongs to the `news` or `uucp` system accounts in order to alter the respective programs' behaviors.

Running Commands with at

Sometimes you don't want programs to execute repeatedly—rather only once at a scheduled time. Although the `cron` daemon could be used for this purpose, it's not ideal. In fact, strictly speaking, there's no way to schedule a program to execute just once with `cron`; even if you specify an exact minute, hour, day, and month, the program will be executed again next year at the specified time, unless you change your `crontab` file in the intervening period.

There's a much simpler solution to this problem: the `at` command. This command allows you to schedule the one-time execution of a single command or a series of commands.

The `at` command executes in conjunction with the `atd` daemon, which is another system daemon that's usually started when the system boots.

The command or commands you want to execute must be placed in a file. The contents of this file will be executed at the scheduled time by the `/bin/sh` shell, just as though you typed the commands yourself at the keyboard. To schedule execution of a command with `at`, at a given time, simply type:

`at HH:MM -f command-file`

Any output produced by the commands thus executed will be mailed to the user who scheduled the execution. For instance, if you want to see the size of user mailboxes in the /var/spool/mail directory at a later time of the day, you could create a file named viewmaildir with the following single line as its contents:

```
ls -al /var/spool/mail
```

You can then schedule execution of this command at 7 p.m. using at, as follows:

```
at 19:00 -f viewmaildir
```

At the scheduled time, the command will run and the directory listing will be emailed to you.

Shell Scripts

The previous section demonstrated how, when scheduling the execution of commands via the at utility, you have to put these commands into a file. This file is actually an example of a shell script—a simple program that contains commands you'd normally enter interactively while working with Linux.

Simple Programs

As the earlier examples used in conjunction with the at command suggest, simple shell scripts are merely lists of commands you'd type if you were at the keyboard. There may be several important reasons why you'd want to record them into a file. Perhaps you just want to make sure you'll remember next time what the commands are. Perhaps you're bored of typing the same 27 commands over and over again. Or, perhaps you want to have these commands executed when you're not at the computer—for instance, by using the at utility.

When I say that these commands are *executed*, what I really mean is that a command interpreter is loaded that then processes the contents of the script file. If you recall from Chapter 2, "The Linux Workhorse," Linux has several versions of the command interpreter, or *shell*. Although throughout this book we've been using the bash shell, many Linux users prefer to use other shells. These shells may use slightly different syntax for carrying out similar tasks; therefore, it's possible that a script written for one would not work under another. This begs the following question: When you have a shell script, is it possible to specify which shell should be used to interpret it? Indeed it is. All you need to do is to add the name of the desired shell as the first line of your script file, in the form of a comment beginning with the pound sign. Therefore, if you want to specify that your script is to be interpreted specifically by the csh shell, for instance, your script file would begin with the following line:

```
#!/bin/csh
```

Note that both the exclamation mark and the full pathname of the shell program are required.

Conditional Execution

The simple scripts discussed so far contain only a sequential set of commands that will be executed unconditionally. Sometimes, however, you may want to make program execution conditional. For instance, when you're creating a directory, you may want to check first whether the directory exists in order to avoid an error message.

The bash shell offers several forms of executing an instruction conditionally. You do not normally encounter these instructions when working with the shell interactively, because in those cases, it's you who'll make the conditional decisions, not the computer. To stick with the previous example, if you want to create a directory, you check for its presence first; if it's already there, you'll simply avoid trying to create it altogether and you'll never type the mkdir command in the first place. However, when it all happens under program control, you might not know in advance whether the mkdir instruction is necessary; therefore, you should make it part of your script, but in such a way that it's only executed when needed.

Enough words, let's see some action. Here's how you make a command execute conditionally:

```
if [ -d mydir ] ; then
  echo Directory already exists.
else
  mkdir mydir
fi
```

> **NOTE**   Note that it's good programming practice to indent lines that follow an if or similar statement to indicate that those lines are part of a conditionally executed block.

Save these lines to a file called `makemydir` and make sure that this file is marked as an executable command (`chmod +x makemydir.`) Then, when you type the name of this file on the command line, the directory will be created. If typed a second time, the following error message will be printed:

```
$ ls -ald mydir
ls: mydir: No such file or directory
$ ./makemydir
$ ls -ald mydir
drwxr-xr-x   2 vttoth   users          1024 Apr 25 18:08 mydir
$ ./makemydir
Directory already exists.
```

OPTIONS   As part of the `bash` shell's `if` statement, you can use many other flags in place of `.d directory-name`. Here are a few:

`-f file`	True if the file exists as a regular file
`-s file`	True if the file exists and its size is nonzero
`-x file`	True if the file is an executable program
`-n string`	True if *string* has a nonzero length
`string1 = string2`	True if the two strings are equal
`string1 != string2`	True if the two strings are equal
`arg1 -gt arg2`	True if *arg1* (a number) is greater than *arg2*

Many more conditional forms exist. The `bash` manual page contains a complete list of these forms (look for the description of the `test` command in the list of internal `bash` commands.)

▲

Variables

Conditional execution becomes especially powerful when used in conjunction with shell variables.

Once again, there are similarities between the Linux shell and MS-DOS batch files. If you've used MS-DOS batch files, you may remember the role *environment variables* play in MS-DOS. These variables, once set, remained accessible to all programs that are subsequently called. It's common practice to configure certain system settings as environment variables, often loaded in the `AUTOEXEC.BAT` file.

Linux, too, has environment variables. Their roles are similar to the roles the environment variables play under MS-DOS, but there are a few key differences as well.

First, Linux environment variables are local to the user. When you log on to a Linux system and set environment variables, these will not affect any other users on the system or the programs they run.

Second, environment variables remain in effect only as long as you're logged on. (Well, strictly speaking, this is also true under MS-DOS, except that *logging on* there simply means booting the system so that COMMAND.COM starts, and *logging off* means turning the power off. Under Linux, this is not so: When you log off, the rest of the system remains operational. However, all your environment variables will be gone.)

The third difference is that Linux shells usually offer local variables in addition to environment variables. The difference is that local variables will *not* be seen by other programs.

Here's a simple example. To set a local variable, simply type its name, followed by the equal sign and the value you want to assign to the variable. (If the value contains blanks, simply surround it with double quotes.) To set an environment variable, precede it with the export keyword. Then, starting a second copy of bash, you can test which of the two variables is inherited:

PART
V

CH
18

```
$ X=1
$ export Y=2
$ bash
$ echo $X

$ echo $Y
2
$ exit
exit
$ echo $X
1
$ echo $Y
2
```

As you can see, when you start a second copy of the bash shell, only the exported variable (Y) remains visible; X disappears. However, when you exit this second shell, returning to the first copy, X reappears. This example also demonstrates the way you can use variables: precede their names with the dollar sign ($) character.

What would happen if you did it the other way around? Create a second copy of the shell, create the two variables, and then return to the first copy? The answer is that both variables will disappear. That's because even though Y is specified as an exported variable, it's exported only to programs called from within the second copy of the shell, not to other programs. When you return from the second copy, terminating its existence, all its variables, whether local or exported, will be wiped out:

```
$ bash
$ X=1
$ export Y=2
$ exit
$ echo $X

$ echo $Y
```

If this last example doesn't work as expected on your system, you may have variables left over from the previous experiment. Variables can be deleted using the unset command. Make sure you type unset X and unset Y before performing a new experiment using the same variable names.

When a variable is used in a shell script, its value is substituted exactly as it appears. Therefore, you may need to protect against situations when the variable has an unexpected value or if it's blank. Here's an example:

```
if [ $X = one ] ; then
   echo X is set to one.
else
   echo X is not one.
fi
```

As long as X holds a simple string, this example will work. However, X may be blank. In this case, the first line will expand to this:

```
if [ = one ] ; then
```

When the shell attempts to execute this line, it will fail with an error message:

```
[: =: unary operator expected
```

There are many ways to protect yourself against situations like this. First, you can use default values, like this:

```
if [ ${X:-null} = one ] ; then
```

The expression ${X:-null} will evaluate to the value of X unless X is empty; in that case, the default value (in this case, null) will be substituted.

Another method is to add an extra character to avoid null values. (This is often seen in MS-DOS batch files, as well.) Here's an example:

```
if [ X$X = Xone ] ; then
```

In this form, the statement will work even when the variable X is blank. However, the statement will still fail if the variable contains blank characters. For instance, try setting X as follows:

```
$ X="one two"
```

With this value of X, the conditional statement will expand to this:

```
if [ Xone two = Xone ] ; then
```

When executed, this statement will fail with the following error:

```
[: too many arguments
```

To protect against situations like this one, you can use double quotes:

```
if [ "$X" = "one" ] ; then
```

> **WARNING**   Unexpected interpretation of variables can be a grave security concern if the variables' values are obtained from users. If a variable contains spaces, newline characters, or control characters, its contents may end up being interpreted as commands, in effect providing a potential intruder a back-door to your system, a means to execute arbitrary commands of their own choosing. Always keep this possibility in mind when you create scripts that accept values from users or any other outside source over which you have no direct control.

Although most of these examples use variables as part of if statements, variables can be used anywhere in a script.

Special Parameters and Predefined Variables

The bash shell has several special parameters that can be accessed via a syntax similar to that used for variables. For instance, the symbol $$ indicates the shell's own numeric process identifier. You can also refer to any command-line parameters passed to the shell script using $1, $2, and so on for the first, second, and subsequent parameters.

The shell also sets the values for a number of variables when it's started. For instance, PWD is set to the name of the current working directory, UID is the numeric user identifier of the current user, and OSTYPE is the type of the operating system on your system (quite useful when a shell script is created that can run on different UNIX versions).

For a simple demonstration, consider the following script:

```
if [ "$1" = "OS" ] ; then
  echo The operating system is $OSTYPE.
elif [ "$1" = "PWD" ] ; then
  echo Your current directory is $PWD.
else
  echo Invalid command. Please use $0 OS or $0 PWD.
fi
```

Note the use of the `elif` command (else if) to chain `if` statements. Also note the use of `$0` to reference the name under which the script itself is invoked. If you save this file under the name vars, make it executable (`chmod +x vars`), and run it from the command line, you should see the following:

```
$ vars
Invalid command. Please use ./vars OS or ./vars PWD.
$ vars OS
The operating system is Linux.
$ vars PWD
Your current directory is /home/vttoth.
$ vars X
Invalid command. Please use ./vars OS or ./vars PWD.
```

Input, Output, and Redirection

The topic of redirecting a program's input and output was discussed briefly in Chapter 2. It's time to look at this feature in a little bit more detail.

When a program, any program, is started under UNIX, it immediately has access to three streams of data: its *standard input*, *standard output*, and *standard error*. When you run a program interactively, the standard input is simply the keyboard; the standard output and standard error are the computer's screen. However, it's possible to *redirect* each of these three data streams to a file; it's also possible to *pipe* the output of one program to become the input of another program.

To redirect the input of a program, use the < character. For instance, you may want to use the `mail` command to send the contents of a file to a mail recipient. To do so, you can use the following command:

```
mail recipient <file
```

Here, `recipient`, of course, stands for the recipient's email address, whereas `file` is the name of the file that you want to send. (In this form, the file must be a human readable text file, because it'll be sent as the message body, not as an attachment.)

Similarly, the output can be redirected using the > character. To redirect the output of the ls command, for instance, you can type this:

```
ls >filelist
```

This example also demonstrates that the behavior of some commands will differ when their input or output is not an interactive terminal. The ls command, for instance, lists files in a multicolumn format on the screen, but when its output is redirected to a file, it'll be formatted as a single column. (Command-line switches exist to alter this behavior; type **man ls** for more.)

When you redirect output to a file, the contents of that file will be lost (that is, *overwritten*). However, you can direct output to a file so that it gets appended to that file by using the >> symbol.

So why do commands have a separate error output? Consider, for instance, the tar command, which was introduced in the previous chapter and is used for backup purposes. This command can produce a backup archive on its standard output, but it may also print error messages or warnings. Clearly, you don't want the two to mix. Fortunately, the error messages are printed on the standard error output of the tar command; therefore, when you redirect the command's output to a file, error messages will still appear on screen, without corrupting the output file.

That said, sometimes you may want to redirect the error messages themselves. To redirect a program's standard error, use the 2> symbol. (In case you're curious about the origin of the number 2 here, a long standing convention under UNIX specifies that a program's standard input is identified by the number 0, its standard output by 1, and its standard error by 2.) It is also possible to redirect standard output and standard error to the same file, as in the following example:

```
ls >filelist 2>&1
```

Lastly, a program's standard output can be piped to become another program's standard input. For instance, if you're looking for a file named myfile, you can type the following:

```
ls -al | grep myfile
```

(Of course, you could have just as easily added myfile as an argument to the ls command, but that's not the point here.) Piping is once again a feature familiar to users of MS-DOS, but there's a crucial difference. When you pipe the output of a command under MS-DOS to become the input of another command, MS-DOS runs the first command to its completion, saving its output in a temporary file. When the first command finishes execution, MS-DOS starts the second command, feeding the contents of that temporary file as input.

Under UNIX, the situation is different. In this multitasking environment, the two commands run simultaneously, and no temporary file is created. This leads to some interesting applications. For instance, recall from Chapter 16, "Logs," the use of the `tail` command with the `.f` command-line switch. This continuously monitors new lines appearing in a log file. If you only want to see log entries containing, for instance, the `kernel` keyword, you could type the following:

```
tail -f /var/log/messages ¦ grep kernel
```

This application would be impossible under MS-DOS. There, the system would wait for the completion of the `tail` command (which never happens, because when used with `.f`, the command waits forever for new lines to appear in the specified file) and the second command would never even be started.

Here Documents

Closely related to the topic of redirection are *here documents*. This funny concept arose because of the need to invoke, within scripts, programs that were originally designed to take parameters interactively. Although these programs' input could be redirected, that would necessitate the use of a second file containing just the parameters to the command. Here documents make it possible to invoke these commands without resorting to secondary files.

By way of an example, consider a shell script that collects information into variables and then mails the results to a user. Without here documents, the variables' values would first have to be saved to a file and then that file mailed to the recipient. With a here document, the solution is much simpler, as the following example demonstrates:

```
MYVAR=value
mail vttoth <<-EOF
Hello,

The value of MYVAR today is $MYVAR.

Sincerely,

Your favorite script
EOF
```

Here, `EOF` is not a keyword. Any word can take its place after the `<<-` symbol, which is what indicates the beginning of a here document. The here document ends when the word found after `<<-` is encountered again. The word `EOF` (standing for *end of file*) is used traditionally, but you're free to use any other word if you so desire.

Using Output As Parameters

Sometimes you may want to use the output of a program not as the input of another program but as a command-line parameter for the input of another command. This is possible through the use of the backquote character (`` ` ``). When a command appears enclosed by backquotes within a script, it will be evaluated and the result will be used in its place.

For instance, consider a script that executes a scheduled task and sends you an email message with the results. The program's output is piped to the email program, but that's the easy part. You also want to see the current date in the email's subject header, but this must be passed as a command-line parameter to the mail utility.

The solution is to use the `/bin/date` command along with the backquote syntax:

```
myscript | mail -s "Script results on `/bin/date +%D`" vttoth
```

This command will execute the program or script named `myscript` and send the results in an email to `vttoth`. The email's subject field will contain text like this:

```
Subject: Script results on 04/25/99
```

Other Often Used Languages

Sometimes the capabilities of the `bash` shell are not sufficient to perform the task at hand. In this case, another shell program is often used. What's more, if other shell programs are also insufficient, a genuine programming language is picked, such as Perl or C.

Other Shells

As mentioned in Chapter 2, several shells, in addition to `bash`, are in common use. When it comes to creating shell scripts, the various shells differ from each other in many ways. That said, for the simple scripts you're likely to create, the differences are more annoying than functional. For instance, if you're using the C shell–compatible `tcsh`, you may find that in order to set a variable, you must use the `set` command.

Perl

Next to shell scripts, Perl is the most often used programming language for simple scripts. In fact, it's the programming language of choice when it comes to creating server-side scripts (CGI scripts) for a Web server. However, Perl has many other uses.

The main strength of Perl lies in its ability to process text strings. This greatly helps in the processing of command-line parameters, user input, and even larger files such as HTML Web pages. However, the syntax of *regular expressions* (Perl's powerful feature used for isolating text in a string) can be difficult to master.

Perl is an interpreted language. In other words, to use a program that's written in Perl, you need to run the Perl interpreter program and feed it the name of the Perl file that contains your instructions. In this respect, Perl works very similarly to shell scripts. To complete the similarity, you can also mark Perl files "executable" using the chmod command, if their first lines contain the name of the Perl interpreter in the standard format:

```
#!/usr/bin/perl
```

Of course, if your copy of Perl is located elsewhere, this line may need to be modified.

Note that Perl might not be installed on your system by default. To learn more about Perl or to obtain the latest version, you may want to visit the Web page of The Perl Institute:

```
http://www.perl.org/
```

C

The *de facto* standard programming language of UNIX is C. The Linux kernel itself is written largely in C, and the same applies to most Linux commands, tools, and utilities.

C is a simple programming language in terms of syntax or the number of keywords, but its conceptual foundations aren't easy to understand. Perhaps the reason is that it's a language that does not hide the gory details; you actually have to understand a lot about the way your computer's processor works in order to make sense out of C language concepts such as *pointers*.

That said, not all C programs are complex. Take, for instance, the infamous Hello, World program from the original C manual, *The C Programming Language*, by Kernighan and Ritchie:

```
#include <stdio.h>

void main(void)
```

```
{
    printf("Hello, World!\n");
}
```

Of course, even if C isn't hard, it's highly idiosyncratic: Using statements such as #include and void or that \n at the end of the printf statement are entirely counterintuitive and make no sense at all at first sight.

However, if you're serious about running a Linux server, learning just a tiny bit of C will be highly beneficial, even if you'll never actually write (or even read) a single line of C code. Why? Because a number of other languages (including scripting and macro languages) borrow their syntax from C. You'll encounter elements of C syntax everywhere when you're using any version of UNIX. C-style syntax is even used in some configuration files! Examples include the Perl language and the new-style configuration files used with a DNS server.

Examples

Needless to say, this short introduction only scratched the surface of the process of script programming. However, even with this introductory information, you should be able to create simple solutions to many complex problems. The remainder of this chapter contains several real-world examples I use on the various live Linux systems I administer.

Note that these solutions are not masterpieces of programming, nor do they necessarily illustrate the best or most efficient programming techniques. However, they did the job when they were needed, and they were easy to put together and use. Hopefully you'll find them educational as well.

crontab Entries

You may recall from the previous chapter how I used tar and des to create an encrypted backup tape on one of my systems. However, I did not tell you the whole story. The actual crontab entry I use is a monster that utilizes many of the techniques described in this chapter. Here it is:

```
0 8 * * sun (/bin/tar -clpvf - —atime-preserve /etc /usr/local/samba
➥/usr/local/majordomo /home /root /var/adm /usr2/src ¦ /usr/local/bin/des
➥-E -k PassWord > /dev/rmt0) 2>&1 ¦ gzip ¦ uuencode tarlist.gz ¦
➥/bin/mail -s "System backup: `/bin/date +%y%m%d`" root
```

This monster is invoked at 8 a.m. every Sunday morning (one side effect being that our cat stares with great curiosity at the machine with the whining tape drive inside for the next half hour).

First, the command /bin/tar is executed. Flags ensure that file ownership and permissions are preserved. The directories include those containing user data files, configuration settings, and customizations. The output of the tar command is piped to the des command, which encrypts the result using a keyword. The result of the des encryption is then redirected to the tape device /dev/rmt0.

But that's not all. This entire command set is enclosed in parentheses so that its standard error can be redirected to standard output which, in turn, is piped. Because the tar command was invoked with the verbose flag (v), it lists all files processed during the archive operation. This list, along with any error messages or warnings, is piped to the gzip command for compression; the result of this is fed to the uuencode program, which packs it in an encoded form suitable for transmission via email.

This compressed, encoded output is then fed to the mail program /bin/mail. The subject will contain the current date to ensure that the message is properly identified. All this is then mailed to the root user.

The result? Figure 18.1 shows the email message I received this morning when the backup executed. Under Microsoft Outlook, my preferred email client application under Windows, the file neatly appears as an icon, ready to be viewed via the popular shareware program WinZip. Quite a large result from a one-liner in my crontab file, isn't it?

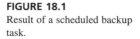

FIGURE 18.1
Result of a scheduled backup task.

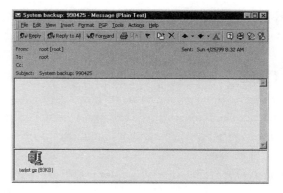

On another system, I have a crontab entry that's used to update the system clock by obtaining the time from an NTP server (see Chapter 14, "Time Services"):

```
5 5,11,17,23 * * * /usr/local/bin/ntpdate -s host2
```

The program runs four times a day, every six hours. The time is obtained from a server named `host2`.

On that NTP server, I have another `crontab` entry that ensures the computer's CMOS clock remains synchronized with the system clock. The reason why this is necessary is that this computer runs for months without rebooting, during which time the CMOS clock's drift becomes significant. When it's rebooted, NTP fails to start because the difference is too great between the local time and the time obtained from remote servers. Other solutions exist to this problem, but my preference is to keep the CMOS clock as accurate as possible, which is accomplished by the following `crontab` entry:

```
0 8 * * * /sbin/clock -wu
```

Cleaning Logs

As explained in Chapter 16, in order to prevent your log files from growing without limit, you must trim them, and even rotate them from time to time. You may be using a utility for this purpose that came with your Linux distribution, but some distributions contain no such tool. What's more, even when a tool is present, it may not do things the way you like them.

On several systems, I use a log-rotation script similar to the one shown in Listing 18.1. This script is run monthly, on the first day of the month, one minute after midnight, via a `crontab` entry like this one:

```
1 0 1 * * /bin/sh /root/cleanlog
```

The script can easily be expanded to rotate other log files, including nonstandard log files created by special server applications that could not be handled by standardized tools.

LISTING 18.1   Rotating logs

```
# !/bin/sh
cd /var/log
mv messages messages.old
touch messages
chmod 0640 messages
kill -HUP `/bin/cat /var/run/syslogd.pid`
mv wtmp wtmp.old
touch wtmp
chmod 0644 wtmp
cd /tmp
rm log_mg.ttyS0
```

Network Backup

In Chapter 17, "Backups," I discuss a system on which a daily backup is performed across the network. This backup is accomplished via the script shown in Listing 18.2.

LISTING 18.2   Network backup

```
#!/bin/sh
if [ -d /backup/mudgod ]; then
  MOUNTED="YES"
else
  MOUNTED="NO"
  mount host1:/home/backup /backup
fi

rm -rf /backup/*
cd /home
tar -clpf - —atime-preserve —exclude mudgod/LOGS . |
➥tar -C /backup -xlpf - —atime-preserve

if [ $MOUNTED = "NO" ]; then
  umount /backup
fi
```

This script first mounts the remote file system. The previous state is recorded in the MOUNTED variable, in order, so that at the end, the file system will only be unmounted if it wasn't mounted when the script began. (For instance, if I have that file system mounted for another reason, the script won't unmount it.)

Next, the actual backup is performed. All relevant files are copied from their source locations to the remote destination using two invocations of the tar command. One directory that contains large log files is excluded: These files do not contain any data that needs preserving.

When the backup is complete, the remote file system is unmounted.

Checking for Server Operation

A while ago, I had a problem with the Internet superserver on one of my Linux systems. If you recall, the Internet superserver daemon, inetd, is a program that accepts incoming Internet connection requests and activates other servers as and when needed. In this case, the system in question is host to the online game MUD2, and inetd is essential in order to allow players to log on via telnet. Therefore, when inetd died, the game was, in effect, unavailable.

Although my preference was to find the cause of the problem, in the meantime, I had to create a quick-and-dirty fix. This fix came in the form of a shell script that was used to find out whether the `inetd` daemon was operational and restarted it if necessary. The script also sent email to alert me to this occurrence.

Listing 18.3 shows the script I created for this purpose.

LISTING 18.3   Monitoring `inetd`

```
#!/bin/sh
inetd_owner=`ps axuw ¦ grep inetd ¦ grep -v grep ¦ grep -v checkinetd ¦
➥cut -f 1 -d " "`
if [ ${inetd_owner:-''} != "root" ]; then
  ( /bin/cat <<-EOF
    From: MUD2
    Subject: MUD2 EMERGENCY: inetd down
     The process inetd is down; attempting restart.
    -----------------------------------------------
    EOF
    /bin/netstat -t
    echo .
  ) ¦ /usr/sbin/sendmail root
  /usr/sbin/inetd
fi
```

Note the use of a here document, explained earlier in this chapter, to generate the email notification. The output of the `netstat` command is also appended to the email, which helped me identify the cause of the problem.

The No-Shell Shell

On another system, I had to establish user accounts with no shell access but with full access to the system otherwise. The simplest solution would have been to assign a nonexistent shell program to their user identifiers, but this wasn't satisfactory. Other programs, most notably the FTP server on this system, verify whether a user's shell is a valid one (that is, an existing program listed in `/etc/shells`) and deny access if it isn't.

The solution was to create the simple program shown in Listing 18.4. This program is the no-shell shell; I added it to the list of shell programs in `/etc/shells`. Really, though, it's just a tiny program that tells the user that his account has no shell access.

PART

V

CH

18

LISTING 18.4   The No-Shell Shell

```
#include <stdio.h>

int main(void)
{
        printf("Sorry, you are not permitted to have shell access.\n");
        sleep(1);
}
```

Because this is a C language program, it must be compiled before use. Assuming that the source program is saved to a file named nosh.c, you can compile it as follows:

```
cc nosh.c -o nosh
```

The executable program will be named nosh. On the system where this program is used, I copied the executable to /usr/local/bin and added /usr/local/bin/nosh to the list of shells in /etc/shells.

Password Generation

One of the most common security problems on all networks is that users tend to pick passwords that are easy to remember. Unfortunately, this also means passwords that are easy to guess. With today's powerful computers, one can launch a *vocabulary attack* that tries tens, even hundreds of thousands of known words and phrases as passwords in order to crack a target system.

One solution is to ensure that users use truly random passwords. If users cannot change the passwords themselves (for example, if they're denied shell access via the nosh program shown in the previous section), they won't be able to change their passwords to another, more easily remembered value. These random passwords are especially useful when users do not need to type the passwords by hand (for instance, when the passwords are stored as configuration settings for their email program, news reader, or dial-up logon script).

The program in Listing 18.5 is a simple C program I created for this purpose. The program generates a random 8-character password containing uppercase and lowercase letters as well as digits, at least one from each of the three groups.

LISTING 18.5   Random password generator

```c
#include <stdio.h>
#include <ctype.h>
#include <sys/times.h>

char validchr[] =
        "ABCDEFGHIJKLMNOPQRSTUVWXYZ0123456789abcdefghijklmnopqrstuvwxyz";

void main(void)
{
    char newpwd[9];
    int i;
    int l, u, d;
    struct tms tp;

    srand(times(&tp));
    newpwd[8] = '\0';
    l = u = d = 0;
    while (!l || !u || !d)
    {
        for (i = 0; i < 8; i++)
        {
            newpwd[i] = validchr[rand() % strlen(validchr)];
            l |= islower(newpwd[i]);
            u |= isupper(newpwd[i]);
            d |= isdigit(newpwd[i]);
        }
    }
    printf( "New random password: %s\n", newpwd);
}
```

Summary

Many system administration tasks occur repetitively. Other tasks may not occur on an exact schedule, but the steps are sufficiently complex that you may want to automate their execution. Task scheduling with the cron daemon and simple shell scripts are the answer in these situations.

The cron daemon can be used to schedule any number of tasks that occur on a repeated schedule. Separate lists exist for each individual user; the lists can be edited using the crontab command. These scheduled tasks are executed in the background by the crond daemon.

Similar in function to `crond` is the `atd` daemon, which allows for the one-time execution of a task at a scheduled time. Such tasks can be scheduled using the `at` command.

Commands normally typed at the keyboard can be recorded into files. These files are usually called *shell scripts*. In addition to regular commands, the scripts can contain conditional execution commands, variables, and special features such as redirection and so-called *here documents*.

In addition to shell scripts, other programming languages are also sometimes used to perform system administration tasks. These include Perl, a popular language with powerful text-processing features, and, of course, C, the ubiquitous programming language of UNIX systems.

Manual Pages

For additional information on the topics discussed in this chapter, refer to the following manual pages:

- `man cron`
- `man crontab`
- `man 5 crontab`
- `man at`
- `man bash`
- `man tcsh`
- `man ksh`
- `man perl`

Configuring Workstations

The **reason why servers exist** is quite simple: They provide functions that you utilize from client workstations. Therefore, any book that's about using Linux as a server system would be incomplete if it didn't contain information about configuring client systems.

Then again, client systems come in many flavors, and their configurations can be quite complex. Tomes, many times the size of this one, have been written about configuring Windows, Macintosh, and OS/2 workstations. In order to limit its size, the present chapter is focused on the use of 32-bit versions of Windows, most notably Windows 95/98, in conjunction with your Linux server. What you'll learn here is how you can configure your Windows workstation to access specific services on your Linux server, including IP routing, email, network news, and SMB file services. Because of this limited focus, it's possible to present instructions here in reasonable detail—these instructions can be of use as examples even if you're installing a workstation using different software from what's described here.

One application that does not require any special configuration steps is your Web browser. Once you've successfully established a local area network connection to your Linux server and properly configured TCP/IP networking, your Web browser will work "out of the box"—no extra configuration steps are needed.

This chapter begins at a well-defined starting point: It's assumed that you already have a fully functional Linux router and server. You'll be guided through the steps of setting up Windows-based workstations to operate with this server and obtain all types of Internet services.

Using a Linux Router

The first step in connecting workstations to the Internet via a Linux router is configuring the workstation's TCP/IP settings to use the router as its gateway to the external network (as you see in Figure 19.1). The router can be a regular router, which simply passes data traffic between workstations and the external network, or it can be a firewall gateway that hides your workstations behind a firewall address, performing IP masquerading and other protective functions (see Chapter 11, "Firewalls").

FIGURE 19.1
Routing for your workstation.

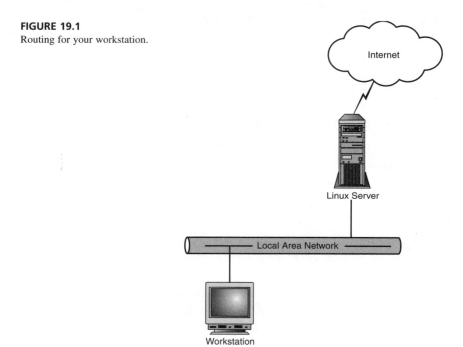

It's assumed here that the Linux router is already fully functional and either maintains a permanent connection to the Internet or performs dialing on demand (see Chapter 7, "Making the Connection").

Setting Up the TCP/IP Protocol

If your Linux router is configured as an ordinary (nonfirewall) router, all workstations on your network must have their own registered IP addresses. Usually, you'll be able to obtain a block of IP addresses from your Internet Service Provider, which you can then assign to your workstations as needed. If you only have a single IP address (worse yet, if your IP address changes every time you connect to the ISP), the steps described in this section will *not* work! What you need to do in this case is either obtain a block of IP addresses or set up your Linux router as a masquerading firewall gateway and use work-station addresses from a reserved range, such as 192.168.*xxx*.*yyy*.

To connect a Windows workstation to the Internet via your Linux router, you must per-form the following steps:

1. If not done already, install a network card and the TCP/IP protocol.
2. Set up the IP address, gateway address, and DNS server address for the workstation.

Installation of most network cards under Windows 95/98 is straightforward. Unless Plug-and-Play becomes Plug-and-*Pray*, all you need to do is insert the card, turn on the com-puter, and keep clicking until you're through with the installation steps. Here, let's assume that the card is already installed and functional. Now what needs to be done is to configure the card with the appropriate IP settings in order for the workstation to prop-erly function with your Linux server.

In the following paragraphs, the steps required to set up a Windows 95 machine for TCP/IP networking are described. The procedure is very similar under Windows 98 and Windows NT.

Network settings can be changed through the Network applet of the Windows Control Panel. When you invoke this applet by double-clicking the Network icon in the Control Panel, the Network dialog box is displayed (see Figure 19.2). It shows all your current network settings. Locate the settings labeled TCP/IP -> *adapter name*, where the adapter name corresponds with the network card you want to configure. (Most systems would have at least another network adapter, the *dial-up adapter*—this refers to the modem on your system when used to make dial-up Internet connections. Some systems may have additional network cards as well.)

If you do *not* have a TCP/IP entry for your network adapter, it may be necessary to install the TCP/IP protocol first. Click on the Add button, select Protocol, and find Microsoft's TCP/IP among the network protocols, as you see in Figure 19.3.

PART

V

CH

19

FIGURE 19.2
The Windows 95 Network dialog box.

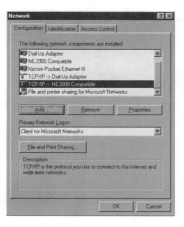

FIGURE 19.3
Adding the TCP/IP protocol.

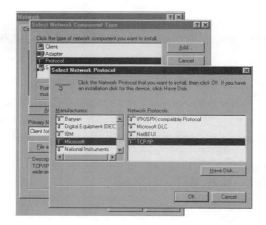

Configuring the IP Address

To change TCP/IP settings, click on the Properties button. This activates the TCP/IP Properties dialog box (this dialog box also appears if you're installing a fresh copy of the TCP/IP protocol). This is where you begin entering settings that correspond with your Linux server.

First, take a look at the address (see Figure 19.4). Make sure the Obtain an IP Address Automatically setting is off. (For this setting to work, you need a functioning DHCP server on your network.) The IP address should be the address assigned to your workstation or an address from the 192.168.*xxx*.*yyy* range if you're behind a masquerading firewall or on a private network with no Internet connection. The subnet mask would normally be either the standard subnet mask for a Class C IP network (255.255.255.0) or a subnet mask that corresponds with the address block you received from your ISP. For instance, if you received a block of 16 IP addresses, the subnet mask would be 255.255.255.240. (Refer to Chapter 5, "Internet Concepts," for more information.)

FIGURE 19.4
Setting the IP address.

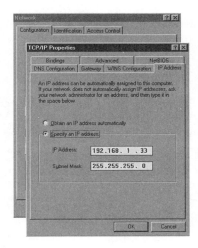

Setting Up the Network Gateway

Next, you need to configure the default router, or gateway, for this Windows machine (see Figure 19.5). This gateway is used for traffic with a destination that's outside your local network. Consequently, you only need to enter an address here if you actually provide a connection to the outside world; if the workstation is used in an intranet-only configuration with no external connection, no network gateway is required.

PART
V

CH
19

FIGURE 19.5
Configuring the gateway.

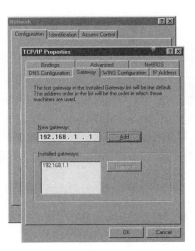

If you have a more complex network topology with several routers, you may not be able to configure them using this interface. Instead, it may be necessary to use ROUTE.EXE, the Windows equivalent of the Linux route command. To find out how you can use ROUTE.EXE to list or configure network routing, simply type **ROUTE** in an MS-DOS window; this will display a help screen.

NOTE	You can verify your Windows workstation's network routing using the PING.EXE and TRACERT.EXE command-line utilities. These are Windows versions of the UNIX ping and traceroute tools, and they work very similarly. Although you can use these programs through the Run command in the Start menu, they are best invoked from an MS-DOS window.

Setting Up Name Service

In order for your network connection to be fully functional, you must also specify a DNS server (take a look at Figure 19.6). When a standalone Windows machine is connected to the Internet, the DNS server is usually that of your ISP. However, in a local area network configuration, you'll probably be running DNS on the Linux server; if so, make sure you specify this machine's address here.

FIGURE 19.6
Adding the DNS server.

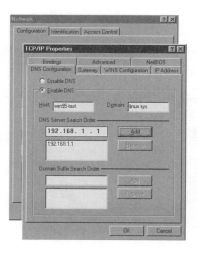

For more information about setting up DNS service under Linux, refer to Chapter 6, "The Domain Name System."

If you have more than one computer on your network that provides DNS service, you can specify multiple DNS servers here. Alternatively, if you enjoy a permanent high-speed Internet connection, you may add, as a secondary DNS server, the address of your ISP's DNS server; this will provide you with redundancy in case your own DNS server fails for any reason.

Using a Linux Mail Server

When you're configuring a workstation for mail service, you usually need to enter two pieces of information: the name of your SMTP server and the name of your POP3 server.

SMTP and POP3 Service

As explained in Chapter 8, "Running a Mail Server," SMTP is a protocol used for sending mail; POP3 is a protocol used for accessing your mailbox on a remote system.

Consequently, you must configure the SMTP address to be that of a computer on which a properly configured mail server is running. POP3, on the other hand, must point to a system that has a running copy of a POP3 server program and a mailbox that you can access. In other words, whereas the identity of the SMTP server is unimportant (as long as it accepts outgoing mail from you), the POP3 server must be the server where your mailbox is located.

If you configured your Linux server with user accounts and a copy of the sendmail server, this machine will act both as your SMTP server (courtesy of sendmail) and as your POP3 server (courtesy of the POP3 daemon or another daemon with similar functionality). If you aren't using a sendmail server, or if users have their mailboxes at your ISP, for instance, your SMTP and POP3 addresses, or both, may point to your ISP's server.

Setting Up Microsoft Outlook Express

Because it's distributed with Microsoft Internet Explorer, Windows 98, and Windows 2000, Outlook Express is one of the most popular email applications today. It's also the email application most likely to be present on newly configured Windows 95/98 workstations. That said, if you're installing another email application, the procedure to follow is probably very similar to that presented here.

PART

V

CH

19

What's described here are the steps required to configure an existing Outlook Express installation so that it works with your Linux server. If you're installing a fresh copy of Outlook Express, follow these procedures, as appropriate, when you get to the point of setting up an email account.

> **NOTE** The steps presented here describe the exact procedure with Outlook Express version 4.72 under Windows NT. Because there are several different versions of this application in circulation, the installation procedure you need to follow may be slightly different.

To view your existing email accounts or add accounts, select the Accounts command from the Outlook Express Tools menu. Click the Add button and select Mail (as you see in Figure 19.7).

FIGURE 19.7
Adding a mail account in Outlook Express.

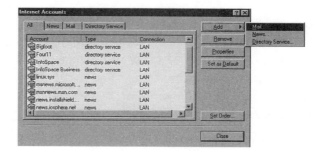

This command activates the Internet Connection Wizard, as shown in Figure 19.8. The first step is to enter the desired *display name*; this will be the human-readable name of the user, not an email address.

FIGURE 19.8
Entering the display name.

When you click the Next button, another dialog box appears where you can enter the desired email address (see Figure 19.9). This address will be the user's return address in outgoing email. In this dialog box, it's actually possible to enter an address from another system or a completely bogus address. However, under most circumstances, you're advised to enter the user's correct return address here. This is because when the user sends mail, this address will show up as the sender address on outgoing messages; when recipients reply, their reply will go to the address entered here. If you enter an address that is not a valid address for this user, replies to his mail will never reach his mailbox.

FIGURE 19.9
Entering the email address.

When you click the Next button again, things get interesting. This is where you finally arrive at the dialog box where you can specify the identity of your mail servers, as shown in Figure 19.10.

FIGURE 19.10
Entering server names.

PART
V

CH
19

First of all, the mailbox server type, in the case of a Linux server, will almost always be POP3.

Next, you enter the name of the incoming mail server. This is the name of the computer that holds user mailboxes. There's no confusion, of course, if you're operating a single Linux server that does everything. The confusion begins in configurations where the incoming and outgoing mail function is separated, implemented on different computers.

The outgoing mail server can be any computer that runs sendmail or an equivalent mail server application, as long as it's prepared to relay messages from your workstation. It can be your own Linux sendmail server, or it can be your ISP's mail server machine (see Chapter 8). In the latter case, check with your ISP as to whether its system is actually configured to accept outgoing mail from your workstations. If it isn't, users on your network won't be able to send mail with this configuration.

Clicking the Next button brings up the Internet Mail Logon dialog box, which you see in Figure 19.11. SPA is a three-letter acronym that you can safely ignore since Linux mail servers do not normally use it; however, you still must specify the user's mailbox name and password. The mailbox name is the user's name on your Linux system, and the password is, of course, the regular Linux password. This information is used when the user's mailbox is accessed for the purpose of retrieving messages; it's *not* used when outgoing mail is being sent.

FIGURE 19.11
Mailbox identification.

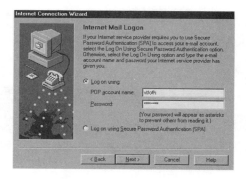

When you click the Next button again, Outlook Express lets you assign a "friendly name" to the newly configured account (see Figure 19.12). This step is cosmetic in nature; the name you use here will in no way affect the user's access to the mail system.

Clicking the Next button one more time brings up a dialog box for you to specify the connection type (see Figure 19.13). The significance of this dialog box is that it lets you configure Outlook Express to automatically dial a remote system in order to deliver mail. However, if the server is a Linux server on your local area network, such dialing is not necessary; select the Connect Using My Local Area Network (LAN) option.

FIGURE 19.12
Naming the new account.

FIGURE 19.13
Specifying the connection type.

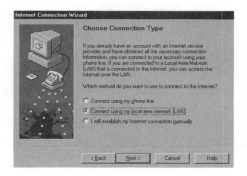

This is it. Clicking the Next button brings up a congratulatory dialog box; when this dialog box is dismissed, your new mail account is usable.

If you ever need to modify any of these settings at a later time, you once again begin with the Accounts command under the Tools menu. Select the desired account and click the Properties button to bring up a tabbed dialog box, like the one shown in Figure 19.14, when any of the settings can be altered. It's also possible to change parameters that were not modifiable during the initial wizard-based setup of the mail account (for example, security and advanced settings).

To summarize, configuring a mail account consists of setting up the user's display name, the return address, the identity of the incoming and outgoing mail server, the mailbox protocol used, and the user's mailbox name and password.

FIGURE 19.14
Changing an existing account.

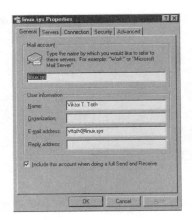

Accessing Network News

If you're operating a news server, you'll probably want to configure user workstations so that they can access this server. Whether you have your own news server or not, you might be interested in setting up user workstations to access your ISP's news server or another public news server that provides access to the nearly 30,000 Usenet newsgroups.

The NNTP Server

As explained in Chapter 9, "Mailing Lists and Newsgroups," a news server is accessed through the Network News Protocol (NNTP). This protocol allows a client application to both read and post news messages.

Some NNTP servers are public, meaning that they can be accessed by anyone on the Internet. Other NNTP servers provide restricted access. Access can be restricted to machines on specific networks or to users with valid passwords.

When you set up a client program to work with a news server, you need to know in advance the identity of the server and whether access is protected by a password. If this is a news server using the INN software suite on your Linux machine, access restrictions are defined in the nnrp.access configuration file.

Adding a News Account to Outlook Express

The steps to adding a news account are very similar to the steps you followed when adding an email account to Outlook Express. Once again, you need to invoke the Accounts command from the Tools menu and click the Add button. This time, select News, as you see in Figure 19.15.

FIGURE 19.15
Adding a news account in
Outlook Express.

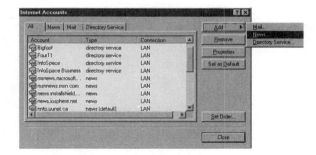

The first dialog box that appears is one you've already seen, where Outlook Express asks
you to enter a display name (refer to Figure 19.8). When you click Next, Outlook
Express asks you to enter an email address for this news account (see Figure 19.16).

FIGURE 19.16
Entering the news account email
address.

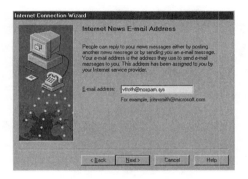

PART
V

CH
19

When setting up an email account, you were advised to provide the user's correct email
address as the return address. This time, the contrary may be the case. When posting
messages to public news servers, many users opt to use fake addresses to avoid having
their real email addresses fall victim to *harvesting* (that is, being collected by unscrupu-
lous individuals who then use, or sell, the mailing lists they compiled for junk mail purposes). Some newsgroup users provide completely bogus addresses, whereas others
simply add a part to their address that can be easily noticed and removed by human
beings but is enough to mislead harvesting programs. (For instance, using
`vttoth@linux.dontspamme.sys` in place of `vttoth@linux.sys`.)

When you click Next again, you're asked to enter the name of the news server you're
connecting to. Additionally, you're asked to specify whether this news server requires
you to log on (see Figure 19.17). Typically, public news servers don't, but privately operated servers often do, especially those that contain confidential information.

FIGURE 19.17
Specifying the news server name.

The remaining two dialog boxes are already familiar to you. Outlook Express asks you to name the new account with a "friendly name" (previously shown in Figure 19.12); it also asks you to specify the type of the connection you're using (refer to Figure 19.13).

That's it. When you're done with these steps, Outlook Express can make an attempt to connect to the news server and download a list of newsgroups. To modify the parameters of this account at a later time, you should once again begin with the Accounts command under the Tools menu, select the desired account, and click the Properties button, as you see in Figure 19.18.

FIGURE 19.18
Modifying a news account.

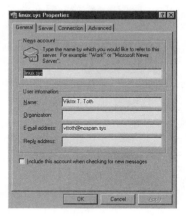

In summary, in order to set up a news account, you must specify the name of the news server, optionally specify a valid username and password combination, and enter a return address.

Using Samba Services

As described in Chapter 13, "File Services for Windows: Samba," Samba for Linux provides SMB-style file and printer services. In plain language, this means your Linux server can be configured to provide access to shared directories and printers over a Windows network.

Accessing Remote Directories

If everything is configured correctly, a Samba server with its shared directories should appear no different from other Windows machines on the network. In other words, you should be able to see the Samba system when you double-click the Network Neighborhood icon on the Windows desktop (see Figure 19.19). You'll be able to browse files on the shared directories just as you're able to browse local items or shared directories on Windows systems.

FIGURE 19.19
Samba shared directories in Windows Explorer.

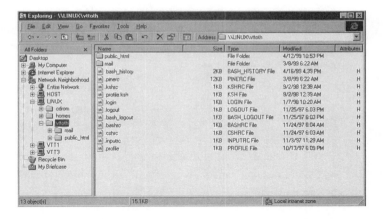

It's also possible to access the Samba server from the MS-DOS command line. This is especially useful if you want to configure network settings from a batch file under program control.

To view the list of shares on a remote server, you'd use the following command:

```
C:\>net view \\linux
```

```
Shared resources at \\LINUX

Sharename       Type            Comment
------------------------------------------------------------------------
cdrom           Disk
homes           Disk
lp              Print
printers        Print
vttoth          Disk            Home directory of vttoth
The command was completed successfully.
```

Needless to say, you should use the actual name of your Linux server in place of \\linux; this name is specified during Samba configuration (see Chapter 13).

To associate a shared directory with a local drive letter, you need the net use command:

```
C:\>net use n: \\linux\vttoth

The command completed successfully.
```

Note that it's not always necessary to associate network shares with drive letters. You can use the so-called UNC (Universal Naming Convention) pathname instead. Here's an example:

```
C:\>dir \\linux\vttoth

 Directory of \\linux\vttoth
PUBLI~34        <DIR>           04-12-99 10:53p public_html
MAIL            <DIR>           03-08-99  6:22a mail
```

UNC pathnames work with almost all 32-bit applications; however, older 16-bit DOS and Windows programs may require that the remote directory be mapped to a drive letter before they can access the files there.

You may encounter problems with accessing directories with net use or via UNC paths if your Windows password is not the same as your password on your Linux system (and sometimes, problems occur even when they're identical). Most commonly, you'll receive an error message indicating an invalid password. To connect to a remote server using the correct password, use another form of the net use command:

```
C:\>dir \\linux\vttoth

Invalid password
C:\>net use \\linux\vttoth Password
The command was completed successfully.
C:\>dir \\linux\vttoth
 Directory of \\linux\vttoth
PUBLI~34        <DIR>           04-12-99 10:53p public_html
MAIL            <DIR>           03-08-99  6:22a mail
```

Needless to say, you should use your actual password in place of *Password* with the net use command.

If the user ID you use to log on to your Windows system is not the same as your user ID on the Linux machine, things get even more difficult. If changing your Windows username is impractical for any reason, I recommend you map your username to your Linux username via Samba's username_map parameter and smbusers file. For more information, refer to Chapter 13.

Printing over the Network

Installing a printer is a bit more complicated than accessing a shared directory, simply because a printer needs a driver. It's the printer driver software that translates generic graphical commands and text into commands that the printer understands—for example, PostScript, PCL (the Printer Control Language of Hewlett-Packard printers), and other forms of control codes.

When a printer is used on a Windows network, in principle, you can install the driver on the machine that has the printer attached; alternatively, the driver can be installed on the workstation that would connect to this server and its printer. The difference is that, in the first case, generic graphic instructions are sent across the network and translated into the printer's control language at the server. In the second case, the translation occurs at the workstation, and the server merely passes on the translated commands to the printer in a transparent fashion.

When using a printer attached to a Linux server, only this second option is available. In other words, the printer driver must be installed on each workstation that you intend to use with the shared Linux printer.

> **NOTE**
> Some printers come with driver software that needs to be installed before you begin the process of adding a printer through the Windows Printers control panel. Also, note that many newer printers come with software that only works when the printer is attached locally (through a bi-directional parallel port). When you're using the printer across the network, an alternate driver is required, also usually supplied by the manufacturer. These alternate drivers, however, might not provide a means to access all of the printer's advanced functions.

PART
V

CH
19

To install a Linux printer, shared via Samba, on your Windows 95/98 or NT workstation, you need to invoke the Printers control panel under Settings from the Start menu. Double-clicking the Add Printer button invokes the Add Printer Wizard (see Figure 19.20).

FIGURE 19.20
The Add Printer Wizard.

Clicking Next brings up the second part of this wizard, where you can specify whether the printer you're adding is local or networked. Select Network Printer and click the Next button, as shown in Figure 19.21.

FIGURE 19.21
Selecting a network printer.

The third panel of this wizard, shown in Figure 19.22, lets you specify the network printer using a UNC pathname. Alternatively, you can click the Browse button and select the printer from the list of available network printers (as you see in Figure 19.23). You can also specify whether you want to print from MS-DOS–based programs; if so, the wizard will let you associate the network printer with an MS-DOS–style printer device name (for example, LPT1).

FIGURE 19.22
Specifying the printer's network path.

FIGURE 19.23
Browsing for a printer.

When you close the Browse for Printer dialog box and click the Next button, the Add Printer Wizard lets you capture a printer port. This is where you associate the desired MS-DOS printer port name with the newly added printer (see Figure 19.24).

PART
V
CH
19

FIGURE 19.24
Capturing the printer port.

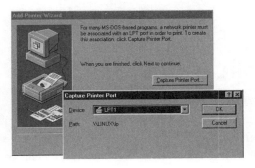

When you click Next again, the Add Printer Wizard lets you select the printer type, as shown in Figure 19.25. Drivers for the printer you select here will be installed on the computer if they aren't already present.

FIGURE 19.25
Specifying the printer type.

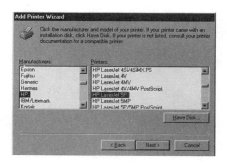

Lastly, when you click Next, the Add Printer Wizard lets you name the newly added printer (see Figure 19.26). At this point, when you click the Next button, Windows will begin loading the necessary printer drivers. It may ask you to insert the original Windows CD-ROM or floppy disks, and it may also reboot the computer before the printer becomes usable. When you're asked whether a test page should be printed, click Yes; this will let you verify whether your network printer setup is correct and complete.

FIGURE 19.26
Naming the printer.

Other Applications

Email, news, access to remote files and directories, and the ubiquitous Web browser all can be considered core applications when utilizing the Internet. However, other applications are also frequently used in conjunction with a Linux server. I'll mention two in particular: Web-authoring tools let you maintain the contents on a Web server using WYSIWYG tools, and X servers let you use full-screen graphical Linux programs from your Windows workstation.

Web Authoring Tools

Web pages can be created by hand or by using any one of the numerous Web page–authoring programs available. Some of these tools integrate authoring features with server-side support, thus eliminating the need to upload and organize files by hand.

One such tool that supports the Apache Web server under Linux is Microsoft FrontPage. (Yes, the Redmond giant does support our favorite operating system!) Although it's possible to host Web pages created with FrontPage on a stock Apache server, added functionality is available if you install the FrontPage Server Extensions for Apache/Linux. You'll be able to upload Web pages from within FrontPage, manage access security, and perform other maintenance functions. FrontPage Server Extensions can be downloaded from the Web site `http://officeupdate.microsoft.com/frontpage/wpp/`.

Installation of the Server Extensions is a complex process. The Server Extension kit actually installs a modified (patched) version of the Apache Web server and also installs scripts and programs that are used when you connect to the server using a FrontPage client.

If you're maintaining a simple Web site that only you modify, installing FrontPage extensions or other toolkits of similar functionality is probably overkill. The complexity of the installation process outweighs any benefits gained in the form of extra functionality. However, if you have multiple authors maintaining your Web pages, or if authors regularly access the Web server remotely, the effort may be worthwhile.

X Applications

Being able to run X applications on a Linux server simplifies your life, because you can use the full-screen graphical interface to interact with the system. It's also possible to extend this capability to the Windows desktop, making your life a lot easier when administering the system remotely. (Remote, in this sense, may simply mean that you're accessing the Linux system from across the room, sitting at your Windows workstation.)

One of the oddities of the X Window System is that the roles of servers and clients suffer an apparent reversal. Your workstation becomes the server (providing graphical services) to clients (application programs, that is), which run on the remote Linux system. Consequently, software packages that implement X capability on your workstation are referred to as *X server software*.

Setting up the X server also reflects this shift in roles. When you configure the X server on your workstation, it's actually on the workstation where you need to enable access to clients that access it from a remote system—that is, your Linux server.

One such X server software package is X-Win32, an excellent package created by StarNet Communications (`http://www.starnet.com/`). This package has an auxiliary utility called X-Util32, which is where configuration settings can be made. Here, you must add the address of any remote UNIX system that will run applications making use of your Windows workstation's display (see Figure 19.27).

FIGURE 19.27
Configuring the X-Win32 server.

X-Win32 allows you to start up a session with the UNIX program of your choice through commands in a user-configurable menu. If you configure the remote shell (rsh) facility on your Linux system, it may be possible for you to configure X-Win32 in such a way so that, for instance, a single mouse-click invokes a terminal session with the remote Linux machine.

Summary

One of the main reasons for a Linux server's existence is so that it can be used from workstations. In most environments, the term *workstation* probably refers to a Windows computer.

To configure a Windows computer to work seamlessly with your Linux server, you must perform the following steps:

- Establish basic Internet routing and connectivity.
- Set up mail and news software and configure user accounts.
- Optionally connect to any Samba shared directories and printers.
- Install any other network applications that you may want to use.

Configuring Internet settings involves establishing the machine's IP address, specifying the default gateway (probably your Linux machine) and the DNS server (again, probably your Linux machine). When these steps are complete, you should be able to access the Linux server via a Web browser, and, if the server is configured to provide Internet routing, access other Web sites as well.

When setting up an email application (such as the commonly used Microsoft program Outlook Express), you must, at a minimum, specify the user's display name, the return address, the identities of the incoming and outgoing mail servers, the mailbox protocol used, and the user's mailbox name and password. For news servers, you need the name of the news server, the user's name and password (if required by the server), and a return email address.

The Samba software suite lets your Linux machine provide file and printer services to Windows clients. Connecting to a Samba shared directory is no different from connecting to any other shared directories on a Windows network. You can browse shared directories via the Windows Explorer, or you can establish connections to them from the MS-DOS command line via the `net use` command. You may need to specify a password when connecting, and, if your Linux and Windows usernames aren't identical, you may also need to add username mappings to Samba.

When connecting to a Samba printer, you must install the printer driver on your Windows computer. Connecting to the printer requires going through the steps of the Add Printer Wizard, found in the Printers control panel, located under Settings in the Windows Start menu.

You can also configure other applications on a Windows workstation. These include Web-authoring tools, such as FrontPage, or X servers, such as X-Win32. The latter is especially useful if you want to administer your Linux system remotely, because you can take advantage of X graphical applications without having to physically access the server.

Manual Pages

For additional information on topics discussed in this chapter, you can type the following MS-DOS commands to obtain online help:

- NET HELP
- PING
- ROUTE
- TRACERT

Security Revisited

Throughout **this book you've read** dire warnings about various security risks. This is no accident: When you're running a server, you're by definition maintaining a machine that's routinely accessed by others. Therefore, security is an ongoing concern.

This chapter will not teach you how to set up a server for guarding national secrets. However, it will give you a chance to review common security problems, learn about the signs of security problems on your system, understand how security can be compromised either intentionally or by mistake, and also learn about recovering from an attack.

Access Security

First, let me state the obvious: Your system must be physically secure in order for it to be trusted. When someone can walk up to the server and boot it from a floppy disk or appear with a screwdriver and take a hard disk out, no security measures can keep your system from being damaged or your data from being stolen.

Physical Security

If I can boot your computer using a floppy disk of my own making, I can at the very least corrupt data on your computer's hard disk. Probably, I'll also be able to read data off your hard disk, unless you're using an encrypted file system (which is a rarity.)

If I have physical access to your computer, I can open its case and remove or replace components. I can remove your computer's hard disk and take it away, along with your valuable data. I can remove your backup tapes. Worse yet, I may even be able to replace the hard disk with another one—say, one that contains a program that appears like a normal Linux login program, except that any passwords it accepts, it immediately transmits over the Internet for me to record and use.

Consequently, any computer that should not be compromised must be physically protected. Placing your Linux server on the receptionist's desk just a few feet from your office's front doors is probably a terrible idea! (No, this is not something I just dreamt up: I've actually seen servers located this way.)

Dial-up Security

Even if your system is physically secure, it may be just as naked if it's connected to a telephone line. In fact, a system hooked up to a modem presents a number of serious risks, some of which aren't that obvious.

First, if your system is configured to answer incoming calls, that provides a means for strangers to access the system. Usually this shouldn't represent a problem, unless they have access to passwords on your system, or they were able to guess the passwords.

However, sometimes, even when you didn't configure your modem to answer calls, you're still at risk. Some modems can be configured to autoanswer; that is to say, they'll answer an incoming call even when not specifically controlled by software. That means a caller, without your knowledge, has gained some form of interactive access to your system.

Sometimes this doesn't represent a problem, because when there's no application controlling the modem line, an intruder has nothing to interact with. But what if there is such an application? What if the intruder can make that application execute another program, such as a shell program that gives the intruder full interactive access?

The situation becomes especially troublesome if you do provide dial-up access via modem for legitimate users (or for yourself, to perform remote system administration). For example, let's say that due to a software or hardware failure, your system doesn't detect when your connection drops. If the modem answers the next call all by itself, an intruder would be able to continue where you left off, possibly gaining root access to your system (if you were doing something as the root user when you lost connection).

So how can you protect against these situations? Testing is most important. Sometimes you can only test your system fully when you have access to two telephone lines (and another computer with a modem of course), but this may be a necessity. You must ensure that your system behaves as expected under unusual circumstances and that, most importantly, the following conditions are always true:

- When a connection is terminated in any way, the system recognizes it, terminates all running programs on that terminal, and reinitializes the terminal.

- The modem only answers incoming calls when instructed to do so by software.

- When a call is answered, a login screen or some other authentication procedure is presented to the user.

Is this just a hypothetical discussion about something that never happens? Not so. I've seen quite a number of popular modems that did not provide the correct indicator signals to the host computer when, for instance, the carrier was lost. Sometimes, the modem's firmware required upgrading before the problem was eliminated.

However, these problems can occur even when the modem is functioning perfectly. For instance, modems can be configured by software never to present a carrier-loss signal to the host computer. Cheap modem cables for external modems are sold everywhere that do not have the necessary connections for these signals. Therefore, it's imperative that you thoroughly test a modem before putting it into service.

> **NOTE**   Technically, the same problems exist under other operating systems, such as Windows, but in practice, the danger is far less significant. That's because other operating systems do not routinely have the capability to perform all functions via a dial-up line. Under Windows, you must explicitly start bulletin board software or similar utilities before an incoming telephone connection can be put to any use. Under Linux, however, this capability is inherent; everything you can do with Linux, you can do via a terminal connected to the machine's serial port and, by consequence, via a terminal connected through a modem line.

Network Security

When you connect a server to a network, you open up many potential security holes. Your machine is no longer isolated; a high-speed interface with the outside world exists, which is designed from the outset to allow you to perform complex functions remotely.

Note that the problem is not with the network card *per se*—it's the fact that behind the network card are several layers of software protocols, each with their own configuration traps, that an intruder can potentially use to gain access to higher-level functions.

Another problem arises from the fact that networks are usually there in order to be used, and when they're being used, they can potentially be monitored.

Local Area Networks

One of the key characteristics of local area networks is that they're broadcast-type networks: Data sent by one computer can be heard by all computers on the network.

Under normal circumstances, a computer only picks up those bits and pieces of data that are addressed to it and simply ignores the rest. However, it's possible to write network-monitoring software that can record *all* data traffic on the network. For instance, when you're sitting at Computer A, typing your secret password in order to log on to Computer B across the network, a malicious user at Computer C may be monitoring the entire session, thus obtaining a copy of the master password (see Figure 20.1).

FIGURE 20.1
Network monitoring.

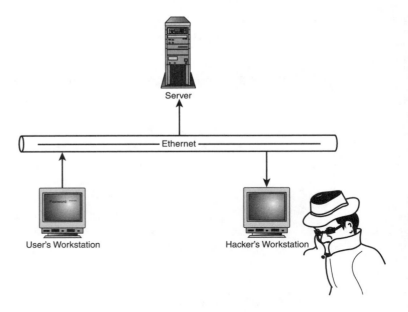

If your network is physically secure and the only computers on it are those in the hands of trusted colleagues, this is not really a problem. However, you must be careful and ensure that no unauthorized persons can gain access to it, even momentarily.

This is not as trivial as it seems. In many offices, network connections are prewired, and such wiring may extend to rooms such as boardrooms and meeting rooms, which are frequently accessed by nonemployees. Although it's unlikely that your bank manager will attempt to hack into your system when he visits you to discuss your loan application, can you say the same about that young hacker who came applying for a job with a portable computer under his arm?

Remote Connections

Security wise, a remote connection differs from a local area network connection in two ways. The good news is that on a remote connection, only data explicitly meant to be sent there will be transmitted. Traffic between your local computers will not be reflected beyond your local network, and, specifically, it will not be sent out over the remote connection (see the warning later in this chapter for one exception from this rule concerning cable modems).

On the bad side, whereas you have some degree of control over who has access to your local area network, the same isn't true when you establish an Internet connection. Anybody in the world with a computer and Internet access is at your doorstep, so to speak. It's a large world out there; how many from this crowd will be carrying picklocks?

You may think that this is of no concern to you; your system is adequately protected by passwords. But passwords alone aren't sufficient. You see, a would-be attacker can do a lot more than trying to log on to your system via telnet.

In fact, a would-be attacker has at least 131,072 different holes to probe. These are, of course, the 65,536 TCP and 65,536 UDP ports on your machine, behind any of which there might be a server program lurking, any of which may be having a security problem.

When a hacker probes your system, the vast majority of these ports will come up with no result; however, your attacker only has to find one. Or perhaps he won't even use a TCP or UDP port; he may be aware of a vulnerability with your operating system's handling of low-level ICMP packets, for instance.

The answer to this problem is simple: Don't run any server software you don't need and always know what server applications are installed on your system. In particular, familiarize yourself with the contents of `/etc/inetd.conf`, which, of course, is the file that controls what applications might be started by `inetd`, the Internet superserver, in response to incoming requests (see Chapter 4, "Internet Configuration and Basic Security").

PART
V

CH
20

Personnel Security

Most often, security is compromised not because you're using defective software or because your local area network has been penetrated by a sophisticated hacker. No, the most frequent cause behind security-related problems is people.

The Case of the Disgruntled Employee

The case of the disgruntled employee causing grave harm to your computer systems after leaving his job has been portrayed in the media many times. Still, small organizations and businesses often believe that they're immune to this problem. This is not so. Even in my personal experience, I encountered situations where a disgruntled employee left behind a "back door" on a company's UNIX server, only to exploit it a few weeks later. His intent was not to cause harm—he just didn't feel like "letting go." He believed that he still had a right to access a system that he helped build. Needless to say, his former employers disagreed.

Of course, there's no surefire way to protect against a situation that might occur when a trusted employee leaves, short of reinstalling all your systems from scratch. Still, a few precautionary measures, such as changing all your system passwords, can help mitigate the risk.

Carelessness and Ignorance

Even employees with no evil intent can cause grave harm to your systems through carelessness coupled with ignorance. Leaving behind a slip of paper with your Linux server's dial-up telephone number and the root password in a college cafeteria is just one of the many examples that come to mind. If users are not educated about the importance of keeping secret passwords secret, problems are bound to occur.

Application Security

Some security problems arise simply due to the nature of certain applications—namely that either intentionally or accidentally, they provide a means for external users to run arbitrary commands on your system.

It must be said that this is not necessarily a security risk just by itself. There are thousands of Internet Service Providers out there that supply users with "shell accounts" (that is, the ability to log on, via telnet, to a UNIX system and execute programs there, including programs of their own making).

Shell Accounts

It's important to note that there's a difference between intentionally letting users access your system this way and finding out after the fact that such access has taken place. If you plan to offer shell access to untrusted (external) users from the outset, presumably you're aware of the risk this entails and have made sure that such users will not be able to access material they're not authorized to see.

Web Scripts and Other Utilities

Ill-designed Web scripts represent a particularly dangerous security hole. Given the ease with which a shell's script can be created to process Web forms, it's no wonder that a lot of them are around; unfortunately, not all of them have been written by expert hands.

Let me show you a simple example. Suppose you create a simple Web page, shown in Figure 20.2, which processes a user's email. The HTML code for this Web page may look like the following:

```
<HTML>
<BODY>
<FORM METHOD="GET" ACTION="http:cgi-bin/test.cgi">
  E-mail: <INPUT TYPE="text" NAME="Email"><INPUT TYPE="submit">
</FORM>
</BODY>
</HTML>
```

FIGURE 20.2
A simple Web form calling a script.

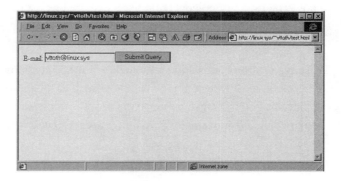

When the user clicks the Submit button, his browser makes another connection to your server, this time invoking the script `test.cgi`, shown here:

```
#!/bin/sh
EMAIL=`echo $QUERY_STRING | cut -d= -f2`
echo Content-type: text/plain
echo
echo $EMAIL
```

PART

V

CH

20

This is about as simple as it gets. This script does nothing special; it simply sends back to the user the information that the user provided. Absolutely nothing can go wrong with a script like this, right?

Wrong.

The script echoes back normal email addresses fine. But what if I submit, as my email address, a single asterisk? The result is shown in Figure 20.3.

FIGURE 20.3
A Web script and its unexpected output.

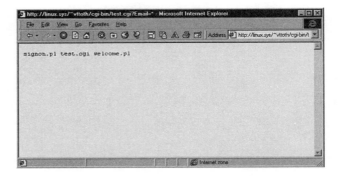

Just what has happened here?

The answer is simple: The script, or rather the shell that executed the script, expanded the wildcard character, *, into a list of files in the current directory, just as it's designed to do. Perhaps it's of no concern if users can see this list of files; perhaps it is. In any case, this should not have happened. And if this can happen, just what other security holes exist on your system, ready to be exploited by clever hackers?

These types of problems are not limited to Web scripts. In fact, Web scripts are relatively safe because most "dangerous" characters (such as the redirection characters < and > and the pipe character ¦) are supplied to the script in encoded form. When a script runs in another context (for example, if you offer access to your system via telnet and let users run scripts), the danger is far greater.

In the end, a hacker's goal is to *break out* of the confines of the scripts or programs that you designed and be able to execute programs of his own choosing. When you design your Web site or applications that you offer on your server, it's your job to ensure that no methods exist that the hacker can use for this purpose.

Malicious Programs

One security problem that is often prominently featured in the news is the problem of computer viruses. Actually, not all malicious programs are viruses. There appears to be some confusion with regard to the terminology, no doubt due to insufficient understanding on behalf of the journalists writing the articles. So what, exactly, are viruses, Trojan horses, and worms, and how can they affect your Linux system?

Viruses

A biological virus is a nonliving piece of DNA or RNA. When it gets inside a living cell, it modifies the behavior of that cell, its chemical factories, causing the cell to produce more copies of the virus. As a side effect, the cell may also eventually self-destruct, release toxins into the host's body, or exhibit other forms of behavior not related to its original function.

Computer viruses work much the same way. They're fragments of program code that cannot be executed by themselves; however, when attached to a regular program, they cause that program to create more copies of the virus and propagate them by infecting other programs. While the host program executes the virus code, it may also perform other functions encoded in the virus, such as damaging your hard disk, popping up offensive messages on your screen, and so on.

One common Linux myth is that Linux is immune to viruses because it does not run DOS programs. This is true to the extent that DOS viruses indeed cannot work under Linux, at least not without the help of third-party tools such as MS-DOS emulators. However, there are three points to consider:

- Viruses written specifically for Linux exist.
- Some viruses infect the boot sector of your hard disk or, specifically, the program that executes when the system is booted; this program is operating system independent, so it can be infected no matter which operating system you use.
- Malicious code exists nowadays in the form of Java code, which executes the same way under all operating systems.

PART
V

CH
20

In other words, myths to the contrary notwithstanding, Linux isn't immune. Precautionary measures, such as not running programs of uncertain origin, not using the root account, and scanning the system with antivirus software are warranted.

Trojan Horses

Unlike a virus, which is just a code fragment ready to attach itself to other applications, a Trojan horse is a full-featured program. However, like its wooden counterpart from Greek mythology, a software Trojan horse bears unwanted guests in its belly. In other words, a Trojan horse program, in addition to performing its advertised function, may also perform other things hidden from the user.

A classic example of a Trojan horse is a modified version of the login program. When used, it behaves exactly the same way as the original version, with no hints as to its real nature. However, in the background, it collects all password information that has been entered and delivers the information to its creator.

This means that if I ever manage to pass you a Trojan version of the login program, eventually I'll be in possession of all the passwords used to log on to your system, including the root password. Not a pleasant prospect, is it?

Of course, Trojan horses can be used for purposes other than information collection. The hidden function can be destructive (such as destroying your hard disk) or simply annoying (such as displaying an obscene message). Trojan horses are somewhat easier to get rid of or to protect against than viruses, because they do not infect other programs.

Worms

Worms represent yet another category of malicious software code. Unlike a virus, a worm is a full-featured program; unlike a Trojan horse, a worm doesn't pretend to be something else. Like true worms burrowing underground, a worm finds its way around a network by exploiting some vulnerability, which allows it to create copies of itself on remote machines.

One of the most famous cases occurred about 10 years ago, when the Internet was much smaller than it is today. A worm created by a student exploited an obscure bug in the popular sendmail server, which allowed it to propagate over the network. According to folklore, the worm was originally intended to propagate slowly, simply as a "proof of concept"; however, due to a bug in its code, it escaped and penetrated the Internet at a very high speed, multiplying exponentially. It caused a major disruption in worldwide Internet email communications.

Protective Measures

Protecting yourself against the many ways through which a would-be attacker can gain access to your system sounds like a nearly impossible task at first. Indeed, government security guidelines often prescribe that a truly secure system must have no external connections and no physical access by unauthorized users. Of course, this would neatly defeat the purpose of a Linux server that you specifically configured to provide your office with better Internet connectivity.

Fortunately, such Draconian measures are rarely necessary. Attacks are few and far between, and if you take a few sensible precautions, you'll be protected against most forms of intrusion.

Password Policies

Your first line of defense is an effective password policy. At minimum, you should ensure that all users, including yourself, observe the following precautions:

- Use passwords that cannot be easily guessed; using the name of a mother or spouse is definitely a bad idea.
- Use passwords that aren't simple words, which can be successfully guessed by a program performing a dictionary-style attack.
- Never reveal passwords to anyone.
- Never use the same password on more than one system.

You should also ensure that unauthorized users cannot gain access to passwords in encrypted form, by utilizing the shadow password suite, introduced in Chapter 15, "User Accounts."

Lastly, you may opt to enforce stronger policies regarding the changing of user passwords. The shadow password suite lets you specify how frequently passwords need to be, or can be, changed. Personally, I believe that such policies are at best ineffective, at worst counterproductive; if users are forced to change their passwords often, they're more likely to pick passwords that are easy to remember (hence, also easy to guess) and also more likely to write their passwords down.

PART

V

CH

20

Access Rights

Here's a catchy phrase often heard in James Bond movies or read in Tom Clancy novels: *need to know*. It so happens that this phrase has direct applicability even with a small office Linux server.

The basic idea is this: When it comes to privileges assigned to individual users, you should only give them privileges they really need. This is not a question of trust—in fact, if you don't trust them, why are you working with them in the first place?—just a question of common sense: The fewer the people who have access to sensitive resources, the lesser the chance your system will be compromised.

For instance, consider a user whose password is stolen by his teenage son, who then passes it on to his friends. By the time you discover the problem, 50 high-school students have attempted to hack into your system with a valid password. Wouldn't you be happy to realize that because this user never had a need for shell privileges on your system, these juveniles were never able to log on via telnet and wreak havoc there?

Files should only have read and write access by those who need them. Passwords should only be disclosed to those who have a need for them. User accounts should only have shell privileges if the user has a need for such privileges. With these simple measures, you can save yourself an awful lot of trouble later on.

The best way to ensure that, by default, user files remain accessible only to the user who created them is by using the umask command. This command takes a parameter similar to that used by the chmod command introduced in Chapter 4. It defines the *default* file permissions for a file that the user creates. The difference between umask and chmod is that umask works backwards; the value you set tells you which permissions will *not* be available when a file is created.

For instance, consider the following commands:

```
$ umask 0077
$ touch myfile
$ ls -al myfile
-rw-------   1 vttoth   users          0 May  4 06:14 myfile
```

As you'll recall from Chapter 4, 0077 means read/write/execute permissions for group users and other users. When the file is created after this mask has been set, read/write/execute permissions are *denied* to group users and other users. Therefore, the file will be created with permissions only for its owner.

The best place for a systemwide umask setting (for users of the bash shell) is in /etc/profile, which is where common shell initialization commands are stored.

Secure Protocols

If you cannot secure your local area network to your satisfaction and exclude the possibility of unauthorized access, you may require a software solution. One such solution is Kerberos, an authentication mechanism specifically designed for unsecured local networks such as those that exist at college campuses. Most popular UNIX tools have "kerberized" versions that work well when the Kerberos authentication scheme is installed. Kerberos basically ensures that no critical information such as passwords ever travels on the network in unencrypted form.

Kerberos is complex and difficult to master. If you think you have a need for it, a good place to start is the Kerberos Web site at `http://web.mit.edu/kerberos/www/index.html`. In the meantime, my recommendation is to simply keep your network physically secure. This may be as simple as unplugging unused network connections from your LAN concentrator.

> **WARNING**
>
> A special case of a local area network connection is a cable modem. Many cable television companies offer cable modem solutions that, in effect, extend your local area network to encompass the local cable segment. In other words, you'll be sharing a LAN with all your neighbors. For this reason, a cable modem should never be placed on the same segment with more than one of your computers, because communication between these computers will then become visible to others. For more information, see Chapter 12, "Using External Routers."

Another secure protocol is SSL, the Secure Sockets Layer. SSL is used mainly between Web browsers and clients and provides a means for secure communication even when the data stream can be overheard by unauthorized users. SSL capability is built into most Web browsers. To add SSL to your Web server, it may be necessary to download and install a free or commercial extension. Such extensions for the Apache Web server are described in Chapter 10, "Web Service."

PART
V

CH
20

Note that commonly, Web browsers are equipped only with exportable versions of SSL, which is a weakened implementation. However, U.S. software manufacturers do make full-strength versions available to North American users. Also, browser applications developed in other countries exist that do not fall under American export restrictions and support full-strength encryption by default.

Software Upgrades

There's a long-standing debate over the Internet about a particular aspect of system security: Should known flaws in commonly used software be publicized?

The arguments go like this: If you publicize a flaw in a common tool, hackers will learn about it, possibly before legitimate users do. They'll be able to exploit the vulnerability before legitimate users have a chance to implement protective measures. On the other hand, if you don't disclose such information, hackers may learn about them anyway, and legitimate users would never even know that there's a problem until they experience an attack.

Experience shows that *security through obscurity* doesn't work; you cannot make vulnerabilities go away by simply not talking about them. Even software giants such as Microsoft recognize this fact nowadays and regularly issue informational security bulletins.

This is where you come in. If you're running a Linux server, consider it your sacred duty to regularly check for security-related warnings and software upgrades. If your system ever gets broken into due to a known vulnerability in a software package for which an upgrade is available, you have only yourself to blame!

So where do you go for security information? Several Web sites and mailing lists exist. For the Linux kernel itself, the best place to monitor are the Linux-related newsgroups on Usenet (the `comp.os.linux` hierarchy.) For server software, newsgroups may exist, or you can pay regular visits to the Web sites of the servers in question.

There are also general security-related Web sites that often contain up-to-date information about known security defects in popular software packages. These include the Computer Incident Advisory Capability (CIAC) Web site operated by the U.S. Department of Energy (`http://ciac.llnl.gov/ciac/`.)

When a security bulletin suggests that a particular software package be upgraded, don't wait until you can get a new Linux distribution containing the updated version. If at all possible, download and install the upgraded version yourself. Note that this may require you to learn how to build and install a software package from source archives. This is a valuable skill; the time spent learning and experimenting will not be wasted.

If you're attempting to upgrade the Linux kernel itself, take a peek at Appendix A, "Configuring the Kernel," which contains some information about building and installing a custom kernel version.

User Education

Most security problems are a result of the human factor: Ill-educated users are often to blame when an intruder gets hold of a password or other confidential information and gains access to your system.

Users must be warned of the importance of keeping passwords secure. You need to explain to them that when they're given access privileges to your systems, it's like getting a copy of the office key; just as they are expected to keep that key safe, not leaving it behind in a public place, they're similarly expected to keep passwords and other confidential information about your system secure.

Another area of user education concerns program code of uncertain origin. This is true whether users are logged on to the Linux server or use Windows workstations on your network. Programs downloaded from unknown Web sites and cute little executable files attached to email messages have no place on a well-managed network.

Firewalls

Firewall routers provide enhanced security by limiting the type of data traffic that can flow between your local area network and the Internet. As explained in Chapter 11, "Firewalls," use of a firewall can be a controversial practice; although it indeed protects you from some types of attacks, it also limits your users' ability to use the Internet to its fullest potential. The use of some firewall-like features (such as packet filtering) is always recommended; however, whether you use a full-featured firewall depends on your evaluation of the risks versus the drawbacks.

If you do decide to use a firewall, keep in mind that even the best firewall only protects you against certain types of attacks—typically attacks that exploit known software bugs or configuration issues. The best firewall in the world won't protect you if your system is not maintained well or if your users don't keep their passwords secret.

PART
V

CH
20

About the Root Account

It was mentioned before, but because it's such an important security issue, it ought to be mentioned again: When it comes to protecting your system, one of the best defenses you have is not using the root account unless you really must.

Resist the temptation. It's nice to be "in charge" all the time, and it's convenient not having to type su every time you need to run a privileged command. However, when you use the root account, you open up the following possibilities:

- Buggy software you run will execute with root privileges, wreaking havoc within your system.

- Viruses and other malicious programs will execute with root privileges, enjoying full access to your system.

- Any mistakes you make can have disastrous consequences.

- If you fail to log off (or get disconnected due to a telephone line problem, for instance) and another user gains control of your session, that user will inherit your root-privileged shell.

Need I say more? The root account is there for you to use when you need it, but when you don't...well, don't!

The Truth About Email Attachments

Frequently, you hear dire warnings about malicious email messages that will destroy your system if you but only look at them. Then others assure you that this can never happen: In order for an email to wreak that kind of havoc with your computer, you must actually open and execute the programs that came with it in the form of attachments.

As usual, the truth is somewhere in between. It's quite true that an email message is just a block of data (usually text). If attachments exist, they must be extracted, and the resulting files, if they're executable programs, must be executed before anything malicious can happen.

Unfortunately, with the advent of HTML email programs, these steps are often performed automatically. These email programs interpret email messages as Web pages containing formatted text. However, HTML text can contain a lot more than character formatting instructions; among other things, it can contain embedded blocks of executable code, or *scripts*. Although safeguards exist that usually prevent malicious code from executing on your system, they can potentially be circumvented.

Fortunately, most malicious attachments are written for Windows and remain inactive under Linux. (You can still forward them inadvertently to others, including Windows users.) Still, Linux users have no reason for complacency; attachments that can affect Linux systems do exist, and as Linux becomes increasingly popular, they'll likely become more prominent.

Bogus Warnings

Unless you've never actually had an email account before, you've probably received numerous warnings from friends and acquaintances regarding a dangerous virus. Usually, the warnings are about email messages with recognizable titles, and you're told not only to refrain from opening these but also to send out the warning to everyone on your mailing list.

The fact is that the vast majority of these warnings are bogus. The purported malicious email usually doesn't even exist. Unfortunately, well-meaning users follow the instructions contained in the warnings and, as requested, forward the bogus messages to all their friends and acquaintances.

At this point, it's the warning itself that becomes a virus of sorts. Some of these warnings, such as the infamous "Good Times Virus" hoax, survive for many years, occasionally wreaking havoc with the mail systems at various organizations. Imagine what happens when such a message arrives at an office that employs, say, 50 people. First, the person who received it forwards it to everyone else in the office; next thing you know, everyone forwards the message to everybody else except for the sender. Within a short time, your system is forced to handle 2,352 (49×48) identical email messages. Such a volume, although not excessive, can easily overwhelm a smaller server, at least temporarily.

But this is not all. These 50 users will probably forward the message to recipients outside the office as well. Let's say that the message is 10 kilobytes in size, and each of the 50 users forwarded it to 20 different addresses. That's a grand total of 50×20×10KB, or 10MB, of data that your mail server must send out that morning; if you're connecting to your Internet Service Provider via a dial-up connection, this may tie down the connection for several hours!

In larger offices, the situation is even worse, because the amount of messages generated increases roughly in proportion with the square of the number of people at your site. If 500 employees at an organization forward the message to each other, you may end up with up to a quarter million messages, which is bound to overwhelm even the largest email server.

This is why, at several large organizations, Draconian policies were put in place. I'm aware of at least one department at the Canadian government where employees have been threatened with being fired if they forward any virus or similar warnings (whether hoax or real) that they receive from the Internet.

PART

V

CH

20

Once again, this is a matter of educating users. They should be made to understand that because they're not Internet security experts, they have no business evaluating and forwarding warnings to others. They should also be told of the signs by which bogus warnings can be recognized; most importantly, for reasons that should be obvious to anyone after reading this section, a genuine warning never contains the suggestion that it should be forwarded to everyone on your mailing list.

If you receive a warning that appears authentic, you should check available Internet resources for its authenticity. There are also Web pages devoted to Internet hoaxes: for instance, the CIAC Web site, mentioned earlier, contains a list of some of the better known hoaxes at `http://ciac.llnl.gov/ciac/CIACHoaxes.html`.

Summary

Security begins with restricting physical access to your Linux system. When unauthorized persons can gain access to the computer, they can damage it, remove its components, or boot another operating system from a floppy disk and steal your data.

Next to physical security, you must ensure that dial-up modem lines and network connections are properly configured. A bad modem and an ill-configured network application can provide backdoors for potential attackers.

However, by far the most significant source of security-related problems is represented by your system's users. Carelessness, ignorance, or malice play a role when users inadvertently or intentionally disclose passwords, run malicious applications, or cause other forms of damage. Your best line of defense is an educated user community; when you operate a server, ensure that users who access the server guard their passwords and are generally aware of the security risks present.

Existing applications can also represent a security problem. Even innocent-looking Web scripts can open gaping security holes if you do not understand their implications and do not protect your system adequately. Even worse are malicious programs such as viruses, Trojan horses, and worms.

To protect your system, establish a solid password policy. Also, make sure that file system access permissions are properly configured, secure protocols are used when needed, and software packages are upgraded regularly. You can further protect your system with a firewall router and, of course, by reducing the use of the root account.

When Something Goes Wrong

21 Diagnosing Your System

22 Moving to Backup Hardware

Diagnosing Your System

Imagine this: **One morning you** enter your office, turn on your Windows workstation, and expect to read the morning's email. Instead, you're presented with an error message stating that your email program could not log you on to your Linux server. You try to access the server via telnet, but this fails, too. Your Web browser doesn't work either. You walk over to the server itself, flick on its monitor, and see nothing. What do you do?

Obviously, something is wrong. But what? How can you identify the nature of the problem and go about recovering your system?

Pre-Boot Diagnostics

One of the most important pieces of advice I can provide when you're faced with a dysfunctional system is also the simplest: avoid haste. The pressure can be overwhelming with users, colleagues (or even worse, bosses) banging on your door, demanding that the system be brought back online immediately. Ignore them. You're not going to do anyone much good if the system you bring up crashes again a few seconds later, only to destroy more data.

In line with this, the first step to take when your Linux system fails is to attempt to find out as much as possible about the nature of the problem before you even reboot the system. Don't touch that power switch, don't hit that reset button just yet; first, try to understand what's happening with your system. The information you collect will help you diagnose the system later and determine the proper cause of action.

Signs of Life

So what happens when all you have is a blank screen to stare at?

First, watch for and listen for signs of life coming from the Linux box. Is the power light on? Do you hear the fan? Does the hard disk make noise?

In many ways, the easiest problems to deal with are the ones with the most dramatic effects. A system that's completely dead may have nothing wrong with it at all; perhaps it's just your dog, cat, or a fellow employee who tripped over a loosely inserted power cord.

If the system has power (the fan whirrs and the power light is on) check the keyboard. If you click the Caps Lock or Num Lock keys, do the corresponding keyboard lights come on? If so, the operating system is still somewhat alive and its keyboard driver is functioning.

Does the hard disk make any noise? Do you hear seek activity? Does the hard disk light come on from time to time? If this is the case, you have software activity, so the operating system isn't completely dead yet. Try to log on to the system from the console, over the network, or via a modem.

The Blank Screen

Most Linux installations are preconfigured to blank your screen after a predetermined period of inactivity. I find this a particularly annoying feature, for a simple reason: When the system fails, it often prints diagnostic messages on the console; however, on a failed system, the display driver may no longer be responsive, so the screen remains blank, and those useful diagnostic messages are lost forever.

You can avoid this, of course, by properly configuring the console in advance. Console blanking can be turned off using the `setterm` command. Make sure `setterm .blank 0` is issued on the console every time you boot the system (or better yet, add it to your `rc.local` file). Because Linux servers usually sit in server rooms with no monitor or a monitor that's not turned on more than once every month or so, burn-in isn't going to be a problem (burn-in doesn't usually affect newer color monitors anyway).

Of course, if you've turned off screen blanking, and the computer appears to function normally anyway, a blank screen may simply be the indication of a broken monitor!

Remote Access

If the system shows some signs of life (for example, the power light is on) it's a good idea to test whether it remains accessible remotely. Actually, sometimes this may be your only option (for instance, when you're diagnosing a system remotely over the network or a modem).

First, try to access the system with the ping utility from another computer (a Windows or a Linux machine would suffice). It's best to use the numeric address of the Linux server, just in case you'd normally use the very same server you're diagnosing as your DNS server. (Obviously, a dead or near-dead system may not be able to resolve symbolic addresses for you.) If the system responds with echoes to your ping requests, this indicates that the kernel still functions, and low-level network drivers are healthy. You can then try to log on to the system via telnet.

Another thing to try if the system has a modem attached is to dial into the system. If calls are normally answered by software, an answer indicates that the software (for example, uugetty) is operational, along with many high-level system functions. If your modem is configured to autoanswer, a successful connection tells you nothing (the modem would answer even if the computer behind it is frozen up). However, if you actually get a login prompt, that again indicates that high-level system functions are present.

If You Can Get In

So what if you can log on to the system? If you manage to get a shell prompt (preferably as the root user), you suddenly have many more diagnostic options at your disposal.

When I diagnose a dysfunctional system, I normally try the following commands: df, dmesg, free, and uptime.

The free command tells you the amount of memory available on your system. This is a very important piece of information. If your system is low on memory, it can behave in strange and mysterious ways.

The df command gives you the amount of free space available on your various disk partitions. If the root partition (which is mounted as /) has insufficient disk space, many applications can fail unpredictably.

The dmesg command lists the most recent messages in the kernel's internal buffer. If you're experiencing a hardware failure but the system still responds to your commands, this is the most likely spot where you'll find some indication as to the nature of the problem.

PART

VI

CH

21

The uptime command lets you know how long the system has been up and running as well as its load averages.

These commands are covered in more detail later in this chapter in the "Software Problems" section. If you can log on to your system without rebooting, your problems are likely caused by a software failure, so I suggest you read that section first.

Hardware Problems

If your system behaves erratically, one of the first questions is whether the problem is due to a faulty hardware component. If it is, you ought to know about it as soon as possible in order to avoid wasting precious time trying to fix a nonexistent software configuration issue.

Although this book is not a PC hardware repair manual, I think a few common-sense notes are not out of place here. Presumably, if you're reading this book, you've opened computer cases in the past and you can tell a hard disk from a power supply. Therefore, you may be able to spot and fix a number of problems. The hints and suggestions that follow often helped me out when I was trying to bring a sick Linux system back to life.

> **WARNING**   If a failing computer emits smoke or a burning smell, turn it off and disconnect it immediately! Do not attempt to repair such a unit without qualified help. Certain types of failures and short circuits can cause higher than normal voltages to appear inside the case, burning out components—and possibly you—if you poke your fingers in there without knowing what you're doing.

I think this section is especially appropriate because many Linux computers these days are older systems that are getting a second lease on life as Linux servers, taking advantage of Linux's low hardware requirements. My own Linux machines are no exception!

Power Supply

Is the computer completely dead? If the system is plugged in, turned on, and still doesn't make any discernible noise, it's likely that the power supply is blown—which is not at all unheard of given the cheap power supplies that are in use these days.

This is the easiest problem to fix. If you haven't done so already, check the power cord, ensure that the unit is turned on (just in case a helpful cleaning staff member did you a favor last night after the office closed) and check whether the power-on light is lit. Turn the unit off for a few minutes and try again; dying power supplies sometimes come back to life briefly when they're allowed to cool a bit.

None of this helped? The last thing to check is the power supply connectors inside the case. If all of them are seated properly, there's a good chance you have a power supply failure. These are relatively simple and cheap to replace if you can find a module that fits, both electrically (for instance, you cannot use an ATX power supply with an AT-type motherboard) and physically. Just make sure you unplug the power cord before you begin messing with the unit; some parts, such as an externally attached power switch, may contain high voltages.

> **WARNING**   Unless you're familiar with power supply repair, never ever actually open up the power supply's metal case. Like any switching power supply, it contains quite deadly DC voltages (up to 300 volts or more) that can kill you in less than a blink of an eye. (Even when unplugged, power supplies can give you a nasty shock due to the high-valued capacitors inside.)

Dead Motherboard

So what if your power supply checks out fine, the power-on LED is lit on the front of the case, but the computer refuses to work? You may have a major problem on the system's motherboard.

The easiest one to spot is a nonspinning fan on top of the CPU (if your system has one; older, slower 486 systems do not). This can cause intermittent failures, erratic behavior, or even destruction of the processor. If the CPU fan is not spinning, the system should be turned off immediately. (Did you know that a modern Pentium-class processor emits more heat per unit area than an electric burner on your kitchen stove?) This fan must be replaced before the unit can be turned back on again.

A seemingly dead motherboard could also be the result of an ill-fitted or faulty extension card or connector. By removing all cards and connectors, except for the display adapter, you can test the system again to see if any BIOS startup messages appear. Also try to reseat the display adapter, just in case it might be the culprit.

Another potential cause is a badly inserted or damaged memory chip. Try to remove some memory and boot the system. Swap around the memory chips and try again. When you do this, make sure you consult the motherboard's manual (you do have it, don't you?) to ensure that you don't insert memory chips in an illegal configuration.

If none of this helps, you may actually have a bad processor or a broken motherboard. One or the other (or both) may need to be replaced. However, there's one more possibility: You may have a system with a broken BIOS chip, which you can repair yourself.

Flash BIOS

Most newer motherboards have their BIOS (Basic Input Output System) software stored in a so-called *flash memory chip*. The contents of such a chip can be updated using the proper utility program. Under rare circumstances, the BIOS may become corrupted. If this is the case, often your only recourse is to request a replacement BIOS from the manufacturer. However, sometimes you may be able to apply an emergency recovery procedure.

The actual details of the procedure vary from one manufacturer to another, but the essence is the same: Some BIOSes contain a bootstrap code that's capable of loading a new flash copy from a floppy disk even when your current BIOS is corrupted. To perform the procedure, you need the emergency flash software from the manufacturer, usually downloadable from its Web site. Follow the instructions to create an emergency flash floppy.

> **WARNING** Never perform a flash BIOS upgrade unless you really have to. A failed upgrade can render a perfectly functional motherboard absolutely useless, necessitating repair or replacement by the manufacturer.

Before you flash the BIOS, it's a good idea to disconnect all internal hardware components (hard disks, adapter cards, and so on) with the exception of a single floppy drive and a video card. It's also important to keep in mind the fact that a broken BIOS may fail to initialize a PCI graphics card; you may have to use an old, ISA video card in order to communicate with your system. For this reason, I actually keep a couple of old ISA video cards around, just in case I need them to diagnose a system that otherwise shows no signs of life on the screen.

If you're lucky, you'll be able to complete the flash procedure without problems, and your system will be functional again. If not, or if the problem is not with the motherboard or its BIOS, you may be able to use the BIOS's built-in diagnostics to find the actual problem.

Beep Codes and Diagnostic Codes

Ever since the original IBM PC was released in the early 80's, the BIOSs of PC-compatible computers contained extensive startup diagnostics. When the system is powered up, the BIOS checks itself, the processor, the motherboard, and other main components. If the test succeeds, the BIOS emits a single beep, which is the beeping sound you hear when you turn on a PC. If the test fails, the BIOS produces a diagnostic code.

If you turn your system on and hear some kind of beeping, it means that the processor actually came to life and successfully began executing the BIOS code, only to fail during a diagnostic check sometime later. If you can find out what the diagnostic code means, you may be able to fix your system in no time, even if no visible messages appear onscreen indicating the nature of the problem.

Some, but unfortunately not all, BIOSs actually produce many different beep codes, depending on the nature of the failure. If your system is like this, you need to find out the meaning of the code you hear. The easiest way to find out is by looking it up in the motherboard's manual; of course, not all manuals contain this information, and even if yours does, you may have misplaced that manual years ago when the system was originally purchased.

Other BIOSs have only one failure code. They remind me of that gang of space-faring aliens in a Star Trek: The Next Generation episode who kidnapped Lieutenant Commander Geordi LaForge from the starship Enterprise and told him: "Our spaceship is broken! Fix it!"

Fortunately, even these BIOSes aren't as stupid as Geordi's alien friends. They do produce a diagnostic code, just not in a visible way. However, low-cost diagnostic cards exist that can read this code and display it (see Figure 21.1). The numeric code displayed by these cards, usually a two-digit hexadecimal number, can help you trace the various phases of BIOS initialization; if the code stops before reaching 00 or FF, you have a problem. As with beep codes, the actual meaning of the code varies from one BIOS to the next, but this information is once again available from the BIOS manufacturer. The maker of the diagnostic card you use may also have supplied you with a manual containing the description of diagnostic codes for many common BIOS versions.

PART

VI

CH

21

FIGURE 21.1
A diagnostic card.

So what do you do with the failure code once you have it? Often, replacing the component indicated by the failure code can cure the problem. However, this is not always the case; a floppy disk failure code may, for instance, indicate a faulty flash BIOS that tries to read an emergency flash disk. If you haven't inserted such a disk, you may get a floppy failure code even though your floppy drive is in perfect working order.

Swapping Components

If your system passes the diagnostic test when no components are plugged in other than the keyboard and a video card, yet it fails when other components are connected, it's swapping time. Try removing components one by one in order to pinpoint the bad component by elimination. First, remove nonessential pieces of hardware, such as your sound card or modem. Next, disconnect your hard disk and CD-ROM drives; if they're connected through an interface card (IDE or SCSI), remove that as well. Also disconnect floppy drives, remove the network card, and continue stripping the machine until nothing else remains but the video card and keyboard (without which, most systems will fail to boot).

> **WARNING**   Before removing or inserting a component, always turn off
> the power first! Also be careful not to damage a component
> with static electricity. Although the standard safety advice is
> to unplug the computer before fiddling with its insides, I usu-
> ally keep mine plugged in (so that the case remains
> grounded through the standard three-prong connector) and
> touch the power supply's metal case to statically discharge
> electricity from my body. I only unplug the system when I'm
> actually working on the power supply or the power switch,
> which are the components that contain high voltages.

If the system comes to life after a particular component has been removed, try reinserting all other components. If the system continues to work, you have your suspect. However, you still cannot be certain. For instance, if your system fails if a hard disk is connected but comes to life if it isn't, the problem may be with the hard disk, but it's just as likely that you have a faulty hard disk adapter. In order to fully identify the faulty component, it may be necessary to replace it with a similar or identical unit and try to turn the system on. If the system still fails, the problem may be elsewhere. If it works, you've got your culprit.

Intermittent Failures

The hardest problems to diagnose are intermittent in nature. Your system may work fine for days, without showing any signs of a problem; then suddenly, it may reboot itself for no apparent reason. Or it may suddenly behave erratically, spewing out error messages you've never seen before.

Believe it or not, the vast majority of intermittent failures are caused by faulty connections. Inside your PC are literally dozens of mechanical connectors for power and data, connecting the various components. Any one of these connectors can have a problem, which may render your entire system unreliable.

The solution is to reseat all cable connectors. That is, unplug them and plug them back in again. If you have a suspect (for instance, if the intermittent failure affects only your CD-ROM drive), it's not necessary to reseat all connectors, just the relevant ones.

Pay particular attention to power connectors (usually white plastic connectors with four wires—one red, one yellow, two black); the prongs inside these connectors often pop out, resulting in an unreliable connection.

Also, make sure that IDC connectors (black rectangular connectors with two rows of pins) are never connected backwards; doing so can cause severe damage to the computer! Many IDC connectors can only be plugged in one way (for example, they're missing a pin, or the socket has a groove on one side), but this is not always true. If by any chance you've disconnected an IDC connector and no longer remember its proper orientation, look for a red stripe along the ribbon cable; this side of the cable should be matched against pin number 1 on the socket. Whether a socket is on a circuit board or in the back of a unit such as a disk drive, there are usually markings indicating which side is pin 1; when you reconnect the cable, its red stripe should be on this side.

BIOS Settings

If your system comes to life after it's powered up, passes the BIOS diagnostics, but still fails to boot, the cause may be an incorrect or corrupt BIOS setting.

Most BIOSs allow you to activate a setup screen by pressing a key (for example, Delete) during boot. If the BIOS settings are so corrupt that even this doesn't work (for example, if the BIOS contains memory timing settings that prevent even the BIOS setup screen from coming up) another key (for example, Insert) can be used to reset the BIOS to default values.

The most typical conflicts in the BIOS that can cause system lockups include conflicting interrupt and DMA settings, bad memory settings (for example, "overclocking" your memory by setting wait state values below the recommended settings) or bad settings for your disk drives.

Disk drive settings can be especially problematic with BIOSes that offer different translation modes for IDE disks. Changing the translation mode from the values used when you installed Linux renders your system unbootable. Because it effectively changes the disk geometry (the number of heads, tracks, and sectors), the boot loader will not even find the operating system image; file system drivers will also fail.

Software Problems

More often than not, a seemingly dead system has no faulty component; the problem is the result of a software configuration error or a runtime software problem.

Boot Failures

When your system simply fails to boot, the first question you must find an answer for is exactly at what point during the boot sequence does the system fail.

Are you booting your system with LILO, the Linux Loader? If so, does the word *LILO* appear when you reboot your computer? If it doesn't, LILO has been removed from your system. Windows is notorious about replacing LILO with its own boot loader on your hard disk. The solution is to reboot your system from a floppy disk and rerun LILO so that it restores the boot loader.

Perhaps the word *LILO* does begin to appear but it's incomplete? If all you see is the first two letters, one likely culprit is the disk geometry. If you've changed the disk translation settings in your computer's BIOS, this will be the result. Note that this problem applies only to IDE hard disks (but not all models), not to SCSI hardware.

Maybe *LILO* appears fine and the boot process begins, only to get stuck at one point. Watch carefully to see what messages appear as the system boots. Does the kernel report a hardware failure? Is there any indication that a software component failed to initialize?

If the problem is with the kernel and you're using a customized kernel, try to boot from your backup copy (see the next section for more information). If the problem is with a software component, you may need to boot the system from a disk and manually edit `/etc/inittab` or the files in `/etc/rc.d` and remove references to the offending software.

Low Memory

If a system that has been working fine suddenly begins spewing out incomprehensible error messages, it isn't necessarily an indication of broken hardware: You may simply be running low on memory. One possible indication is error messages such as `can't map '/lib/libc.so.5'`, indicating a failure to load a shared library component. Of course, such messages may also be a sign that the component is genuinely missing (big trouble), but more often than not, this message simply indicates that there isn't enough memory to load the component.

To verify whether you're indeed having a problem with insufficient memory, use the `free` command. Here's an example:

```
$ free
              total        used        free      shared     buffers
cached
Mem:          63316       24892       38424        7940         232
6344
-/+ buffers:               18316       45000
Swap:         88352        2960       85392
```

PART
VI
CH
21

If the numbers under the free column are close to zero, you have a problem.

Of course, when you have so little memory, you may not even be able to run the `free` command or other diagnostic tools. To free up some memory—at least temporarily—try to terminate all unused sessions (for instance, if you're logged on via multiple consoles, log off all of them except one). A couple of megabytes is all you need to run your tools.

So why would such a condition occur? There are several possible reasons, actually.

One is a runaway program that gobbles up memory with no limit. Such a program can be found using the `ps` command. Type **ps axu** and search for an application that has an excessively high amount in the %MEM, %SIZE, or %RSS column. Here's a real-world example:

```
USER       PID %CPU %MEM  SIZE   RSS TTY STAT START    TIME COMMAND
root       153  0.2 60.0 99872 37992  ?  S    Apr 23  25:23 java
```

(Yes, many versions of the famous Java interpreter contain hideous memory leaks.) When you encounter such a program, you should terminate it as soon as possible. If the problem occurs repeatedly, you may have to quit using the offending program or write a script that's invoked regularly and terminates the offending application, perhaps starting up a fresh copy.

Another reason may be that you simply don't have enough memory in the first place! If your system is heavily loaded, you may simply have to increase your swap space or add additional RAM to ensure reliable operation.

Insufficient Disk Space

Running out of disk space can, of course, also affect the way your system operates. When disk space is insufficient, many applications fail; furthermore, many fail unpredictably because their authors never designed them to handle this type of situation.

Fortunately, Linux has a built-in safeguard: A certain amount of disk space is always reserved. Applications cannot access this part of the disk unless they're owned by the root user. This safeguard usually allows critical system applications to continue functioning. This also includes the system log so that log entries continue being made even when a "disk full" condition exists. At least until the disk gets really full (that is, until the reserved space is filled up by applications running under the root user's account identifier), after which not even log files can grow any further.

To find out how much disk space you have available, use the df command. This command lists all mounted file systems, their size, the amount of space used and available, and a percentage value that indicates the used capacity:

```
$ df
Filesystem              1024-blocks  Used Available Capacity Mounted on
/dev/sda1                    237943 195950     29706     87%   /
/dev/sdb1                   1138543 254497    825218     24%   /home
/dev/sda3                    237959 177171     48500     79%   /usr2
```

Usually five percent of space is reserved for root on most file systems. Therefore, if the figure in the Capacity column exceeds 95 percent, you know you have a problem.

When you encounter a "disk full" condition, the first place to check is the /tmp directory. Many applications leave files (sometimes quite large files) in this directory as a result of bugs or crashes. Sometimes you'll be able to free up several megabytes just by removing junk files found here. As a general rule, it's usually safe to remove files from /tmp; however, if you remove a file that's currently in use, it may cause the corresponding application to fail. To find out if any files in /tmp are presently in use, you can use the fuser command, as in the following example:

```
$ fuser /tmp/*
/tmp/elv_214b.1:        8523
```

What this example reveals is that there's one file presently in use in this directory, owned by process 8523. You can find out the identity of this process using the ps command.

Another place to look is /var/log. If a system condition exists that causes an excessive amount of log entries to be made, files in this directory can become quite large. Ten megabyte (and larger) copies of /var/log/messages are not unheard of, even if logs are rotated on a daily basis. Running your log-rotation utility (see Chapter 16, "System Logs") can help alleviate the problem, but what you should really do is find the root cause. Examine the logs and identify the types of messages that appear with great frequency.

Needless to say, log files other than the main system logs are also suspect. These include log files generated by your Web server, Samba server, UUCP server, or any other server application you use.

Processor Overload

In the multitasking Linux environment, applications typically spend most of their time waiting. They may be waiting for data to arrive on the network, for the user to hit a key, or for a disk operation to complete. What's important is that they're idle, not consuming any time on the computer's processor.

However, occasionally applications start using the CPU excessively, sometimes by design (for example, a compression or encryption utility can be using computationally intensive algorithms), and other times due to a bug. When the CPU is under heavy load, other applications become noticeably slower. If several applications compete for the CPU, the system can slow to a crawl.

To find out whether your system is under such load, you can use the uptime command:

```
$ uptime
  5:12pm   up 62 days,   2:46,   1 user,   load average: 0.08, 0.03, 0.00
```

The numbers to check are the load average numbers at the end of the single line of output produced by this command. The three numbers here are values representing the processor's load average during the last minute, last five minutes, and last 15 minutes.

Basically, the load average tells you how many running jobs are competing for the system's processor. If a process runs full time but all other processes are paused (perhaps waiting for user input), you'll have a load average of 1. When two processes compete for the processor, the load average is 2. If only one process is active, but it waits for hardware 50 percent of the time, you'll have a load average of 0.5. In essence, the load average tells you how many processors you need to let all running processes work full time, without having to wait for other processes to finish their jobs with the processor.

Normally, your system's load average is a fractional number. Quite often, it's 0.00 on a quiescent system. If the load average is above 0.50 on a lightly loaded system, I always investigate. A high load average does not necessarily indicate an abnormal condition, but it's a good idea to know what processes cause such a load on your system. It could be that your Web server suddenly became more popular; it could be that a user who uses your system to develop applications managed to write a program that entered an infinite loop, consuming processing power as fast as it's allowed to. Or, it could be that you have a problem (a runaway process, for instance).

How do you find out which process is responsible for the higher-than-normal load average? By taking a closer look at the output of the ps command, of course. When you type **ps axu** (or **ps axuw** to avoid the truncating of lines at the right edge of the screen), you'll see that the third column is labeled *CPU%*. This tells you how much of the processor's time a given process consumes, as a percentage of the total available processor time. You can actually sort by this column as follows:

```
$ ps u ¦ sort +2 -n
USER         PID %CPU %MEM   SIZE    RSS TTY STAT START     TIME COMMAND
vttoth      5918  0.0  1.0   1112    640 p1  S    Apr 30    0:01 -bash
vttoth      8867  0.0  0.5    824    360 p1  R    21:15     0:00 ps u
vttoth      8868  0.0  1.0   1112    640 p1  R    21:15     0:00 -bash
vttoth      8758 97.3  0.2    756    168 p1  R    21:05     9:45 ./x
```

In this example, the +2 parameter tells sort to sort by column 2 (column numbering starts with 0), whereas the .n parameter tells sort to interpret what's found in this column as a numeric value (not as text). Note that I used ps u instead of ps axu (to list only my own processes, as opposed to all processes on the system) to keep the list shorter; normally, you'd use ps axu to find the offending process.

Clearly seen is the program "x" at the end of the list, consuming 97.3 percent of processor time. The TIME column also shows that in the 10 minutes or so since the process started, it managed to actually run up 9 minutes and 45 seconds with the system's processor, so it's pretty much running continuously. Were it not for the fact that I created this program specifically to demonstrate the use of ps to find a runaway process, this would be a bad sign indeed. Normally, if a process consumes processor time at such a ferocious rate, something is very wrong and needs to be corrected. Often, correction means shutting down the offending process using the kill command. If you recall from Chapter 2, "The Linux Workhorse," I always recommend using kill.HUP first, because this gives many commands a chance to clean up after themselves. Here's an example:

```
$ kill -HUP 8758
$ ps u
USER         PID %CPU %MEM   SIZE    RSS TTY STAT START     TIME COMMAND
vttoth      5918  0.0  1.0   1112    644 p1  S    Apr 30    0:01 -bash
vttoth      8871  0.0  0.5    824    360 p1  R    21:20     0:00 ps u
```

So what can cause a perfectly normal application to become a runaway process? One frequent problem occurs when a user logs on to the system interactively and then loses the connection. Sometimes, programs the user was running do not terminate but instead get into an infinite loop waiting for user input that can no longer arrive, thus consuming processor time excessively.

Missing or Corrupt DLLs

DLLs, or *dynamic load libraries*, are shared program components. Basically, the idea is this: Most programs contain common code components such as libraries with system functions. Rather than including one copy with each program on your system, why not just have a single, shared copy that's loaded into memory along with the first program that needs it and remains available to the rest? This saves memory, reduces the programs' loading times, and saves on disk space as well.

Of course, there's a catch. If an important DLL goes missing or becomes corrupted, many programs will fail to execute. If these programs include such essential tools such as login or the shell program, you're facing a serious problem: Your system is, for all intents and purposes, dead.

So what can you do?

First of all, learn to recognize the problem: Missing DLLs are indicated by messages such as `can't map '/lib/libc.so.5'`.

Second, keep in mind that not all such messages indicate a DLL problem; often, they're an indication of low memory, as explained earlier in this chapter.

If you can verify that the problem is truly a DLL problem, you need to restore the original DLLs. Boot your system (perhaps from a floppy disk) and find the missing files on the installation CD-ROM or your backup disks. The command `ldconfig .v` can help you ensure that the restored libraries are properly recognized.

Disk Corruption

A genuine disk error, of course, can throw a monkey wrench into the workings of even the best designed operating system.

It all depends on where the error occurs on the disk and the nature of the error. Corruption of the swap areas can cause the system to freeze; corruption of areas containing critical programs can cause core system functions to fail. Corruption elsewhere may remain unnoticed for a long time, only to come back and haunt you later when, for instance, the system attempts to move a critical file to the affected area.

It's rare (but not unheard of) these days for a hard disk to develop actual physical surface defects. The reason is that almost all hard disks in use these days have the capability to detect bad areas before complete failure and remap them to reserved areas, also called *spare cylinders*. To the end user, the only noticeable sign is a tiny amount of excess disk activity when the remapping occurs. The disk will not actually fail until all reserve areas are exhausted, which is a highly unlikely occurrence; other components (such as motors and head actuators) are far more likely to wear out first.

That said, even newer hard disks sometimes develop surface defects (possibly due to a failure of the remapping algorithm). Far more often, though, disk corruption is caused by file system errors, which in turn are usually the result of system crashes.

In the case of a genuine hardware defect, you'll see error messages in the system logs to the effect that specific sectors on the disk cannot be read from or written to. A disk that develops defects like these should be removed from service as soon as possible. As a temporary solution, you may be able to map the defective area using the .c option of the e2fsck utility (or the mkswap utility if the defect is in a swap partition). This invokes another program named badblocks, which scans the disk surface and records bad sectors; the list generated by badblocks is used by e2fsck to mark these sectors as "unavailable." Note that this does not actually repair the error but rather merely masks it; also, if the defective area contains part of a file, that file will remain corrupt. However, you may be able to continue using the bad disk, at least for a while, until new defects develop.

NOTE	The e2fsck utility is specific to Linux's native file system type, the *second extended file system*. If you're using another file system, use of a different utility is required. However, it's strongly recommended that you use the native file system on production machines.

If the error is due to a corrupt file system, the situation is far simpler. The solution is to boot into single-user mode (hitting the Ctrl key when the LILO prompt appears and typing **linux single** usually does the trick), ensure that the affected disk drive is mounted read-only, and invoke the e2fsck utility to repair the errors.

During the course of its repair activity, e2fsck may place files and directories in a special directory named lost+found. This, in principle, is similar to what MS-DOS's CHKDSK utility does when it creates files with the name FILE0000.CHK (and so on). Chains of allocated blocks are found on disk with no corresponding filename in any directory; in order to recover the data that might be lost in these, the utility creates a file entry in this special directory and attaches to it the chain of blocks found. Upon examining the files and directories placed in lost+found, you can determine whether they can be safely deleted.

PART

VI

CH

21

A special type of disk corruption may occur if you're using a dedicated swap partition for virtual memory. When this area is corrupted, you may see messages such as this:

```
swap_duplicate: trying to duplicate unused page
```

Often, simply rebooting the system solves the problem. However, if the problem reoccurs, it's best to reboot into single-user mode, turn off the swap space using the `swapoff` command, and use the mkswap utility to reinitialize the swap area.

Kernel Panics

A review of Linux software failures wouldn't be complete without a mention of *kernel panics*. Kernel panics are the Linux equivalents of the dreaded "blue screen of death" under versions of Microsoft Windows. They essentially indicate that something seriously went wrong in the kernel and that the operating system may not be able to continue to function.

After you see a kernel panic, it's best to reboot immediately and analyze the system afterwards. Review the log files and try to determine what lead to the panic in the first place.

Apart from genuine hardware failures, kernel panics can be caused by software bugs in the kernel or its drivers. This is more likely if you're using experimental (beta test) versions of hardware drivers.

Kernel panics are rare. With several Linux systems running 24 hours a day, I haven't seen one in a very long time. (I hope this will continue to be the case.)

Boot Options

Sometimes, in order to correct a problem that affects your system's operation, you need to reboot the computer. Perhaps you were unable to locate the application that consumed all the system memory. Perhaps the corruption was so great, you were not able to execute any meaningful commands from the system console. Or perhaps the system is simply frozen.

If the system reboots normally, fine. You can then proceed to perform a post-mortem analysis, examining the various log files and trying to find out what caused the abnormal condition to develop. But what if the attempt to reboot the system fails?

Your goal then is simple: Bring some version of Linux up on the hardware so that you can access the failed system's hard drive, analyze its logs, and replace or repair files if necessary.

Booting from the Backup Kernel Image

If you have more than one kernel image installed on your system (see Appendix A, "Configuring the Kernel"), and the problem is specific to the kernel image you're trying to use, you may be able to bring your system back to life using the backup kernel image. To do so, you need to type the name of the backup image when the LILO prompt appears (again, Appendix A provides a more detailed explanation of this procedure).

If the backup image works and you're planning to compile a new kernel, don't forget that your current default kernel (the dysfunctional one) will replace the backup image (the working one) when a new image is created. To avoid this, you may want to copy the backup image over the default image before compiling a new kernel.

Note that if the problem you're experiencing is due to a system-configuration issue, booting with the backup kernel is unlikely to help you.

Booting from Floppy

There are two ways to boot Linux from a floppy disk.

First, you can have a "naked" kernel image on the floppy. Booting with this image is much like booting a backup kernel image from the hard disk. Still, such a floppy can come in handy when, for instance, the master boot record on your computer's hard disk is overwritten by another operating system and you can no longer boot LILO, the Linux Loader.

You can actually create such a naked boot floppy quite easily. All you need to do is copy the kernel image (usually /vmlinuz) to a raw floppy disk (that is, a floppy disk that contains no file system). First, however, the floppy disk needs to be formatted. Assuming that you're starting with a blank 1.44MB floppy in drive A, you need to use the following commands:

```
# fdformat /dev/fd0H1440
# dd bs=8192 if=/vmlinuz of=/dev/fd0
```

The floppy you create this way will not be readable in any conventional sense; it will contain no directory and no files. The kernel image simply occupies consecutive sectors on the disk starting from sector 0. (You'll recall from Chapter 17, "Backing Up Your

System," that magnetic tapes are used in a similar fashion.) Despite this apparent unread-ability, you'll be able to boot your system with this floppy inserted, even if the kernel images on the hard disk are corrupt. In fact, if you experiment a lot with various kernel versions, keeping a floppy handy with a "known good" kernel version on it might be a very good idea.

An alternative to naked boot floppies is the creation of a boot floppy/root floppy set like the one found in many Linux distribution kits. The main advantage of such a kit is that it lets you boot into your system regardless of the state of the hard disk. In other words, such a floppy set is the perfect diagnostic/repair tool when you're faced with a corrupted hard disk that prevents you from booting the system. In effect, this will be your Linux version of the Windows 95/98 Emergency Repair Disk.

Creating such a disk set is not an easy undertaking, however. Fortunately, you rarely need to create them from scratch. It's much easier to use the disks provided with your installation kit, as shown in the next section. You may also start with such a disk set and modify its contents to best suit your needs.

Booting from Installation Disks

Since installation kits are meant to be used on computers that don't even have an operat-ing system installed, they're by definition bootable. What is less known is that most installation kits offer a "breakout" option: At a certain point, you can bring up a shell and begin manipulating the system as the root user. More often than not, this is as simple as hitting Alt+F2 to switch to another virtual console and logging on as the root user (no password required).

This capability is present whether you're booting from floppy disks or CD-ROMs. Therefore, both types of installation media are suitable as a diagnostic/repair tool.

Case Studies

The remainder of this chapter contains a few real-life cases that I've encountered recently.

A Bad Hard Disk

Some of the scariest messages that ever appear in a Linux system's log files are those that indicate read or write errors on your main system disk. This is precisely what hap-pened on my Linux machine that hosts the online game MUD2.COM.

The messages in the log files indicated that a specific sector on the hard drive had a defect. Whenever the system attempted to use this sector as part of a file, an error occurred. If the file in question was a key system file, the system crashed.

As a temporary solution, I attempted to mark the bad areas of the disk using the .c option with e2fsck. However, this proved to be insufficient; soon, additional defects developed. Because the system was also used by several users, I feared that the problem may have more serious consequences if it remained unfixed.

I had spare hard drives that I could use with this system, but there was a catch—whereas the failed drive was an IDE unit, my spare drives were all SCSI. Therefore, I not only needed to replace the disk, I also had to update the kernel (the system in question used a custom kernel image with no SCSI drivers).

First, I created a new kernel image, adding a driver for the SCSI card I intended to use. With this new kernel image installed, I shut down the system, inserted the new SCSI card and hard drive (without removing the old IDE card and drive), and rebooted. Initially, boot messages indicated that the new SCSI card was *not* found by the driver. A search on the Internet with the correct keywords revealed a possible cause, namely that the driver in question cannot always detect the proper hardware parameters. Armed with this information, I booted the kernel with a boot parameter, and the SCSI card this time was successfully initialized.

Second, I formatted the new SCSI disk and placed a file system there. I also reserved space for a swap area.

Third, I copied the entire contents of the old IDE drive to the new SCSI drive. I also used the lilo command with a special option to initialize the new drive:

```
lilo -r /mnt
```

Here, /mnt is the empty directory I used as the mount point for the newly installed SCSI drive. The .r option basically tells lilo to pretend that the system's root directory is the specified directory and perform its operations there. Therefore, instead of installing a bootable image on the real root drive / (which was still the old IDE drive), the command installed an image on the freshly mounted SCSI drive at /mnt.

Now it was time to shut down the system, remove the IDE hardware, and make an attempt to reboot the system from the SCSI drive. There were a few glitches, but shortly, the system was up and running with the new drive and kernel image.

After some tests to ensure that everything worked as expected, I booted the system in multiuser mode, and it has been working reliably ever since.

PART

VI

CH

21

The Case of the Broken Tape Drive

As chance would have it, just as I was writing this chapter, one Linux system under my care went dead. This is a system located elsewhere, one that I manage remotely (over the Internet or using a modem). The first indication of trouble came early one Sunday morning when, instead of receiving the usual weekly email about a successful backup, I received a boot message instead. (This system is configured to send me email every time it reboots.)

"What the devil?" I asked. Was it yet another unannounced power test in the building that houses the system? Night owl that I am, I was still awake when this happened, so I immediately connected to the system via telnet and examined its log files. Looking into /var/log/messages, I found messages describing not one, but two separate boot events, less than a minute apart. Obviously, the first of these boots didn't successfully complete, which is why I only received email after the second occurrence.

I was still cursing and calling the building management company names when it occurred to me to log on to another machine located with the Linux system. I found out that the other machine had been up for several days without interruption. No power failure there, after all. So what?

Since the reboot event occurred at the time when the weekly backup is usually taking place, the next obvious suspect was the system's tape drive. I logged on again, listed the root user's crontab entries, and with some copy-and-paste magic I extracted the weekly backup command. I entered it at the command line and guess what? Within seconds, I lost my connection to the system, and when I was able to reconnect, I found that it just rebooted again.

A bad tape drive, I thought. Just recently, they began rotating tapes at this office (previously, they used a single tape over and over again, which, of course, isn't a very smart idea). Could it be that the sudden mechanical stresses caused a short circuit or something in the tape unit? Probably.

Because this occurred on a Sunday, I couldn't do much to further diagnose the problem. But the next day, I performed some diagnostics over the telephone with the help of the onsite technical staff. I asked them to reseat the tape to ensure that it was inserted properly; to our surprise, the system rebooted when they touched the tape drive. Worse yet, it began a boot cycle, going through the BIOS boot messages over and over again. Therefore, I suggested that the system be turned off and the tape drive be disconnected internally. After this was done, the system failed to even power up anymore.

So it wasn't the tape drive after all. The next suspect was the power supply; sure enough, after it was replaced, the machine powered up fine, even when the tape drive was reattached. I once again issued the usual weekly backup command by hand, and the backup successfully ran to completion.

As an added quirk, however, I noticed something unusual in the most recent boot sequence: Messages pertaining to the parallel port and one serial port were missing. So once again, I called the onsite staff, who powered down the system and reseated the interface cards inside. That cured the problem, and the system has been working reliably since. The "broken" tape drive executes its weekly backups without a glitch.

Swap File Trouble

Yet another problem that occurred as I was writing this book affected the swap file on a Linux system. Having been out of my office for a few hours, I knew immediately that there was trouble when I returned, seeing that the disk activity light was continuously lit on this machine, and there was a regular clickety-click sound coming from it.

First, I suspected a hard drive failure. But when I turned on the attached monitor and saw screen after screen scrolling by, containing messages such as

```
swap_free: swap-space map bad (entry 00022a00)
```

I knew what the clickety-click sound was: The system kept adding entries to the system logs on a continuous basis, and what I heard was the disk activity as these new entries were written out.

I'd seen enough. Corrupt swap space means trouble, and the sooner the system is rebooted, the better. Hitting Ctrl+Alt+Delete invoked /sbin/shutdown normally (so the system wasn't quite dead yet), and I rebooted into single-user mode. First, I made sure that all hard disks were mounted read-only, and then I checked them for corruption:

```
$ mount -n /dev/sda1 -o remount,ro
$ /sbin/e2fsck /dev/sda1
```

The check didn't find anything significant (complaints about a "zero dtime" on deleted blocks and minor bitmap differences are not abnormal for a file system that's in use), so I knew the disks were probably alright. An examination of the log files in /var/log showed that the problem began a few hours earlier, with the following message being the first sign of trouble:

```
Hmm.. Trying to use unallocated swap (00020700)
```

Because the system has been up for more than two months, experiencing moderate-to-heavy use at times, I concluded that I was probably the victim of a software bug; the system "lost its marbles," for lack of a more scientific term. After rebooting into multiuser mode, the system continued to operate normally.

Note that during these few hours, several megabytes of log entries were produced, with many error messages appearing in the log files every *second*.

The Case of the Dead CD-ROM

On yet another Linux system, I was testing an old CD-ROM drive. When the CD-ROM drive was connected, the system completely failed to boot; not even the initial BIOS messages appeared. This situation demonstrates why it's imperative that you remove all nonessential components when diagnosing your system: A faulty component can cause unusual behavior in seemingly unrelated parts of the system. Were it not for the fact that I just inserted that CD-ROM drive myself, this system would have appeared, for all intents and purposes, like one with a dead processor or motherboard.

A Broken BIOS

My last Linux war story concerns an older Pentium motherboard that I was hoping to reuse in a Linux system. Unfortunately, I found that the board was completely broken; when I installed it, it showed no signs of life.

Rather than giving up, I decided to investigate. I attempted to boot this motherboard with an ISA video card, but it still failed; no image ever appeared on the monitor. I used a diagnostic card, and it showed some activity; the BIOS initialization stopped with a code that, according to the manual, referred to the system's floppy drive. However, I was driving blind, because the monitor remained dark.

Then it occurred to me to use another ISA video card, a really old one with no acceleration features. Surprise! With this card, I suddenly saw messages appear on the monitor that informed me of a BIOS checksum failure and that the system was attempting to boot from a recovery floppy. Quickly, I visited the Web site of the motherboard manufacturer, where I found out the details for the emergency BIOS recovery procedure. I made a bootable floppy disk according to the manufacturer's instructions and booted the old motherboard with this floppy. I was able to launch the BIOS flash utility, which successfully updated the motherboard's BIOS. The board has been functioning ever since in one of my Linux boxes.

Summary

When you're dealing with a dysfunctional or misbehaving Linux system, make no haste. Also, don't reboot. Instead, attempt to diagnose the system by observing its life signs and, if you can log on, by issuing simple diagnostic commands.

Simply checking whether the power light is on, listening for a whirring fan or seek noises from the hard disk can tell you a lot about the state of your system. You can determine whether it has power, whether the processor is active, and whether the operating system is still functioning.

Of course, the easiest way to diagnose the system is by interacting with it. Often, the system displays log messages when it encounters a fatal error, but these messages may never be seen if the console is configured to blank the monitor in screen-saving mode.

If your system fails to boot due to a hardware failure, you can still find out a lot about it by watching for any messages that may appear on screen or by listening for diagnostic beep codes. You can also begin a process of elimination, disconnecting system components one by one to identify the faulty component. If you have one available, you can also try using a diagnostic board that plugs into your computer's motherboard.

If the hardware checks out fine, the system may be experiencing a software failure. It may refuse to boot because of a corrupt operating system image or a boot sector that has been overwritten by another operating system. Erratic operation may be due to a low-memory condition, missing key system files, or a problem with your hard drive.

When the problem prevents you from booting into the faulty system, you may be able to utilize a backup operating system image, a boot floppy or boot floppy set, or the original installation disks or CDs. Once you gain control of your system this way, you'll be able to perform the needed diagnostics and, if all goes well, correct the problem and make your system functional again.

Manual Pages

For additional information on topics discussed in this chapter, refer to the following manual pages:

- man df
- man dmesg
- man free

- `man fuser`
- `man ld.so`
- `man ldconfig`
- `man lilo`
- `man mkswap`
- `man mount`
- `man swapoff`
- `man swapon`
- `man uptime`

Moving to Backup Hardware

Sometimes, due to a hardware or software failure, it may be necessary to move your Linux server to backup hardware, at least on a temporary basis.

As you can imagine, this is far from a trivial undertaking. Even if the two systems are physically identical, the move can be a long procedure; if the systems are different, requiring different drivers and configuration options, that just compounds the difficulties.

So how can you transplant your Linux server into another box?

Anatomy of a Transplant

Call it brain surgery. When you move to another computer, what you're really transplanting is not any physical component (although the transfer of such components may be part of the process) but rather the *identity* of your server—its soul, if you like.

So what defines your server's identity? What are the components you need to transplant in order to move your system's identity from one box to another? Conversely, which components can be replaced without affecting the identity of your computer?

The Processor and the Motherboard

The motherboard (including the processor and memory) is often referred to as the "brain" of your computer system. This image may imply that it's these components that give your computer its unique identity. This is not so; these components merely execute instructions and provide transient storage, but the actual identity comes from somewhere else.

That said, processors, motherboards, and even memory aren't completely interchangeable between one system and another. The reason is that an operating system may be configured with a specific driver for a particular motherboard chipset or a certain BIOS. It can even contain code that can only be executed on Pentium-class processors, for instance. Nevertheless, most systems will survive "motherboard surgery" and remain bootable afterwards.

Replacing the motherboard of a system is not hard (usually, the most sophisticated tool you need is a Phillips screwdriver), but it is time consuming. You have to remove all adapter boards and disconnect all electrical connections. You may also need to remove parts such as disk drives or even the power supply, simply to make room so that you can remove the motherboard without bending or breaking it.

> **WARNING**   Be very careful with static electricity when you remove the motherboard. This is by far the most static-sensitive component in your system. Also make sure you don't bend or strain the board; these large, multilayer circuit boards are quite fragile, and if a connection breaks, the board has had it because repair is almost impossible.

If your system is functional prior to performing motherboard surgery, make sure you have a kernel image available that contains generic motherboard chipset drivers. This is not usually a problem unless you're using a customized kernel (see Appendix A, "Configuring the Kernel"). This will maximize your chances that the system will be bootable after surgery is complete.

If you're only replacing the processor or memory, you should usually not experience any difficulties afterwards when booting the system. Just make sure you configure all motherboard switches correctly *before* applying power; setting the wrong voltage, for instance, can quickly fry that expensive CPU you just purchased.

The Hard Disk

The motherboard and its processor may be called your computer's brain, but the true soul of the machine exists on the system's hard disk in the form of software. Remove the hard disk and your system is dead. Replace the hard disk with another one, and your system's identity changes completely. Indeed, you may recall that the test system I used to develop examples for this book has just such a removable cartridge hard drive in it; by swapping cartridges, I can turn the computer into a Linux box, a Windows 98 or NT machine, or an OS/2 testbed system. (At least that's the theory; reliability problems with that Iomega JAZ drive often make reality far less simple.)

With that in mind, you might expect that simply moving the hard disk from one computer to another is all you need to do to transplant your computer's identity. If all other components in the two boxes are identical (or at least sufficiently similar), this may indeed be the case. However, if there are significant differences between the two boxes, the transplant may not be this simple.

First, the hard disk may be of an incompatible type. You cannot transfer an IDE hard drive to a computer with a SCSI disk controller, and vice versa.

Second, even one SCSI hard disk may differ from the next, because of the many variants (Wide-SCSI, SCSI-2, and so on) that exist.

Third, booting a computer with an operating system configuration that's tailored for another machine can present numerous problems. During the boot process, failures may occur when an incompatible driver is loaded, when a network configuration cannot be established, when another disk, floppy, CD-ROM, or tape drive isn't where it's supposed to be, when the video graphics hardware is of a make different from what your X server is configured for, and so on.

However, it *is* possible to move a Linux configuration to another machine by moving the hard disk, but a few precautions must be observed.

First, if at all possible, make sure *before* the move that the hard disk contains a bootable kernel that's compatible with the target machine's hardware components. If the new machine contains a different hard disk controller (for instance, if you're moving your hard disk from a system with a BusLogic SCSI controller to another containing a Future Domain one) you may need to build a customized kernel first in order to ensure that the new configuration will be bootable.

Second, verify that the machine can be booted into a single-user configuration. This is usually accomplished by typing `linux single` when the LILO prompt appears at the beginning of the boot process. This will let you boot up Linux on the target system, without unnecessary drivers or server applications, so that you'll be able to continue your testing and configuration efforts there.

Third, make sure the hard disk can be hooked up inside the target system. While you may be able to connect an IDE connector to a SCSI hard disk using a suitable large hammer, the results are unlikely to please you, and you'll probably end up with many costly components in the dumpster. Instead, you may have to add the necessary adapters and cables first, to ensure that the hard disk will be operational in the new case.

The fourth step is especially important for IDE hard drives: Before attempting to boot the target system with the new hard drive, make sure the system's BIOS is properly configured for the new drive. This is especially important with older motherboards and BIOSs that do not have an autoconfiguration option.

If all goes well, you'll see the LILO prompt appear when you attempt to reboot. Hit the Ctrl key so that a colon appears, type `linux single` to ensure a single-user boot, and watch the system come to life. If you only see the first few letters of the word LILO appear, and the hard disk contained a bootable copy of Linux, the problem is quite possibly with the disk geometry settings in the BIOS.

If there are problems during the boot, watch for any messages during the boot process. If you can log on, you can also make use of the `dmesg` command to check for error messages. These may indicate that a driver failed to load due to a missing hardware component or unexpected hardware configuration. In rare cases, it may be necessary to supply a boot-time parameter to the Linux kernel before you can boot your system properly.

If you're using a modular kernel, such as the Caldera OpenLinux kernel found on the CD-ROM included with this book, all (or at least *most*) of the hardware components on the new system should come to life after rebooting. If your kernel is customized, however, you may need to recompile the kernel to match the new hardware configuration (see Appendix A).

When you're satisfied with the kernel and the system configuration, it's time to test multiuser mode. Reboot the system and watch for any error messages as they come up.

Other Peripherals

Unlike the processor, motherboard, and main hard disk, other components have little to do with your system's identity. When you perform the electronic equivalent of today's medical miracle—a multiple organ transplant—and move the motherboard, processor, and main hard disk to a new case, your machine in the new box should come to life just as before. Some other peripherals, however, may present annoying problems—for instance, a CD-ROM drive not functioning or the network drivers not coming to life, but these are unlikely to prevent Linux from booting.

If you transplant most of your computer's innards, including the motherboard, hard disks, CD-ROM drives, and adapter cards, to a new case, this will be the same computer as before inasmuch as the operating system is concerned. Certain components, such as the power supply and floppy disk drives, have no vendor-specific software drivers whatsoever, so when these change, Linux will not be affected the slightest.

> **WARNING**
>
> When you're reconfiguring your computer's hardware, or building a new system to be used as a Linux server, the problem of heat must always be kept in mind. A system with a high-capacity hard drive, fast processor, high-end graphics card or DVD decoder can easily produce enough heat to overload a single power supply fan. Overheating is a frequent cause of unreliable system operation. What is a mere annoyance for a workstation can become a major headache with a server that is expected to work reliably 24 hours a day, 7 days a week. Sometimes adding a second fan is sufficient; other times, you may wish to acquire a better case with improved cooling. Or, you might consider removing components that really aren't necessary for a server system, such as a high-end graphic accelerator.

Moving Software

Because the true soul of a machine is the information stored on its hard disk, you can actually "move" your Linux system to another box without ever moving a single physical component. However, it's rarely as simple as just copying all files from one machine to the other and expecting it to work.

In fact, about the only instance when I'd expect such a software transplant to yield a functional result is when the target system has an identical, or nearly identical, hardware configuration to that of the source system. When the configurations are sufficiently different, the transplant becomes so problematic that often, starting with a fresh installation is easier, only moving configuration settings and user files selectively.

Moving the System

So how, exactly, do you move system files? It's not like you can just copy them between two machines, especially if the target machine doesn't even have an operating system installed.

The easiest method I've found is to temporarily remove the target machine's hard disk drive and attach it to the source system. You can then format this drive, copy all needed files to it, and run `lilo` to ensure that the Linux Loader is installed properly so that the new drive will become bootable. This method, by the way, can also be used when you're replacing a failing hard drive; in a sense, that also qualifies as transplanting your system, even though you're only replacing a single component!

The actual steps you need to carry out this cloning procedure vary from one system to the next. The situation is further complicated by the fact that often a hard drive contains more than one partition; if you expect the copy to work, you might have to replicate the partitioning scheme or resort to another method, such as the use of symbolic links, in order to create a directory structure similar to that on the original drive.

Broadly speaking, you'll need to perform the following operations, starting with a virgin hard drive:

1. Insert the new drive.
2. Partition the drive (using `fdisk`).
3. Format the partitions (create the file systems using `mkfs`).
4. Initialize swap partitions, if any (using `mkswap`).
5. Copy all files (using `tar` or `cpio`).
6. Make a partition on the new drive bootable (using `lilo`).
7. Replace and test.

All this, of course, can only be done if the source system functions well. Often, however, you want to move the system to another box because the hardware does not work reliably. Another possibility is that the source system may not be compatible with the target machine's hard drive. In this case, the simple steps described here will not do the trick.

Instead, you're faced with the paradox described in Chapter 17, "Backups." In order to use the target system to copy anything to its hard drive, you already need a working copy of the operating system, which means that rather than copying an existing installation, you must begin by installing a fresh copy of Linux.

At this point, I suggest you give up on the idea of actually copying the system in its entirety. Instead, install a suitable Linux system from a distribution and begin copying configuration options, customizations, and user data. The source of this copy operation can be your backup (you *do* have a regularly updated backup, don't you?) or the old machine's hard drive, if you can hook it up with the target machine temporarily. Alternatively, if both machines work, you may attempt to copy the relevant files across the network. One problem with this approach is that if you're configuring the new system to assume the old one's identity, both may believe that they're "the" Linux server on your network, with identical IP numbers and other configuration settings; you'll need to temporarily change one or the other in order for the two to coexist.

Moving the Kernel

Sometimes, rather than moving a complete operating system configuration, you may simply want to move a working copy of the Linux kernel, leaving all other settings, configuration options, and system components unchanged. Perhaps you're copying a known good kernel from a floppy disk to a system whose kernel has been damaged. Perhaps you created a custom kernel on a fast, high-end computer, and you're copying it over to a slower machine, on which a kernel recompilation would have taken hours. Whatever the reason, copying the kernel is not a complicated task, but you must make sure that the resulting system remains bootable.

The kernel is usually stored in the file /vmlinuz. It's possible to simply overwrite this file with a new copy. However, if you're using LILO to boot the system, you must make sure that LILO is informed of the change.

To refresh your LILO configuration, it's usually sufficient to rerun the `lilo` command with no parameters. The command reads the configuration file /etc/lilo.conf and sets up the system's boot parameters accordingly (see Appendix A).

Moving Applications

So how do you move an installed application from one system to another? Often enough, the answer is that you don't—reinstalling is a far easier option. The reason is that once an application is installed, it may have executable files, manual pages, and configuration and data files all over the place; often, there's no reliable inventory as to which files need to be moved. Furthermore, the application's installation scripts may have configured the program to match your system's hardware configuration, so moving the application in an unaltered form to another machine may not be appropriate even if you know exactly what needs to be moved.

If the application was installed from CD-ROM or some other distribution media, reinstallation shouldn't present a problem.

Many applications are downloaded from the Internet. These applications are usually distributed in source code form. As standard practice, every time you install such an application, you should leave a copy of its source tree on your system under the /usr/src directory hierarchy. Perhaps in the past, when disk space was at a premium, this wasn't a popular option. Now, however, in the day of low-cost multigigabyte disk drives, this really shouldn't present a problem.

When you need to move an application to another system, simply move its source tree, where all the installation files can be found in one place. When the source tree has been re-created on the target system, you're ready to repeat the installation there. Note that this doesn't mean that you need to start from scratch. The source directory in all likelihood contains the last interim result of your previous installation; often, a `make install` or similar command is all that's needed, and the application is reinstalled on the new system.

Note that this doesn't mean that if you're using multiple Linux systems, you need a copy of every application's source archive in `/usr/src` on all such systems. It's sufficient to have just one copy that you can access through the network. Multiple copies are only needed if the application is recompiled with different configuration settings on different machines, which is a rare occurrence.

Moving User Data

As is the case with backups, when you're moving data from one system to another, user data is by far the easiest to move. This is because the system's operations do not depend on the presence, absence, or condition of these files.

In other words, these files can be copied unconditionally from the source to the target system, using a command such as `tar` or `cpio`. The operation is no different from what you'd do when you're preparing a backup of your system (see Chapter 17).

More Case Studies

Over the years since I've been running Linux systems, I've had my share of broken hardware; on a few occasions, this required major surgery. Perhaps it's appropriate to wrap up this book with a few more war stories; allow me to express my hope that you'll not have to deal with situations like these anytime soon.

Screaming Gamers

It was over two years ago that as a result of a long chain of events, I inherited the game MUD2 and began operating the server `mud2.com` out of my home office. For a short while, the game shared my main Linux server with other Internet applications, but it obviously needed its own server badly, so a new machine was installed soon afterwards.

The server ran fine for several weeks, at which time I received a software upgrade from the game's author. The upgrade was tested on another system and seemed to work well, so I installed it on the game system. Within hours, the game began experiencing hideous crashes, the likes of which I've never seen before. Some crashes actually caused the game software to endlessly dump log entries, eventually filling up the system's hard drive! No sooner did the system recover from one crash when another followed. This was unprecedented.

On a production system, I always follow the practice of leaving open a way to back out of an upgrade. This case was no different; the old copy of the game software was still there, so I was able to back out and restore this version. I expected the system to return to normal, and at first it seemed to do just that. However, a few hours later another big crash followed.

This made it clear that the problem wasn't with the new game version. I made a mental apology to MUD2's author whose name I'd been cursing earlier, and I got to work. At this point, I had no choice: It was necessary to shut down the game and begin testing every part of the system systematically. By this time, I was beginning to suspect that I had more than a simple software bug to deal with; I was, in fact, suspecting hardware failure.

That suspicion was confirmed spectacularly when during an attempt to reboot the system, even its BIOS failed to come up! When a motherboard cannot get to the point of displaying its initial BIOS startup screen, you know your search is over: All that was left to do was to remove all peripheral components (that is, everything with the exception of the keyboard and a video card) and try again. When the motherboard failed to boot even in this stripped-down configuration, there was no question about it—the culprit wasn't Linux or MUD2 but rather faulty hardware.

A replacement motherboard arrived the next day, and I promptly exchanged it with the old one. Although the two motherboards were of a different make, I didn't expect much trouble with Linux. I was not disappointed; after the replacement was completed, Linux booted fine on the first attempt, and it has been running on that motherboard ever since, without further trouble.

An April Morning

It was a bright April morning some three years ago, and my wife and I were about to depart on what eventually turned out to be a fabulous transcontinental car trip across the United States. At the time, I used to operate a single Linux server in my home office; this machine handled all my email, incoming faxes, and my Internet connection via a dial-up modem. The modem also accepted incoming data calls, and I intended to connect to it with my portable computer regularly while on the road, in order to retrieve my email.

All sounds nice in theory, except for a not-so-insignificant glitch. Before leaving, I decided to check my email one last time; however, when I turned on the monitor, what I saw instead was repetitive error messages. A reboot didn't cure the problem; from the messages it was obvious that I had a major problem with the system's hard drive.

Fearing the worst, I shut down the system, opened the case, and attempted to reseat the hard disk's controller card and all connecting cables. This didn't help. Shortly after reboot, the error messages reappeared. I realized at this time that any further attempt to "fix" the system would likely just cause data loss; what I really needed was a new hard drive.

I promptly telephoned my supplier, who fortunately had a hard drive of an identical make. That way, at least I didn't need to worry about any software or configuration changes! Two hours later, the drive arrived and I began attacking my system with a screwdriver.

I was facing a dilemma, however. What should I try to do? Should I simply install the new drive as the boot drive and start with a fresh copy of Linux installed on it, salvaging whatever I can from the failing drive (or my backups) afterwards? I had a better solution in mind. I inserted the new drive as a *secondary* drive and, hoping for the best, rebooted the system. What I was hoping for, specifically, was that the system would come to life just long enough for me to make a full copy of the old hard drive onto the new one.

The system indeed came to life. I booted into single-user mode and wasted no time partitioning and formatting the new drive. It worked. Next, I used a `tar` command combination to transplant all the contents from the old drive to the new one (see Chapter 17). This full copy took the better part of an hour; all the while, I was watching the screen intently, hoping that the dreaded error messages wouldn't reappear.

They didn't. The old drive held together this last time just long enough for the dump to complete. I used `lilo` with the `.r` command-line switch to install the Linux Loader on the new drive. Then, I shut down the system, removed the faulty drive, and reconfigured the new drive as the boot drive.

Upon reboot, the system came back normally. I did a few checks and everything seemed to work fine—no important system files appeared corrupt. It was now three o'clock in the afternoon, but we left anyway, to begin what turned out to be one of the most fabulous vacations we ever had. During the three weeks we spent on the road, I called this system in my home office every day, and it worked flawlessly. In the end, I was grateful; had this failure occurred a couple of days later, when we were already more than a thousand miles from home, I would not have been able to fix the problem this easily.

Summary

In case of a major failure, it may be necessary to transplant your Linux system's identity to new hardware.

Despite being the brain of the computer, the motherboard, and the processor it contains, does not carry your system's identity. Instead, that identity is encoded in the form of software code and system configuration settings on your computer's hard drive. Consequently, moving components from one system to another, which is not always straightforward, will not transplant a system's identity until you actually move its main hard disk or its contents.

Moving the hard disk is easy if you're moving it along with most other system components, or when you're moving it to another machine with identical or near-identical specifications. However, when you move a hard disk to a different machine, you cannot always expect Linux to simply boot up and work. This is especially true if the system is configured with a customized kernel instead of a modular one.

Rather than moving the hard disk physically, you can simply move data from one hard disk to another and transplant your system's identity that way. Once again, this solution is unlikely to work unless the source and the target system have very similar specifications. If the target drive can be hooked up to the source system, the move can be performed by booting Linux on the source machine, formatting the new drive, and copying the files. However, if the source machine isn't bootable, you may need to install a fresh copy of Linux on the target system first, which makes the whole idea of simply transplanting the contents of the old system's hard drive questionable. Instead, you may be better off starting with a freshly installed copy of Linux on the target system and only copying data files and configuration information selectively.

When you move a copy of the Linux kernel from one disk to another, make sure that the target disk remains bootable by invoking the `lilo` command. When it comes to applications, these are often easier to install either from distribution disks or from source archives that were used to perform the original installation. Lastly, user data files can usually be moved with impunity, similar to the way backups are performed.

Manual Pages

For additional information on topics discussed in this chapter, refer to the following manual pages:

- `man cpio`
- `man dmesg`
- `man fdisk`
- `man lilo`
- `man lilo.conf`
- `man mkfs`
- `man mkswap`
- `man tar`

Part **VII**

Appendixes

A Configuring the Kernel

B Linux Resources on the Internet

C Linux Publications

D Linux Support Organizations

Configuring the Kernel

Having completed a Linux installation, you should be able to boot your system and log on to it either as root, or using the username that you specified for your non-privileged account. Once you're logged on you're running a shell program, from which commands can be issued and other programs can be run. At this point, you have a fully functional Linux system on your hands. There is, however, a critical configuration step left: You need to create a kernel that matches your system configuration.

The kernel is the core of the operating system. It usually exists on your system in the form of the file /vmlinuz. Essentially it is a program that implements the operating system's essential features. By its very nature, the kernel is hardware dependent, and must be configured to work on a particular computer. The desired configuration can be achieved using kernel modules or by recompiling the kernel.

Knowing how to recompile the kernel is important for another reason as well: You might decide to obtain a newer version of the kernel from the Internet. These new versions are distributed in source form, and to create a running copy, you must compile the package.

Modules and Kernel Customization

Modern versions of Linux support the concept of a *modular* kernel. A modular kernel consists of the core kernel file and a variety of additional modules, each implementing support for a specific device or feature. Kernel modules can be loaded and unloaded dynamically.

This is, in fact, how Caldera OpenLinux can be installed on any system using only a pair of floppy disks. Older Linux distributions often used dozens of different floppy disk images containing *stock* kernels so, as the first installation step, you needed to pick the image that best matched your system. Caldera OpenLinux uses a modular kernel instead, which can be booted on any system as long as the proper modules are present.

Kernel Recompilation

Kernel customization is called *recompiling the kernel* because it in fact re-creates the kernel image from the original Linux sources using a C compiler and associated tools. For this reason, many assume that in order to recompile the kernel, you must be a C programmer yourself. Not true! Kernel recompilation is automatic, and kernel configuration is aided by a script that, while not exactly intuitive, is nevertheless fairly foolproof. Furthermore, you can take a few simple precautionary steps to ensure that even if the recompiled kernel doesn't work, you can revert to the old kernel configuration.

Note that you don't have to perform this step if you don't feel comfortable with it. In all but the most heavily loaded or esoteric situations, a modular stock kernel will do every bit as good a job as a customized one, and the amount of work saved can be considerable.

Preparing LILO to Boot the Old Kernel

When you create a new kernel image, there is always a possibility that it will not work. For instance, you might have forgotten to include a driver that is required for the system to run or you might have added a driver that causes the system to crash. Whatever the reason, it is essential to retain the capability of booting the system using the old (last known good) kernel image.

It so happens that when you recompile the kernel using standard scripts, the new kernel is copied to /vmlinuz, but the old kernel is saved first as /vmlinuz.old. All you need to do then is tell LILO about this alternative kernel image.

This is accomplished by modifying the LILO configuration file, /etc/lilo.conf. This file can be edited by hand; it can also be updated using the LISA utility of Caldera OpenLinux. This is the same utility that performed initial installation. LISA can be started from the command line (if you are root) by typing the lisa command.

LISA, however, has a limitation. It cannot install support for kernel images that do not yet exist. If you have never recompiled the kernel before, there is no /vmlinuz.old file on your system yet. The solution is the simplest imaginable: Create a copy of /vmlinuz. That is, log on to the system as root, and type the following:

```
cd /
cp vmlinuz vmlinuz.old
```

Now you can use LISA to add this new image to the LILO configuration.

TEST SYSTEM   On my test system, I created a copy of /vmlinuz. Then I ran lisa from the command line, selected the System Configuration option, and in the menu that followed, selected the Configure Boot Manager command.

LISA displayed the result of a boot analysis. As expected, it showed that LILO was already installed on my system. Pressing the Enter key took me to an already familiar screen (refer to Figure 3.12) where I confirmed that LILO was to be (re-)installed on /dev/sda, my first SCSI hard disk.

In the next screen, LILO offered a series of operating system image choices, including the newly created /vmlinuz.old file (see Figure A.1).

FIGURE A.1
Adding a LILO boot image.

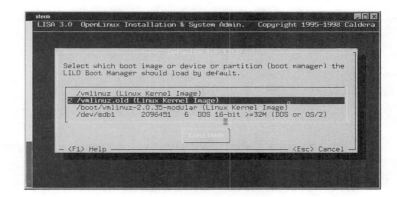

Because LISA creates a new lilo.conf file, I had to specify /vmlinuz first, as the default boot image. As before, I accepted LISA's choices for a RAM disk image and boot parameters.

Next I proceeded to add /vmlinuz.old as a second boot image. Again, I accepted LISA's defaults for a RAM disk. When LISA asked for a name for the new entry, I entered oldlinux.

In the end, my /etc/lilo.conf file (as generated by LISA) looked like this:

```
#
# general section
#
boot = /dev/sda
install = /boot/boot.b
message = /boot/message
prompt

# wait 20 seconds (200 10ths) for user to select the entry to load
timeout = 200
```

▼

▼
```
#
# default entry
#


image = /vmlinuz
        initrd = "/boot/initrd.gz"
        label = linux
        root = /dev/sda1
        read-only
        append = "load_ramdisk=1 ramdisk_size=2880"

#
# additional entries
#


image = /vmlinuz.old
        initrd = "/boot/initrd.gz"
        label = oldlinux
        root = /dev/sda1
        read-only
        append = "load_ramdisk=1 ramdisk_size=2880"
```

▲   Having installed a backup boot image, I was ready to configure a new kernel.

Running the Kernel Configuration Scripts

Here is what you need to do to create a new kernel image. Logged on as root, type the following commands:

```
cd /usr/src/linux
make config
make dep
make clean
make zlilo
```

Now reboot the system and enjoy the new kernel.

Sounds too simple? Maybe so, but it's also true; these are the only commands you need to type. Of course this description conveniently neglects the fact that after you type make config, you'll be presented with possibly several hundred cryptic configuration questions. Your answer to these questions determines the configuration of the new kernel.

Does that mean you need to know the meaning of each of the options presented? Nothing could be further from the truth. Don't let the cryptic nature of these questions intimidate you; a few simple rules of thumb can help you through this phase and let you create a well configured kernel image.

First rule: Defaults work. If you go through the configuration script pressing Enter all the time, you'll get a kernel image that matches the one you already have, that is, a kernel that is known to work.

Second rule: Know your hardware configuration. This way you can confidently make selection choices during kernel configuration, picking only devices that your system actually contains.

Third rule: If a kernel failed to boot and you reverted to booting with `/vmlinuz.old`, your first action should be to copy this backup image over `/vmlinuz` and run the command `/sbin/lilo`. This restores the working kernel image as the default image. If you omit this step and recompile the kernel again, `/vmlinuz.old` will be replaced by the previous, dysfunctional `/vmlinuz`. If the new `/vmlinuz` also fails to boot, you have a problem!

Fourth rule: If all else fails, use the question mark option! Most configuration questions let you respond with a question mark, which causes a brief help text to be displayed.

TEST SYSTEM   When recompiling the kernel, my goal on the test system was to turn off kernel module support and instead build a kernel that matches the test system's hardware configuration accurately, and also implements all kernel services I need.

What follows is a transcript of my interactive session started with the `make config` command, with occasional comments describing the reasoning behind my selection choices.

```
#make config
/bin/sh scripts/Configure arch/i386/config.in
#
# Using defaults found in arch/i386/defconfig
#
*
* Code maturity level options
*
Prompt for development and/or incomplete code/drivers (CONFIG_
➥EXPERIMENTAL) [Y/n/?] n
```

You should generally not require experimental or incomplete drives unless an essential device on your system is not (yet) supported by a production driver.

```
Enable loadable module support (CONFIG_MODULES) [Y/n/?] n
```

I know that I do not need loadable modules, so I disabled this feature. If you leave it on, you'll be able to reply with an M to many of the subsequent questions, meaning that the desired feature will be compiled as a loadable module. In this case, you will also need to

▼   do a `make modules`, followed by a `make modules_install` at the end of the recompilation process.

```
*
* General setup
*
Kernel math emulation (CONFIG_MATH_EMULATION) [Y/n/?] n
```

Enabling math emulation is a safe choice on a *stock* kernel because it allows that kernel to function without a coprocessor (for example, on older 80386 or 80486SX based systems.) However, because I am compiling a kernel specifically for a Pentium system, math emulation is not required.

```
Networking support (CONFIG_NET) [Y/n/?] y
Limit memory to low 16MB (CONFIG_MAX_16M) [N/y/?] n
PCI bios support (CONFIG_PCI) [Y/n/?] y
System V IPC (CONFIG_SYSVIPC) [Y/n/?] y
Kernel support for a.out binaries (CONFIG_BINFMT_AOUT) [Y/n/?] y
Kernel support for ELF binaries (CONFIG_BINFMT_ELF) [Y/n/?] y
Compile kernel as ELF - if your GCC is ELF-GCC (CONFIG_KERNEL_ELF)
➥[Y/n/?] y
Processor type (386, 486, Pentium, PPro) [386] Pentium
  defined CONFIG_M586
*
* Floppy, IDE, and other block devices
*
Normal floppy disk support (CONFIG_BLK_DEV_FD) [Y/n/?] y
Enhanced IDE/MFM/RLL disk/cdrom/tape/floppy support (CONFIG_ BLK_DEV_IDE)
➥[Y/n/?] y
*
* Please see Documentation/ide.txt for help/info on IDE drives
*
   Use old disk-only driver on primary interface (CONFIG_BLK_DEV_HD_IDE)
➥[N/y/?] n
   Include IDE/ATAPI CDROM support (CONFIG_BLK_DEV_IDECD) [Y/n/?] y
   Include IDE/ATAPI TAPE support (CONFIG_BLK_DEV_IDETAPE) [Y/n/?] n
   Include IDE/ATAPI FLOPPY support (new) (CONFIG_BLK_DEV_IDEFLOPPY)
➥[Y/n/?] n
   SCSI emulation support (CONFIG_BLK_DEV_IDESCSI) [N/y/?] n
   Support removable IDE interfaces (PCMCIA) (CONFIG_BLK_DEV_IDE_PCMCIA)
➥ [Y/n/?] n
   CMD640 chipset bugfix/support (CONFIG_BLK_DEV_CMD640) [Y/n/?] n
   RZ1000 chipset bugfix/support (CONFIG_BLK_DEV_RZ1000) [Y/n/?] n
   Intel 82371 PIIX (Triton I/II) DMA support (CONFIG_BLK_DEV_TRITON)
➥[Y/n/?] y
   Other IDE chipset support (CONFIG_IDE_CHIPSETS) [Y/n/?] n
```

▼   The last four options concern specific IDE devices. I know that the motherboard I use (ASUS TX-97E) carries the Intel Triton chipset on board. You might be able to find out

▼   what IDE chipset you have by typing dmesg from another virtual console. This shows
messages generated during the boot process, which might include a line identifying the
IDE interface type.

When in doubt, leave these four options on. They won't do any harm, they only make
your kernel a tiny bit bigger.

```
*
* Additional Block Devices
*
Loopback device support (CONFIG_BLK_DEV_LOOP) [Y/n/?] y
Multiple devices driver support (CONFIG_BLK_DEV_MD) [Y/n/?] n
RAM disk support (CONFIG_BLK_DEV_RAM) [Y/n/?] n
```

When using a modular kernel, I need a RAM disk from which drivers essential to the
boot process can be loaded. With a customized kernel with no kernel module support, the
RAM disk will no longer be needed. However, after the kernel is recompiled, I will need
to modify the LILO configuration file as well.

```
XT harddisk support (CONFIG_BLK_DEV_XD) [Y/n/?] n
Parallel port IDE device support (CONFIG_PARIDE) [Y/n/?] n
*
* Networking options
*
Network firewalls (CONFIG_FIREWALL) [Y/n/?] y
Network aliasing (CONFIG_NET_ALIAS) [Y/n/?] y
TCP/IP networking (CONFIG_INET) [Y/n/?] y
IP: forwarding/gatewaying (CONFIG_IP_FORWARD) [Y/n/?] y
IP: multicasting (CONFIG_IP_MULTICAST) [Y/n/?] n
IP: syn cookies (CONFIG_SYN_COOKIES) [Y/n/?] y
IP: firewalling (CONFIG_IP_FIREWALL) [Y/n/?] y
IP: firewall packet logging (CONFIG_IP_FIREWALL_VERBOSE) [Y/n/?] y
IP: masquerading (CONFIG_IP_MASQUERADE) [Y/n/?] y
*
* Protocol-specific masquerading support will be built as modules.
*
IP: ICMP masquerading (CONFIG_IP_MASQUERADE_ICMP) [Y/n/?] n
IP: always defragment (CONFIG_IP_ALWAYS_DEFRAG) [Y/n/?] y
IP: accounting (CONFIG_IP_ACCT) [Y/n/?] y
IP: optimize as router not host (CONFIG_IP_ROUTER) [N/y/?] n
        IP: tunneling (CONFIG_NET_IPIP) [Y/n/?] n
        IP: aliasing support (CONFIG_IP_ALIAS) [Y/n/?] y
```

The preceding set of options enable standard IP networking features as well as support
for firewall functions.

```
*
* (it is safe to leave these untouched)
▼      *
```

▼   IP: PC/TCP compatibility mode (CONFIG_INET_PCTCP) [N/y/?]
```
IP: Reverse ARP (CONFIG_INET_RARP) [N/y/?]
IP: Disable Path MTU Discovery (normally enabled) (CONFIG_NO_PATH_MTU_
➥DISCOVERY) [N/y/?]
IP: Drop source routed frames (CONFIG_IP_NOSR) [Y/n/?]
IP: Allow large windows (not recommended if <16Mb of memory) (CONFIG_
➥SKB_LARGE) [N/y/?]
```

I left these options untouched, as the script suggested.

```
*
* IPX options
*
The IPX protocol (CONFIG_IPX) [Y/n/?] n
Appletalk DDP (CONFIG_ATALK) [Y/n/?] n
Amateur Radio AX.25 Level 2 (CONFIG_AX25) [N/y/?] n
Kernel/User network link driver (CONFIG_NETLINK) [N/y/?] n
```

The preceding set of network drivers is needed only under specific circumstances.

```
*
* SCSI support
*
SCSI support (CONFIG_SCSI) [Y/n/?] y
*
* SCSI support type (disk, tape, CD-ROM)
*
SCSI disk support (CONFIG_BLK_DEV_SD) [Y/n/?] y
SCSI tape support (CONFIG_CHR_DEV_ST) [Y/n/?] n
SCSI CD-ROM support (CONFIG_BLK_DEV_SR) [Y/n/?] n
SCSI generic support (CONFIG_CHR_DEV_SG) [Y/n/?] n
*
* Some SCSI devices (e.g. CD jukebox) support multiple LUNs
*
Probe all LUNs on each SCSI device (CONFIG_SCSI_MULTI_LUN) [Y/n/?] n
Verbose SCSI error reporting (kernel size +=12K) (CONFIG_SCSI_CONSTANTS)
➥[Y/n/?] n
*
* SCSI low-level drivers
*
7000FASST SCSI support (CONFIG_SCSI_7000FASST) [Y/n/?] n
Adaptec AHA152X/2825 support (CONFIG_SCSI_AHA152X) [Y/n/?] n
Adaptec AHA1542 support (CONFIG_SCSI_AHA1542) [Y/n/?] n
Adaptec AHA1740 support (CONFIG_SCSI_AHA1740) [Y/n/?] n
Adaptec AIC7xxx support (CONFIG_SCSI_AIC7XXX) [Y/n/?] y
    Override driver defaults for commands per LUN (CONFIG_OVERRIDE_CMDS)
➥[N/y/?] n
    Collect statistics to report in /proc (CONFIG_AIC7XXX_PROC_STATS)
➥[N/y/?] n
    Delay in seconds after SCSI bus reset (CONFIG_AIC7XXX_RESET_DELAY)
➥[15] 5
```
▼   `AdvanSys SCSI support (CONFIG_SCSI_ADVANSYS) [Y/n/?] n`

▼
```
Always IN2000 SCSI support (CONFIG_SCSI_IN2000) [Y/n/?] n
AM53/79C974 PCI SCSI support (CONFIG_SCSI_AM53C974) [Y/n/?] n
BusLogic SCSI support (CONFIG_SCSI_BUSLOGIC) [Y/n/?] n
DTC3180/3280 SCSI support (CONFIG_SCSI_DTC3280) [Y/n/?] n
EATA-DMA (DPT, NEC, AT&T, SNI, AST, Olivetti, Alphatronix) support
➥(CONFIG_SCSI_EATA_DMA) [Y/n/?] n
EATA-PIO (old DPT PM2001, PM2012A) support (CONFIG_SCSI_EATA_PIO)
➥[Y/n/?] n
EATA ISA/EISA/PCI (DPT and generic EATA/DMA-compliant boards)
➥support (CONFIG_SCSI_EATA) [Y/n/?] n
Future Domain 16xx SCSI support (CONFIG_SCSI_FUTURE_DOMAIN) [Y/n/?] n
Generic NCR5380/53c400 SCSI support (CONFIG_SCSI_GENERIC_NCR5380)
➥[Y/n/?] n
NCR53c406a SCSI support (CONFIG_SCSI_NCR53C406A) [Y/n/?] n
NCR53c7,8xx SCSI support (CONFIG_SCSI_NCR53C7xx) [Y/n/?] n
NCR53C8XX SCSI support (CONFIG_SCSI_NCR53C8XX) [Y/n/?] n
IOMEGA Parallel Port ZIP drive SCSI support (CONFIG_SCSI_PPA) [Y/n/?] n
PAS16 SCSI support (CONFIG_SCSI_PAS16) [Y/n/?] n
Qlogic FAS SCSI support (CONFIG_SCSI_QLOGIC_FAS) [Y/n/?] n
Qlogic ISP SCSI support (CONFIG_SCSI_QLOGIC_ISP) [Y/n/?] n
Seagate ST-02 and Future Domain TMC-8xx SCSI support (CONFIG_SCSI_
➥SEAGATE) [Y/n/?] n
Tekram DC-390(T) SCSI support (CONFIG_SCSI_DC390T) [Y/n/?] n
Trantor T128/T128F/T228 SCSI support (CONFIG_SCSI_T128) [Y/n/?] n
UltraStor 14F/34F support (CONFIG_SCSI_U14_34F) [Y/n/?] n
UltraStor SCSI support (CONFIG_SCSI_ULTRASTOR) [Y/n/?] n
GDT SCSI Disk Array Controller support (CONFIG_SCSI_GDTH) [Y/n/?] n
```

The only SCSI driver I enabled is the AIC7xxx driver. (This is the driver required for the Adaptec 2940 family of SCSI adapters.) I only enabled support for SCSI disks because I have no SCSI tape drives, CD-ROMs, or other SCSI devices on this system.

```
*
* Network device support
*
Network device support (CONFIG_NETDEVICES) [Y/n/?] y
Dummy net driver support (CONFIG_DUMMY) [Y/n/?] y
EQL (serial line load balancing) support (CONFIG_EQUALIZER) [Y/n/?] n
PLIP (parallel port) support (CONFIG_PLIP) [Y/n/?] n
PPP (point-to-point) support (CONFIG_PPP) [Y/n/?] y
*
* CCP compressors for PPP are only built as modules.
*
SLIP (serial line) support (CONFIG_SLIP) [Y/n/?] y
 CSLIP compressed headers (CONFIG_SLIP_COMPRESSED) [Y/n/?] y
 Keepalive and linefill (CONFIG_SLIP_SMART) [N/y/?] n
 Six bit SLIP encapsulation (CONFIG_SLIP_MODE_SLIP6) [N/y/?] n
Radio network interfaces (CONFIG_NET_RADIO) [N/y/?] n
Ethernet (10 or 100Mbit) (CONFIG_NET_ETHERNET) [Y/n/?] y
3COM ISA, EISA and PCI cards (CONFIG_NET_VENDOR_3COM) [Y/n/?] n
```
▼
```
Western Digital/SMC ISA and EISA cards (CONFIG_NET_VENDOR_SMC) [Y/n/?] n
```

▼
```
PCI Ethernet adapters (CONFIG_NET_PCI) [Y/n/?] n
Other ISA cards (CONFIG_NET_ISA) [Y/n/?] y
AMD LANCE and PCnet (AT1500 and NE2100) support (CONFIG_LANCE) [Y/n/?] n
AT1700 (Fujitsu 86965) support (CONFIG_AT1700) [Y/n/?] n
Cabletron E21xx support (CONFIG_E2100) [Y/n/?] n
DEPCA, DE10x, DE200, DE201, DE202, DE422 support (CONFIG_DEPCA) [Y/n/?] n
EtherWORKS 3 (DE203, DE204, DE205) support (CONFIG_EWRK3) [Y/n/?] n
EtherExpress 16 support (CONFIG_EEXPRESS) [Y/n/?] n
HP PCLAN+ (27247B and 27252A) support (CONFIG_HPLAN_PLUS) [Y/n/?] n
HP PCLAN (27245 and other 27xxx series) support (CONFIG_HPLAN) [Y/n/?] n
HP 10/100VG PCLAN (ISA, EISA, PCI) support (CONFIG_HP100) [Y/n/?] n
NE2000/NE1000 ISA support (CONFIG_NE2000) [Y/n/?] y
SK_G16 support (CONFIG_SK_G16) [N/y/?] n
EISA, VLB and other board controllers (CONFIG_NET_EISA) [Y/n/?] n
Pocket and portable adapters (CONFIG_NET_POCKET) [Y/n/?] n
Token Ring driver support (CONFIG_TR) [Y/n/?] n
FDDI driver support (CONFIG_FDDI) [N/y/?] n
ARCnet support (CONFIG_ARCNET) [Y/n/?] n
```

I enabled network support for my network card (an NE2000-compatible device), and for the PPP and SLIP protocols that work on serial lines.

```
*
* ISDN subsystem
*
ISDN support (CONFIG_ISDN) [Y/n/?] n
```

ISDN support is only needed if your system actually contains an ISDN device. If you're connecting via ISDN but use an external router, this option can be left off.

```
*
* CD-ROM drivers (not for SCSI or IDE/ATAPI drives)
*
Support non-SCSI/IDE/ATAPI CDROM drives (CONFIG_CD_NO_IDESCSI) [Y/n/?] n
*
* Filesystems
*
Quota support (CONFIG_QUOTA) [N/y/?] y
```

Quota support lets you specify an upper limit to the disk space individual users can use. This option is useful if you allow users to log on to the system and execute arbitrary programs that might create data files.

```
Minix fs support (CONFIG_MINIX_FS) [Y/n/?] y
Extended fs support (CONFIG_EXT_FS) [Y/n/?] n
Second extended fs support (CONFIG_EXT2_FS) [Y/n/?] y
xiafs filesystem support (CONFIG_XIA_FS) [Y/n/?] n
Native language support (Needed for FAT and ISO9660) (CONFIG_NLS)
➡[Y/n/?] y
```
▼
```
ISO9660 cdrom filesystem support (CONFIG_ISO9660_FS) [Y/n/?] y
```

```
▼   DOS FAT fs support (CONFIG_FAT_FS) [Y/n/?] y
    MSDOS fs support (CONFIG_MSDOS_FS) [Y/n/?] y
    umsdos: Unix like fs on top of std MSDOS FAT fs (CONFIG_UMSDOS_FS)
    ➥[Y/n/?] y
    VFAT (Windows-95) fs support (CONFIG_VFAT_FS) [Y/n/?] y
```

The Minix file system is used with Linux-formatted floppy disks. The Extended File System is largely obsolete. The Second Extended File System is the format used with Linux hard drives.

```
Codepage 437 (CONFIG_NLS_CODEPAGE_437) [Y/n/?] y
Codepage 737 (CONFIG_NLS_CODEPAGE_737) [Y/n/?] n
Codepage 775 (CONFIG_NLS_CODEPAGE_775) [Y/n/?] n
Codepage 850 (CONFIG_NLS_CODEPAGE_850) [Y/n/?] n
Codepage 852 (CONFIG_NLS_CODEPAGE_852) [Y/n/?] n
Codepage 855 (CONFIG_NLS_CODEPAGE_855) [Y/n/?] n
Codepage 857 (CONFIG_NLS_CODEPAGE_857) [Y/n/?] n
Codepage 860 (CONFIG_NLS_CODEPAGE_860) [Y/n/?] n
Codepage 861 (CONFIG_NLS_CODEPAGE_861) [Y/n/?] n
Codepage 862 (CONFIG_NLS_CODEPAGE_862) [Y/n/?] n
Codepage 863 (CONFIG_NLS_CODEPAGE_863) [Y/n/?] n
Codepage 864 (CONFIG_NLS_CODEPAGE_864) [Y/n/?] n
Codepage 865 (CONFIG_NLS_CODEPAGE_865) [Y/n/?] n
Codepage 866 (CONFIG_NLS_CODEPAGE_866) [Y/n/?] n
Codepage 869 (CONFIG_NLS_CODEPAGE_869) [Y/n/?] n
Codepage 874 (CONFIG_NLS_CODEPAGE_874) [Y/n/?] n
NLS ISO 8859-1 (CONFIG_NLS_ISO8859_1) [Y/n/?] n
NLS ISO 8859-2 (CONFIG_NLS_ISO8859_2) [Y/n/?] n
NLS ISO 8859-3 (CONFIG_NLS_ISO8859_3) [Y/n/?] n
NLS ISO 8859-4 (CONFIG_NLS_ISO8859_4) [Y/n/?] n
NLS ISO 8859-5 (CONFIG_NLS_ISO8859_5) [Y/n/?] n
NLS ISO 8859-6 (CONFIG_NLS_ISO8859_6) [Y/n/?] n
NLS ISO 8859-7 (CONFIG_NLS_ISO8859_7) [Y/n/?] n
NLS ISO 8859-8 (CONFIG_NLS_ISO8859_8) [Y/n/?] n
NLS ISO 8859-9 (CONFIG_NLS_ISO8859_9) [Y/n/?] n
NLS KOI8-R (CONFIG_NLS_KOI8_R) [Y/n/?] n
```

These code pages are required to read VFAT filenames that might contain foreign language characters. Generally it is sufficient to enable code page 437, the U.S. code page.

```
/proc filesystem support (CONFIG_PROC_FS) [Y/n/?] y
```

The /proc file system is a must; many applications depend on its presence.

```
NFS filesystem support (CONFIG_NFS_FS) [Y/n/?] y
    Root file system on NFS (CONFIG_ROOT_NFS) [N/y/?] (NEW) n
SMB filesystem support (to mount WfW shares etc..) (CONFIG_SMB_FS) [Y/n/?]
y
SMB Win95 bug work-around (CONFIG_SMB_WIN95) [Y/n/?] y
▼   OS/2 HPFS filesystem support (read only) (CONFIG_HPFS_FS) [Y/n/?] n
```

▼   System V and Coherent filesystem support (CONFIG_SYSV_FS) [Y/n/?] n
     UFS filesystem support (read only) (CONFIG_UFS_FS) [Y/n/?] n
     *
     * Character devices
     *
     Standard/generic serial support (CONFIG_SERIAL) [Y/n/?] y
     Digiboard PC/Xx Support (CONFIG_DIGI) [N/y/?] n
     Cyclades async mux support (CONFIG_CYCLADES) [Y/n/?] n
     Stallion multiport serial support (CONFIG_STALDRV) [N/y/?] n
     SDL RISCom/8 card support (CONFIG_RISCOM8) [Y/n/?] n
     Parallel printer support (CONFIG_PRINTER) [Y/n/?] y
     Specialix IO8+ card support (CONFIG_SPECIALIX) [Y/n/?] n
     Mouse Support (not serial mice) (CONFIG_MOUSE) [Y/n/?] y
     ATIXL busmouse support (CONFIG_ATIXL_BUSMOUSE) [Y/n/?] n
     Logitech busmouse support (CONFIG_BUSMOUSE) [Y/n/?] n
     Microsoft busmouse support (CONFIG_MS_BUSMOUSE) [Y/n/?] n
     PS/2 mouse (aka "auxiliary device") support (CONFIG_PSMOUSE) [Y/n/?] y
     C&T 82C710 mouse port support (as on TI Travelmate) (CONFIG_82C710_MOUSE)
     ➥[Y/n/?] n
     Support for user misc device modules (CONFIG_UMISC) [N/y/?] n
     QIC-02 tape support (CONFIG_QIC02_TAPE) [N/y/?] n
     Ftape (QIC-80/Travan) support (CONFIG_FTAPE) [Y/n/?] n
     Advanced Power Management BIOS support (CONFIG_APM) [N/y/?] n
     Watchdog Timer Support (CONFIG_WATCHDOG) [N/y/?] n
     Enhanced Real Time Clock Support (CONFIG_RTC) [N/y/?] n
     *
     * Sound
     *
     Sound card support (CONFIG_SOUND) [Y/n/?] y
     ProAudioSpectrum 16 support (CONFIG_PAS) [Y/n/?] n
     100%% Sound Blaster compatibles (SB16/32/64, ESS, Jazz16) support
     ➥(CONFIG_SB) [Y/n/?] y
     Generic OPL2/OPL3 FM synthesizer support (CONFIG_ADLIB) [Y/n/?] y
     Gravis Ultrasound support (CONFIG_GUS) [Y/n/?] n
     MPU-401 support (NOT for SB16) (CONFIG_MPU401) [Y/n/?] n
     PSS (ECHO-ADI2111) support (CONFIG_PSS) [Y/n/?] n
     Microsoft Sound System support (CONFIG_MSS) [Y/n/?] n
     Ensoniq SoundScape support (CONFIG_SSCAPE) [Y/n/?] n
     MediaTrix AudioTrix Pro support (CONFIG_TRIX) [Y/n/?] n
     Support for OPTi MAD16 and/or Mozart based cards (CONFIG_MAD16) [Y/n/?] n
     Support for Crystal CS4232 based (PnP) cards (CONFIG_CS4232) [Y/n/?] n
     Support for Turtle Beach Wave Front (Maui, Tropez) synthesizers
     ➥(CONFIG_MAUI) [Y/n/?] n
     Yamaha OPL3-SA1 audio controller (CONFIG_OPL3SA1) [Y/n/?] n
     SoftOSS software wave table engine (CONFIG_SOFTOSS) [Y/n/?] n
     FM synthesizer (YM3812/OPL-3) support (CONFIG_YM3812) [Y/n/?] y
     I/O base for Audio Excel DSP 16 220 or 240 (AEDSP16_BASE) [220]
     I/O base for SB Check from manual of the card (SBC_BASE) [220] (NEW)
     Sound Blaster IRQ Check from manual of the card (SBC_IRQ) [7] (NEW) 5
     Sound Blaster DMA 0, 1 or 3 (SBC_DMA) [1] (NEW) 1
     Sound Blaster 16 bit DMA (SB16, Jazz16, SMW) 5, 6 or 7 (use 1 for
▼   ➥8 bit cards)(SB_DMA2) [5] (NEW) 5

▼   MPU401 I/O base of SB16, Jazz16 and ES1688 Check from manual of the card
➥(SB_MPU_BASE) [330] (NEW) 300
*
* MPU401 IRQ is only required with Jazz16, SM Wave and ESS1688.
*
*
* Enter -1 to the following question if you have something else such
➥as SB16/32.
*
SB MPU401 IRQ (Jazz16, SM Wave and ES1688) Check from manual of the card
➥(SB_MPU_IRQ) [-1] (NEW) -1
I/O base for the 16 bit daughtercard of GUS 530, 604, E80 or F40
➥(GUS16_BASE) [530]
GUS 16 bit daughtercard IRQ 3, 4, 5, 7, or 9 (GUS16_IRQ) [7]
GUS DMA 0, 1 or 3 (GUS16_DMA) [3]
make[1]: Entering directory `/usr/src/linux-2.0.35/drivers/sound'
Compiling Sound Driver v 2 for Linux
rm -f configure
gcc -I/usr/src/linux-2.0.35/include -o configure configure.c
./configure fixedlocal > local.h
./configure fixeddefines > .defines
make[1]: Leaving directory `/usr/src/linux-2.0.35/drivers/sound'
Additional low level drivers (CONFIG_LOWLEVEL_SOUND) [Y/n/?] n
*
* Kernel hacking
*
Kernel profiling support (CONFIG_PROFILE) [N/y/?] n
*
* STREAMS subsystem
*
Include STREAMS subsystem (CONFIG_STREAMS) [Y/n/?] n

The linux kernel is now hopefully configured for your setup.
Check the top-level Makefile for additional configuration,
and do a 'make dep ; make clean' if you want to be sure all
the files are correctly re-made

After completing the configuration, I ran the make dep and make clean commands,
which executed without errors. Had they failed, the make process would have been
interrupted with an obvious error message.

Next I proceeded to run make zlilo. Execution of this command takes considerable time
(10–15 minutes on a modern Pentium system, 6–8 hours or more on an older, low-end
machine). If this phase completes without an error, the /vmlinuz file will be replaced
with a new version.

One possible problem you might encounter is that the resulting kernel becomes too large.
In this case, an error message is displayed. In such a case, the solution is to run make

▼   bzlilo instead of make zlilo, producing a *big* kernel image instead of a standard one.

▼ This will not adversely affect performance and will only slightly increase the kernel's memory footprint. It is not necessary to repeat the preceding steps when this error message is encountered; run `make bzlilo` and the problem will correct itself.

I had no such problems and the kernel compiled correctly. Before rebooting the system to test the new kernel, I once again ran the LISA utility and reconfigured LILO. This time, I did not specify a RAM disk for `/vmlinuz`. I continued to specify `/boot/initrd.gz` as the RAM disk image for `/vmlinuz.old`.

▲ After reset, the system rebooted successfully. I now have a fully optimized kernel for this computer.

Linux Resources on the Internet

Web Sites

> **NOTE**
>
> The Web addresses presented in this section are up to date as of May, 1999. Although the sites listed here have been in business for many years, due to the constantly changing nature of the Internet, it's possible that some of the addresses will no longer be valid by the time you read this book. In that case, you're advised to utilize one of the many search engines (for example, `http://www.altavista.com/`) to find alternative sites.

- `http://freshmeat.net/`. Contains valuable up-to-date information about Linux-related updates and fixes.
- `http://metalab.unc.edu/metalab.shtml`. MetaLab, also known as *SunSITE*, is one of the oldest servers on the Internet for downloadable software. Linux related software can be located here at `http://metalab.unc.edu/pub/Linux/!INDEX.html`.
- `http://www.apache.org/`. Home of the Apache Web server.
- `http://www.cdrom.com/`. Home of Walnut Creek CDROM, official distributors of Slackware Linux.

- `http://www.gnu.org/`. Home of the GNU project, which produced many of the best software packages used under Linux.
- `http://www.kde.org/`. Home of the K Desktop Environment.
- `http://www.kernel.org/`. The Linux Kernel Archives, the primary site of the Linux kernel source as well as many other Linux-related software packages. Note the links to many country-specific mirrors here.
- `http://www.linuxgazette.com/`. Home of the online *Linux Gazette*.
- `http://www.linuxfocus.org`. An online multilingual Linux magazine.
- `http://www.loonie.net/~eschenk/diald.html`. Home of the diald automatic dialing daemon.
- `http://web.mit.edu/kerberos/www/index.html`. Home of the Kerberos secure authentication suite.
- `http://www.ntp.org/`. Home of the Network Time Protocol and related software.
- `http://www.perl.org/`. Home of the Perl text-processing language, an essential tool for Web site builders.
- `http://www.rootshell.com`. Contains valuable information and news about security-related matters.
- `http://www.samba.org/`. Home of Samba, the Linux-based file and printer server software for Windows networks.
- `http://www.sendmail.org/`. Home of the sendmail mail server.
- `http://www.slackware.com/`. Home of the Slackware Linux distribution.

FTP Sites

> **NOTE**
>
> Traditionally, Linux kernels and other Linux software were distributed via publicly accessible FTP sites. These sites still play an important role for exchanging Linux-related software. The sites listed in this section can be accessed using the `ftp` command, and they accept anonymous logins (log on as "anonymous," using your email address as your password).

- `sunsite.unc.edu`. The venerable SunSITE archive, one of the largest and oldest FTP archives on the Internet. It can also be accessed through `http://metalab.unc.edu/metalab.shtml`.

- `tsx-11.mit.edu`. Another one of the "grand old" Internet archives. This one is operated at the Massachusetts Institute of Technology.

- `ftp.psy.uq.oz.au`. This is an Australian location of encryption-related software packages not bound by U.S. export restrictions. The `libdes` library, used with packages such as the Apache Web server to obtain secure socket support, can be found in the directory `pub/Crypto/DES`.

Newsgroups

PART
VII

APP
B

> **NOTE** When you need quick assistance with a Linux-related problem, often the best place to turn to is a Usenet newsgroup. There are a large number of newsgroups dedicated to Linux and to the software packages, network protocols, and standards discussed in this book.

- `alt.os.linux.*`. An unregulated hierarchy of alternative Linux newsgroups.

- `comp.infosystems.www.*`. A hierarchy of newsgroups related to the World Wide Web.

- `comp.lang.perl.*`. A hierarchy of newsgroups related to the Perl programming language.

- `comp.mail.sendmail`. Configuring and using sendmail.

- `comp.mail.uucp`. Mail in the UUCP environment.

- `news.*`. A hierarchy of newsgroups related to Usenet and news server administration and maintenance.

- `comp.os.linux`. A core hierarchy of Linux-related newsgroups.

- `comp.os.linux.announce`. Contains announcements important to the Linux community.

- `comp.protocols.dns.*`. A hierarchy of newsgroups related to the Domain Name System

- `comp.protocols.kerberos`. The Kerberos authentication server.

- `comp.protocols.ppp`. A discussion of the Internet Point-to-Point Protocol.
- `comp.protocols.smb`. The SMB file-sharing protocol and the Samba suite.
- `comp.protocols.tcp-ip.*`. A hierarchy of newsgroups related to the TCP/IP family of network protocols.
- `comp.protocols.time.ntp`. The Network Time Protocol.
- `comp.windows.x.*`. A hierarchy of newsgroups about the X Window System.
- `de.comp.os.linux.*`. A hierarchy of German-language Linux-related newsgroups.
- `es.comp.os.linux`. Spanish language discussions on Linux.
- `fr.comp.os.linux.*`. A hierarchy of French-language Linux-related discussions.
- `gnu.*`. A hierarchy of newsgroups related to GNU software.

Whois Databases

NOTE	These databases are for use with the Linux whois utility. By default, this utility accesses the North American registry of sites in the .com, .net, and .org domains. For other domains, you need to specify the database. For instance, when using whois to obtain contact information for the White House's Web site, you'd type the following: `whois whitehouse.gov@whois.nic.gov`

- `whois.apnic.net`. Asia Pacific IP address allocations
- `whois.arin.net`. American Registry for Internet Numbers
- `whois.nic.gov`. U.S. government
- `whois.nic.mil`. U.S. military
- `whois.ripe.net`. European IP address allocations

Linux Publications

Useful Books

Here's a list of a few books about Linux, UNIX in general, and networking that I find particularly useful. In fact, I use many of these regularly as valuable references. For additional books, `http://www.amazon.com`, `http://www.barnesandnoble.com` and `http://www.fatbrain.com` are excellent starting points.

- *CGI Programming on the World Wide Web*, by Shishir Gundavaram

  O'Reilly & Associates, Inc.

  ISBN: 1-56592-168-2

- *DNS and BIND*, by Paul Albitz and Cricket Liu

  O'Reilly & Associates, Inc.

  ISBN: 1-56592-010-4

- *Dr. Linux: The Linux Documentation Project*

  Linux System Labs

  ISBN: 1-885329-02-4

- *Essential System Administration*, by Æleen Frish

  O'Reilly & Associates, Inc.

  ISBN: 0-937175-80-3

- *Firewalls and Internet Security*, by William R. Cheswick and Steven M. Bellovin

  Addison-Wesley Publishing Company

  ISBN: 0-201-63357-4

- *HTML 3.2 & CGI Unleashed*, by John December and Mark Ginsburg
  Sams Publishing
  ISBN: 1-57521-177-7
- *Learning the UNIX Operating System*, by Grace Todino and John Strang
  O'Reilly & Associates, Inc.
  ISBN: 0-937175-16-1
- *Learning the vi Editor*, by Linda Lamb
  O'Reilly & Associates, Inc.
  ISBN: 0-937175-67-6
- *Network Protocol Handbook*, by Matthew Naugle
  McGraw-Hill, Inc.
  ISBN: 0-07-046461-8
- *Programming Perl*, by Larry Wall and Randal L. Schwartz
  O'Reilly & Associates, Inc.
  ISBN: 0-937175-64-1
- *Running Linux*, by Matt Welsh and Lar Kaufman
  O'Reilly & Associates, Inc.
  ISBN: 1-56592-151-8
- *sendmail*, by Bryan Costales with Eric Allman
  O'Reilly & Associates, Inc.
  ISBN: 1-56592-222-0
- *Special Edition Using Linux*, by Jack Tackett, Jr.
  Que
  ISBN: 0-7897-1746-8
- *Special Edition Using TCP/IP*, by John Ray
  Que
  ISBN: 0-7897-1897-9
- *TCP/IP & Related Protocols*, by Uyless Black
  McGraw-Hill, Inc.
  ISBN: 0-07-005560-2
- *TCP/IP Network Administration*, by Craig Hunt

O'Reilly & Associates, Inc.

ISBN: 0-937175-82-X

- *UNIX Unleashed*, by Robin Burk

  Sams Publishing

  ISBN: 0-672-31411-8

- *Using & Managing uucp*, by Ed Ravin, Tim O'Reilly, Dale Dougherty, and Grace Todino

  O'Reilly & Associates, Inc.

  ISBN: 1-56592-153-4

Magazines

- *The Linux Journal*

  `http://www.linuxjournal.com/`

  Self-described as "The Premier Linux Magazine," *The Linux Journal* celebrates its fifth birthday in 1999. It's an excellent resource of Linux-related information.

PART

VII

APP

C

Linux Support Organizations

The **number of organizations worldwide** that offer Linux support in one form or another is growing rapidly. Rather than presenting a complete list that's likely to become obsolete by the time this book is on store shelves, I've provided a list of the names of a few companies I have experience with.

Caldera Systems, Inc.

Maker of Caldera OpenLinux.

> http://www.calderasystems.com/
> 240 West Center Street
> Orem, UT 84057
> USA
> Phone: +1 (801) 765-4999
> Fax: +1 (801) 765-1313

Corel Corporation

Manufacturer of the WordPerfect office suite. Free Linux version for non-commercial use is available for download.

> http://linux.corel.com/
> 1600 Carling Avenue
> Ottawa, ON K1Z 8R7
> Canada
> Phone: +1 (613) 728-3733
> Fax: +1 (613) 761-9176

Dell Computer Corporation

Supplier of computer systems. Offers workstations with Linux preinstalled.

> http://www.dell.com/products/workstat/ISV/linux.htm
> One Dell Way
> Round Rock, TX 78682
> USA
> Phone: +1 (800) 999-3355 (WWW-DELL)
> Fax: +1 (800) 225-4893 (small business customers)

InfoMagic

Publisher of the outstanding Linux Developer's Resource CD-ROM set and other Linux CD-ROM kits.

> http://www.infomagic.com/
> 11950 N. Highway 89
> Flagstaff, AZ 86004
> USA
> Phone: +1 (800) 800-6613 or +1 (520) 526-9565

Linux System Labs

Publisher of Linux-related books and magazines.

> http://www.lsl.com/
> 49884 Miller Court
> Chesterfield, MI 48047
> USA
> Phone: +1 (888) 546-8988 (LINUX-88) or +1 (810) 716-1704
> Fax: +1 (810) 716-1703

Linuxcare, Inc.

Organization offering Linux support for corporations.

> http://www.linuxcare.com
> 650 Townsend Street
> San Francisco, CA 94103
> USA
> Phone: +1 (888) 546-4878 (LIN-GURU)
> Fax: +1 (415) 701-7457

Red Hat Software

Publisher of the Red Hat Linux distribution.

> http://www.redhat.com/
> 2600 Meridian Parkway
> Durham, NC 27713
> USA
> Phone: +1 (888) 733-4281 (REDHAT1) or +1 (919) 547-0012
> Fax: +1 (919) 547-0024

Specialized Systems Consultants (SSC)

Publishers of *The Linux Journal*.

> http://www.ssc.com/
> P.O. Box 55549
> Seattle, WA 98155-0549
> USA
> Phone: +1 (206) 782-7733
> Fax: +1 (206) 782-7191

Walnut Creek CD-ROM

Official distributor of the famous Slackware Linux distribution and manufacturer of other operating system toolkits.

> http://www.cdrom.com/
> 4041 Pike Lane, Suite F
> Concord, CA 94520-1207
> USA
> Phone: +1 (800) 786-9907 or +1 (925) 674-0783
> Fax: +1 (925) 674-0821

INDEX

Symbols

$ (dollar sign), system prompt, 41
& (ampersand), backgrounding commands, 39
> (greater than), redirecting output, 39
—system command-line switch, 218
/ (forward slash), root file systems, 33
\ (backslash), MS-DOS, 33
~ (tilde), Web pages (Apache server), 221

A

A (Address) record, 138
Accelerated-X, 49
access
    backup hardware, 326-327
    ownership
        assigning, 34
        files, 34
        root users, 36
    remote hosts, verifying, 121
    restrictions, 226, 295-296
    rights, assigning, 25, 34
    root users, 35
    shared directories (Samba), 375-377
    users, 396
accounting, IP (firewalls), 238-239
accounts
    news (Outlook Express), 372-374
    root
        creating, 80
        passwords, 80, 91
        security, 91-92, 399-400
    shell, security, 391
    user, 293, 296
        adding, 296-298
        creating, 80
        deleting, 296-298
        email addresses, 295
        etc/passwd files, 296
        home directories, 294
        managing, 20

names, 80
restricting interactive access, 295-296
startup shells, 295-296
switching, 89
user IDs, 86, 294
Accounts command (Tools menu), Outlook Express, 368, 371-372
active partitions, 58
adapters, dial-up, 363
Add Printer Wizard, 276, 378-380
adding
news accounts (Outlook Express), 372-374
password policies, 300-301
user accounts, 296-298
users, 89
adduser command, 90, 296-298
LISA, 90, 297-298
useradd command, 90, 296-297
Address (A) record, 138
address resolution. *See* **addresses**
addresses
Caldera Systems, Inc., 467
Corel Corporation, 467
Dell Computer Corporation, 468
DNS
address resolution, 126
AlterNIC, 128
country-level domains, 128
hierarchy, 127
InterNIC, 128
Network Solutions, 128
top-level domains, 127-128
email
harvesting, 373
user accounts, 295
etc/hosts file, 126
hacks, 287
InfoMagic, 468
IP, 70-71, 79, 109
aliasing, 114, 237-238
dynamic address assignments, 112-113
forged, 242
multiple, 109
obtaining, 153-154
portability, 112
private networks, 113
problems, 111
setting, 364-365
Linux System Labs, 468
Linuxcare, Inc., 468

local host, 71
name servers, reverse lookups, 135
netmasks, 110
Red Hat Software, 469
Specialized Systems Consultants (SSC), 469
subnets, 109-110
blocks, 112
loopback, 110
reserved, 110
Walnut Creek CD-ROM, 469
adduser command, 90, 296-298
aliasing, firewalls, 114, 237-238
allocation units (hard drives), 64
AltaVista search engine, 459
AlterNIC, 128
Amazon.com Web site, 46, 463
ampersand (&), backgrounding commands, 39
anonymous access, FTP, 215-216
Apache, 12, 217-219. *See also* **networks**
configuring, 219-221
FrontPage, Server Extensions, 380-381
Linux installation, 18
log files, 229, 315
restarting, 225
Web pages, setting up, 221-223
Web site, 459
Apache-SSL, 226
applets, Network, 363
applications. *See also* **processes; utilities**
boot loaders, 59
email, sendmail, 12, 18, 28
firewalls, 239-240
ISPs, 12-13
killing, 40
minicom
testing modems, 149-150
testing passwords, 159-160
moving, 437-438
ps command
high-memory applications, 416
processor overload, 419
security, 390
shell accounts, 391
software, 398
Trojan horses, 394
viruses, 393
Web scripts, 391-392
worms, 394
source trees, 437
suspended, 41

X, 13

X server software (X-Win), 32, 381-382

assigning

email addresses, 295

IP addresses, 112-113

permissions, unnecessary, 92

rights, 25, 34

user IDs, 294

at command, 341-342

atd daemon, 341

attachment (email), security, 400

authentication service, inetd daemon, 101

auto-answer setting (modems), 155

automation, scheduling tasks, 339

at command, 341-342

cron daemon, 340-341

crontab entry examples, 353-355

autoprobing hardware, 68, 73-74

B

backbone providers, 108

backbone routers, 108

backdoors, variables, 347

background printing, 268-269

backgrounding

applications, suspended 41

commands, & (ampersand), 39

backing up. *See* **backups**

backquote character (shell scripts), 351

backslash (\), MS-DOS, 33

Backspace key, 41

backups

automatic, 20

backup systems, 21

cartridge drives, 326

CD-Recordable drives, 325

CD-RW drives, 325

cp command, 330

cpio command, 330-331

encryption, des command, 334-335

file systems, 327

files, 323-325

frequency, 333

incremental, 333-334

kernel, booting, 423

Linux drivers, 326

media rotation, 333

networks, 335-336

planning, 321-323

restoring files, 331-332

shell script example, 356

tape drives, 325, 330

tar command, 327-329

compressed files, 328, 331

cpio command comparison, 330

filename extensions, 331

hard drives, 327

restoring files, 332

Barnes and Noble Web site, 46, 463

bash shell, 37

COMMAND.COM comparison, 37-40

commands, 37-39

parameters, 347

predefined variables, 347-348

scripts, conditional execution, 343-344

Basic Input Output System. *See* **BIOS**

basis series (software), 78

beep codes (BIOS), 411

Berkeley sockets (UNIX), 11

Berkeley Standard Distribution (BSD), 11

bg command, 41

BIOS (Basic Input Output System), 59

beep codes, 411

configuration, replacing hard drives, 434

diagnostic codes, 411-412

flash memory chips, 410-411

settings, 414

troubleshooting example, 428

blank passwords, 91

block devices, 30

books

CGI Programming on the World Wide Web, 463

DNS and BIND, 125, 463

Dr. Linux: The Linux Documentation Project, 463

Essential System Administration, 463

Firewalls and Internet Security, 463

HTML 3.2 & CGI Unleashed, 464

Learning the UNIX Operating System, 23, 464

Learning the vi Editor, 46, 464

Network Protocol Handbook, 464

Programming Perl, 464

Running Linux, 464

sendmail, 464

Special Edition Using Linux, 464

Special Edition Using TCP/IP, 464

TCP/IP & Related Protocols, 103, 464

TCP/IP Network Administration, 465

UNIX Unleashed, 465
Using and Managing uucp, 465
boot CD-ROMs, 21, 66, 72
boot disks, 21, 67, 72
boot loaders, 59
boot managers
    LILO, 59-60
        LISA, 80- 82
            refreshing configuration, 437
            troubleshooting, 415
    OS/2, 59
boot sectors, 59
boot signatures, 59
booting, 66. *See also* **loading; running**
    BIOS, 59, 434
    boot CD-ROMs, 21, 66, 72
    boot loaders, 59
    floppy disks
        boot disks, 21, 67, 72
        boot sectors, 59
        boot signatures, 59
        naked kernel images, 423-424
        rescue disks, 424
    init
        configuration files, 95-96
        runlevels, 96
    installation disks, 424
    kernel
        backup image, 423
        old kernel boot, 446-448
        replacing hard drives, 433
        troubleshooting, 415
    LILO, 59-60
        LISA, 80- 82
            refreshing configuration, 437
            troubleshooting, 415
    LOADLIN.EXE, 67-68, 72
    master boot record, 59
    notification email (dmesg command), 310
    operating systems, 59-60
    OS/2, 59
    partition table, 60
    pre-boot troubleshooting, 405
        observation, 406
        remote access, 407
    rebooting, 422-423
    startup services, selecting, 82
bootps, inetd daemon, 101
Bourne Again Shell. *See* **bash shell**
Bourne shell, 37

Bourne, Steve, 37
brute force attacks (passwords), 300
BSD (Berkeley Standard Distribution), 11
buffers, ring (kernel), 310
burning smells, 408

C

C, 352-353
    The C Programming Language, 352
    no-shell shells script, 357-358
    password generation script, 358-359
C shell, 37
cable connectors, 413
cable modems, 257-258
    firewalls, 258
    security, 397
Caldera OpenLinux. *See* **OpenLinux**
Caldera Systems, Inc., 467
Canonical name (CNAME) record, 138
cards
    diagnostic, 411
    motherboards, troubleshooting, 409
Carrier Detect settings (modems), 155
Carrier Sense Multiple Access/Collision Detect
  (CMSA/CD), 104
cartridge drives, 326
CD-Recordable (CD-R) drives, 325
CD-ROMs
    booting, 21, 66, 72
    CD-ROM drives, troubleshooting, 428
    loading, 66, 72
CD-RW (rewritable) drives, 325
certificates, 227
Certification Authority (CA), 227
CGI
    CGI Programming on the World Wide Web, 463
    HTML 3.2 & CGI Unleashed, 464
    script location, 228
Change LISA Setup dialog box, 73
character devices, 30
chat utility (pppd daemon), 151
chfn command, Comment fields (users), 89
chgrp command, 93-94
chips, memory, 410-411, 431-432
chmod command
    mnemonic form, 94
    numeric form, 93-94

Perl files, 352
recursive mode, 94
chown command, 93-94
chsh command, setting login shells, 89
CIAC (Computer Incident Advisory Capability)
Web site
bogus warnings, 402
software defects, 398
classes, records (zone files), 137
cleaning log files, 355
clients
communications, managing, 20
X, 48
clocks
CMOS, 282
hwclock command, 283
system time, 282
configuration (LISA), 79
clusters (hard drives), 64
CMOS clocks, 282
hwclock command, 283
system time, 282
CMSA/CD (Carrier Sense Multiple
Access/Collision Detect), 104
CNAME (Canonical name) record, 138
code pages, recompiling kernels, 455
command interpreters. *See* **shells**
command lines (shells), 36
command mode (vi), 45-46
command processors. *See* **shells**
command-line tools, 48
COMMAND.COM (MS-DOS), 36-40
commands. *See also* **daemons; scripts**
adduser, 90, 296-298
anonymous FTP access, 216
at, 341-342
bash shell, 37-39
bg , 41
chfn, editing Comment fields (users), 89
chgrp, 93-94
chmod
mnemonic form, 94
numeric form, 93-94
Perl files, 352
recursive mode, 94
chown, 93-94
chsh, setting login shell, 89
compress, 328
cp, 330

cpio, 330-331, 438
crontab, 341
date, 282
des, encrypting files, 334-335
df, 407, 417
dmesg, 407
boot notification email, 310
replacing hard drives, 434
viewing kernel messages, 310
edquota, 302
elif, 348
fg, 41
find, 39
free, 407, 415-416
ftp, 211, 460
getty, 154-156
gpasswd, setting groups, 89
grep, 38, 313
groups, listing user groups, 89
gzip
errors, 331
filename extensions, 331
PK-ZIP comparison, 328
head, 313
hostname, 129
hwclock, 283
ifconfig, 119
info, 44
ipfwadm
options, 244-247
policy keywords, 245
startup files, 246
kill
HUP (hang-up) signal, 29
KILL signal, 29-30
PID, 29
killall, inetd configuration files, 101
last, wtmp files, 314
lastlog, 315
ldconfig -v, 420
lilo, -r option, 425
lpq, 269
lpr, 269
ls -a, 194
mail command, 171
man, 42-43
mgetty, 158-159
mount, 33
MS-DOS, 37-38

named
  configuring name servers, 134
  root cache, 136
  root domains, 135
  setting configuration files, 134-135
  testing configuration files, 139-142
net time, synchronization, 288
net use, 274-276, 376-377
net view, 274
netstat, 120
newaliases, 221
newgrp, setting groups, 89
nslookup, 129, 140-142
ntpdate, synchronization, 287-288
output, redirecting, 39, 348
passwd, setting passwords, 89
ping, 121, 161
ps, 26, 97
  high-memory applications, 416
  processor overload, 419
  ps ajx, 26-27
  ps ax, 97-98
  ps j, 26
quota, 302
recompiling kernels, 448
  make bzlilo, 457
  make clean, 457
  make config, 449
  make dep, 457
  make zlilo, 457
repquota, 302
route, 120, 255
set type, 140
setterm, 406
shells, backgrounding, 39
smbmount, 278
su, switching accounts, 89
swapoff, 422
tac, 313
tail, 313
tar, 327-329
  compressed files, 328, 331
  cpio command comparison, 330
  filename extensions, 331
  hard disks, 327
  moving user data files, 438
  restoring files, 332
telnet, HTTP, 213
time, MS-DOS, 282

Tools menu (Outlook Express), Accounts, 368,
  371-372
traceroute, 121, 61
umask, user access, 396
unset, 346
uptime, 408, 418
useradd, 90, 296-297
userdel, 296-297
uucico, 177
uugetty, 156-157
uustat, 190
vi editor, 45-46
who, utmp files, 314
whois, 130-133
Comment fields
  chfn command, 89
  users, 87
components, swapping, 412-413
compress command, 328
compressing files
  compress command, 328
  gzip command, 328, 331
Computer Incident Advisory Capability (CIAC)
  Web site
  bogus warnings, 402
  software defects, 398
conditional execution, shell scripts, 343-344
conduits (WANs), 105
conf files (Apache server), 220
configuration, kernel, 445
configuration files
  Apache server, 220
  inetd, 99-101
  init, 95-96
configuring. *See also* **selecting**
  Apache server, 219-221
  configuration files, backups, 324
  diald (dialer daemon), 162-163
  firewalls, 243-247
    ipfwadm command, 244-247
    kernel configuration, 244
  getty command, 155-156
  hardware
    installation, 58
    LISA, 73-75
    manually, 69
  INN package (Caldera OpenLinux), 205
  LILO (LISA), 80-82, 446-448
  mouse (LISA), 79

name servers
  named command, 134
  reverse lookups, 135
  root cache, 136
  root domains, 135
  setting named configuration files, 134-135
  testing named configuration files, 139-142
  zone files, 137-139
network parameters, 69-71
  DNS servers, 71, 79
  hardware drivers, 70
  high-level protocols, 70
  HTTP, 70
  IP, 70-71, 79
  IPX, 70
  layers, 70
  LISA, 78-79
  local host address, 71
  low-level protocols, 70
  NetBIOS, 70
  network cards, 70
  NIS, 79
  TCP, 70
news servers, 201-202
NTP daemon, 285-286
  hacks, 287
  standalone servers, 286-287
Outlook Express, 367-371
  connection type, 370
  editing existing configuration, 371
  Internet Connection Wizard, 368
  Internet Mail Logon dialog box, 370
printers (LISA), 79
routers
  external, 250-252
  ISDN, 257
  segmented networks, 252-255
Samba
  configuration files, 263-264
  global configuration settings, 264-266
  shared directories configuration settings,
    267-268
  shared printers settings, 268-271
sendmail program, 178-182
  m4 macro language, 180
  message filtering, 181-182
  rulesets, 179
  sendmail.cf file, 179-180
  test system, 183-190
  UUCP, 188-191

startup files (LISA), 97-98
syslogd daemon, 307-309
time (LISA), 79
connections. *See also* **Internet; modems; networks**
  dial-up, security, 386-387
  Internet, installation, 17
  remote
    security, 389
    troubleshooting systems, 407
connectors
  cable, 413
  IDC, 414
  motherboards, troubleshooting, 409
  power, 413
consoles, virtual, 40-41
cooperative operating systems, 25-26
copying system files, 435-436. *See also* **moving**
copyleft license, 10
Corel Corporation, 467
corruption, file (hard drives), 421-422
cost, Linux/UNIX comparison, 10
cp command, 330
cpio command, 330-331, 438
CPUs
  overload, 418-419
  replacing, 431-432
  troubleshooting, 410
crashes, 14, 21
**create mode parameter (Samba configuration),
  267**
cron daemon
  crontab entries, 340-341
    editing, 341
    examples, 353-355
  format, 340
  scheduling tasks, 340-341
crontab command, 341
crontab entries (cron daemon), 340-341
  editing, 341
  examples, 353-355
crontab utility, 190
cross-posting (newsgroups), 198
ctlinnd program, 206
Ctrl+C, 40
Ctrl+D, 41
Ctrl+Z, 41
customizing kernels, 83, 434

D

daemons. *See also* **commands; scripts**
atd, at command, 341
cron
crontab entries, 340-341
examples, 353-355
format, 340
scheduling tasks, 340-341
defined, 97
diald
configuring, 162-163
Web site, 152, 460
inetd, 29, 99
authentication service, 101
bootps, 101
configuration files, 99-101
finger service, 101
Gopher, 100
monitoring shell script example, 356-357
POP3 protocol, 101
reinitializing, 102
Telnet, 99
TFTP, 101
klogd, 310
named
configuring name servers, 134
root cache, 136
root domains, 135
setting configuration files, 134-135
testing configuration files, 139-142
NTP
configuring, 285-286
downloading, 285
hacks, 287
installing, 284-285
ntpdate command, 287-288
standalone servers, 286-287
pppd, 150
chat utility, 151
crtscts option, 158
incoming connections, 157-158
modem option, 158
passive option, 158
setting default routes, 152-153
silent option, 158
testing, 160, 162
sendmail, 28

syslogd, 305
configuring, 307-309
flushing log files, 309
network logging option, 306-307
OpenLinux, 309
running, 306
data
hard drives, installation issues, 56
headers (IP), 109
Internet, routing, 107-108
user, moving, 438
databases, whois, 462
date command, MS-DOS, 282
Date header (email), 175
default document, Web pages, 221
defaults, recompiling kernels, 449
Del key, 41
deleting
user accounts, 296-298
users, userdel command, 296-297
variables, unset command, 346
delivery process (email), 169-173
MTAs (mail transport agents), 172
MUAs (mail user agents), 171-172
Dell Computer Corporation, 468
demand-dial capability, modems, 151-152
denial of service attacks, 100
des command, encrypting files, 334-335
desktops, X, 13
detecting hardware, 68-69
autoprobing, 68, 73-74
plug and play, 68
develop series (software), 78
device names, tape drives, 330
devices. *See also* **hardware**
block, 30
character, 30
device dependence/independence, 30
identifying, 31
list, 31-32
df command, 407, 417
DHCP (Dynamic Host Configuration Protocol), 258
diagnosing crashes, 21
diagnostics. *See* **troubleshooting**
diagnostic codes (BIOS), 411-412
dial-up adapters, 363
dial-up security
testing, 386-387
Windows comparison, 387

diald (dialer daemon), 152
  configuring, 162-163
  download site, 152
  Web site, 460
dialing, modems, 151, 160-162
dialog boxes
  Change LISA Setup, 73
  Internet Mail Logon (Outlook Explorer), 370
directories
  anonymous FTP access, 216
  CGI scripts, 228
  home, 87, 294
  newsgroups, 201
  ownership, 92
  permissions, 92
  shared
    net use command, 376
    passwords, 376-377
    Samba, 267-268, 375-377
    UNC pathnames, 376
  URLs, 222
DirectoryIndex configuration entry, 222
disabling blank screen option, 406
disk space, quotas, 302-303
disks. *See* **floppy disks; hard drives**
distributions
  GNU Public License, 10
  OpenLinux
    installation, 71-83
    LISA, 71-79
  rights, 10
DLLs (dynamic load libraries), 420
dmesg command, 407
  boot notification email, 310
  replacing hard drives, 434
  viewing kernel messages, 310
DNS (domain name system), 71, 113, 125
  address resolution, 126
  AlterNIC, 128
  DNS and BIND, 125, 463
  domains
    Canadian domain names information Web site,
      133
    checking existing names, 131-133
    country-level, 128, 133
    RIPE Web site, 133
    root, 135
    selecting names, 131
    top-level, 127-128
    U.S. domain names information Web site, 133
  dynamic address assignments, 113
  hierarchy, 127
  hostname command, 129
  InterNIC, 128, 132-133
  ISPs, registering domain names, 133
  Network Solutions, 128
  nslookup command, 129, 140-142
  servers, 71
    LISA, 79
    routers, 366-367
  virtual hosts, 223
  whois command, 130-133
DNS and BIND, 125, 463
documents, here, 350-351
doku series (software), 78
dollar sign ($), system prompt, 41
domain name system. *See* **DNS**
domain names. *See* **names**
domains. *See* **DNS**
DOS, environment variables, 344-345
dotted notation (IP addresses), 109
downloading
  FrontPage Server Extensions, 381
  newsgroups, 198
  NTP daemon, 285
Dr. Linux: The Linux Documentation Project, **463**
drivers
  hardware, network configuration, 70
  Kernel Module Manager (LISA), loading, 74-75
  Linux, backup hardware, 326
  network, recompiling kernels, 452
  printer, installing (Samba), 377-380
  SCSI, recompiling kernels, 452-453
drives. *See also* **specific drive types**
  experimental, recompiling kernels, 449
  incomplete, recompiling kernels, 449
  partitions, 33-34
  shared drives, Windows access (Samba), 275
dual boot computers, 16
**Dynamic Host Configuration Protocol (DHCP),
  258**
dynamic load libraries (DLL)s, 420

E

e2fs (Ext-2 File System), 33, 64, 421, 455
e2fsck utility, 421

ed (line editor), 47
editing
   Comment fields, chfn command, 89
   crontab entries, 341
   etc/passwd files, 296
   files
      ownership, 93-94
      permissions, 93-94
      startup, 96
      text, 44-47
   inetd, configuration files, 99-101
   network status, ifconfig command, 119
   Outlook Express, configuration, 371
   root accounts, 35
   source code, 14-15
Editing Macros (Emacs), 47
editors
   elvis, 44
   Emacs, 47
   line, 45-47
   Pico, 47
   text, 44
   vi, 44-46
   vim, 44
edquota command, 302
educating users, 399, 402
electricity, static, 432
elif command, 348
elvis editor, 44
Emacs (Editing Macros), 47
email
   addresses, user accounts, 295
   attachments, security, 400
   bogus warnings, 401
      Computer Incident Advisory Capability
         (CIAC) Web site, 402
      educating users, 402
   boot notification (dmesg command), 310
   etc/aliases file, 177
   forwarding, 177
   harvesting, 373
   headers, 175
   mail servers, delivery process, 169-173
   mailing lists, 194-196
      etc/aliases, 195
      .forward file, 194-195
      list manager programs, 195-196
      requirements, 194
   message filtering, 182, 187-188

   MIME, 122
   Outlook Express
      configuring, 367-371
      connection type, 370
      editing existing configuration, 371
      Internet Connection Wizard, 368
      Internet Mail Logon dialog box, 370
   Pine, 47
   POP3 protocol, 101, 118, 367
   RFC-822, 121
   servers, sendmail, 12, 28, 169, 172-173, 177
   SMTP (Simple Mail Transfer Protocol), 118,
      173-174, 367
   spam, 182-183, 187-188
   UUCP, 122
employee security concerns, 390
enabling PPP, 150-151
encrypted passwords
   Samba configuration, 265-266
   Samba support, 271-273
      SMB passwords, 272-273
      Windows NT compatibility, 271-272
encryption, 299
   backups, 334-335
   brute force attacks, 300
   one-way, 299-300
   salting, 300
   software, Australian FTP site, 461
   SSL, 227
   vocabulary attacks, 300
end of file (EOF), 351
end-of-line conventions, 42
environment variables, 344-345
errors. *See also* **crashes**
   gzip command, 331
   standard, redirecting 348-349
Essential System Administration, **463**
etc directory, Apache server, 218
etc/aliases file, 177, 195
etc/group files (group information), 88-89
etc/hosts file, 126. *See also* DNS
etc/named.boot file. *See* **named command**
etc/named.conf file. *See* **named command**
etc/passwd files (user information), 86-87
   editing, 296
   example, 87
   user accounts, 296
etc/printcap file, 268
etc/resolv.conf file, 128-129
etc/shells file, 87

Ethernet
    CSMA/CD, 104
    interfaces, virtual hosts, 225
execute permissions, 92
executing shell scripts
    bash shell parameters, 347
    bash shell predefined variables, 347-348
    conditional execution, 343-344
    variables, 344-347
expressions, regular (Perl), 352
Ext-2 File System (e2fs), 33, 64, 421, 455
Extended File System, recompiling kernels, 455
extensions, 331
external routers. *See* **routers**
external synchronization, 282

F

facility identifiers (log messages), 307
fans
    overheating, 435
    troubleshooting, 409
FAT(file allocation table) file system, 34, 63
FAT16 file system, 64
FAT32 file system, 64
fatbrain.com Web site, 463
fax servers, mgetty+sendfax, 158-159
fdisk (LISA), 76
fg command, 41
fields
    Comment
        editing, 89
        users, 87
    record class, 137
    record name, 137
    record type, 137-138
file allocation table file system (FAT file system),
    34, 63,
file formats, Web content, 211
file systems
    backup hardware, 327
    Extended File System, 455
    FAT file system, 34, 63
    FAT16file system, 64
    FAT32 file system, 64
    hierarchy, 32
    HPFS, 64

    Linux recognition, 32
    Minix, 455
    mounting, 32-34
    NTFS, 64
    /proc, 455
    read-only, 34
    root, 32-33
    second extended file system, 33, 64, 421, 455
    UMSDOS, 34, 63-65, 75
File Transfer Protocol. See FTP
filename extensions, 331
files
    backups, 323
    compressing
        compress command, 328
        gzip command, 328, 331
    configuration
        backups, 324
        inetd, 99-101
    configuration (named)
        setting, 134-135
        testing, 139-142
    customizations, backups, 324-325
    drives, partitions, 33-34
    etc/aliases file, 177, 195
    etc/hosts, 126
    etc/passwd, user accounts, 296
    etc/printcap, 268
    etc/resolv.conf, 128-129
    etc/shells, 87
    file systems, 25, 63
        backup hardware, 327
        Extended File System, 455
        FAT file system, 34, 63
        FAT16file system, 64
        FAT32 file system, 64
        hierarchy, 32
        HPFS, 64
        Linux recognition, 32
        Minix, 455
        mounting, 32-34
        NTFS, 64
        /proc, 455
        read-only, 34
        root, 32-33
        second extended file system,33, 64, 421, 455
        UMSDOS, 34, 63-65, 75
    .forward file, 177, 194-195
    group information, 88-89
    hard drives, corruption, 421-422

hidden
  MS-DOS, 39-40
  UNIX, 39-40
  viewing, 194
init, runlevels, 96
location, searching, 39
lock, 156
log, 305-306
  cleaning, 355
  flushing, 309
  INN, 316
  lastlog, 315
  monitoring, 313
  processing, 313
  reading, 311-312
  rotating, 316-317, 355
  test system example, 317
  transfer, 315
  utmp, 314-315
  UUCP, 315
  Web servers, 315
  wtmp, 314-315
ownership, 34, 92-94
password file (Samba), 273
permissions
  editing, 93-94
  execute, 92
  group, 92
  read, 92
  user, 92
  world, 92
  write, 92
restoring, 331-332
root cache, 136
root file systems, 32-33
Samba configuration file, 263-264
  global section, 264-266
  homes section, 267
  shared printers, 268-271
sendmail.cf, 179-180, 185-186
shadow password, 300-301
startup
  editing, 96
  init, 95-96
  LISA, 97-98
swap, 427-428
system, moving, 435-436
text
  editing, 44-47
  searching, 38

user
  backups, 323-324
  information, 86-87
  data, moving, 438
Web pages, Apache server, 221
zone, 137
  (name servers), 134
  records, 137-138
  test system examples, 138-139
filtering email messages, 182, 187-188
find command, 39
finger service, inetd daemon, 101
firewalls, 235-236, 399. *See also* **routers**
  aliasing, 237-238
  application support, 239-240
  cable modems, 258
  configuring, 243-247
  dial-up systems, 240
  difficulties, 240-241
  external routers, 256
  Firewalls and Internet Security, 463
  IP accounting, 238-239
  ipfwadm command
    options, 244-247
    policy keywords, 245
    startup files, 246
  kernel configuration, 244
  kernel features, 12
  Linux installation, 18
  packet filtering, 236-237
  recompiling kernels, 451
Firewalls and Internet Security, **463**
flash memory chips
  recovering, 410-411
  upgrading, 410
floppy disks
  booting
    boot disks, 21, 67, 72
    boot sectors, 59
    boot signatures, 59
    naked kernel images, 423-424
    rescue disks, 424
  configuration files, 324
flushing log files, 309
foregrounding applications, suspended, 41
formatting partitions (LISA), 77
forms (Web servers), processing, 227-229
forward file, 177, 194-195
forward slash (/), root file systems, 33
forwarding email, 177

free command, 407, 415-416
freshmeat.net Web site, 459
From line (email headers), 175
FrontPage, Server Extensions
    Apache, 380-381
    installing, 381
FTP (File Transfer Protocol), 13, 118, 212
    Linux installation, 18
    setting up service, 214
        anonymous access, 215-216
        installing server, 214
        Internet superserver, 214
        server management, 216
    transfer log files, 315
    URLs, 211
ftp command, 211, 460
FTP sites. *See* **sites**
ftpaccess file, 215

G

gateways, network, 365-366
getty command, 154
    configuring, 155-156
    mgetty command, 158-159
    uugetty command, 156-157
GIF, 210
global configuration settings (Samba), 264-266
    logging, 265
    password encryption, 265
    printing, 266
    security, 264-265
    system identification, 264
    test system example, 266
GNU project Web site, 460
GNU Public License, 10
Gopher, inetd daemon, 100
gpasswd command, setting groups, 89
graphical user interfaces (GUIs), 48
graphical utilities, command-line tools comparison, 48
greater than (>), redirecting output, 39
Greenwich Mean Time (UTC), selecting, 79
grep command, 38, 313
groups. *See also* **users**
    gpasswd command, 89
    group information files, 88-89
    group numbers, users, 86
    listing users, 89
    permissions, 88, 92
    setting users, 89
groups command, listing user groups, 89
guest account parameter (Samba configuration), 265
GUIs (graphical user interfaces), 48
gzip command
    errors, 331
    filename extensions, 331
    PK-ZIP comparison, 328

H

hackers, 85
hacks, NTP servers, 287
hang-up (HUP) signal, kill command, 29
Hangup on DTR settings (modems), 155
hard drives
    clusters, 64
    errors, 420
        e2fsck utility, 421
        file corruption, 421-422
        physical defects, 420-421
    installation, existing data, 56
    insufficient space, 416-417
    master boot record, 59
    partitions, 58
        active, 58
        e2fs, 64
        FAT file system, 63
        FAT16 file system, 64
        FAT32 file system, 64
        formatting, 77
        HPFS, 64
        LISA, 75-77
        logical, 63
        MS-DOS, 62
        NTFS, 64
        partition managers, 59
        partition table, 60
        partitioning schemes, 55, 60, 63-66
        repartitioning utilities, 63, 75
        root, 77
        single, 60
        swap, 60-62, 65, 76

replacing, 432-434
  BIOS configuration, 434
  bootable kernels, 433
  compatibility issues, 433
  example, 439-440
  kernel issues, 434
  single-user configuration, 433-434
tar command, 327
troubleshooting example, 424-425
UMSDOS file system, 63-65, 75
virtual memory, 60-62, 65, 76
hardware. *See also* **devices**
autoprobing, 68, 73-74
configuration
  installation, 58
  LISA, 73-75
  manual, 69
  recompiling kernels, 449
detecting, 68-69
devices
  block, 30
  character, 30
  device dependence/independence, 30
  identifying, 31
  list, 31-32
drivers, network configuration, 70
hard drives, replacing, 432-434, 439-440
heat issues, 435
inventory, installation, 57
motherboards, replacing, 431-432, 438-439
network cards, configuration, 70
operating systems, managing, 24-25
peripherals, replacing, 434
plug and play, 68
troubleshooting, 408
  beep codes (BIOS), 411
  BIOS settings, 414
  cable connectors, 413
  cards, 409
  CD-ROM drives, 428
  connectors, 409
  diagnostic codes (BIOS), 411-412
  fans, 409
  flash memory chips, 410-411
  hard drives, 420-425
  IDC connectors, 414
  memory chips, 410
  motherboards, 409-410, 428
  power connectors, 413

power supplies, 408-409
processors, 410, 418-419
swapping components, 412-413
tape drives, 426-427
harvesting email addresses, 373
head command, 313
headers
email, 175
IP, 109
heat issues (hardware), 435
help
BIOS
  beep codes, 411
  diagnostic codes, 411-412
  flash memory chips, 410-411
  settings, 414
  troubleshooting example, 428
booting, 422-423
  backup kernel image, 423
  floppy disks, 423-424
  installation disks, 424
burning smells/smoke, 408
cable connectors, 413
The C Programming Language, 352
CD-ROM drives, 428
CGI Programming on the World Wide Web, 463
DLLs, 420
DNS and BIND, 125, 463
Dr. Linux: The Linux Documentation Project, 463
Essential System Administration, 463
Firewalls and Internet Security, 463
hard drives, 420
  e2fsck utility, 421
  file corruption, 421-422
  physical defects, 420-421
  troubleshooting example, 424-425
HTML 3.2 & CGI Unleashed, 464
IDC connectors, 414
insufficient disk space, 416-417
intermittent problems, 413-414
kernel panics, 422
Learning the UNIX Operating System, 464
Learning the vi Editor, 464
The Linux Journal, 469
low memory, 415-416
man pages, 42
  etc/resolv.conf file, 129
  navigating, 42
  organization, 43

Network Protocol Handbook, 464
newsgroups, listing, 461-462
power connectors, 413
processor overload, 418-419
Programming Perl, 464
recompiling kernels, 449
Running Linux, 464
sendmail, 464
Special Edition Using Linux, 464
Special Edition Using TCP/IP, 464
swapping components, 412-413
TCP/IP & Related Protocols, 103, 464
TCP/IP Network Administration, 465
Texinfo pages, 44
troubleshooting
    cards, 409
    connectors, 409
    df command, 407, 417
    disabling blank screen option, 406
    dmesg command, 407
    fans, 409
    free command, 407, 415-416
    hardware, 408
    kernel, 415
    LILO, 415
    memory chips, 410
    motherboards, 409-410, 428
    observation, 406
    power supplies, 408-409
    pre-boot, 405
    processors, 410
    remote access, 407
    swap files, troubleshooting, 427-428
    tape drives, troubleshooting, 426-427
    uptime command, 408, 418
UNIX Unleashed, 465
Using and Managing uucp, 465
whois databases, 462
here documents, 350-351
hidden files
    MS-DOS, 39-40
    UNIX, 39-40
    viewing, 194
hierarchies
    newsgroups, 198
    processes, 26-28
High Performance File System (HPFS), 64

history
    Linus Torvalds, 10
    system development, 10-11
hoaxes, 401-402
home directories, 87, 294
home pages. *See* **sites**
hostname command, 129
hostnames
    fully qualified, 126
    hostname command, 129
hosts
    ping command, 121
    synchronization, 281
    traceroute command, 121
hosts allow parameter (Samba configuration), 265
HPFS (High Performance File System), 64
htaccess file, 226
HTML (Hypertext Markup Language), 122, 210
    forms, 227
    HTML 3.2 & CGI Unleashed, 464
    SGML, 122
***HTML 3.2 & CGI Unleashed*, 464**
http, 211-213
HTTP (Hypertext Transfer Protocol), 70, 118
httpd, 217
httpd.conf, 220
HTTPS, 213
HUP (hang-up) signal
    kill command, 29
    reinitializing inetd, 102
hwclock command, 283
Hypertext Markup Language. *See* **HTML**
Hypertext Transfer Protocol (HTTP), 70, 118

I

IANA (Internet Assigned Numbers Authority) Web site, 122
ICMP (Internet Control Message Protocol), 117
IDC connectors, 414
IDE devices, recompiling kernels, 450
identifiers
    account, users, 86
    facility (log messages), 307
    priority (log messages), 308
identifying devices, 31
IDs, users. *See* **users**
ifconfig command, 119, 224

implementations (X), 49
IN class (zone file records), 137
incoming connections, 154
    getty command, 154-156
    mgetty command, 158-159
    pppd daemon, 157-158
    uugetty command, 156-157
incremental backups, 333-334
inetd, 99, 215
    authentication service, 101
    bootps, 101
    configuration files
        editing, 99-101
        killall command, 101
    finger service, 101
    Gopher, 100
    HUP, reinitializing, 102
    POP3 protocol, 101
    Telnet, 99
    TFTP, 101
inetd daemon, 29, 356-357
info command, 44
InfoMagic, 468
init, 27
    booting, 95
    configuration files, 95-96
    runlevels, 96
INN package (Caldera OpenLinux), 201-202
    configuring to start automatically, 205
    log files, 316
    managing, 206
input, standard, 348
input mode (vi), 46
installation, 15, 55
    dual boot computers, 16
    email servers, 18
    firewalls, 18
    hard drives, 58
        e2fs, 64
        existing data, 56
        FAT file system, 63
        FAT16 file system, 64
        FAT32 file system, 64
        HPFS, 64
        logical partitions, 63
        MS-DOS partitions, 62
        NTFS, 64
        partitioning schemes, 55, 60, 63-66
        partitions, 58
        repartitioning utilities, 63, 75

        single partitions, 60
        swap partitions, 60-62, 65
        UMSDOS file system, 63-65, 75
    hardware
        configuring, 58, 73-75
        inventory, 57
    Internet connection, 17
    kernel, recompiling, 16
    LISA, 71-72
        autoprobing, 73-74
        Change LISA Setup dialog box, 73
        fdisk, 76
        formatting partitions, 77
        hardware configuration, 73-75
        Kernel Module Manager, 74-75
        LILO configuration, 80-82
        loading configurations, 82
        mouse configuration, 79
        network configuration, 78-79
        partitioning, 75-76
        previous configurations, 73
        printer configuration, 79
        root accounts, 80
        saving configurations, 82
        selecting root partitions, 77
        software packages, 76-78
        startup services configuration, 82
        supported languages, 72
        swap partitions, 76
        time configuration, 79
        time zone configuration, 79
        user accounts, 80
    network configuration, 69-71
        DNS servers, 71, 79
        hardware drivers, 70
        high-level protocols, 70
        HTTP, 70
        IP, 70-71, 79
        IPX, 70
        layers, 70
        local host address, 71
        low-level protocols, 70
        NetBIOS, 70
        network cards, 70
        NIS, 79
        TCP, 70
    newsgroups, 18
    OpenLinux, 71-83
    planning, 55-58
    routers, 19

Samba, 19
security, 16-17
software, 69
synchronizing computer clocks, 19
Web servers, 18
installation disks, booting, 424
installing
FrontPage Server Extensions, 381
NTP daemon, 284-285
printers, Samba, 377-380
routers
cable modems, 257-258
ISDN, 256
shadow password suites, 301-302
Integrated Services Digital Network (ISDN), 256-257, 454
interfaces
ifconfig command, 119
netstat command, 120
interfaces parameter (Samba configuration), 265
intermittent system problems, 413-414
Internet. *See also* **WWW**
authentication service, 101
bootps, 101
connectivity, Linux installation, 17
Apache server, 217-223
file formats, 210-211
FTP, 211-216
HTTP, 212-213
secure sockets, 213
URLs, 211
Web browsers, 209
Web servers, 209, 223-229
DHCP, 258
DNS, 125
address resolution, 126
AlterNIC, 128
Canadian domain names information Web site, 133
checking existing domain names, 131-133
country-level domains, 128, 133
hierarchy, 127
hostname command, 129, 140-142
InterNIC, 128, 132-133
Network Solutions, 128
registering domain names, 132-133
RIPE Web site, 133
root domains, 135
selecting domain names, 131
top-level domains, 127-128

U.S. domain names information Web site, 133
whois command, 130-133
domain names, 17
etc/hosts file, 126
etc/resolv.conf file, 128-129
finger service, 101
firewalls, 235-236, 399
aliasing, 114, 237-238
application support, 239-240
cable modems, 258
configuring, 243-247
dial-up systems, 240
difficulties, 240-241
external routers, 256
IP accounting, 238-239
kernel configuration, 244
kernel features, 12
Linux installation, 18
packet filtering, 236-237
recompiling kernels, 451
FTP, 13, 18, 118
Gopher, 100
hackers, 85
help, TCP/IP and Related Protocols, 103
hostnames, fully qualified, 126
HTML, 122
HTTP, 118
IANA Web site, 122
ICMP, 117
inetd, 29, 99
configuration files, 99-101
reinitializing, 102
IP, 103
addresses, 109-112, 153-154
aliasing, 114, 237-238
dotted notation, 109
dynamic address assignments, 112-113
headers, 109
netmasks, 110
networking, 12, 451
private networks, 113
subnet blocks, 112
subnets, 109-110
ISPs, registering domain names, 133
kernel features, 12
LANs
Ethernet, 104
kernel features, 12
security, 388-389
MIME, 122

NetBIOS, 242
NetWare, 13
newsgroups, 18
NNTP, 118
PLIP, 116
POP3 protocol, 101, 118, 367
PPP, 17, 116
protocols
    application-level connectivity, 116-117
    connectionless, 116-117
    development, 115
    diversity, 114
    modems, 115-116
    multiple layers, 118
    RFCs (Request for Comments), 115
providers, 108
RFC-822, 121
routers, 12, 105-106, 249-250
    backbone, 108
    cable modems, 257-258
    default routes, 152-153
    DNS servers, 366-367
    external, 164, 250-256
    IP addresses, 364-365
    IP forwarding, 153
    ISDN, 256-257
    ISPs, 108
    Linux installation, 19
    network gateways, 365-366
    route command, 120, 255
    routing data, 107-108
    TCP/IP settings, 362-363
    traceroute command, 121
security, 85-86
server applications features, 12-13
services, setting, 99-102
SLIP, 115
SMTP, 118, 367
SSL, Linux installation, 18
TCP, 116-117
Telnet, 13, 99, 118
TFTP, 101
UDP, 116-117
WANs, 12, 104-105
Internet Connection Wizard (Outlook Express), 368
Internet Control Message Protocol (ICMP), 117
Internet Mail Logon dialog box (Outlook Explorer), 370
Internet Protocol. *See* **IP**

Internet service providers. *See* **ISPs**
Internet Software Consortium Web site, 202
Internet Superserver. *See* **inetd daemon**
InterNIC, 128
    domain names, 132-133
    Web site, 133
intranets, 13. *See also* **Apache; networks**
Iomega, 326
IP (Internet protocol), 103
    accounting, 238-239
    addresses, 70-71, 79, 109
        aliasing, 114, 237-238
        dotted notation, 109
        dynamic address assignments, 112-113
        forged, 242
        multiple, 109
        netmasks, 110
        obtaining, 153-154
        octets, 109
        portability, 112
        private networks, 113
        problems, 111
        routers, 364-365
        subnet blocks, 112
        subnets, 109-110
        virtual hosts, 224
    aliasing, 224
    etc/hosts file, 126
    headers, 109
    LISA, 79
    network configuration, 70
    networking, 12, 451
    Special Edition Using TCP/IP, 464
    TCP/IP & Related Protocols, 464
    TCP/IP Network Administration, 465
ipfwadm command
    options, 244-247
    policy keywords, 245
    startup files, 246
IPX network configuration, 70
ISDN (Integrated Services Digital Network), 256-257, 454
ISPs (Internet service providers), 12, 145
    DHCP, 258
    domain names, 17, 133
    dynamic address assignments, 112-113
    IP subnets, blocks, 112
    kernel features, 12
    PPP connection, testing, 159

routers, 108
selecting, 145-149
server applications features, 12-13
virtual hosts, 223

J-K

JAZ drives, 326
JPEG, 210
junk email, harvesting, 373

KDE, Web site, 460
Kerberos
    security, 397
    Web site, 460
kernel
    backup image, 423
    boot, troubleshooting, 415
    bootable, replacing hard drives, 433
    configuration, 445
    customized, 83
    firewall configuration, 244
    ISP features, 12
    Linux Kernel Archives Web site, 460
    log messages, 309-310
    math emulation, 450
    modular, 83, 445
    moving, 437
    naked kernel images (floppy disks), 423-424
    old, 446-449
    panics, 422
    quota support, 302
    recompiling, 16, 446
        code pages, 455
        commands, 448
        defaults, 449
        example, 449-458
        experimental drives, 449
        Extended File System, 455
        firewalls, 451
        hardware configuration, 449
        help, 449
        IDE devices, 450
        incomplete drives, 449
        IP networking, 451
        ISDN support, 454
        loadable modules, 449

make bzlilo command, 457
make clean command, 457
make config command, 449
make dep command, 457
make zlilo command, 457
Minix file system, 455
network drivers, 452
network support, 453-454
/proc file system, 455
quota support, 454
RAM disk support, 451
SCSI drivers, 452-453
second extended file system, 455
testing, 458
    replacing hard drives, 434
    ring buffer, 310
    source code, 14-15
    stock, 83, 445
    upgrading newsgroups, 398
Kernel Module Manager (LISA), loading drivers, 74-75
keyboards, 40
    Backspace key, 41
    Ctrl+C, 40
    Ctrl+D, 41
    Ctrl+Z, 41
    Del key, 41
    virtual consoles, 40-41
keywords, policy (ipfwadm command), 245
kill command
    HUP (hang-up) signal, 29
    KILL signal, 29-30
    PID, 29
killall command, 101
killing
    applications, 40
    processes, currently running, 29-30
klogd daemon, 310
Korn shell, 37

L

languages
    C, 352-353
        The C Programming Language, 352
        no-shell shells script, 357-358
        password generation script, 358-359
    Perl, 352

LANs (local area networks)
kernel features, 12
Ethernet, 104
routers, 105-106
security, 388-389
last command, wtmp files, 314
lastlog command, 315
lastlog files, 315
layers (network configuration), 70
ldconfig –v command, 420
Learning the UNIX Operating System, **23, 464**
Learning the vi Editor, **46, 464**
Lempel-Ziv compression method, 210
libraries, DLLs, 420
LILO (Linux Loader), 59-60
configuration (LISA), 80-82, 446-448
old kernels, booting, 446-448
refreshing configuration, 437
troubleshooting, 415
lilo command, -r option, 425
line editors, 45-47
Linux. *See also* **UNIX**
distribution rights, 10
file system recognition, 32
GNU Public License, 10
history, 10
installation, 15
dual boot computers, 16
email servers, 18
firewalls, 18
Internet connection, 17
newsgroups, 18
routers, 19
Samba, 19
security, 16-17
synchronizing computer clocks, 19
Web servers, 18
kernel, recompiling, 16
Open Source software, 12
reliability, 14
source code, 14-15
system development, 10-11
UNIX compatibility, 11
UNIX cost comparison, 10
Linux Documentation Project, 463
Linux Gazette Web site, 460
The Linux Journal, **469**
Linux Kernel Archives Web site, 460
Linux Loader. *See* **LILO**

Linux Support Team's Installation and System Administration utility. *See* **LISA**
Linux System Labs, 468
Linuxcare, Inc., 468
LinuxFocus Web site, 460
LISA (Linux Support Team's Installation and System Administration), 71-72, 183, 218
autoprobing, 73-74
Change LISA Setup dialog box, 73
fdisk, 76
hardware configuration, 73-75
IP forwarding, setting, 153
Kernel Module Manager, loading drivers, 74-75
LILO configuration, 80-82, 446-448
loading configurations, 82
mouse configuration, 79
network configuration, 78-79
partitioning, 75-77
previous configurations, 73
printer configuration, 79
root accounts, 80
saving configurations, 82
software installation, 76-78
startup configuration, 82, 97-98
supported languages, 72
time configuration, 79
time zone configuration, 79
user accounts, 80
users, adding, 90, 297-298
list manager programs, 195-196
listing
groups, users, 89
head command, 313
processes, currently running, 97-98
tac command, 313
tail command, 313
listings
backup shell script, 356
monitoring inetd shell script, 357
newsgroups, 461-462
no-shell shells script, 357
password generator script, 358-359
rotating log files shell script, 355
lists, common devices, 31-32
load averages (processors), 418
load printers parameter (Samba configuration), 266
loadable modules, recompiling kernels, 449

loading. *See also* **booting; running**
   BIOS, replacing hard drives, 434
   boot disks, 67, 72
   bootable CD-ROMs, 66, 72
   drivers, Kernel Module Manager (LISA), 74-75
   floppy disks
      naked kernel images, 423-424
      rescue disks, 424
   init
      configuration files, 95-96
      runlevels, 96
   installation disks, 424
   kernel
      backup image, 423
      replacing hard drives, 433
      troubleshooting, 415
   LILO, 59-60
      LISA, 80-82
      refreshing configuration, 437
      troubleshooting, 415
   LOADLIN.EXE, 67-68, 72
   operating systems, 59-60
   OS/2 boot manager, 59
   rebooting, 422-423
   startup services, selecting, 82
   system configurations (LISA), 82
LOADLIN.EXE, 67-68, 72
local area networks. *See* **LANs**
local host addresses, 71
local time, selecting, 79
local variables, 345
location files, searching, 39
location, systems, 385-386
lock files, 156
log file parameter (Samba configuration), 265
log files, 305-306
   cleaning, 355
   flushing, 309
   INN, 316
   lastlog, 315
   monitoring, 313
   processing, 313
   reading, 311-312
   rotating, 316-317, 355
   test system example, 317
   transfer, 315
   utmp, 314-315
   UUCP, 315
   Web servers, 229, 315
   wtmp, 314-315

log messages, 305-306
   facility identifiers, 307
   kernel logging, 309-310
   monitoring, 313
   priority identifiers, 308
   processing, 313
   reading, 311-312
logging, Samba configuration, 265
logical partitions, 63
login names, 86
login shells, 87-89
logins, root, 91-92
logs, system
   INN log files, 316
   lastlog files, 315
   log messages, 305-306
      facility identifiers, 307
      kernel logging, 309-310
      monitoring, 313
      priority identifiers, 308
      processing, 313
      reading, 311-312
   managing, 20
   rotating log files, 316-317
   syslogd daemon, 305
      configuring, 307-309
      flushing log files, 309
      network logging option, 306-307
      OpenLinux, 309
      running, 306
   test system example, 317
   transfer log files, 315
   utmp files, 314-315
   UUCP log files, 315
   Web server log files, 315
   wtmp files, 314-315
loopbacks, subnets (IP addresses), 110
lossy compression, 210
low memory, 415-416
lpq command, 269
lpr command, 269
ls -a command, 194

M

m4 macro language, 180, 185-186
macros, 180, 185-186

mail command, 171
Mail Exchanger (MX) record, 138
mail servers
  delivery process, 169-170, 172-173
    MTAs (mail transport agents), 172
    MUAs (mail user agents), 171-172
  Outlook Express
    configuring, 367-371
    connection type, 370
    editing existing configuration, 371
    Internet Connections Wizard, 368
    Internet Mail Logon dialog box, 370
  POP3 protocol, 176, 367
  sendmail, 12, 18, 28, 169, 172-173, 177
  SMTP (Simple Mail Transfer Protocol), 173-174,
    367
  UUCP log files, 315
mail transport agents (MTAs), 172
mail user agents (MUAs), 171-172
mailboxes, UNIX-style, 174
mailing lists, 194-196
  etc/aliases file, 195
  .forward file, 194-195
  list manager programs, 195-196
  requirements, 194
Majordomo, 196
make bzlilo command, 457
make clean command, 457
make config command, 449
make dep command, 457
make zlilo command, 457
man command, 42-43
man pages, 42
  etc/resolv.conf file, 129
  navigating, 42
  organization, 43
managing
  clients, 20
  hardware, 24-25
  partitions, 59
  system logs, 20
  user accounts, 20
manual pages. *See* **man pages**
map archive parameter (Samba configuration),
  267
masquerading, firewalls, 114, 237-238
Massachusetts Institute of Technology (MIT) FTP
  site, 461
master boot record, 59
math emulation (kernels), 450

max log size parameter (Samba configuration),
  265
memory
  low, 415-416
  shared, UNIX, 11
  virtual, 60-62, 65, 76
memory chips
  flash
    recovering, 410-411
    upgrading, 410
  replacing, 431-432
  troubleshooting, 410
messages, log, 305-306
  facility identifiers, 307
  kernel logging, 309-310
  monitoring, 313
  priority identifiers, 308
  processing, 313
  reading, 311-312
MetaLab Web site, 459
Metro-X, 49
mgetty command, 158-159
mouse, configuring (LISA), 79
Microsoft FrontPage, Server Extensions
  Apache, 380-381
  installing, 381
Microsoft Outlook Express. *See* **Outlook Express**
MIME (Multipurpose Internet Mail Extensions),
  122, 175
minicom
  modems, testing, 149-150
  passwords, testing, 159-160
Minix file system, 455
misc series (software), 78
MIT (Massachusetts Institute of Technology) FTP
  site, 461
modems
  auto-answer setting, 155
  cable, 257-258
    firewalls, 258
    security, 397
  Carrier Detect settings, 155
  demand-dial capability, 151-152
  dialing, 151, 160-162
  Hangup on DTR settings, 155
  incoming connections, 154
    getty command, 154-156
    mgetty command, 158-159
    pppd daemon, 157-158
    uugetty command, 156-157

minicom, 149-150
protocols, 115-116
security
    testing, 386-387
    Windows comparison, 387
modular kernels, 445
OpenLinux, 83
replacing hard drives, 434
modules, loadable, 449
monitoring
inetd daemon, 356-357
log files, 313
monitors, blank screen option, 406
motherboards
replacing, 431-432, 438-439
static electricity, 432
troubleshooting, 409-410
    cards, 409
    connectors, 409
    example, 428
    fans, 409
    memory chips, 410
    processors, 410, 418-419
mount command, 33
mount points, 33
mounting
backup hardware, 327
file systems, 32-34
moving
applications, 437-438
kernel, 437
system files, 435-436
user data files, 438
MS-DOS
\ (backslash), 33
COMMAND.COM, 36-40
commands, 37-38
Ctrl+Z, 41
date command, 282
end-of-line conventions, 42
FAT file system, 34, 63
FAT16 file system, 64
FAT32 file system, 64
hidden files, 39-40
LOADLIN.EXE, 67-68, 72
NetBIOS, 242
partitions, 62
time command, 282
UMSDOS, 63, 75
MTAs (mail transport agents), 172

MUAs (mail user agents), 171-172
multimedia
RealPlayer, firewalls, 239-240
UDP, 116
Multipurpose Internet Mail Extensions (MIME), 122, 175
multitasking operating systems, 24
cooperative, 25-26
preemptive, 25
multiuser operating systems, 25
MX (Mail Exchanger) record, 138

N

naked kernel images (floppy disks), 423-424
Name Server (NS) record, 138
named command, 134
configuration files
    setting, 134-135
    testing, 139-142
name servers, configuring, 134
root cache, 136
root domains, 135
names
device, tape drives, 330
DNS
    AlterNIC, 128
    Canadian domain names information Web site, 133
    checking existing domain names, 131-133
    country-level domains, 128, 133
    hierarchy, 127
    InterNIC, 128, 132-133
    Network Solutions, 128
    registering domain names, 132-133
    RIPE Web site, 133
    selecting domain names, 131
    top-level domains, 127-128
    U.S. domain names information Web site, 133
    whois command, 130-133
domain, 17
hostnames
    fully qualified, 126
    hostname command, 129
ISPs, registering domain names, 133
login, 86
pseudo domain names, 135

records (zone files), 137
servers
    etc/resolv.conf file, 128-129
    named command, 134
    nslookup command, 129, 140-142
    registering domain names, 132
    reverse lookups, 135
    root cache, 136
    root domains, 135
    running, 133
    setting named configuration files, 134-135
    testing named configuration files, 139-142
    zone files, 134, 137-139
user accounts, 80
naming conventions, newsgroups, 198
navigating man pages, 42
net time command, synchronization, 288
net use command, 274, 276, 376-377
net view command, 274
NetBIOS
    network configuration, 70
    security, 242
netiquette, 198
netmasks (IP addresses), 110
netstat command, 120
NetWare, 13
network, LANs, 12, 388-389
Network applet, 363
network configuration, 69-71. *See also* **networks**
    DNS servers, 71, 79
    hardware drivers, 70
    high-level protocols, 70
    HTTP, 70
    IP numbers, 70-71
    IPX, 70
    layers, 70
    LISA, 78-79
    local host address, 71
    low-level protocols, 70
    NetBIOS, 70
    network cards, 70
    NIS, 79
    TCP, 70
Network File System (NFS), 13
network gateways, routers, 365-366
Network Information System (NIS), 79
network interfaces, virtual hosts, 224
Network News Transfer Protocol (NNTP), 118,
    200-201, 372
network printers (Samba), 275-277

Network Protocol Handbook, **464**
network series (software), 78
Network Solutions, 128
Network Time Protocol. *See* **NTP**
networks. *See also* **Apache**
    authentication service, 101
    backbone providers, 108
    backups, 335-336
    bootps, 101
    cards, 70
    DHCP, 258
    DNS servers, 71, 79
    drivers, 452
    finger service, 101
    firewalls
        aliasing, 114, 237-238
        application support, 239-240
        configuring, 243-247
        dial-up systems, 240
        difficulties, 240-241
        IP accounting, 238-239
        kernel configuration, 244
    FTP, 13, 118
    Gopher, 100
    hackers, 85
    HTTP, 118
    ICMP, 117
    ifconfig command, 119-120
    IP, 103
        addresses, 70-71, 79, 109-112, 153-154
        aliasing, 114, 237-238
        dotted notation, 109
        dynamic address assignments, 112-113
        headers, 109
        netmasks, 110
        networking, 12, 451
        private networks, 113
        subnet blocks, 112
        subnets, 109-110
    LANs, 104
    local host addresses, 71
    NetBIOS, security, 242
    NetWare, 13
    Network Protocol Handbook, 464
    NFS, 13
    NIS, 79
    NNTP, 118
    NTP, 13
        daemon, 284-287
        hacks, 287

ntpdate command, 287-288
synchronization, 283-284
PLIP, 116
POP3 protocol, 101, 118, 367
POPs, 108
PPP, 116
protocols
application-level connectivity, 116-117
connectionless, 116-117
development, 115
diversity, 114
high-level, 70
HTTP, 70
IP, 70-71, 79
IPX, 70
low-level, 70
modems, 115-116
multiple layers, 118
NetBIOS, 70
RFCs (Request for Comments), 115
TCP, 70
routers, 12, 105-106, 249-250
backbone, 108
cable modems, 257-258
default routes, 152-153
DNS servers, 366-367
external, 164, 250-252, 256
IP addresses, 364-365
IP forwarding, 153
ISDN, 256-257
ISPs, 108
Linux installation, 19
network gateways, 365-366
route command, 120, 255
routing data, 107-108
TCP/IP settings, 362-363
traceroute command, 121
RPC, 13
Samba, 13, 19
accessing shared directories, 375-377
installing printers, 377-380
synchronization, 288
Web site, 460
security, 85-86, 387-389
segmented, 252-255
SLIP, 115
SMTP, 118, 367
status, 119-120
port, recompiling kernels, 453-454
TCP, 116-117

Telnet, 13, 99, 118
TFTP, inetd daemon, 101
UDP, 116-117
WAN (wide area network) systems, 12, 104-105
New Technology File System (NTFS), 64
newaliases command, 221
newgrp command, 89
news servers, 372
configuring, 201-202
INN, 316
managing, 206
NNTP (Network News Transfer Protocol), 372
Outlook Express, adding news accounts, 372-374
test system example, 202-205
newsgroups, 18, 197-206
cross-posting, 198
directories, 201
downloading, 198
hierarchies, 198
listing, 461-462
naming convention, 198
netiquette, 198
news servers
configuring, 201-202
managing, 206
test system example, 202-205
NNTP (Network News Transfer Protocol), 118,
200-201
private newsgroups, 200
propagation, 199
public newsgroups, 199-200
upgrade information, 398
Usenet, 197
UseNet News, 18
NFS (Network File System), 13, 335-336
NIS (Network Information System), 79
**NNTP (Network News Transfer Protocol), 118,
200-201, 372**
no-shell shells, 357-358
Novell NetWare, 13
NS (Name Server) record, 138
nslookup command, 129, 140-142
NTFS (New Technology File System), 64
NTP (Network Time Protocol), 13
daemon
configuring, 285-286
download Web site, 285
installing, 284-285
standalone servers, 286-287
hacks, 287

ntpdate command, 287-288
synchronization, 283-284
Web site, 460
ntpdate command, synchronization, 287-288

O

obtaining IP addresses, 153-154
octets (IP addresses), 109
one-way password encryption, 299-300
Open Source software, 12
OpenLinux (Caldera)
Apache server, 219
Caldera Systems, Inc. Web site, 467
FTP server, installing, 215
INN package, 201-202
configuring automatic start, 205
managing, 206
installation, 71-83
kernel, modular, 83
LISA, 71-72
adding users, 90, 297-298
autoprobing, 73-74
Change LISA Setup dialog box, 73
configuring LILO, 446-448
configuring startup files, 97-98
fdisk, 76
formatting partitions, 77
hardware configuration, 73-75
IP forwarding, setting, 153
Kernel Module Manager, 74-75
LILO configuration, 80- 82, 446-448
loading configurations, 82
mouse configuration, 79
network configuration, 78-79
partitioning, 75-77
previous configurations, 73
printer configuration, 79
root accounts, 80
saving configurations, 82
selecting root partitions, 77
software installation, 76-78
startup configuration, 82, 97-98
supported languages, 72
swap partitions, 76
time configuration, 79
time zone configuration, 79

user accounts, 80
shadow password suites, 302
syslogd daemon, 309
operating systems
access
ownership, 34-36
rights, 25, 34
booting, 59-60
backup kernel image, 423
BIOS, 59, 434
boot loaders, 59
boot sectors, 59
floppy disks, 423-424
installation disks, 424
master boot record, 59
partition table, 60
rebooting, 422-423
cooperative, 25-26
device dependence/independence, 30
file systems, 25, 63
backup hardware, 327
e2fs, 64
e2fsck utility, 421
Extended File System, 455
FAT file system, 34, 63
FAT16file system, 64
FAT32 file system, 64
hierarchy, 32
HPFS, 64
Linux recognition, 32
Minix, 455
mounting, 32-34
NTFS, 64
/proc, 455
read-only, 34
root, 32-33
second extended file system, 33, 455
UMSDOS, 34, 63-65, 75
hardware
autoprobing, 68, 73-74
detecting, 68-69
managing, 24-25
manual configuration, 69
plug and play, 68
multitasking, 24
multiuser, 25
preemptive, time-slices, 25
system configuration, security issues, 95, 99
tasks, scheduling, 24

OS/2
    boot manager, 59
    HPFS, 64
Outlook Express
    commands, Accounts (Tools menu), 368, 371-372
    configuring, 367-371
    connection type, 370
    editing existing configuration, 371
    Internet Connection Wizard, 368
    Internet Mail Logon dialog box, 370
    news accounts, adding, 372-374
output
    commands, redirecting, 39, 348
    standard, 348
        backquote character, 351
        piping, 349-350
        redirecting, 349
overheating issues, 435
overloading processors, 418-419
ownership
    assigning, 34
    directories, 92
    files, 34, 92-94
    root users
        access, 35
        security issues, 35-36

P

packages (software), 69
    basis series, 78
    develop series, 78
    doku series, 78
    installation, 69, 76-78
    misc series, 78
    network series, 78
packet filtering, 236-237
panics, kernel, 422
Parallel Line Internet Protocol (PLIP), 116
parameters
    backquote character, 351
    bash shell, 347
    Samba configuration parameters
        create mode, 267
        encrypt password, 265
        guest account, 265
        hosts allow, 265

        interfaces, 265
        load printers, 266
        log file, 265
        map archive, 267
        max log size, 265
        path, 267-269
        printcap name, 266
        public, 267-268
        read only, 267
        security, 265
        server string, 264
        smb passwd file, 265
        username map, 265
        workgroup, 264
Parent Process ID (PPID), 26
partition table, 60
partitions
    active, 58
    drives, 33-34
    file systems
        e2fs, 64
        FAT, 63
        FAT16, 64
        FAT32, 64
        HPFS, 64
        NTFS, 64
        UMSDOS, 63-65, 75
    formatting, 77
    LISA, 75-77
    logical, 63
    MS-DOS, 62
    partition managers, 59
    partition table, 60
    partitioning schemes, 55, 60, 63-66
    repartitioning utilities, 63, 75
    root, 77
    single, 60
    swap, 60
        LISA, 76
        location, 62, 65
passwd command, 89
password encryption. *See* **passwords**
password file (Samba), 273
passwords
    backups, 335
    blank, 91
    encryption, 91, 299
        brute force attacks, 300
        one-way, 299-300
        salting, 300

Samba configuration, 265
Samba support, 271-273
vocabulary attacks, 300, 358
minicom, testing, 159-160
passwd command, 89
password generation example script, 358-359
policies, 300-301, 395
root accounts, 80, 91
shadow, 91, 299
    shadow password file, 300
    shadow password suites, 301
shared directories, 376-377
user, 86, 90
path parameter (Samba configuration), 267-269
performance, Apache Web server, 217
periodicals, *The Linux Journal*, 469
peripherals, replacing, 434
Perl, 228, 352
chmod command, 352
interpreted language, 352
Programming Perl, 464
regular expressions, 352
Web site, 460
permissions
execute, 92
files, editing, 93-94
group, 88, 92
read, 92
unnecessary, 92
user, 92
world, 92
write, 92
personal Web pages, Apache server, 221
personnel security concerns, 390
physical security, 385-386
Pico (Pine Composer) editor, 47
PID (Process ID), 26
Pine Composer (Pico) editor, 47
pine email application, 47, 172
ping command, 121, 161
PING.EXE utility, 366
piping, standard output, 349-350
PK-ZIP, gzip command comparison, 328
planning
backups, 321-323
installation, 55-58
    configuring hardware, 58
    hard drives, 58
    hardware inventory, 57
    network configuration, 69-71

partitioning, 58
partitioning schemes, 55, 60, 63-66
software, 69, 78
PLIP (Parallel Line Internet Protocol), 116
plug-and-play hardware, 68
Point-to-Point Protocol. *See* PPP
Pointer (PTR) record, 138
policy keywords (ipfwadm command), 245
POP3 (Post Office Protocol 3), 101, 118, 176, 367
POPs (Points of Presence), 108
port 21, 215
port 443, 213
port 80, 213, 218
port numbers, 117
Post Office Protocol 3 (POP3), 101, 118, 176, 367
power connectors, 413
power supplies
swapping components, 413
troubleshooting, 408-409
PPID (Parent Process ID), 26
PPP (Point-to-Point Protocol), 17, 116
connection, testing, 159
diald (dialer daemon)
    configuring, 162-163
    download Web site, 152
enabling, 150-151
pppd daemon, 150
    chat utility, 151
    crtscts option, 158
    incoming connections, 157-158
    modem option, 158
    passive option, 158
    setting default routes, 152-153
    silent option, 158
    testing, 160-162
SLIP comparison, 150
pppd daemon, 150
chat utility, dialing modems, 151
crtscts option, 158
default routes, setting, 152-153
incoming connections, 157-158
modem option, 158
passive option, 158
silent option, 158
testing, 160, 162
pre-boot troubleshooting, 405
observation, 406
remote access, 407
predefined variables, bash shell, 347-348
preemptive operating systems, 25

printcap name parameter (Samba configuration), 266

printers
LISA, 79
Samba
  installing, 377-380
  network, 268-271, 277

printing, 266-269
background printing, 268-269
etc/printcap file, 268
Samba configuration, 266

priority identifiers (log messages), 308

private newsgroups, 200

/proc file system, recompiling kernels, 455

process IDs, 26, 156

processes. *See also* **applications; utilities**
currently running
  killing, 29-30
  listing, 97-98
  viewing, 26-27
hierarchy, 26-28
init, 27
multiple, running, 25
PID, 26
PPID, 26
preemptive operating systems, 25

processing log files, 313

processors
overload, 418-419
replacing, 431-432
troubleshooting, 410

programming languages
C, 352-353
  The C Programming Language, 352
  no-shell shells script, 357-358
  password generation script, 358-359
Perl, 352

***Programming Perl*, 464**

programs. *See* **applications**

propagation (newsgroups), 199

protocols
application-level connectivity, 116-117
connectionless, 116-117
development, 115
diversity, 114
FTP, 118
HTTP, 70, 118
ICMP, 117

IP, 103
  addresses, 70-71, 109-112, 153-154, 364-365
  aliasing, 114, 237-238
  dotted notation, 109
  dynamic address assignments, 112-113
  headers, 109
  LISA, 79
  netmasks, 110
  private networks, 113
  subnet blocks, 112
  subnets, 109-110
IPX, 70
modems, 115-116
multiple layers, 118
NetBIOS, 70
network, 70
Network Protocol Handbook, 464
NNTP, 118, 200-201, 372
NTP. *See* NTP
PLIP, 116
POP3, 101, 118, 176, 367
PPP. *See* PPP
RFCs (Request for Comments), 115
security, 397
SLIP, 115
SMB (Server Message Block), 262
SMTP (Simple Mail Transfer Protocol), 118, 173-174, 367
TCP, 70, 116-117, 215, 218
TCP/IP
  networking (Samba), 262
  settings, routers, 362-363
  Special Edition Using TCP/IP, 464
  TCP/IP & Related Protocols, 103, 464
  TCP/IP Network Administration, 465
Telnet, 118
UDP, 116-117
URLs, 211

ps ax command, 97-98

ps command, 97
high-memory applications, 416
processor overload, 419
ps ajx, 26-27
ps j, 26

pseudo domain names (reverse lookups), 135

PTR (Pointer) record, 138

public directories, 215

public newsgroups, 199-200

public parameter (Samba configuration), 267-268

Q-R

quotas
quota command, 302
support, 302-303, 454

Raven, 226
read only parameter (Samba configuration), 267
read permissions, 92
read-only file systems, 34
reading
diagnostic codes, 411-412
log files, 311-312
RealPlayer, firewalls, 239-240
rebooting, 422-423
recompiling kernel, 16, 446
code pages, 455
commands, 448
defaults, 449
example, 449-458
experimental drives, 449
Extended File System, 455
firewalls, 451
hardware configuration, 449
help, 449
IDE devices, 450
incomplete drives, 449
IP networking, 451
ISDN support, 454
loadable modules, 449
make bzlilo command, 457
make clean command, 457
make config command, 449
make dep command, 457
make zlilo command, 457
Minix file system, 455
network drivers, 452
network support, 453-454
/proc file system, 455
quota support, 454
RAM disk support, 451
SCSI drivers, 452-453
second extended file system, 455
testing, 458
records (zone files)
class, 137
names, 137

set type command, 140
type
A, 138
CNAME, 138
MX, 138
NS, 138
PTR, 138
SOA, 137-138
recovering flash memory chips, 410-411
recurring tasks, 339
recurring tasks, 339-341, 353-355
Red Hat Software, 469
redirecting
log message, kernel, 310
output, 39, 348-349
standard error, 349
standard input, 348
Regional Internet of Europe (RIPE) Web site, 133
registering domain names
country-level domains, 133
InterNIC, 132-133
ISPs, 133
regular expressions, Perl, 352
reinitializing inetd, 102
remote connections
security, 389
troubleshooting systems, 407
remote hosts, ping command, 121
Remote Procedure Call (RPC), 13
removing. *See* **deleting**
repartitioning utilities, 63, 75
replacing
CPUs, 431-432
hard drives, 432-434
BIOS configuration, 434
bootable kernels, 433
compatibility issues, 433
example, 439-440
kernel issues, 434
single-user configuration, 433-434
memory chips, 431-432
motherboards, 431-432, 438-439
peripherals, 434
processors, 431-432
repquota command, 302
Request for Comments (RFCs), 115
rescue disks, 424
restarting Apache server, 225
restoring systems. *See* **backups**

restricting access
disk space
quota support, 302-303
user quotas, 302
root logins, 91-92
user accounts, 295-296
Web servers, 226
reverse lookups (name servers), 135
RFC Web site, 115
RFC-822 (email), 121, 175
RFCs (Request for Comments), 115
rights, assigning, 25, 34
ring buffer (kernel), 310
RIPE Web site (Regional Internet Registry of Europe), 133
root accounts
LISA, creating 80
passwords, 80, 91
security, 91-92, 399-400
root cache files, 136
root domains, 135
root file systems, 32
root logins, 91-92
root partitions (LISA), 77
root users, 35-36
rootshell.com Web site, 460
rotating
logs, 316-317, 355
media (backups), 333
route command, 120, 255
routers, 12, 105-106, 249-250. *See also* **firewalls**
backbone, 108
default routes, 152-153
DNS servers, setting, 366-367
external, 164
cable modems, 257-258
configuring, 250-252
firewalls, 256-258
ISDN, 256-257
segmented networks, 252-255
IP addresses, setting, 364-365
IP forwarding, 153
ISPs, 108
Linux installation, 19
network gateways, setting, 365-366
route command, 120, 255
routing data, 107-108
TCP/IP settings, 362-363
traceroute command, 121
routing data, Internet, 107-108

RPC (Remote Procedure Call), 13
rulesets (sendmail program), 179
runlevels, 96
running. *See also* **booting; loading**
name servers, 133
processes
killing, 29-30
multiple, 25
viewing, 26-27
syslogd daemon, 306-307
Running Linux, 464

S

salting passwords, 300
Samba, 13, 261
components, 262
configuration files, 263-264
global section, 264-266
homes section, 267
shared printers, 268-271
encrypted passwords, 271-273
SMB passwords, 272-273
Windows NT compatibility, 271-272
Linux installation, 19
obtaining, 263
printers
installing, 377-380
network, 275-277
shared directories
accessing, 375-377
net use command, 376
passwords, 376-377
UNC pathnames, 376
shared drives, Windows access, 274-275
shared resources, Linux access, 277-279
SMB (Server Message Block) protocol, 262
synchronization, 288
TCP/IP networking, 262
Web site, 263, 460
saving
kernels, old, 449
system configurations (LISA), 82
scheduling tasks, 339
at command, 341-342
cron daemon, 340-341
crontab entry examples, 353-355
operating systems, 24

screens, blank option, 406
scripts. *See also* **commands; daemons**
    C, 352-353
        The C Programming Language, 352
        no-shell shells example, 357-358
        password generation example, 358-359
    Perl, 352
    shell, 39, 342
        backquote character, 351
        backup example, 356
        bash shell, 347-348
        cleaning log files example, 355
        conditional execution, 343-344
        here documents, 350-351
        monitoring inetd daemon example, 356-357
        rotating log files example, 355
        shell differences, 351
        specifying, 343
        standard error, 348-349
        standard input, 348
        standard output, 348-350
        variables, 344-347
    startup, route command, 120
    Web, security, 391-392
SCSI drivers, recompiling kernels, 452-453
search engines, 459
searching
    files
        location, 39
        text, 38
    grep command, 313
    ps command
        high-memory applications, 416
        processor overload, 419
    record types (zone files), set type command, 140
second extended file system (e2fs), 33, 64
    e2fsck, 421
    recompiling kernels, 455
secure sockets, 213
secure sockets layer (SSL), 18, 226-227, 397
secure transactions, SSL support, 226
security, 241, 393
    applications, 390
    backups
        automatic, 20
        backup systems, 21
        cartridge drives, 326
        CD-Recordable drives, 325
        CD-RW drives, 325
        configuration files, 324

        cp command, 330
        cpio command, 330-331
        customizations, 324-325
        encryption, 334-335
        file systems, 327
        filename extensions, 331
        files, 323-324
        frequency, 333
        incremental, 333-334
        kernel, booting, 423
        Linux drivers, 326
        media rotation, 333
        networks, 335-336
        planning, 321-323
        restoring files, 331-332
        shell script example, 356
        tape drives, 325
        tar command, 327-332
    bogus warnings, 401-402
    boot disks/CD-ROMs, 21
    denial of service attacks, 100
    dial-up, 386
        testing, 386-387
        Windows comparison, 387
    directories, 92
    email, attachments, 400
    files, 92-94
    firewalls, 18, 235-236, 399
        aliasing, 114, 237-238
        application support, 239-240
        cable modems, 258
        configuring, 243-247
        dial-up systems, 240
        difficulties, 240-241
        external routers, 256
        IP accounting, 238-239
        kernel configuration, 244
        kernel features, 12
        packet filtering, 236-237
        recompiling kernels, 451
    Firewalls and Internet Security, 463
    forged IP addresses, 242
    groups, 88-89
    installation, 16-17
    Internet, 85-86, 99-102
    modems, cable, 397
    NetBIOS, 242
    networks, 85-86, 387
        LANs, 388-389
        remote connections, 389

passwords
  blank, 91
  brute force attacks, 300
  encryption, 91, 299-300
  password generation script, 358-359
  policies, 300-301, 395
  selecting, 90
  shadow, 91, 299-301
  shared directories, 376-377
  testing, 159-160
  vocabulary attacks, 300, 358
physical, 385-386
protocols, 397
root accounts, 91-92, 399
root users, 35-36
Samba configuration, 264-265
shell accounts, 391
software, 398
syslogd daemon, network logging option, 306-307
system configuration, 95, 99
system management issues, 21
Trojan horses, 394
users, 86
  access, 396
  account identifiers, 86
  Comment fields, 87, 89
  education, 399, 402
  group numbers, 86
  home directory, 87
  login names, 86
  login shells,87- 89
  passwords, 86, 89
  personnel issues, 390
  restricting interactive access, 295-296
  root accounts, 400
  umask command, 396
  user information files, 86-87
viruses, 393
Web scripts, 391-392
worms, 394
security parameter (Samba configuration), 265
sed (line editor), 47
segmented networks, 252-255
selecting. *See also* **configuring**
  backup hardware, 325-326
  domain names, 131-133
  email addresses, 295
  Greenwich Mean Time (UTC), 79
  IP numbers, 70-71, 79
  ISPs, 145-149

local time, 79
partitioning schemes, 65-66
passwords, 80, 90
root partitions, 77
software, 77-78
startup services, 82
time zones, 79
user IDs, 294
sendmail, 12, 28, 464
  configuring, 178-182
    m4 macro language, 180
    message filtering, 181-182
    rulesets, 179
  Linux installation, 18
  sendmail.cf file, 179-180, 185-186
  server, 12, 18, 28, 169, 172-173, 177
  test system configuration, 183-190
    activating sendmail, 183-184
    sendmail.cf file, creating, 184-186
    spam filtering rules, 186-187
    UUCP delivery, 188-190
  Web site, 183, 188, 460
Serial Line Internet Protocol (SLIP), 115, 150
server applications, 12-13
Server Extensions (FrontPage)
  Apache, 380-381
  installing, 381
Server Message Block (SMB) protocol, 262
server string parameter (Samba configuration), 264
servers
  Apache, 12, 217-219
    configuring, 219-221
    FrontPage Server Extensions, 380-381
    Linux installation, 18
    log files, 315
    Web pages, setting up, 221-223
    Web site, 459
  applications, 12-13
  demand-dial capability, 151-152
  DNS, 71
    LISA, 79
    routers, 366-367
  fax, mgetty command, 158-159
  firewalls, 12, 235-236, 399
    aliasing, 114, 237-238
    application support, 239-240
    cable modems, 258
    configuring, 243-247
    dial-up systems, 240

difficulties, 240-241
external routers, 256
IP accounting, 238-239
kernel configuration, 244
Linux installation, 18
packet filtering, 236-237
recompiling kernels, 451
FTP, 214
configuring anonymous access, 215-216
configuring Internet superserver, 214
server management, 216
incoming connections, 154
getty command, 154-156
mgetty command, 158-159
pppd daemon, 157-158
uugetty command, 156-157
inetd, 99
authentication service, 101
bootps, 101
configuration files, 99-101
finger service, 101
Gopher, 100
POP3 protocol, 101
reinitializing, 102
Telnet, 99
TFTP, 101
INN, 316
kernel features, 12
log files, 229
mail servers
delivery process, 169-173
Linux installation, 18
Outlook Express, 367-371
POP3 protocol, 176, 367
sendmail, 12, 18, 28, 169, 172-173, 177
SMTP (Simple Mail Transfer Protocol),
173-174, 367
UUCP log files, 315
name
etc/relov.conf file, 128-129
named command, 134
nslookup command, 129, 140-142
registering domain names, 132
reverse lookups, 135
root cache, 136
root domains, 135
running, 133
setting named configuration files, 134-135
testing named configuration files, 139-142
zone files, 134, 137-139

news, 372
configuring, 201-202
managing, 206
NNTP, 372
Outlook Express, 372-374
test system example, 202-205
NTP
configuring, 285-286
download Web site, 285
installing, 284-285
ntpdate command, 287-288
standalone servers, 286-287
synchronization, 283-284
processing forms, 227-229
restricting access, 226
Samba, 13, 375
accessing shared directories, 375-377
installing printers, 377-380
Linux installation, 19
synchronization, 288
Web site, 460
security, 387
LANs, 388-389
remote connections, 389
SSL support, 226-227
time, synchronizing computer clocks, 19
virtual hosts, 223-225
Web
Linux installation, 18
log files, 315
X, 48
viewing X windows, 49-50
X server software, 381-382
set type command, 140
setterm command, 406
setting
configuration files (named), 134-135
date, date command, 282
default route (pppd daemon), 152-153
groups, 89
Internet services, 99-102
IP addresses, 364
IP forwarding, 153
login shells, 89
passwords, 89
routers
DNS servers, 366-367
IP addresses, 365
network gateways, 365-366
TCP/IP settings, 362-363

time, hwclock command, 283
variables
    local, 345
    security, 347
    unset command, 346
settings
    BIOS, troubleshooting, 414
    umask command, 396
SGML (Standard Generalized Markup Language), 122
shadow passwords, 91, 299
    shadow password file, 300-301
    shadow password suites, 301-302
shared directories
    net use command, 376
    passwords, 376-377
    Samba
        accessing, 375-377
        configuration settings (Samba), 267-268
    UNC pathnames, 376
shared drives, Windows access (Samba), 274-275
shared memory, UNIX, 11
shared printers configuration settings (Samba), 268-271
    background printing, 268-269
    test system example, 269-271
shared resources, Linux access (Samba), 277-279
    SMB file system, 278-279
    smbclient utility, 277-278
shell scripts, 39, 342
    backquote character, 351
    backup example, 356
    bash shell
        parameters, 347
        predefined variables, 347-348
    C, 352-353
    conditional execution, 343-344
    here documents, 350-351
    monitoring inetd daemon example, 356-357
    no-shell shells example, 357-358
    password generation example, 358-359
    Perl, 352
    specifying, 343
    standard error, 348-349
    standard input, 348
    standard output, 348-350
    variables, 344-347
shells, 36
    accounts, security, 391
    bash, 37

COMMAND.COM comparison, 37-40
    commands, 37-39
    conditional execution, 343-344
    parameters, 347
    predefined variables, 347-348
benefits, 37
Bourne, 37
C, 37
command line functionality, 36
commands
    backgrounding, 39
    redirecting output, 39, 348
Korn, 37
login
    setting, 89
    users, 87
MS-DOS
    COMMAND.COM, 36-40
    commands, 37-38
    Ctrl+Z, 41
    end-of-line conventions, 42
    hidden files, 39-40
    restricting interactive access, 295-296
    scripts, 39, 342
        backquote character, 351
        backup example, 356
        bash shell, 347-348
        C, 352-353
        conditional execution, 343-344
        here documents, 350-351
        monitoring inetd daemon example, 356-357
        no-shell shells example, 357-358
        password generation example, 358-359
        Perl, 352
        specifying, 343
        standard error, 348-349
        standard input, 348
        standard output, 348-350
        variables, 344-347
    shell programming, 39
    startup, user accounts, 295-296
    UNIX
        end-of-line conventions, 42
        hidden files, 39-40
    Z, 37
Simple Mail Transfer Protocol (SMTP), 118, 173-174, 367
single partitions, 60
single-user configuration, replacing hard drives, 433-434

sites, 46
  AltaVista search engine, 459
  Amazon.com, 46, 463
  Apache, 459
  Australian encryption software FTP site, 461
  Barnes and Noble, 46, 463
  Caldera Systems, Inc., 467
  Canadian domain names information, 133
  Computer Incident Advisory Capability (CIAC)
    Web site
      bogus warnings, 402
      software defects, 398
  Corel Corporation Linux Web site, 467
  Dell Computer Corporation, 468
  diald (dialer demon)
    download site, 152
    Web site, 460
  fatbrain.com, 463
  freshmeat.net, 459
  FrontPage Web site, 381
  GNU project, 460
  IANA, 122
  InfoMagic, 468
  Internet Software Consortium, 202
  InterNic Web site, 133
  KDE, 460
  Kerberos, 397, 460
  Linux Gazette, 460
  Linux Kernel Archives Web site, 460
  Linux System Labs, 468
  Linuxcare, Inc., 468
  LinuxFocus, 460
  MetaLab, 459
  MIT (Massachusetts Institute of Technology), 461
  NTP Web site, 285, 460
  Perl, 460
  Red Hat Software, 469
  RFC Web site, 115
  RIPE Web site, 133
  root cache file downloads, 136
  rootshell.com, 460
  Samba, 263, 460
  search engines, 459
  sendmail, 183, 188, 460
  Slackware, 460
  Specialized Systems Consultants (SSC), 469
  StarNet Communications, 381
  SunSITE, 459, 461
  Sunsite FTP site, 302-303

  U.S. domain names information, 133
  Walnut Creek CD-ROM, 459, 469
size, hard drives, 416-417
Slackware Web site, 460
SLIP (Serial Line Internet Protocol), 115, 150
smart hosts, 177
SMB (Server Message Block) protocol, 262
SMB file system, 278-279
smb passwd file parameter (Samba configuration), 265
SMB passwords (Samba), 272-273
smbclient utility, 277-278
smbmount command, 278
smbpasswd utility, 272
smoke, 408
SMTP (Simple Mail Transfer Protocol), 118, 173-174, 367
SOA (Statement of Authority) record, 137-138
sockets, Berkeley (UNIX), 11
software
  applications
    moving, 437-438
    source trees, 437
  basis series, 78
  develop series, 78
  doku series, 78
  encryption, Australian FTP site, 461
  installation, 69, 76-78
  kernel, moving, 437
  misc series, 78
  network series, 78
  Open Source, 12
  security, 398
  system files, moving, 435-436
  troubleshooting
    BIOS, 428
    DLLs, 420
    hard drives, 420-425
    insufficient disk space, 416-417
    kernel, 415
    kernel panics, 422
    LILO, 415
    low memory, 415-416
    processor overload, 418-419
    swap files, 427-428
  user data files, moving, 438
source code, 14-15
source trees (applications), 437

spam
 filtering, 182-183, 187-188
 harvesting, 373
Special Edition Using Linux, 464
Special Edition Using TCP/IP, 464
Specialized Systems Consultants (SSC), 469
specifying sections, man command, 43
srm.conf, 220-222
SSC (Specialized Systems Consultants), 469
SSL (secure sockets layer), 18, 226-227, 397
standard error, 348-349
**Standard Generalized Markup Language
 (SGML), 122**
standard input, 348
standard output, 348
 backquote character, 351
 piping, 349-350
 redirecting, 349
**StarNet Communications, X-Win32 software
 package, 381-382**
starting. *See* **booting; loading; running**
startup
 files
  editing, 96
  init, 95-96
  LISA, 97-98
 scripts, route command, 120
Statement of Authority (SOA) record, 137-138
static electricity, motherboards, 432
stock kernels, 83, 445, 450
stopping. *See* **killing**
Stronghold, 226
su command, switching accounts, 89
Subject header (email), 175
subnets (IP addresses), 109-110
 blocks, 112
 loopback, 110
 reserved addresses, 110
SunOS, 11
SunSITE
 FTP site, 461
  quota support tools, 303
  shadow password suites, 302
 Web site, 459
superservers, inetd, 215
superusers, 35-36
suspending applications, 41
swap files, troubleshooting, 427-428

swap partitions, 60
 LISA, 76
 location, 62, 65
swapoff command, 422
swapping components, 412-413
switching
 accounts, su command, 89
 virtual consoles, 41
symbolic domain names, virtual hosts, 225
synchronization
 computer clocks, 19
 external sources, 282
 hosts, 281
 importance, 281
 net time command, 288
 NTP, 283-284
 ntpdate command, 287-288
 Samba, 288
 TimeServ (Windows NT), 288
syntax, commands
 bash shell, 38-39
 MS-DOS, 38
syslogd daemon, 305
 configuring, 307-309
 log files, flushing, 309
 network logging option, 306-307
 OpenLinux, 309
 running, 306
system boards
 replacing, 431-432, 438-439
 static electricity, 432
 troubleshooting, 409-410
  cards, 409
  connectors, 409
  example, 428
  fans, 409
  memory chips, 410
  processors, 410, 418-419
system components, swapping, 412-413
system configuration, security issues, 95, 99
system files, moving, 435-436
system identification (Samba configuration), 264
system inventory, planning installation, 57
system logs
 INN log files, 316
 lastlog files, 315
 log messages, 305-306
  facility identifiers, 307
  kernel logging, 309-310
  monitoring, 313

priority identifiers, 308
    processing, 313
    reading, 311-312
managing, 20
rotating log files, 316-317
syslogd daemon, 305
    configuring, 307-309
    flushing log files, 309
    network logging option, 306-307
    OpenLinux, 309
    running, 306
test system example, 317
transfer log files, 315
utmp files, 314-315
UUCP log files, 315
Web server log files, 315
wtmp files, 314-315
system management
    backups, 20-21
    boot disks/CD-ROMs, 21
    client communications, 20
    crashes, diagnosing, 21
    security issues, 21
    system logs, 20
    user accounts, 20
system time, 282
System V (UNIX), 11

T

tac command, 313
tail command, 313
tape drives
    backups, 325
    device names, 330
    file systems, 327
    tar command, 327-329
        compressed files, 328, 331
        cpio command comparison, 330
        filename extensions, 331
        restoring files, 332
    troubleshooting example, 426-427
tar command, 327-329
    compressed files, 328, 331
    cpio command comparison, 330
    filename extensions, 331
    hard disks, 327

moving user data files, 438
restoring files, 332
tasks, scheduling, 339
    at command, 341-342
    cron daemon, 340-341
    crontab entry examples, 353-355
    operating systems, 24
TCP (Transmission Control Protocol), 116
    network configuration, 70
    port numbers, 117
    TCP port 21, 215
    TCP port 80, 218
TCP/IP
    networking (Samba), 262
    settings, routers, 362-363
    Special Edition Using TCP/IP, 464
    TCP/IP & Related Protocols, 103, 464
    TCP/IP Network Administration, 465
***TCP/IP & Related Protocols*, 103, 464**
***TCP/IP Network Administration*, 465**
telephone lines, security issues, 386-387
Telnet, 13, 99, 118
telnet command, 213
test systems
    Samba
        global configuration settings, 266
        shared directories configuration settings, 268
        shared printers configuration settings, 269-271
    sendmail program, 183-190
        activating, 183-184
        sendmail.cf file, creating, 185-186
        spam filtering rules, 186-187
        UUCP delivery, 188-190
testing
    configuration files (named), 139-142
    kernels, 458
    modems, minicom, 149-150
    news servers, 202-205
    passwords, minicom, 159-160
    ping command, 161
    PPP connection, 159
    security, dial-up, 386-387
    traceroute command, 161
Texinfo pages, 44
text editors
    difficulties, 44
    elvis, 44
    Emacs, 47
    Pico, 47

vi, 44
  command mode, 45-46
  commands, 45-46
  input mode, 46
  Learning the vi Editor, 46
  line editor origins, 45
vim, 44
text files
  editing, 44-47
  searching, 38
TFTP, inetd daemon, 101
tilde (~), Web pages (Apache server), 221
time
  configuration (LISA), 79
  services (UNIX), 283
  synchronizing computer clocks, 19
  time command, MS-DOS, 282
  time-slices, 25
  zones, selecting (LISA), 79
TimeServ (Windows NT), synchronization, 288
To line (email headers), 175
tools
  command-line, 48
  quota support, 302-303
  TimeServ (Windows NT), 288
**Tools menu commands (Outlook Express),
  Accounts, 368, 371-372**
Torvalds, Linus, 10
traceroute command, 121, 161
TRACERT.EXE utility, 366
transfer log files, 217, 315
Transmission Control Protocol. *See* **TCP**
Trojan horses, 394
troubleshooting
  BIOS
    beep codes, 411
    diagnostic codes, 411-412
    example, 428
    flash memory chips, 410-411
    settings, 414
  blank screen option, disabling, 406
  booting, 422-423
    backup kernel image, 423
    floppy disks, 423-424
    installation disks, 424
  cable connectors, 413
  cards, 409
  CD-ROM drives, 428

  connectors, 409
  df command, 407, 417
  DLLs, 420
  dmesg command, 407
  fans, 409
  free command, 407, 415-416
  hard drives, 420
    e2fsck utility, 421
    example, 424-425
    file corruption, 421-422
    physical defects, 420-421
  hardware, 408
  IDC connectors, 414
  insufficient disk space, 416-417
  intermittent problems, 413-414
  kernel
    booting, 415
    kernel panics, 422
  LILO, 415
  low memory, 415-416
  memory chips, 410
  motherboards, 409-410, 428
  power connectors, 413
  power supplies, 408-409
  pre-boot, 405
    observation, 406
    remote access, 407
  processors, 410, 418-419
  swap files, 427-428
  swapping components, 412-413
  tape drives, 426-427
  uptime command, 408, 418
types, records (zone files), 137-138
  A, 138
  CNAME, 138
  MX, 138
  NS, 138
  PTR, 138
  set type command, 140
  SOA, 137-138

U

UDP (Universal Datagram Protocol)
  multimedia, 116
  port numbers, 117
umask command, user access, 396

UMSDOS file system, 34, 63-65, 75
UNC (Universal Naming Convention), 376
UNIX. *See also* **Linux**
    BSD, 11
    end-of-line conventions, 42
    hidden files, 39-40
    Learning the UNIX Operating System, 23, 464
    Linux compatibility, 11
    Linux cost comparison, 10
    shell programming, 39
    shells, 36
    System V, 11
    time services, 283
    UNIX Unleashed, 465
    UUCP, 122
    windowing systems, 48
UNIX to UNIX Copy standard. *See* **UUCP**
UNIX Unleashed, **465**
UNIX-style mailboxes, 174
UnixWare, 11
unset command, 346
upgrading
    flash memory chips, 410
    kernels, 398
    software, security, 398
uptime command, 408, 418
URLs, 211
    form data, 228
    indicating directories, 222
Usenet, 197, 461-462
UseNet News, 18
user accounts. *See* **users**
useradd command, 90, 296-297
userdel command, 296-297
UserDir directive, personal Web pages, 221
username map file (Samba), 273
username map parameter (Samba configuration), 265
users, 86. *See also* **groups**
    access, 396
    accounts, 293, 296
        adding, 296-298
        creating, 80
        deleting, 296-298
        email addresses, 295
        etc/passwd files, 296
        home directories, 294
        managing, 20
        names, 80
        restricting interactive access, 295-296

        startup shells, 295-296
        switching, 89
        user IDs, 86, 294
    adding, 89
        adduser command, 90, 296-298
        LISA, 90, 297-298
        useradd command, 90, 296-297
    Comment fields, 87-89
    data, moving, 438
    deleting, userdel command, 296-297
    files, backups, 323-324
    FTP server access, 214
    group numbers, 86
    groups, 89
    home directory, 87
    login names, 86
    login shells, 87-89
    passwords, 86
        blank, 91
        encryption, 91
        policies, 300-301, 395
        selecting, 90
        setting, 89
        shadow, 91, 299-300
        shadow password suites, 301
    quotas, 302
    root
        access, 35
        editing root accounts, 35
        security issues, 35-36
    security
        education, 399, 402
        personnel issues, 390
        root accounts, 399-400
    shell accounts, security, 391
    user information files, 86-87
    user permissions, 92
Using and Managing uucp, **465**
UTC (Greenwich Mean Time), selecting, 79
utilities. *See also* **applications; processes**
    chat (pppd daemon), 151
    e2fsck, 421
    graphical, 48
    LISA, 71-72
        adding users, 90, 297-298
        autoprobing, 73-74
        Change LISA Setup dialog box, 73
        configuring LILO, 446-448
        configuring startup files, 97-98
        fdisk, 76

formatting partitions, 77
hardware configuration, 73-75
Kernel Module Manager, 74-75
LILO configuration, 80, 82
loading configurations, 82
mouse configuration, 79
network configuration, 78-79
partitioning, 75-76
previous configurations, 73
printer configuration, 79
root accounts, 80
saving configurations, 82
selecting root partitions, 77
software installation, 76-78
startup services configuration, 82
supported languages, 72
swap partitions, 76
time configuration, 79
time zone configuration, 79
user accounts, 80
PING.EXE, 366
repartitioning, 63, 75
TRACERT.EXE, 366
whois databases, 462
utmp files, 314-315
uucico command, 177
UUCP (UNIX to UNIX Copy standard), 122
configuring (sendmail program), 188-190
log files, 315
mail delivery, 177-178
uugetty command, 156-157
uustat command, 190

V

variables, 345-347
environment, 344-345
local, 345
predefined (bash shell), 347-348
security, 347
unset command, 346
verifying access, remote hosts, 121
vi editor, 44
command mode, 45-46
commands, 45-46
elvis, 44
input mode, 46

Learning the vi Editor, 46
line editor origins, 45
vim, 44
viewing
files
hidden, 194
startup, 95-98
kernel messages, 310
man pages, 42-43
network status
ifconfig command, 119
netstat command, 120
processes, currently running, 26-27, 97-98
Texinfo pages, 44
windows, X, 49-50
vim editor, 44
virtual consoles, 40-41
virtual hosts, 223-225
virtual memory, 60-62, 65, 76
virtual terminals, Telnet, 99
viruses, 393
vocabulary attacks (passwords), 300, 358

W

Walnut Creek CD-ROM, 459, 469
WANs (wide area networks), 104
kernel features, 12
conduits, 105
point-to-point connections, 105
routers, 105-106
warez, 215
warnings, bogus, 401-402
Web. *See* **WWW**
Web browsers, 209
Web pages
Apache server, 221-223
FrontPage Server Extensions, 380-381
Web scripts, security, 391-392
Web servers, 209
Apache, 217-219
configuring, 219-221
Web pages, setting up, 221-223
Linux installation, 18
log files, 229, 315
processing forms, 227-229
restricting access, 226

SSL support, 226-227
virtual hosts, 223-225
Web sites. *See* **sites**
who command, utmp files, 314
whois command, 130-133
whois utility, databases, 462
wide area networks. *See* **WANs**
Windows
Add Printer Wizard, 276, 378-380
GPFs, 14
modem security, 387
NetBIOS, security, 242
network printers, setting up (Samba), 277
PING.EXE utility, 366
reliability comparison, 14
shared drives, accessing (Samba), 275
TRACERT.EXE utility, 366
UAEs, 14
X comparison, 13
windows
command-line tools, 48
UNIX, 48
X, viewing, 49-50
Windows 3.1, cooperative operating systems, 25-26
Windows NT
encrypted passwords, 271-272
GUIs, 48
NTFS, 64
TimeServ, synchronization, 288
wizards
Add Printer Wizard, 276, 378-380
Internet Connection Wizard (Outlook Express),
368
**WordPerfect, Corel Corporation Linux Web site,
467**
workgroup parameter (Samba configuration), 264
world permissions, 92
World Wide Web. *See* **WWW**
worms, 394
write permissions, 92
wtmp files, 314-315
WWW (World Wide Web), 12, 18. *See also*
Internet
Apache, 12
FrontPage Server Extensions, 380-381
Linux installation, 18
log files, 315
Web site, 459
HTML, 122

X-Z

X
Accelerated-X, 49
application support, 13
benefits, 48
clients, 48
limitations, 13, 48
Metro-X, 49
server
servers, 48
viewing X windows, 49-50
X server software, 381-382
Windows comparison, 13
windows, viewing, 49-50
X-Win32, 49, 381-382
XFree86, 49
X Window System. *See* **X**
X-Win32, 49, 381-382
XFree86, 49

Yellow Pages (YP), 79

Z shell, 37
Zip drives, backups, 326
zipping files
compress command, 328
gzip command, 328, 331
zone files, 137
(name servers), 134
records, 137-138
test system examples, 138-139

What's on the Disc

The companion CD-ROM contains Caldera's OpenLinux 1.3.

Install from Boot Floppies

CD-ROM Boot

1. Insert CD-ROM in CD drive.
2. Restart your computer.
3. You may need to change your BIOS settings to boot from the CD-ROM. Typically, you enter your BIOS setup program with the F2 or DEL keys.
4. Make your changes (if any) and exit the BIOS setup utility.
5. If your CD drive is capable of booting from CD-ROMs, you will boot into the Caldera setup program.
6. Follow the onscreen prompts to complete the installation.

Install from DOS or Windows 95 or 98

1. If you are in Windows 95 or Windows 98, go to Start ->. Restart the computer in MS-DOS mode.
2. Navigate to your CD drive and go to the directory \COL\LAUNCH\DOS.
3. Type INSTALL and press <ENTER>.
4. Your computer will start the Caldera setup program.
5. Follow the onscreen prompts to finish the installation.

Install from Boot Floppies

1. While in DOS or Windows, format two 1.44 MB floppies or 1 2.88 MB floppy.
2. Navigate to your CD drive and go to the directory \COL\LAUNCH\FLOPPY.
3. Type RAWRITE3 and press <ENTER>.
4. When prompted to do so, type in the name INSTALL.144 if you are using 1.44 MB floppies, or INSTALL.288 if using a 2.88 MB floppy, and press <ENTER>.
5. When prompted to do so, type in the drive letter of the disk(s) you are going to prepare and press <ENTER>. Since you are going to be booting from this disk, it's typically A:
6. If you are creating a 1.44 MB boot disk, you need to create a second disk. Repeat step 3. When prompted to do so, type in the name MODULES.144 and press <ENTER>.
7. Repeat step 5.
8. If you don't already have the boot floppy in your disk drive, insert it now.
9. Restart your computer.
10. You may need to change your BIOS settings to boot from the floppy drive. Typically, you enter your BIOS setup program with the F2 or DEL keys.
11. Make your changes (if any) and exit the BIOS setup utility.
12. If your computer is set up properly, you will boot into the Caldera setup program.
13. Follow the onscreen prompts to complete the installation.

GNU GENERAL PUBLIC LICENSE

Version 2, June 1991

Copyright (C) 1989, 1991 Free Software Foundation, Inc.

675 Mass Ave, Cambridge, MA 02139, USA

Preamble

The licenses for most software are designed to take away your freedom to share and change it. By contrast, the GNU General Public License is intended to guarantee your freedom to share and change free software—to make sure the software is free for all its users. This General Public License applies to most of the Free Software Foundation's software and to any other program whose authors commit to using it. (Some other Free Software Foundation software is covered by the GNU Library General Public License instead.) You can apply it to your programs, too.

When we speak of free software, we are referring to freedom, not price. Our General Public Licenses are designed to make sure that you have the freedom to distribute copies of free software (and charge for this service if you wish), that you receive source code or can get it if you want it, that you can change the software or use pieces of it in new free programs; and that you know you can do these things.

To protect your rights, we need to make restrictions that forbid anyone to deny you these rights or to ask you to surrender the rights. These restrictions translate to certain responsibilities for you if you distribute copies of the software, or if you modify it.

For example, if you distribute copies of such a program, whether gratis or for a fee, you must give the recipients all the rights that you have. You must make sure that they, too, receive or can get the source code. And you must show them these terms so they know their rights.

We protect your rights with two steps: (1) copyright the software, and (2) offer you this license which gives you legal permission to copy, distribute and/or modify the software.

Also, for each author's protection and ours, we want to make certain that everyone understands that there is no warranty for this free software. If the software is modified by someone else and passed on, we want its recipients to know that what they have is not the original, so that any problems introduced by others will not reflect on the original authors' reputations.

Finally, any free program is threatened constantly by software patents. We wish to avoid the danger that redistributors of a free program will individually obtain patent licenses, in effect making the program proprietary. To prevent this, we have made it clear that any patent must be licensed for everyone's free use or not licensed at all.

The precise terms and conditions for copying, distribution and modification follow.

GNU GENERAL PUBLIC LICENSE TERMS AND CONDITIONS FOR COPYING, DISTRIBUTION AND

MODIFICATION

1. This License applies to any program or other work which contains a notice placed by the copyright holder saying it may be distributed under the terms of this General Public License. The "Program", below, refers to any such program or work, and a "work based on the Program" means either the Program or any derivative work under copyright law: that is to say, a work containing the Program or a portion of it, either verbatim or with modifications and/or translated into another language. (Hereinafter, translation is included without limitation in the term "modification".) Each licensee is addressed as "you". Activities other than copying, distribution and modification are not covered by this License; they are outside its scope. The act of running the Program is not restricted, and the output from the Program is covered only if its contents constitute a work based on the Program (independent of having been made by running the Program). Whether that is true depends on what the Program does.

2. You may copy and distribute verbatim copies of the Program's source code as you receive it, in any medium, provided that you conspicuously and appropriately publish on each copy an appropriate copyright notice and disclaimer of warranty; keep intact all the notices that refer to this License and to the absence of any warranty; and give any other recipients of the Program a copy of this License along with the Program. You may charge a fee for the physical act of transferring a copy, and you may at your option offer warranty protection in exchange for a fee.

3. You may modify your copy or copies of the Program or any portion of it, thus forming a work based on the Program, and copy and distribute such modifications or work under the terms of Section 1 above, provided that you also meet all of these conditions:

   a) You must cause the modified files to carry prominent notices stating that you changed the files and the date of any change.

   b) You must cause any work that you distribute or publish, that in whole or in part contains or is derived from the Program or any part thereof, to be licensed as a whole at no charge to all third parties under the terms of this License.

c) If the modified program normally reads commands interactively when run, you must cause it, when started running for such interactive use in the most ordinary way, to print or display an announcement including an appropriate copyright notice and a notice that there is no warranty (or else, saying that you provide a warranty) and that users may redistribute the program under these conditions, and telling the user how to view a copy of this License. (Exception: if the Program itself is interactive but does not normally print such an announcement, your work based on the Program is not required to print an announcement.)

These requirements apply to the modified work as a whole. If identifiable sections of that work are not derived from the Program, and can be reasonably considered independent and separate works in themselves, then this License, and its terms, do not apply to those sections when you distribute them as separate works. But when you distribute the same sections as part of a whole which is a work based on the Program, the distribution of the whole must be on the terms of this License, whose permissions for other licensees extend to the entire whole, and thus to each and every part regardless of who wrote it.

Thus, it is not the intent of this section to claim rights or contest your rights to work written entirely by you; rather, the intent is to exercise the right to control the distribution of derivative or collective works based on the Program.

In addition, mere aggregation of another work not based on the Program with the Program (or with a work based on the Program) on a volume of a storage or distribution medium does not bring the other work under the scope of this License.

4. You may copy and distribute the Program (or a work based on it, under Section 2) in object code or executable form under the terms of Sections 1 and 2 above provided that you also do one of the following:

a) Accompany it with the complete corresponding machine-readable source code, which must be distributed under the terms of Sections 1 and 2 above on a medium customarily used for software interchange; or,

b) Accompany it with a written offer, valid for at least three years, to give any third party, for a charge no more than your cost of physically performing source distribution, a complete machine-readable copy of the corresponding source code, to be distributed under the terms of Sections 1 and 2 above on a medium customarily used for software interchange; or,

c) Accompany it with the information you received as to the offer to distribute corresponding source code. (This alternative is allowed only for noncommercial distribution and only if you received the program in object code or executable form with such an offer, in accord with Subsection b above.)

The source code for a work means the preferred form of the work for making modifications to it. For an executable work, complete source code means all the source code for all modules it contains, plus any associated interface definition files, plus the scripts used to control compilation and installation of the executable. However, as a special exception, the source code distributed need not include anything that is normally distributed (in either source or binary form) with the major components (compiler, kernel, and so on) of the operating system on which the executable runs, unless that component itself accompanies the executable.

If distribution of executable or object code is made by offering access to copy from a designated place, then offering equivalent access to copy the source code from the same place counts as distribution of the source code, even though third parties are not compelled to copy the source along with the object code.

5. You may not copy, modify, sublicense, or distribute the Program except as expressly provided under this License. Any attempt otherwise to copy, modify, sublicense or distribute the Program is void, and will automatically terminate your rights under this License. However, parties who have received copies, or rights, from you under this License will not have their licenses terminated so long as such parties remain in full compliance.

6. You are not required to accept this License, since you have not signed it. However, nothing else grants you permission to modify or distribute the Program or its derivative works. These actions are prohibited by law if you do not accept this License. Therefore, by modifying or distributing the Program (or any work based on the Program), you indicate your acceptance of this License to do so, and all its terms and conditions for copying, distributing or modifying the Program or works based on it.

7. Each time you redistribute the Program (or any work based on the Program), the recipient automatically receives a license from the original licensor to copy, distribute or modify the Program subject to these terms and conditions. You may not impose any further restrictions on the recipients' exercise of the rights granted herein. You are not responsible for enforcing compliance by third parties to this License.

8. If, as a consequence of a court judgment or allegation of patent infringement or for any other reason (not limited to patent issues), conditions are imposed on you (whether by court order, agreement or otherwise) that contradict the conditions of this License, they do not excuse you from the conditions of this License. If you cannot distribute so as to satisfy simultaneously your obligations under this License and any other pertinent obligations, then as a consequence you may not distribute the Program at all. For example, if a patent license would not permit royalty-free redistribution of the Program by all those who receive copies directly or indirectly through you, then

the only way you could satisfy both it and this License would be to refrain entirely from distribution of the Program.

If any portion of this section is held invalid or unenforceable under any particular circumstance, the balance of the section is intended to apply and the section as a whole is intended to apply in other circumstances.

It is not the purpose of this section to induce you to infringe any patents or other property right claims or to contest validity of any such claims; this section has the sole purpose of protecting the integrity of the free software distribution system, which is implemented by public license practices. Many people have made generous contributions to the wide range of software distributed through that system in reliance on consistent application of that system; it is up to the author/donor to decide if he or she is willing to distribute software through any other system and a licensee cannot impose that choice.

This section is intended to make thoroughly clear what is believed to be a consequence of the rest of this License.

9. If the distribution and/or use of the Program is restricted in certain countries either by patents or by copyrighted interfaces, the original copyright holder who places the Program under this License may add an explicit geographical distribution limitation excluding those countries, so that distribution is permitted only in or among countries not thus excluded. In such case, this License incorporates the limitation as if written in the body of this License.

10. The Free Software Foundation may publish revised and/or new versions of the General Public License from time to time. Such new versions will be similar in spirit to the present version, but may differ in detail to address new problems or concerns.

    Each version is given a distinguishing version number. If the Program specifies a version number of this License which applies to it and "any later version", you have the option of following the terms and conditions either of that version or of any later version published by the Free Software Foundation. If the Program does not specify a version number of this License, you may choose any version ever published by the Free Software Foundation.

11. If you wish to incorporate parts of the Program into other free programs whose distribution conditions are different, write to the author to ask for permission. For software which is copyrighted by the Free Software Foundation, write to the Free Software Foundation; we sometimes make exceptions for this. Our decision will be guided by the two goals of preserving the free status of all derivatives of our free software and of promoting the sharing and reuse of software generally.

Read This Before Opening the Software

By opening this package, you are agreeing to be bound by the following agreement:

Some of the software included with this product may be copyrighted, in which case all rights are reserved by the respective copyright holder. You are licensed to use software copyrighted by the Publisher and its licensors on a single computer. You may copy and/or modify the software as needed to facilitate your use of it on a single computer. Making copies of the software for any other purpose is a violation of the United States copyright laws.

This software is sold as is without warranty of any kind, either expressed or implied, including but not limited to the implied warranties of merchantability and fitness for a particular purpose. Neither the publisher nor its dealers or distributors assumes any liability for any alleged or actual damages arising from the use of this program. (Some states do not allow for the exclusion of implied warranties, so the exclusion may not apply to you.)